Networks in
the Global Village

Life in
Contemporary Communities

Barry Wellman

Westview Press
A Member of the Perseus Books Group

Copyright © 1999 by Westview Press, A Member of the Perseus Books Group

Published in 1999 in the United States of America by Westview Press, 5500 Central Avenue, Boulder, Colorado 80301-2877, and in the United Kingdom by Westview Press, 12 Hid's Copse Road, Cumnor Hill, Oxford OX2 9JJ

Library of Congress Cataloging-in-Publication Data
Networks in the global village : life in contemporary communities /
    [edited] by Barry Wellman.
        p.   cm.
    Includes bibliographical references and index.
    ISBN 0-8133-1150-0 (hc) —ISBN 0-8133-6821-9 (pb)
    1. Social networks.   2. Community.   3. Community life.
I. Wellman, Barry.
HM131.N453   1999
307—dc21   98-29479
                                                                            CIP

The paper used in this publication meets the requirements of the American National Standard for Permanence of Paper for Printed Library Materials Z39.48-1984.

PERSEUS
POD
ON DEMAND   10   9   8   7   6   5   4   3   2

Networks in
the Global Village

Contents

Tables and Figures

Tables

Figures

Preface

The Network City

Most of us have a few defining, "Aha!" moments when the true nature of the universe becomes clear. For example, legend has it that the nineteenth-century English poet Lord Byron once said that he got his best thoughts climbing in and out of bed. I am a sociologist and not a Romantic poet, so my defining moment was not a Byronic sensual experience but an analytic insight brought on by fear. It happened in the late 1950s when I was a teenager in the Bronx, New York City. The "Fordham Baldies," the baddest gang in New York,[1] were going to attack our high school, the erudite but defenseless Bronx High School of Science. The Baldies never showed up, perhaps because we were armed to defend ourselves with the biggest slide rules[2] we could find. Nevertheless, the experience started me thinking about the myth and reality of gangs.

I gradually came to realize that gangs as real entities did not exist. Drawing up a membership list was impossible. Indeed, it was as futile to draw a map cleanly delineating each gang's turf as it is to draw precise ethnic boundaries in Eastern Europe (Magoscsi and Matthews 1993, plate 30). The Bronx consisted of unbounded networks of friends, and friends of friends. When a fight was coming up, groups of friends would call each other and come together to be the Baldies for that night. On another night, when other friends would call, some of the same teens would become members of another gang. Much of organized crime operates in the same way, be it Colombian or Chinese drug cartels, the Cosa Nostra, or the Moscow mafia.

Although the Baldies did not come, my New York childhood prepared me for my life's work: showing how communities, organizations, cities, and societies are organized as networks. Not only were teenage gangs fluid enterprises, so were many businesses in New York's garment industry, where many of my relatives worked. Deals were being made and remade; alliances shifted seasonally. Although we had an active neighborhood life, we were always using the subway or car to drive to friends and relatives in distant parts of New York. When we could not drive, we visited by telephone.

Studying Community as a Social Network

Given these experiences, when I started reading sociology I was surprised to find it full of concern about the supposed loss of community. Too many scholars used the same counterfactual rhetoric that politicians and pundits continue to sell, although now cyberspace has joined inner-city slums as the alleged destroyer of community. Until well into the 1960s, many urban scholars preached that people were isolated and miserable in the city. Yet my own experience had shown me that, in reality, urbanites were heavily—and usually happily—involved in friendship, kinship, and workmate ties. Analysts kept seeing the city as built out of neighborhoods—a set of neatly drawn boxes on a map. Yet I knew that many ties stretched far beyond my corner of the Bronx.

Fortunately, I became a student in the mid-1960s at Harvard's graduate Department of Social Relations, at a time when some younger faculty members were teaching that the world is made up of social networks rather than little boxes. Harrison White was near the start of his career as the seer of social networks as the stuff of social structure. Charles Tilly, although even more junior than Harrison, was already showing how networks worked in cities (an important part of his early work that suffuses his better-known historical analyses of collective political behavior). I was one of a set of students, including Claude Fischer, Mark Granovetter, and Edward Laumann, who used social network analysis to study interpersonal relations. The social network approach provided analysts with ways to study social relationships that are neither groups nor isolated duets. Instead of an either/or distinction between group membership and social isolation, analysts can look at how relationships fit into a variety of patterns of social structure (for example, see Castells 1996).

At first, researchers just used social network analysis and other empirical approaches to show that traditional communities continue to exist. These scholars documented that, despite all assertions to the contrary, urbanites remain connected (see the reviews in Craven and Wellman 1973; Wellman and Leighton 1979). With time, the implications of my teenage experiences became clearer to me. I came to realize that communities did not equal neighborhoods. This is because communities are about social relationships, whereas neighborhoods are about boundaries. Perhaps at one time communities were confined to neighborhoods (although the evidence I summarize in the next chapter suggests that long-distance community ties stretching beyond the neighborhood have always been important). Yet in the late twentieth century, transportation and communication facilities had so improved that people could maintain many nonlocal friendship and kinship relations. In fact, most community ties in the Western world are not neighborhood ties (Wellman 1993).

During the past three decades network analysts have shown that large-scale social changes have neither destroyed community nor eliminated social support. Communities may have been transformed by the industrial and postindustrial revolutions, but network analysis shows that they continue to flourish. It is possible to trace the evolution of the network analytic approach to community by comparing the somewhat traditional orientation of "Community: City: Urbanization" (Tilly 1970), and "The Network City" (Craven and Wellman 1973)—where we were using a rudimentary network perspective to say "yes, community ties persist in the traditional sense"—with more recent works arguing that sociologists should find community wherever it exists: in neighborhoods, in family solidarities, or in networks that reach further out and include many friends and acquaintances (e.g., Fischer 1982; Wellman 1988a).

Consider the traditional approach saying that neighborhood equals community. This implies that successful neighborhood communities are tightly bounded, densely knit groups of broadly based ties:

- Tightly bounded: Most community ties stay within the neighborhood.
- Densely knit: Most neighborhood residents interact with each other.
- Broadly based: Each tie among neighborhood community residents provides a wide range of social support and companionship.

Yet social network analysts have discovered the opposite in the past thirty years. They have shown that communities are usually loosely bounded, sparsely knit networks of specialized ties:

- Loosely bounded: Most community ties do not stay within the neighborhood. Indeed, they do not stay within any social boundary such as a kinship group or community circle. Instead they ramify outward.
- Sparsely knit: Only a minority of personal community members interact with each other.
- Specialized: Most community ties provide a limited range of social support and companionship.

In short, communities are far-flung social networks and not local neighborhood solidarities.

The early network analysts had it easy twenty-five years ago, although we did not realize it then during the long nights of data-gathering, number-crunching, and paper-writing. Once you start using a network perspective, then it is obvious that communities are networks, just as it is obvious that organizations and world-systems are networks. Analysts have shown whoever has cared to look that life is full of networks. Software analysis tools such as UCINet (Borgatti, Everett, and Freeman 1994) have made it almost as easy to play with networks as it is for users of the Statistical Package for the Social Sciences (SPSS) to play with surveys. The trouble is that SPSS (with its companion, Statistical Analysis System [SAS]) has gone from being a research tool to being a worldview—one that assumes that individuals, analytically isolated from each other, are the proper objects of sociological study (Wellman 1998). The thrust of social network analysis has been to reconnect the study of individuals to the *relationships* and *structures* of relationships in which they are embedded. Part of this venture has been to show that large-scale social changes have neither destroyed community nor eliminated the exchange of social support with friends and relatives. The trick has been to conceive of community as an egocentric network, a "personal community," rather than as a neighborhood. With this approach, a traditional densely knit, village-like neighborhood is but one form of personal community.

The rediscovery of community has been one of sociology's greatest victories. Community, of course, had never been lost. Yet since the industrial revolution, most people have believed that large-scale technological and social changes destroyed community in the developed world and were well on their way to killing it in developing countries. Policymakers and pundits echoed and reinforced this belief, and until a generation ago, most social scientists agreed with them.

All this time communities have continued to thrive around the world, if only people knew how to look for them—and how to look at them. The traditional approach of looking at community as existing in localities—urban neighborhoods and rural towns—made the mistake of looking for *community,* a preeminently *social* phenomenon, in *places,* an inherently *spatial* phenomenon. Why assume that the people who provide companionship, social support, and a sense of belonging only live nearby? The question is important for any era, but it is especially important in contemporary times when people can use cars, planes, phones, and electronic mail to see and talk with far-flung friends and relatives.

The trick is to treat community as a social network rather than as a place. Using this social network approach allows the authors in this book to study people's sociable and supportive community ties with friends and relatives, no matter where they live: across the street, across the metropolis, or across the ocean. The principal defining criterion for community is what people do for each other and not where they live. The social network approach enables the authors in this book to study community without necessarily assuming that all communities are local solidarities.

They do so by defining community as *personal community*, a person's set of ties with friends and relatives, neighbors and workmates.

Networks in the Global Village—
What This Book Is About

This book is the first to present a wide range of scholars who have used social network analysis to study community. Until now, most research has gone into documenting the composition, structure, and supportiveness of community networks in North America. Unfortunately the nature of community networks in the rest of the world has not been clear—the result, no doubt, of the habitual view that America *is* the world.

This book goes beyond the existing situation in two ways. It is the first to bring together analyses of communities from around the globe, presenting original research from eight countries in North America, South America, Europe, and Asia—as well as from cyberspace.[3] Each chapter has been written especially for this book by natives of the countries studied so that we can assess how community networks operate in different societies. This book also goes beyond just documenting the existence of supportive community networks—that task has been well-accomplished—to analyzing the implications of these community networks for the societies in which they are embedded.

The book is organized as an around-the-world tour. I have taken the liberty of starting from my home base in North America because North American scholarship is the reference point with which most studies elsewhere compare themselves and because most of this book's readers will be North American.

After my introductory chapter, the first substantive chapter by Stephanie Potter and myself uses social network analysis to come up with a new way of thinking about community. We do not have to abandon typologies of community altogether, even if the evidence says that we must discard the rigid old way of thinking: "solidary traditional community good/everything else disconnected and bad." Potter and I use Toronto data to argue that a multifactorial and combinatorial approach will allow us to think about how the various elements of community fit together as building blocks of a typology. We suggest that typologies such as ours will aid thinking about the circumstances in which different types of communities will flourish and how being in different types of communities will affect people's lives.

The second substantive chapter, by Milena Gulia and myself, builds on this approach to examine which types of community networks provide what kinds of social support. Until now, most studies of social support have looked only at how different types of *social relationships* provide different kinds of social support. For instance, parents give adult children much more financial aid than companionship, extended kin are not very supportive, women exchange emotional support while neighbors exchange small amounts of goods and services. (I review these studies in the Introduction; see also my more detailed review in Wellman 1992, 1999). Yet social relationships do not exist in isolation but are embedded in social networks. A network is more than the sum of its ties because the composition and structure of a network can affect the resources to which network members have access and the ways in which social relationships operate (Wellman 1992; Milardo and Wellman 1992). In this chapter Gulia and I build on the same data our group has used to study the *tie* basis of social support (Wellman and Leighton 1979; Wellman and Wortley 1989, 1990) to study which kinds of *networks* provide what kinds of support. We ask how the characteristics of community networks—who they are composed of and the structural pattern of the community ties in them—affect the kinds of social support they provide. We find that the greater the *range* of a community network—the larger its size and the greater its heterogeneity—the more supportive it is. Moreover, densely knit community networks are more emotionally and instrumentally supportive than sparsely knit ones. Thus both the characteristics and the structure of a community network affect its supportiveness, in addition to the characteristics of the ties within it. The nature of a network is more than the sum of its ties.

The next two chapters show how social network analysis can continue to be used to study ties within neighborhoods. Still in North America, Barrett Lee and Karen Campbell compare the ties of black and white residents of Nashville, Tennessee. They directly address a key theme of this book: How has large-scale social change affected the nature of community networks? Their particular interest is in how black and white Americans interact within and across putative racial boundaries. Has segregation fostered the "compression" of community so that there is intense interaction within tightly bounded African-American neighborhoods? Or, as William Julius Wilson has argued (1987), has it led to social disorganization and cleavage within these neighborhoods? Lee and Campbell find much evidence of compression and little sign of social disorganization and the loss of community among these segregated African-Americans. Indeed, black and white Nashville residents seem to have similar patterns of neighboring, except that the barriers of segregation make neighborhood relationships more important for African-Americans.

By contrast to Lee and Campbell, Vicente Espinoza's examination of community networks is not limited to neighborhood interactions. Yet he, too, discovers much interaction with neighboring kin and friends among the residents of two impoverished neighborhoods in Santiago, Chile.

More than any other chapter in this book, Espinoza's contribution relates the kinds of community networks people have to the political-economic nature of their society. In Chile, the authoritarian Pinochet regime had adopted an extreme form of a market-based economy, throwing many people out of work and wrecking the country's widespread social welfare institutions. As a result the recent migrants to the metropolis whom Espinoza studied need their community networks for different things than the comparatively affluent North Americans of Toronto and even of Nashville. Rather than North American concerns about family, emotional support, and health care, Santiago residents are preoccupied with obtaining resources for day-to-day survival: getting food, obtaining casual jobs, and maintaining their hastily built homes. In such circumstances, neighbors are handy sources of food, child-care, and information about jobs. There are no telephones, and people do not have the cash to routinely travel elsewhere to visit friends or relatives. The few trips people make to other parts of Santiago or to elsewhere in the country are often for obtaining regular employment. More rarely, someone will put on her best clothes and travel to a rich uncle's house to request a relatively large sum of money.[4]

Crossing the Atlantic brings us to a French chapter by Alexis Ferrand, Lise Mounier, and Alain Degenne. Unlike the neighborhood focus of the preceding two chapters, this work ingeniously juxtaposes and analyzes three national samples, concerned with sexual relationships, modes of life, and interpersonal contact. The authors use network analysis to address the same question that preoccupied Émile Durkheim more than a century ago (1893): How do social relationships integrate and separate different parts of France? In so doing, the authors use interpersonal data to address a matter at a much larger scale of analysis: the articulation of different social categories in France through systems of relationships.[5] They discover a complex pattern of linkages among the French in different socioeconomic positions. Moreover, different types of ties create different kinds of connections between social categories. Their research uses interpersonal data to document precisely the classic French rift between the worlds of self-employed workers and wage-earning workers.

Sik and Wellman's chapter studying Hungary under communism and postcommunism provides another way of examining how large-scale social structures intersect with interpersonal community networks. They use data from a variety of studies to show the importance of community networks for accomplishing things under both communism and postcommunism. One might expect East European communism to be inimical to community because of the ruling class's insistence that no intermediate structures stand between the individual and the state. Moreover, the extensive, often-secret internal security apparatus made it difficult to know who to trust. Consequently, people only had close community ties with presumably trustworthy immediate kin and very few trusted friends (Radoeva 1993). Yet community flourished in providing material aid. The structural rigidities and material shortages inherent in bureaucratic communism (Burawoy 1985) made it imperative for community members and organizational leaders to use networks to get the resources they needed. Using case studies gathered by Sik, the authors show that this was so for heads of agricultural organizations, urbanites wanting their own homes, or villagers largely beyond the ken of state apparatchiks.

Has the need for networks disappeared now that communism is gone from Hungary? Sik and Wellman argue that networks have thrived even more in Hungarian postcommunism. While insecurities of personal freedom have disappeared and bureaucratic rigidities have softened, Hungarians now have insecure access to jobs, income, and capital. They rely on networks to get the multiple jobs they need to survive, to protect their way of life from state regulation, and to assemble the capital they need to start small businesses in a society where none had existed under communism. In short, networks seem to be especially important in situations of high rigidity or uncertainty.

The next three chapters look at Asian networks. Are they as different from Western ones as the proponents of a distinct "Asian way of life" are wont to assert? Like Sik and Wellman, Yanjie Bian studies community networks in a society undergoing a transition from state communism to a new form of postcommunism: China. In the new Chinese situation, *guanxi* (good network connections) are an excellent way to obtain decent jobs despite the explicitly egalitarian and bureaucratic ideology at the heart of the Chinese Communist value system. It is not only who you know that is important, but what positions they have and with whom they are connected. In such circumstances of fluid social mobility, the traditional Chinese obligation to kin and neighborhood is being supplanted by ties to well-placed friends of friends. Only strong ties will do, because the favor being asked is an important one involving access to a valuable resource: a good job. Although weak ties might provide more information about jobs (Granovetter 1974, 1995), they will not get you one in such a situation of scarcity. The relationship is one of exchanges of favors and not of information diffusion.

In another explicit challenge to contentions that Asian communities are markedly different from Western ones, Shinsuke Otani's chapter demonstrates many similarities between Japanese community networks and the North American ones studied by Claude Fischer (1982) and by our research group (Wellman, Carrington, and Hall 1988; Wellman and Wortley 1989). Otani's data destroy some myths about Japanese community networks: They are not as heavily based on neighborhood and kinship, as both Western and Japanese scholars have believed (see also Nozawa 1997). Otani reports that the Japanese neighbor less than North Americans because the Japanese tend to remain living in the same socially heterogeneous neighborhoods, whereas the more spatially and socially mobile North Americans keep moving to neighborhoods that are congruent with their current socioeconomic status. Living among similar people, Otani believes, leads Americans to neighbor more than the Japanese do even though neighbors are only a minority of North American's community ties (Wellman 1992). Moreover, long work and travel times have made neighborhood—and even kinship—less important, especially for Japanese men. Like the situation in the West, extended kin have become the most weakly tied of community members, tied in by normative obligations and kinship structures but providing little companionship and support.

But even if kinfolk are not helpful on a regular basis, they remain a source of help in extraordinary circumstances, mobilizable by densely knit kinship structures that can bring normative obligations and social pressures into play. Salaff, Fong, and Wong's chapter show that this has often been the case for emigrating residents of Hong Kong. Concerns about the handover of Hong Kong to the mainland Chinese government have impelled many families to seek a haven in the Western world. Middle-class Hong Kong residents use ties with network members already in Canada (and other Western-oriented countries such as Britain, Australia, and the United States). Their use of friendship as well as kinship ties to emigrate suggests that differences between kin-oriented Asia and friend-oriented West have been overstated.

The authors show that wealthy Chinese eschew network ties altogether when they emigrate. Because they have enough financial and occupational resources to immigrate on their own to Canada, they go it alone and so avoid having future obligations to the network members in Canada who would have helped them. People do not quickly shed old-world ways as they step through the immigration gate. For one thing, East-West similarities are greater than has been asserted. For another, those who emigrate may be the ones who were already less connected to kinship and neighborhood solidarities back home. And third, the kinds of social systems in which people operate significantly affect the nature of their community networks. As people forge community ties, they are not doing so on a tabula rasa; they are operating within the context of existing social relationships and divisions of labor, both interpersonal and interinstitutional.

Chinese businesspeople who commute regularly between Hong Kong and Toronto are called "astronauts" by their community because they seem always to be in space. But what about those who find community in cyberspace—perhaps the ultimate exemplar of a community that is not bound by place? A debate rages about whether the proliferation of computer-mediated communication, such as the Internet and the Web, will destroy community or enhance it. The debate largely rehashes the community question reviewed in the Introduction, although there is little evidence that most of the debaters have ever considered anything since the advent of computer networks. As philosopher/catcher/baseball manager Yogi Berra once said, "It's deja vu all over again."

In the final chapter of this book, Wellman and Gulia review the debate about virtual community. They bring to bear on the debate what we know about community networks in general and about interactions online in particular. Readers of this preface will not be surprised to learn that online communities look much like in-person communities, with specialized, but supportive, relationships flourishing in far-flung, sparsely connected networks. Although virtual communards take advantage of the ability of computer networks to leap over time and space, many online interactions continue to be with people who are seen in-person at work or at leisure. These, after all, are the people with whom most of us have to deal routinely, and computer-mediated communication provides just another means to connect with them conveniently (Haythornthwaite and Wellman 1998). Despite the dazzling portrayals of virtual worlds whose denizens only meet online, in reality, most ties combine in-person with computer-mediated contact. The advent of still another means of communication does not mean that life as we have known it will cease to exist.

The authors of this book tell us *what to look for*: socially defined community networks; not spatially defined neighborhood communities.

They tell us *where to look for it*: anywhere.

They tell us *what to see*: specialized, often fragmented, interpersonal networks, and not (the absence of) solidarity.

And they tell us *how to picture it*: in the context of large-scale social systems whose opportunities and constraints shape the networks and are, in turn, shaped by them.

Barry Wellman

Notes

1. Indeed, Richard Price wrote a novel in which they star, *The Wanderers* (1974), which was later made into a film.

2. An archaic, handheld tool for quantitative calculations, made obsolete by pocket calculators in the 1970s.

3. Unfortunately, two authors never completed the African chapters that were commissioned. Despite network analysis's glorious origins in Britain (Wellman

1988b; Scott 1991; Freeman and Wellman 1995), the only contemporary study of British community networks I was able to find when I started this book was Wenger's (1992) research into caregiving for the aged.

4. Espinoza studied these neighborhoods in the 1980s. By the time that I visited these neighborhoods in 1996, the homes had been upgraded from shacks to neatly painted permanent structures with good roofs. In the decade, the area had been regularized and absorbed into the expanding metropolis. Electricity had been installed, phone lines were going in as I watched, many roads were paved, and buses ran frequently to other parts of Santiago. Yet on the outskirts of Santiago, I observed the same kinds of shacks, poor transportation, and lack of services that characterized Espinoza's neighborhoods a decade earlier. The cycle of migration, informal settlement, and regularization continues.

5. For more focused American efforts to use social network analysis to study social integration, see Granovetter (1995) and Laumann (1973).

References

Borgatti, Stephen, Martin Everett, and Linton Freeman. 1994. *UCINet 4*. Boston: Analytic Technologies.

Burawoy, Michael. 1985. *The Politics of Production*. London: Verso.

Castells, Manuel. 1996. *The Rise of Network Society*. Malden, MA: Blackwell.

Craven, Paul, and Barry Wellman. 1973. "The Network City." *Sociological Inquiry* 43:57–88.

Durkheim, Émile. 1893 [1993]. *The Division of Labor in Society*. New York: Free Press.

Fischer, Claude. 1982. *To Dwell Among Friends*. Berkeley: University of California Press.

Freeman, Linton, and Barry Wellman. 1995. "A Note on the Ancestral Toronto Home of Social Network Analysis." *Social Networks* 15(2):15–19.

Granovetter, Mark. 1974. *Getting a Job*. Cambridge, MA: Harvard University Press.

Granovetter, Mark. 1995. *Getting a Job*. rev. ed. Chicago: University of Chicago Press.

Haythornthwaite, Caroline, and Barry Wellman. 1998. "Work, Friendship and Media Use for Information Exchange in a Networked Organization." *Journal of American Society for Information Systems* 49(12):1101–1114.

Laumann, Edward. 1973. *Bonds of Pluralism*. New York: Wiley.

Magocsi, Paul Robert, and Geoffrey Matthews. 1993. *Historical Atlas of East Central Europe*. Toronto: University of Toronto Press.

Milardo, Robert, and Barry Wellman. 1992. "The Personal Is Social." *Journal of Social and Personal Relationships* 9(3):339–342.

Nozawa, Shinji. 1997. *Marital Relations and Personal Networks in Urban Japan*. Working Paper. Department of Sociology, Shizouka University, May.

Price, Richard. 1974. *The Wanderers*. Boston: Houghton Mifflin.

Radoeva, Detelina. 1993. "Networks of Informal Exchange in State-Socialist Societies." Presented to the International Sunbelt Social Network Conference, Tampa, February.

Scott, John. 1991. *Social Network Analysis*. London: Sage.

Tilly, Charles. 1970. "Community: City: Urbanization." Working Paper, Department of Sociology, University of Michigan.

Wellman, Barry. 1988a. "The Community Question Re-evaluated." Pp. 81–107 in *Power, Community and the City*, edited by Michael Peter Smith. New Brunswick, NJ: Transaction Books.

Wellman, Barry. 1988b. "Structural Analysis: From Method and Metaphor to Theory and Substance." Pp. 19–61 in *Social Structures: A Network Approach*, edited by Barry Wellman and S. D. Berkowitz. Cambridge: Cambridge University Press.

Wellman, Barry. 1992. "Which Types of Ties and Networks Give What Kinds of Social Support?" *Advances in Group Processes* 9:207–235.

Wellman, Barry. 1993. "An Egocentric Network Tale." *Social Networks* 17(2):423–436.

Wellman, Barry. 1998. "Doing It Ourselves: The *SPSS Manual* as Sociology's Most Influential Book." Pp. 71–78 in *Required Reading: Sociology's Most Influential Books*, edited by Dan Clawson. Amherst, MA: University of Massachusetts Press.

Wellman, Barry. 1999. "The Social Network Basis of Social Support." *Advances in Medical Sociology* 10, forthcoming.

Wellman, Barry, and Barry Leighton. 1979. "Networks, Neighborhoods and Communities." *Urban Affairs Quarterly* 14:363–390.

Wellman, Barry, and Scot Wortley. 1989. "Brothers' Keepers: Situating Kinship Relations in Broader Networks of Social Support." *Sociological Perspectives* 32:273–306.

Wellman, Barry, and Scot Wortley. 1990. "Different Strokes from Different Folks: Community Ties and Social Support." *American Journal of Sociology* 96:558–588.

Wellman, Barry, Peter Carrington, and Alan Hall. 1988. "Networks as Personal Communities." Pp. 130–184 in *Social Structures: A Network Approach*, edited by Barry Wellman and S. D. Berkowitz. Cambridge: Cambridge University Press.

Wenger, G. Clare. 1992. *Help in Old Age—Facing Up to Change: A Longitudinal Study*. Liverpool: Liverpool University Press.

Wilson, William Julius. 1987. *The Truly Disadvantaged*. Chicago: University of Chicago Press.

Acknowledgments to
My Intellectual Community

Although I only knew my late Toronto colleague, Marshall McLuhan, casually, much of my work has turned out to be an empirically supported debate with his insightful "probes." Certainly, Marshall's "global village" concept resonates with my independently developed "community liberated" construct. Indeed, this book's entire notion of examining socially defined communities in contexts is in part an effort to see what the global village looks like around the world. And as McLuhan was very much a man of his context—neighborhood, college, university, and city (Marchand 1989)—I believe he would enjoy this book's description of how the large-scale contexts significantly shape—and are shaped by—the personal communities that are embedded in them.

My debts to members of my intellectual network are multiple, long term, and immense. They start with my two principal Harvard mentors in social network analysis: Charles Tilly and Harrison White. At the other end of the baton, I have profited enormously from working since 1967 with many student collaborators, most notably Susan Gonzalez Baker, Paul Craven, Vicente Espinoza, Milena Gulia, Laura Garton, Keith Hampton, Caroline Haythornthwaite, Emmanuel Koku, Barry Leighton, Nancy Nazer, and Scot Wortley. You can get some sense of what we have done together by examining the coauthored articles that appear in this book's reference lists; more work is underway. In addition to the many colleagues acknowledged in specific chapters, I especially appreciate my conversations through the years with Ronald Baecker, Steve Berkowitz, William Buxton, Donald Coates, Dimitrina Dimitrova, Bonnie Erickson, Alexis Ferrand, Claude Fischer, Linton Freeman, Harriet Friedmann, Chad Gordon, Mark Granovetter, Roxanne Hiltz, Leslie Howard, Nancy Howell, Peter and Trudy Johnson-Lenz, Joel Levine, Marilyn Mantei, Joshua Meyrowitz, William Michelson, Gale Moore, Shinji Nozawa, Detelina Radoeva, Janet Salaff, Endre Sik, Richard Stren, Philip Stone, and Charles Wetherell. Throughout all this networking, the Centre for Urban and Community Studies and the Department of Sociology have been supportive University of Toronto homes.

I have learned a great deal from working with all the authors of the chapters in this book. Because the chapters are original and because most authors do not have English as their first language, most chapters went through multiple drafts. As we collaborated on revisions, we obtained new insights into each other, communities, and social network analysis. I thank the authors for their patience, persistence, and competence in this enterprise, as well as the many things that they taught me about how community networks function in their societies. I also appreciate Alexandra Marin's and Anais Scott's help in preparing the final version.

My greatest debt is to Beverly Wellman, a debt that has accrued constantly since we met in 1963 and married in 1965. Not only has Bev been my best friend and infinite supporter, she has been a superb generator of good ideas and a tireless, fearless editor of not-so-good ideas. I am profoundly joyous that we have coauthored our life together.

B. W.

References

Marchand, Phillip. 1989. *Marshall McLuhan*. Toronto: Random House.

Networks in
the Global Village

The Network Community:
An Introduction

"Things Ain't Wot They Used to Be"—
and They Never Were!

Why does a debate about whether community exists persist, when the reality of community pervades our existence? Remember the timeless British music-hall lament: "Things ain't wot they used to be"? Contemporary urbanites perversely flatter themselves by remarking how well they are coping with stressful modern times in contrast to the easy life their ancestors led. They look back to bygone, supposedly golden days when they are sure that their ancestors—twenty, one hundred, three hundred years ago—led charmed lives, basking in the warmth of true solidary community. I suspect that at all times, most people have feared that communities had fallen apart around them, with loneliness and alienation leading to a war of all against all.

A large part of contemporary unease comes from a selective perception of the present. Many people think they are witnessing loneliness when they observe people walking or driving by themselves. Mass media quickly and graphically circulate news about New York subway attacks and Parisian bombings. The public generalizes its fears: The attack could take place next door tomorrow, but disconnected strangers would never call the police, just as they continue to disregard the sounding of strangers' car-theft alarms.

Paradoxically, few people will confess that they, themselves, are currently living lives of lonely desperation. They know that they have supportive communities, and they are aware that most of their friends, neighbors, kin, and workmates also are members of supportive communities. Yet even with these realizations, the same people believe that they are the exceptions, and that the masses around them are lonely and isolated.

At the same time, there is nostalgia for the perfect pastoral past that never was (see the critique in Laslett 1965). This dims awareness of the powerful stresses and cleavages that have always pervaded human society. The inhabitants of almost all contemporary societies have less to worry about than their predecessors with respect to the basics of human

1

life. Without being Pollyannaish, the data show that people now are generally better fed, housed, and clothed, suffer less personal and property crime, and live longer. In their concern about current problems, people often forget about the problems that are no more. AIDS does not rival the Black Death; automobile pollution may cause less illness than streets littered with horse manure. Yet people are often without history; they forget that crime and political violence rates are lower now than they were one and two centuries ago (Gurr 1981; Monkkonen 1995).

Community has never been lost. Yet since the industrial revolution, most people have believed that large-scale technological and social changes had destroyed community in the developed world and were well on their way to killing it in developing countries. Policymakers and pundits echoed and reinforced this belief, and, until a generation ago, most social scientists agreed with them.

Wherever they have looked, researchers have found thriving communities. This is so well documented that there is no longer any scholarly need to demonstrate that community ties exist everywhere, although the alarmed public, politicians, and pundits need to be constantly reassured and re-educated. But there is a pressing need to understand what kinds of community flourish, what communities do—and do not do—for people, and how communities operate in different social systems.

The Community Question

The basic question about the nature of community—which I call the *Community Question*—is how large-scale divisions of labor affect, and are affected by, smaller-scale communities of kith and kin? Thus the Community Question inherently has two parts depending on which causal direction you look:

1. How does the structure of large-scale social systems affect the composition, structure, and contents of interpersonal ties within them? For example, do different countries, ethnic groups, gender relations, or socioeconomic strata affect the nature of community? The authors in this book focus on this aspect of the Community Question in relation to community networks. But much the same issues pertain to the study of other sorts of interpersonal networks: kinship groups, households, and work groups.

2. How does the nature of community networks affect the nature of the large-scale social systems in which they are embedded? This is the reciprocal part of the Community Question. For example, do resources flow freely from one part of society to another? Or are communities isolated from each other in racial or class enclaves (sometimes called "ghettos")? Speaking to this issue, Mark Granovetter's "strength of weak ties" argu-

ment (1973, 1982, 1995) has shown how weak community ties integrate social systems by linking heterogeneous groups of people; Edward Laumann's *Bonds of Pluralism* (1973) has shown how community networks structure relations among ethnic and religious groups in Chicago; while Alexis Ferrand, Lise Mounier, and Alain Degenne's chapter in this book shows how community networks integrate certain socioeconomic strata in France but decouple others (see Chapter 5).

Thus, the Community Question stands at a crucial nexus between societal and interpersonal social systems. It juxtaposes the problem of the structural integration of a social system and the interpersonal means by which the members of this social system have access to scarce resources. The *social capital* vested in ties provide interpersonal resources for people to use to deal with daily life, seize opportunities, and reduce uncertainties. (Kadushin 1981; Bourdieu 1984; Coleman 1990; Wellman and Wortley 1990; Flap 1995; Putnam 1995; Burt 1997; Lin 1997; Ruan et al. 1997; Schweizer, Schnegg, and Berzborn 1998).

Looking for Community

It is likely that pundits have worried about the impact of social change on community ever since people ventured beyond their caves. The Community Question clearly preoccupied biblical prophets from the eleventh century BCE onward (see 1 Samuel 8, for example), concerned then (as now) that the establishment of an Israeli state would lead to communal disintegration (Leach 1966; Buccellati 1967; Zeidman 1985). As the prophet Jeremiah warned the rapidly modernizing Israelites in the sixth century BCE in "all their wickedness" (Jer. 1:16): "Take ye heed every one of his neighbor, and on any brother place ye no reliance; for every brother will surely supplant, and every neighbor will go about as a talebearer (Jer. 9:3)."[1]

Two thousand years later, the Community Question continued to be a major issue to Renaissance intellectuals. Their concerns ranged from Machiavelli's (1532) celebration of the liberation of communal patterns to Hobbes's (1651) fears that the absence of social structures would result in the interpersonal war of all against all. A bit later, the Community Question was a key preoccupation of such eighteenth-century British philosophers as John Locke and David Hume (see also Wills 1978) as they sought to deduce the social basis of larger-scale societies from their understanding of primordial communal relations. Their student, Thomas Jefferson, gave the question an antiurban cast—communal bonds are not viable in industrial, commercial cities—when he asserted: "The mobs of great cities add just so much to the support of pure government, as sores do to the strength of the human body" (1784, p. 86).

In the two centuries since then, many commentators have wrestled to understand the ways in which large-scale social changes associated with the Industrial Revolution may have affected the composition, structure, and operations of communities. Their analyses have reflected the ambivalence with which nineteenth-century pundits faced the impact on interpersonal relations of industrialization, bureaucratization, capitalism, imperialism, and technological developments. Where religion, locality, and kinship could integrate people, the shift to mobile, market societies had the potential to disconnect individuals from the strengths and constraints of traditional societies (Marx 1964; Smith 1979; White and White 1962; Williams 1973).

On the one hand, analysts feared the negative consequences of large-scale changes. The keynote was set by Ferdinand Tönnies (1887) who claimed there were fundamental differences between the communally organized societies of yesteryear (which he called *gemeinschaft*) and the contractually organized societies (*gesellschaft*) associated with the coming of the industrial revolution. As discussed in Chapter 1, Tönnies asserted that communally organized societies, supposedly characteristic of rural areas and underdeveloped societies, would have densely interconnected social relationships composed principally of neighbors and kin. By contrast, he asserted that contractually organized societies, supposedly characteristic of industrial cities, would have more sparsely knit relationships composed principally of ties between friends and acquaintances, rather than between relatives or neighbors. He believed that the lack of cohesion in such *gesellschaft* societies was leading to specialized, contractual exchanges replacing communally enforced norms of mutual support.

This was not only an isolated, nostalgic lament for the supposed loss of the mythical pastoral past where happy villagers knew their place. Many commentators shared Tönnies's fears about the supposed contemporary loss of community, although they offered different reasons for its occurrence, such as industrialization, urbanization, bureaucratization, capitalism, socialism, or technological change. Thus the loss of community was a centerpiece of Karl Marx's (1852) and Friedrich Engels's (1885) communist analyses, asserting that industrial capitalism had created new types of interpersonal exploitation that drove people apart. Capitalism had alienated workers not only from their work but from each other. By contrast, although sociologist Max Weber (1946, 1958) extolled modern rationality, he also feared that bureaucratization and urbanization were weakening communal bonds and traditional authority. Sociologist Émile Durkheim (1897) feared that the loss of solidarity had weakened communal support and fostered social pathology. Some years later, sociologist Georg Simmel (1903) celebrated urban liberation but also worried that the new individualism would lead to superficial relationships.

On the other hand, many of the same commentators noted that the large-scale reorganization of production had created new opportunities for community ties. Thus Marx acknowledged that industrialization had reduced poverty and Engels realized that working-class home-ownership would heighten local communal bonds. Weber argued that bureaucracy and urbanization would liberate many from the traditional, stultifying bases of community, and Durkheim (1893) argued that the new complex divisions of labor were binding people together in networks of interdependent "organic solidarity." In the same article where he worried about the consequences of urban liberation, Simmel argued that in the new cities, individuals were no longer totally enmeshed in one social circle. Therefore, they have greater personal freedom as they maneuver through their partial attachments.

Tönnies's vision was part of a particularly European debate about the transformation of *societies*—aristocrats, intellectuals, and parvenus coming to terms with the transformation of once-ordered, hierarchical societies of peasants and landowners, workers, and merchants. Despite different social conditions, social scientists in the new North American world adapted Tönnies's concerns, debating whether modern times have occasioned the loss of *community* in developed Western societies (e.g., Berger 1960; Gans 1962, 1967; Grant 1969; Nisbet 1962; Parsons 1943; Slater 1970; Stein 1960). Robert Redfield's (1947) *folk-urban* continuum was especially influential, asserting that the possibilities for community varied linearly between highly communal rural villages, through towns, to cities lacking community.

In confronting their own society, many Americans decried the loss of solidary communities of family, kin, and neighbors, bound by custom and tradition. Their analyses reflected the continuing American tension between individualism and communalism originally put forward by the influential historian, Frederick Jackson Turner. Focusing on the populace's march westward to settle the supposedly empty frontier, Turner (1893) asserted that constant movement left little room for community to develop. He argued that what little there was of community in the rural American west consisted of transient groups of settlers helping each other, with instrumental aid overshadowing emotional support, companionship, or a sense of communal belonging. Even American cities were filled with migrants: floating proletarians who were constantly on the move, seeking work that would push them up the ladder (Thernstrom 1964, 1973; Chudacoff 1972; Katz, Doucet, and Stern 1982). The successful rural settlers and urban migrants embodied the Turnerian spirit of individualism and practicality. They had avoided being trapped in traditional community bonds (Starr 1985, 1990).[2]

What Could Have Caused Changes in Community?

Contemporary analysts have debated the causes of changes in community almost as much as they have debated whether community has, in fact, changed and what the nature of these changes might be. This is because associations among the appearance of industrialization, bureaucratization, urbanization, capitalism, socialism, and new transportation and communication technologies have made it difficult to tease out the ultimate cause, if any (see the discussion in Abu-Lughod 1991). Various analysts have pointed to:

1. The increased scale of the nation-state's activities, with a concomitant low level of local community autonomy and solidarity (e.g., Tilly 1973, 1975, 1984a).
2. Increasing globalization, with footloose financial capital creating uncertainty in local communities and encouraging workers to uproot themselves and migrate to places with better employment possibilities (e.g., Burawoy 1976; Castells 1972).
3. The development of narrowly instrumental bureaucratic institutions for production and reproduction that may have lead to the transformation of former, broadly supportive community ties to contractually defined, narrow relations of exchange (Tönnies 1887; Castells 1972; Howard 1988).
4. The large size of cities creates a population and organizational potential for diverse interest groups (Wirth 1938; Fischer 1984).
5. The high social density of interaction among segments of the population (even where spatial density is low) creates complexities of organizational and ecological sorting (Abu-Lughod 1991; Gillis and Hagan 1982).
6. The diversity of persons with whom urbanites can come into contact under conditions of heightened mobility (Jacobs 1961);
7. The proliferation of widespread networks of cheap and efficient transportation and communication facilities that have allowed contact to be maintained with greater ease and over longer distances: in transportation, from railroads through superhighways and planes; in communication, from overnight mail service to direct long-distance telephone dialing to the Internet and the World Wide Web (Meier 1962; see also Chapter 10 in this volume). The increased velocity of transactions has fostered interactional density. The large-scale metropolis is

accessible and links to diverse social networks can be maintained more readily.

Ambivalence about the consequences of large-scale changes has continued through the twentieth century, with scholars and pundits asking if things have, in fact, fallen apart. Unfortunately, the fundamental concerns of the Community Question have become confounded in many analyses with narrower issues:

1. Some researchers continue the habit of looking for community ties only in local areas, reflecting community sociology's origins in studying neighborhoods (Stein 1960). Seeing community in concrete, bounded neighborhoods is easier than seeing community in far-flung networks whose ties spread almost invisibly through the ether.

2. A general preoccupation with identifying the conditions under which solidary sentiments can be maintained. In so doing, they reflect a continuing worry about whether normative integration and consensus persist. People worry whether they can get help from strangers or even from the members of their community; they worry that they will be alone in confronting crime, disease, joblessness, or natural catastrophes (Etzioni 1991; Nisbet 1962). The most recent manifestation of this concern has been Robert Putnam's raising the alarm that Americans are now "bowling alone" (1995); they are much less involved in voluntary organized groups, be they bowling leagues, churches, clubs, or unions. In his Tocqueville-like analysis (e.g., 1835), Putnam fears that this lessened organizational participation means less civic involvement in promoting good government and less "social trust" in governments and fellow citizens. He wonders if amorphous community networks can substitute for participation in more bounded and concrete organizations.

Concerns about the persistence of community are frequently projected onto the future in Manichean debates about whether community will die or flourish in cyberspace (as Chapter 10 documents). Science-fiction novels have echoed fears of the loss of community, providing scenarios ranging from alienation in densely packed (Ballard 1975), hypercapitalistic (Brunner 1968) mass societies, to postatomic holocaust returns to tribal solidarities (Atwood 1985; Lessing 1974). However, a more optimistic genre has foretold wired people in wired cities moving easily among interest groups (Brunner 1975; Delaney 1976; Gibson 1986; Stephenson 1992). Similar to the novels, the predominant depiction of the future in films has been of small, scattered, and impoverished tribal bands trying to survive in a desolate land filled with marauders, a genre popularized in contemporary times by George Miller's (and Mel Gibson's) *Mad Max* (1979) and *The Road Warrior* (1981), and by James Cameron's (and Arnold Schwarzenegger's) *The Terminator* (1984). An alternative futuristic vision has been equally bleak, in a cinematic fashion set by Ridley Scott's (and Harrison Ford's) *Blade Runner* (1982): the squalid, overpopulated, East Asian-influenced landscape of alienated urban masses in a society visually dominated by huge organizations and their equally huge neon signs.

With the growth of the Internet and the Web, what had once been science fiction has become a staple for apocalyptic speculation, although with much less analysis. As Chapter 10 recounts, those on either side of this debate assert that the Internet either will create wonderful new forms of community or will destroy community altogether. This latter side of the debate is Tönnies *nouveau*, warning that meaningful contact will wither without the full bandwidth provided by in-person, in-the-flesh contact. This debate has been unscholarly, presentist, and parochial. Consistent with the present-oriented ethos of computer-users, pundits write as if people and scholars had never worried about community before the Internet arose. Too many analysts treat the Internet as an isolated phenomenon without taking into account how online interactions fit with other aspects of people's lives.

Finding Community

Rediscovering Traditional Community with Flowers in Its Hair

Given its importance to human kind and accessibility to public discourse, it is a safe guess that the Community Question in some form will remain open to the end of time. Yet since World War II important transformations have taken place in scholarly approaches to the question:

1. The new zeitgeist of community optimism born with the student and civil rights movements of the 1960s.
2. The social-scientific turn away from armchair speculation to gathering data systematically. Fieldwork and survey research have each shown the persistence of community (see the reviews in Wellman 1988a; Wellman and Leighton 1979).
3. The development of new ways of studying local social histories that have demythologized notions of stable pastoral villages and have emphasized the strength of community in the transition from the premodern to the modern world (see the review in Wellman and Wetherell 1996; see also Tilly 1984a; Ariès 1962; Shorter 1975; Stone 1977; Bender 1978; Scherzer 1992; Wetherell, Plakans, and Wellman 1994).

4. The discovery by social scientists that violent political conflicts arise more out of the clash of structured communal interests than out of the *cri de coeur* of the disconnected and the alienated (Feagin 1973, Feagin and Hahn 1973; Tilly 1979, 1984a).

One intellectual generation ago the watchwords of community sociologists were documentation and description. The profession was preoccupied with proving that community persisted—dare they say "flourished"? Scholars of the first (Western, developed, nonsocialist) world wanted to show that supportive community ties remained even in allegedly pernicious habitats: inner-city slums (Gans 1962; Liebow 1967; Whyte 1943; Young and Willmott 1957) and middle-class suburbs (Bell 1968; Clark 1966; Gans 1967). Scholars of the third ("underdeveloped") world battled fears that the migrants flooding into industrializing cities would form communally disconnected, politically dangerous hordes.[3] Although the argument that capitalism had shaped urban communities called for comparative approaches (e.g., Castells 1972; see also Fischer 1978), few scholars tackled the Community Question in the second (socialist) world of Eastern Europe and China. To have done so, would have been contradictory to the anti-Tocquevillean (1835) communist ethos that saw each person relating individually to the state, without intermediary structures. Hence community network studies (such as Chapter 6 in this volume) have only developed in postcommunist times.[4]

With hindsight, postwar fears about the "loss of community" came in part from the same sources as some Americans' fear of evil creatures from outer space and U.S. Senator Joe McCarthy's search for covert subversives. The fearful saw alien forces and believed that the Frankensteinian "machine in the garden" (Marx 1964) had run amok and destroyed traditional communities. Beneath the jingoistic celebration of small-town virtues lurked the fear that people were inherently evil: ready to rob, rape, pillage, and turn atheistically communist when communal bonds were loosened.

By the 1960s, urban scholars had started using ethnographic and survey techniques to show that community had survived the major transformations of the industrial revolution. Since then both fieldwork and survey research have shown that neighborhood and kinship ties continue to be abundant and strong. Large institutions have neither smashed nor withered community ties. To the contrary: the larger and more inflexible the institutions, the more people seem to depend on their informal ties to deal with them. For example, Chapters 6 and 7 in this volume report that both people and organizations relied on informal ties to obtain resources in communist China and Hungary (see also Lin 1997; Lin,

Ye, and Chen 1997). To go through channels would have been to wait forever. Sik and Wellman also show (Chapter 6) that another aspect of informal ties, their reliability, is important in hyperflexible, cash-poor, postcommunist Hungary. It is often the only way to get jobs, money, or
favors.

The developing body of research has shown that, while communities
may have changed in response to the pressures, opportunities, and constraints of large-scale forces, they have not withered away. They buffer
households against large-scale forces, provide mutual aid, and serve as
secure bases to engage with the outside world (see reviews in Choldin
1985; Fischer 1976; Gordon 1978; Keller 1968; Smith 1979; Warren 1978).
They provide Kirkian emotional aid, Spockian information, McCoyesque
companionship, and Scottyan instrumental aid: the four archetypes of
the original *Star Trek* television show (Whitfield and Roddenberry 1970).
For example, Espinoza's work in Chapter 4 shows that informal community ties are the keys to daily survival in the impoverished barrios of urban Chile. They provide food, shelter, short-term loans, job leads, and
help in dealing with organizations. In this situation, neighbors (who are
often kin) provide most everyday support. Yet such neighbors are poor
themselves. To get sizeable amounts of money or access to good jobs, the
residents must rely on their weaker ties to wealthier, better-situated relatives who live outside the barrios. The situation fits well with Granovetter's (1973) and Wellman and Leighton's (1979) argument that weak,
ramifying ties are well suited for obtaining access to new resources,
whereas strong, solidary ties are well suited for mobilizing and conserv-
ing existing resources.

This scholarly rediscovery of community resonated strongly with the
political developments of the 1960s. The civil rights movement encouraged more positive evaluations of urban black neighborhoods (e.g., Stack
1974) and, by extension, of lumpenproletariat life everywhere. The neo-
Rousseauian student movement preached the inherent goodness of human kind. Students and anthropologists boarded new low-cost charter
flights to spend five dollars a day (Frommer 1967) discovering that Europe and the third world were full of enjoyable people in interesting villages and cities. Planners turned away from urban renewal toward the
preservation of dense, noisy downtown neighborhoods (as expressed
most vividly in Jane Jacobs's 1961 anthem). Instead of bulldozing neighborhoods to encourage suburban growth and metropolitan expressways,
planners, and politicians started banning large-scale inner-city housing
projects and terminating expressways outside city cores. Renovation and
gentrification became the buzzwords of the 1970s. There were hard-won
battles, fought with demonstrations, sit-ins, court decrees, elections, and
scholarly articles. Despite much migration to the suburbs, the centers of

such cities as Boston, New York, San Francisco, and Toronto remained well populated.

This transformation in thinking became the academic orthodoxy of the late 1960s and the 1970s. Scholars, planners, and some politicians and members of the public no longer thought of cities as evil, permeated with Original Sin. Their Jacobsean cum Rousseauesque celebrations of community had the lingering aroma of the 1960s, seeing urbanites as permeated with Original Good and happily maintaining mutually supportive ties. The rest of the populace was slower to catch on: many policymakers, the media, and the public at large continued to fear the urban, yearn for the pastoral, and settle for suburbia.

How Green Were the Valleys?

In saying that communities are not as local as they used to be, analysts must avoid committing the pastoralist fallacy of thinking that contemporary cities and suburbs are inferior to the villages or cities of yesteryear, with their pestilence, crime, and insecurity. At the same time that sociologists were discovering the existence of contemporary communities, historical analysts started using similar research methods to study preindustrial villages, towns, and cities. Until their work became known, analysts had contrasted the disorderly urban present with the pastoral ideal of bucolic, solidary villages (Poggioli 1975). They assumed that such communities were socially cohesive and stable, with little movement in or out. Yet the supposed communalism of the preindustrial world has turned out to be an artifact of how earlier commentators thought about it. Preindustrial communities were not as locally bounded as tradition has maintained. Whenever scholars have looked for nonlocal ties, they have found far-ranging networks. For example, radioactive analyses of obsidian have found Neolithic spear points and choppers more than one thousand miles from their origin (Dixon, Cann, and Renfrew 1968).

By looking for community in localities and not in networks, analysts had focused on local phenomena and stability rather than on long distances and mobility. For example, Emmanuel Le Roy Ladurie's (1975) rich account of medieval village life in southern France reveals a good deal of geographical mobility as early as the 1300s. To trace networks of Albigensian heretics, Catholic investigators asked all residents of the village of Montaillou to report who their friends were, who had influence, and how they spent their days. They used this information to build up detailed accounts of the village community. These accounts reveal that many villagers travelled widely. Some were shepherds following their flocks over the Pyrenees, some were itinerant soldiers, while others travelled south to the Spanish coast or west along the Mediterranean to northern Italy. The people of Montaillou had frequent contact with other villages, and passing travellers often gave them news of the outside world. With such contact came new ideas, intermarriage, and new alliances.

Montaillou was not a solidary village. Various factions competed within it for wealth and status. Each faction used its ties outside the village to enhance its local standing, and each used its local support to build external alliances. As with preindustrial villages everywhere, their local life was very much a part of the larger world (see also Davis 1975, 1983; Hufton 1974; Tilly 1964; Chapters 4 and 6 in this volume). Nor was Montaillou an unusual place. Consider the protagonist of the *Return of Martin Guerre* (Davis 1983): a soldier returning to his French village with knowledge and a new identity gained from wars in distant parts of Europe. The wanderings continue during the Renaissance and the Reformation: For example, Le Roy Ladurie's *The Beggar and the Professor* (1997) is a biography of three generations of the sixteenth-century Swiss family Platter. The men in all three generations took long journeys around Europe, ranging from Poland to Bohemia, from southern Spain to Paris to northern Germany. They—and the other Swiss described in this remarkable book—combined their social and spatial mobility with far-flung, fluid community networks. They used their networks to settle into distant universities, to obtain knowledge, and to find jobs and spouses.

In the past three decades, social scientists have analyzed the local histories of both preindustrial and newly industrializing communities in Europe and North America. They have concentrated on the period between 1600 and 1900 when emerging national governments began to keep more careful records. By using such sources as parish registers and early censuses, historical demographers have enumerated the gender, marital status, and occupations of all persons living in a household. Record-linkage techniques help trace the social and spatial movement of persons and households (Laslett 1965, 1972; Anderson 1971; Aminzade and Hodson 1982; Thernstrom 1964; Katz 1975; Darroch and Ornstein 1983; Wellman and Wetherell 1996).

These studies suggest that the average preindustrial household was quite small. For example, at the turn of the nineteenth century, the typical adult inhabitant of the Latvian village of Pinkenhof had only three kin and five friends/neighbors/coworkers in their personal communities (Wetherell, Plakans, and Wellman 1994). Contrary to the contemporary pastoralist myth of immutable villages, many families were socially and spatially mobile. They often worked in the city when they were young adults, but retained ties with their rural villages.[5] Artisans and soldiers were frequently on the road. Women married and moved, geographically and socially. Servants' ties to their distant families concurrently linked their masters' families to the servants' rural homes. And, as all readers of Jane Austen know, these complex connections linked far-flung networks of community ties. For example, in *Sense and Sensibility* (1811), the Misses Dashwood made long journeys between their original Sussex home, their new Devonshire house, and the London social milieu. Even while residing at "Barton Cottage," Devonshire, they—and their network members—were forever going to visit each other, apparently oblivious to the many other homes that they went past. They maintained far-flung kinship and friendship networks throughout southern and central England but few ties with their neighbors.

Neighborhood or Community?

Despite these cautionary tales from the past, the fundamentally structural Community Question has often been a search for local solidarity rather than a search for supportive ties, wherever located and however solidary. As a result of the continuing sociological and public fixation on communities as solidary neighborhoods, community studies have usually been neighborhood studies, be they the "symbiotic" communities of Robert Park's treatises (1925) or the empirical studies of street life by Whyte (1943), Liebow (1967), and Anderson (1990). Definitions of community have usually included three ingredients:

1. Interpersonal networks that provide sociability, social support, and social capital to their members;
2. residence in a common locality, such as a village or neighborhood;
3. solidary sentiments and activities (see Hillery 1955).

It is principally the emphasis on common locality, and to a lesser extent the emphasis on solidarity, that has encouraged the identification of "community" with "neighborhood." There are several reasons that the concept of "neighborhood" has been almost synonymous with the concept of "community":

1. Community researchers have to start somewhere. The neighborhood is an easily identifiable research site, while the street corner is an obvious, visible, and accessible place for observing interpersonal interactions. Indeed, Chapters 3 and 4 in this volume start by drawing their samples from one or more neighborhoods.
2. Many urban scholars have seen the neighborhood as the microcosm of the city, and the city as an aggregate of

neighborhoods. They have emphasized the local rather than the cosmopolitan (Merton 1957) in a building-block approach to analysis that has given scant attention to the interpersonal and interorganizational ties that form large-scale social structures.

3. Administrative officials have imposed their own definitions of neighborhood boundaries upon urban maps in attempts to create bureaucratic units. Politicians are even more neighborhood-oriented, in part because they usually have to be elected from local constituencies. Spatial areas, labeled and treated as coherent neighborhoods, have come to be regarded as natural phenomena—by politicians, the public, researchers, and even by the people who live there. In Toronto, downtown street signs proclaim "Little Italy" in a neighborhood that has, ironically, become filled with Portuguese-Canadians after the Italian-Canadian former residents moved to the suburbs. Citizens fight to keep unwanted garbage dumps outside of their municipality, even if they live far from its proposed location (Michelson 1997). In Chicago, politicians, administrators, and bank officials are forever coping with urban problems by announcing neighborhood-development programs (Taub et al. 1977).

4. Urban sociology's particular concern with spatial distributions of social phenomena (e.g., Schwirian and Mesch 1993) has tended to be translated into local area concerns. Census data, originally designed to enumerate populations in electoral districts, provide large quantities of demographic and social data organized in (too-) convenient, territorially defined census tracts and enumeration areas. The easy availability of these data has encouraged researchers to think in terms of spatial patterns. Territory has come to be seen as the inherently most important organizing factor in urban social relations, rather than as just one potentially important factor.

5. Many sociologists have been preoccupied with the conditions under which solidary sentiments can be maintained in cities and societies. Their preoccupation reflects a persistent overarching public, political, and scholarly concern with achieving normative consensus and social solidarity. The neighborhood has been widely seen and studied as an apparently obvious container of normative solidarity in "the community."

This concentration on the neighborhood has had a strong impact on definitions of, research into, and theorizing about community. Neighborhood studies have produced many finely wrought depictions of urban life, and they have given us powerful ideas about how interpersonal relations operate in a variety of social contexts (see review in Fischer 1976). Analyses have taken mappings of local area boundaries as their starting points and then looked into the extent of communal interaction and sentiment within these boundaries. They have thus assumed, a priori, that a significant portion of a person's interpersonal ties are organized by locality. Such a territorial perspective, searching for answers to the Community Question only within bounded population aggregates, has been especially sensitive to the evaluation of community solidarity in terms of shared values and social integration. Consequently, when observers cannot find much solidary local behavior and sentiments, they have too often concluded that "community" has disappeared.

But does the concept of "neighborhood" equal the concept of "community"? Are the two terms synonymous? The contemporary milieu of frequent residential mobility, spatially dispersed relationships and activities, and the movement of interactions from public spaces to private homes have all limited the amount of observable interactions in neighborhoods. This does not mean that community has been lost but that it is much less likely now to be locally based and locally observed.

The paramount concerns of sociologists are social structures and social processes—and not spatial groupings. Concerns about the spatial location of social structures and processes must necessarily occupy secondary positions. To sociologists, unlike geographers, spatial distributions are not inherently important variables. They assume importance only as they affect such social structural questions as the formation, composition, and structure of interpersonal networks; the flow of resources through such networks; and the interplay of such community networks with the division of labor and the organization of power within larger-scale social systems.

The Network Analytic Approach to Studying Community

The authors in this book examine the Community Question from a network analytic perspective. Social network analysis provides a useful way to study community without presuming that it is confined to a local area. The essence of social network analysis is its focus on social relations and social structures—wherever they may be located and whoever they may be with. Social network analysis does not assume that the world is always composed of normatively guided individuals aggregated into bounded groups or areas. Rather, it starts with a set of *network members* (sometimes called *nodes*) and a set of *ties* that connect some or all nodes (Wasserman and Faust 1993).[6] Social network analysis conceives of social structure as the patterned organization of these network members and their relationships (Wellman 1988b). The utility of the network approach is that it does not take as its starting point putative neighborhood solidarities, nor does it seek primarily to find and explain the persistence (or absence) of solidary sentiments. Thus the network approach attempts to avoid individual-level research perspectives, with their inherently social-psychological explanatory bases that see internalized attitudes as determining community relations.

The social network approach provides ways for analysts to think about social relationships that are neither groups nor isolated duets. Instead of the either/or distinction between group membership and social isolation characteristic of those fearing the alleged loss of community, network analysts can study a more diversified set of structural phenomena, such as:

- The density and clustering of a network;
- how tightly it is bounded;
- whether it is variegated or constricted in its size and heterogeneity;
- how narrowly specialized or broadly multiplex are its ties;
- how indirect ties and structural positions affect behavior.

Although all studies have to start somewhere with some populations, most social network analyses do not treat officially defined group or neighborhood boundaries as truly social boundaries, be they departments in organizations or neighborhoods in cities. Instead network analysts trace the relationships of the persons they are studying, wherever these relationships go and whoever they are with. Only then do they look to see if such relationships cross officially defined boundaries. In this way, formal boundaries become important analytic variables rather than a priori analytic constraints.

The network approach allows analysts to go looking for ties that transcend groups or localities. A group is only a special type of social network, one that is *densely knit* (most people are directly connected) and *tightly bounded* (most relations stay within the same set of people). To be sure, there are densely knit and tightly bounded work groups and community groups. Yet there are other kinds of work and community networks whose ties are sparsely knit with only a minority of members of the workplace or community directly connected with each other. These ties usually ramify out in many directions like an expanding spider's web, rather than curling back on themselves into a densely knit tangle.

For example, people who hang out together—at a French café, Canadian hockey rink, New York street corner, or Chilean barrio—can be studied as either a group or a social network. Those who study them as groups assume that they know the membership and boundaries of the groups. They might ask how important each group is to its members, how the groups are governed and make decisions, how the groups control members, and the circumstances under which members enter and leave. By contrast, those who study such entities as social networks can treat membership and boundaries as open questions. Frequent participation in a friendship circle might be treated as the basis for membership, but so might the indirect connections (and resource flows) that friends provide to others outside the circle. The pattern of relationships becomes a research question rather than a given.

Once analysts adopt this perspective, they see that communities, organizations, and world-systems are clearly social networks, and that many communities, organizations, and political systems are not dense, bounded groups. Although what network analysts have often done is *sheer* documentation—demonstrating the existence of networks—much of their work has been more than *mere* documentation. It has shown social scientists ways to shift away from thinking of social structure as nested in little boxes and away from seeing relationships as the product of internalized norms.

The social network approach does not preclude finding that communities are urban villages where everyone knows each other and provides the abundant, broadly based support that Tönnies (1887) thought only to be a nostalgic relic of vanishing villages. Nor does it preclude finding that organizations really function as Weberian hierarchical bureaucracies. But the social network approach allows the discovery of other forms of community—perhaps sparsely knit and spatially dispersed—and other forms of organization—perhaps loosely coupled or virtual.

Social Networks of Community

Social network analysis has freed the community question from its traditional preoccupation with solidarity and neighborhood.[7] It provides a new way to study community that is based on the community relationships that people actually have rather than on the places where they live or the solidary sentiments they have. It offers three advantages:

1. It avoids the assumption that people necessarily interact in neighborhoods, kinship groups, or other bounded solidarities. This facilitates the study of a wide range of relationships, wherever located and however structured. Look in this book at how Otani (in Japan, Chapter 8), our research group (in Toronto, Chapters 1 and 2) and especially, Salaff, Fong, and Wong (in Hong Kong, Chapter 9) find that residential proximity is, at most, only one dimension of community (see also Fischer 1982b; Nozawa 1997). Yet, as Chapters 3 and 4 also show, the network approach also sup-

ports the analysis of those community ties that do remain in neighborhoods. Thus the social network approach is not antineighborhood—the
traditional stuff of community studies—but allows neighborhood ties to
be discovered without an a priori assumption of their importance (see
also Wellman 1996).

2. Its ability to study linkages at all scales, ranging from interpersonal
relations to world systems, facilitates the analytic linkage of everyday
lives with large-scale social change. For example, Espinoza (Chapter 4)
relates massive sociopolitical upheavals in Chile to the kinds of supportive relations that poor people must maintain, Bian (Chapter 7) and Sik
and Wellman (Chapter 6) trace community ties during the transition
from communism to postcommunism, and Otani (Chapter 8) shows the
ways in which Japanese personal communities have come to resemble
North American communities. Moreover, Ferrand, Mounier, and Degenne (Chapter 5) show how interpersonal ties help to structure connections and cleavages between French social classes.

3. It has developed a set of techniques, both qualitative and quantitative, for discovering, describing, and analyzing the presence, composition, structure and operations of interpersonal networks (Scott 1991;
Wasserman and Faust 1993; Wellman 1992a).

By using the social network approach, analysts have discovered that
community has not disappeared. Instead, community has moved out of
its traditional neighborhood base as the constraints of space weakened.
Except in situations of ethnic or racial segregation (e.g., as described by
Lee and Campbell in Chapter 3), contemporary Western communities are
rarely tightly bounded, densely knit groups of broadly based ties. They
are usually loosely bounded, sparsely knit, ramifying networks of specialized ties. Therefore, analysts should be able to find community wherever it exists: in neighborhoods, in family solidarities, or in networks that
reach farther out and include many friends and acquaintances (Oliver
1988; Wellman 1979; Wellman and Leighton 1979; Fischer 1982b)

Community Networks as Personal Communities

There are two ways to look at community networks (or at any social networks, for that matter): as *whole networks* or as *personal communities.* Many
analysts view social networks much as aliens might view the earth's people: hovering above and observing the relationships linking all members
of the population. This alien's-eye (or Copernican) view of an entire social system is the study of *whole networks,* describing the comprehensive
structure of role relationships in a complete population. Analysts can
have simultaneous views of the social system as a whole and of the parts
that make up the system. Through manipulating matrices, they can find

patterns of connectivity and cleavage within social systems, structurally equivalent role relationships among social system members, changes in network structures over time, and the ways in which system members are directly and indirectly connected. For example, analysts can trace horizontal and vertical flows of resources and detect structural constraints operating on flows of resources. They can find densely knit clusters, structural holes (Burt 1992), areas of high interaction or social isolation (Scott 1991; Wasserman and Faust 1993).

Yet whole network studies are not always feasible or analytically appropriate. Those who use them must define the boundaries of a population, compile a list of all the members of this population, and collect a list of all the relationships (of the sort the analyst is interested in) among the members of this population. Therefore, whole network analysis is most appropriate for studying defined, bounded units such as organizations, nation-states, or clearly bounded neighborhoods. However, such an intrinsic assumption of a clearly bounded population is precisely the approach that led many investigators before the 1970s to pronounce community as dead because they had looked for it only in bounded neighborhoods.

Therefore many community network analysts—including the authors in this book—have concentrated on studying smaller *personal (or ego-centered) networks* defined from the standpoint of *focal persons:* a sample of individuals at the centers of their own networks. Rather than showing the universe as it is viewed by an outside observer, personal network studies provide Ptolemaic views of networks as they may be viewed by the individuals at their centers: the world we each see revolving around us. Figure I.1, for example, shows the significant interpersonal ties of a typical North American.[8] She is directly tied with each network member (by definition), and many network members are also significantly tied with each other. (For the sake of clarity, Figure I.1 omits the direct ties between the focal person and her network members.) She has a densely knit cluster of kin—three of whom are her socially close *intimates*—and more sparsely knit ties among a half-dozen friends and neighbors. One workmate stands apart, his isolation reflecting a separation of work and social life in this focal person's life.

Personal network studies enable researchers to study community ties, whoever with, wherever located, and however structured. They focus on the inherently *social* nature of community and avoid the trap of looking for community only in spatially defined areas. These *personal community* studies have meshed well with mainstream survey research techniques. Researchers have typically interviewed an (often large) sample of focal persons, asking about the composition, relational patterns, and contents of "their" networks. To measure network density (the percentage of in-

FIGURE I.1   Typical Personal Network of an East Yorker

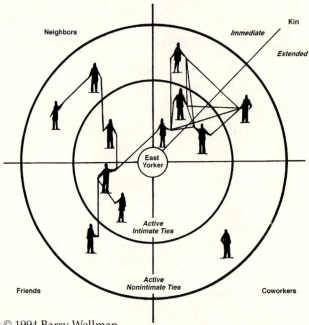

terconnections), researchers typically ask the focal persons in their samples to report about relationships among the members of their networks. Such studies began in Detroit (Laumann 1969a, 1969b, 1973) and Toronto (Casey 1995; Coates 1966; Coates, Moyer, and Wellman 1969; Craven and Wellman 1973; Wellman 1968) in the 1960s and have flourished ever since. Many social scientists concentrated on studying the *social support* that community networks provide: the supportive resources that community ties convey and their consequences for mental and physical well-being and longevity (see reviews in Fischer 1984; Wellman 1990a, 1992c, 1993). For example, researchers have found that people with larger, more diversified personal communities were less susceptible to common colds (Cohen et al. 1997).

By framing analyses in network analytic terms, researchers have been able to show that the fears of a former generation about the loss of community were incorrect. Community, network analysts argue, has rarely disappeared from societies. It has been transformed. Community network analyses—including those represented in this book—have shown the continuing abundance and vitality of interpersonal ties, even as they have been affected by capitalism, socialism, urbanization, industrialization, bureaucratization, and new transportation and communication technology. New forms of community have come into being to replace older ones. The demonstration of the pervasiveness and importance of personal communities has rebutted contentions that large-scale social transformations have produced widespread social isolation in an alienated "mass society" (e.g., Kornhauser 1959). It raises questions about those who see an identity between the loss of community and the loss of formal civic institutions (e.g., Putnam 1995).

If analysts focus on social ties and systems of informal resource exchange rather than on people living in neighborhoods and villages, community can be seen. The discovery that most ties extend well beyond the neighborhood and the village has redressed the common tendency to identify communities with neighborhoods. In the Western world and perhaps elsewhere, most community ties stretch across a metropolitan region, with many extending across the nation or to another continent.

Conceptualizing a person's community life as the central node linking complex interpersonal relationships leads to quite different analytic concerns from conceptualizing it as a membership in a discrete solidarity. The transmutation of "community" into "personal community" is more than a linguistic trick. It frees analysts from searching for Brigadoons: vestigial traditional solidarities hanging on into the twentieth century. Treating communities as social networks makes such solidarities only one possible pattern among many. Rather than looking to see if what they find measures up to the traditional ideal of densely knit, tightly bounded, broadly based solidarities, analysts can evaluate the ways in which different kinds of social structural patterns affect flows of resources to community members.

This shift in perspective from neighborhood community to community network allows analysts to examine the extent to which large-scale social changes have created new forms of association and altered traditional kinship and neighboring structures. It leaves open the extent to which community ties are intimate, frequent, or broadly based. It facilitates the linkage of community networks with analyses of other social systems: in the household, at work, with voluntary organizations, or with bureaucratic institutions.

The definition of "the community" in community network studies is a matter of how investigators define ties, where they draw boundaries, and how high they raise the level of analytic magnification to take into account internal links within clusters.

1. *Do analysts look at all types of relationships or only at those that provide specific types of support?* For example, Chapter 4 looks only at ties that provide material aid—goods and services. Espinoza decided that emotional support and sheer sociability are not important for his tale of survival in poor Chilean neighborhoods.

2. *Where do analysts draw boundaries?* Although researchers may draw samples from a national population (see Ferrand, Mounier, and De-genne's study of France in Chapter 5), studying the total personal networks of many respondents is impractical. Each respondent would have to be questioned about 1,000 ties. Therefore analysts almost always look only at ties with either:

- a few close confidants (Laumann 1973; Fischer et al. 1977; Burt 1984, 1986; Marsden 1987);
- a handful of socially close intimates (e.g., Chapters 3, 5, and 8);
- or a score or so of active network members (e.g., Chapters 1, 2, and 4).

Moreover, researchers have to start somewhere. In community network studies, they typically select a random sample from a neighborhood or metropolitan area, even though they trace the residents' ties to wherever they may be found.

3. *How detailed are the analyses?* Several studies have looked only at "community ties," dropping all the ties of all the respondents into one *tiewise* data-set. Such studies are useful for showing that few ties stay within the neighborhood (Wellman, Carrington, and Hall 1988), parents and adult children disproportionately exchange emotional aid (Wellman 1979; Wellman and Wortley 1989, 1990), and Japanese community networks resemble North American ones (Chapter 8; see also Nozawa 1997). Other studies treat the personal community as the unit of analysis. For example, Wellman and Gulia's Chapter 2 shows the effect of network size on the provision of social support, while other research using the same data shows that women exchange more emotional support than men (Wellman 1988a). Few studies have looked at internal structural variation within the personal community, although there are often densely knit clusters within sparsely knit communities. Thus, our research group (Wellman et al. 1991) found married people to have densely knit clusters of their own kin within communities that were generally sparsely knit. This is because in-laws rarely interact with the other side of the family.

Thinking of communities as personal communities has its costs:

- It concentrates only on strong ties—and sometimes only on strong, *supportive* ties—neglecting the weaker ties that Mark Granovetter has argued (1973, 1982, 1995) transmit new information between groups and integrate social systems.
- It ignores the ecological juxtapositions with which all people must deal in their residential and social spaces. Even if they are not in my network, I am disturbed by the young men who party

and play drums at night in the park near my house, and I am aided by the daytime residents who keep an eye on my street (Jacobs 1961).

- Analyzing the network structure of each personal community is procedurally difficult. This is because software for social network analysis such as UCINet is designed to analyze only one network at a time. Although each personal community can be treated as a whole network, the lack of provision for batch processing means that the data-crunching of hundreds of personal networks must be undertaken one at a time.[9]
- In a sample survey of any size, interviewing the members of a person's personal community is impractical because such an approach would increase the sample size enormously. (For example, a sample of 300 focal persons, each with an average of 20 network members, would require 6,000 interviews.) Hence community network studies usually rely on surveyed respondents' reports about their network members. This hinders reliability (Bernard et al. 1984) although no more so than the respondents' reports about other aspects of their behavior. Our group has found that the least reliable and valid survey data are the respondents' reports about the nature of the relationships among the members of their personal communities. Many people just do not know how Cousin Betty relates to Uncle Henry.

The Nature of Community Networks

The authors in this book—along with other scholars—have already discovered much about the composition, structure, dynamics, and operation of community networks. As an introduction to the chapters in this book, this section reviews what we now know:

1. **Community Ties Are Narrow, Specialized Relationships, not Broadly Supportive Ties.**

Both scholars and the public have traditionally thought of communities as composed of broadly based relationships in which each community member felt securely able to obtain a variety of help. Yet a good deal of research (including the work in this volume by Otani; Bian; Ferrand, Mounier, and Degenne; Wellman and Gulia [Chapter 2]; Espinoza; and Lee and Campbell) has shown that most community ties are specialized, with community network members usually supplying only a few kinds of social support (see also the reviews in Wellman 1988a, 1992c). In France, kin and neighbors engage in mutual aid, but friends and neighbors are the confidants (see Chapter 5). In California, there are differences between trouble-shooting kin and companionable friends (Fischer 1982b; Schweizer, Schnegg and Berzborn 1997). In Toronto, active community members usually supply only one or two out of five types of social support, for example, small services and emotional aid but not large services, companionship, or financial aid (Hall and Wellman 1985; Wellman and Wortley 1989, 1990). (By contrast, Toronto spouses supply each other with all types of social support [Wellman and Wellman 1992]). Those network members who provide small services or emotional aid rarely provide large services, companionship or financial aid (Wellman, Carrington, and Hall 1988; Wellman and Wortley 1989, 1990). Parents and adult children provide the widest range of support although they rarely supply sociable companionship. Accessible ties—people living or working nearby, or otherwise in frequent face-to-face or telecommunications contact—provide important goods and services (Wellman and Wortley 1990). The strength of ties is important, with socially close voluntary and multiple-role ties providing high levels of support. Yet Granovetter (1973, 1982) has cogently argued the importance of weak ties for linking sparsely knit communities and providing people with a wider range of information.

The specialized provision of support in communities means that people must maintain differentiated portfolios of ties to obtain a variety of resources. They can no longer assume that any or all of their network members will help them, no matter what the problem. In market terms, people must shop at specialized boutiques for needed resources instead of casually dropping in at a general store. Like boutique shoppers, people who only have a few network members supplying one kind of support have insecure sources of supply. If the tie ends—if the boutique closes—the supply of that particular type of support may disappear.

2. **People Are Not Wrapped Up in Traditional Densely Knit, Tightly Bounded Communities but Are Manuevering in Sparsely Knit, Loosely Bounded, Frequently Changing Networks.**

As we have seen, the traditional view has been that communities are densely knit solidarities with tight boundaries. In such a situation, almost all community members would interact with each other and almost all informal interaction would take place within the community. Densely knit and tight boundaries make it easy for communities to control their members and coordinate their behavior, whether this be supplying aid to those in distress or punishing those who transgress (see Chapters 3 and 4).

In reality, personal communities are usually sparsely knit and loosely bounded. For example, the density of 0.33 we found in one Toronto study means that only one-third of a person's intimates network have close ties with each other. Moreover, these networks become even more sparsely knit as people age and their networks get more complex: Mean network density declined from 0.33 to 0.13 over a decade (Wellman et al. 1997). As Chapters 1 and 2 show, variation in the composition and structure of these community networks is more complex than the traditional Tönniesian dichotomy of communal versus contractual social organization.

The complex and specialized nature of personal communities means that these are fragmented networks. In both Japan (Chapter 8, this volume; Nozawa 1997) and North America (Chapter 2, this volume; Wellman 1979; Wellman and Wortley 1989, 1990; Fischer 1982b), the kinship system as such does not supply much social support: Extended kin are rarely supportive, although a few immediate kin—parents, children, and siblings—are quite supportive. Moreover, the tendency of computer-mediated communication to emphasize ties based on shared interests rather than ties based on kinship or neighborhood may mean that most online ties will also be specialized, based on a single shared interest, and transitory, as interests change (see Chapter 10).

The fragmentation, specialization, and low density suggests that the nature of individual ties may be more important than the nature of the networks for the provision of social support. This means that to receive support people must actively maintain each tie rather than rely on solidary communities to do this for them. It also means that tie characteristics may have more effect than network characteristics on the provision of social support. Although tie characteristics are important (Wellman 1992c), Chapter 2 shows that the characteristics of community networks are also important. Larger, more heterogeneous, and denser networks provide more support. A network is more than the sum of its ties: The composition and structure of community networks affect the provision of support beyond the effects of the characteristics of the specific ties in these networks. Emergent properties are alive and well and living in Toronto.

Few people have stable community networks. Our group has found that only 28% of Torontonians' intimate ties were still intimate a decade later. Thirty-six percent of the once-intimate ties became less active over the decade, while the rest became very weak or disappeared. Although kinship ties are more stable, only 34% of intimate kinship ties remained intimate a decade later while another 28% continued as active, but not intimate, relationships (Wellman et al. 1997).

It is not that people's communities are disintegrating, but that they are in flux. Rather than locking people into one tightly bounded social circle, 1,000 or so community ties ramify across changing, fragmented communities to connect people to the diverse resources of multiple social arenas (Kochen 1989). Many of the chapters in this book show how people make use of these ramified connections. They are useful for getting jobs in

China (Bian, Chapter 7; see also Lin 1997; Lin, Ye, and Chen 1997) and Chile (Espinoza, Chapter 4), finding financial capital in Hungary (Sik and Wellman, Chapter 6), and helping Hong Kong immigrants to settle into Canada (Salaff and Wong 1995). Indeed Stanley Milgram's (1967) and Harrison White's (1970) observations that the entire world is linked by paths of five or fewer indirect ties are the basis for John Guare's (1990) play and the 1993 movie version, *Six Degrees of Separation*.

Just because community networks ramify does not mean that they connect all persons randomly. "Birds of a feather flock together" whether they flock by gender, socioeconomic status, ethnicity, or race (see Chapters 3 and 5; Laumann 1966, 1973; Wellman 1992b). These clusters organize flows of resources and norms. Even when ties connect people with different social characteristics, they do so unevenly. Moreover, high rates of social mobility leave in their wake cross-cutting ties between people with different social characteristics. Low rates of mobility foster more tightly bounded clusters (see Chapter 5; Herting, Grusky, and Van Rompaey 1997).

As future technology becomes present reality, Chapter 10 on virtual communities shows the potential for computer networks to extend the reach of social networks. It is not only that time and space become less important in computer-mediated communication, but that it is easy to communicate with large groups of community members (using lists) and to bring unconnected community members into direct contact. Yet the ease by which computer-mediated communication connects friends of friends may also increase the density of interconnections among clusters of network members within communities.

Sparsely knit, fragmentary, loosely bounded communities make it possible to reach many people through short chains of "friends of friends" (Boissevain 1974). Yet in such sparsely knit and loosely bounded networks, people cannot depend on the goodwill or social control of a solidary community. Instead, they must actively search and manipulate their separate ties, one by one, to deal with their affairs. Indeed, Chapter 7 shows this to be true even in reputedly solidary China (see also Freeman and Ruan 1997; Ruan et al. 1997).

3. **Communities Have Moved Out of Neighborhoods to Be Dispersed Networks that Continue to Be Supportive and Sociable.**

As well as contemporary communities being fragmentary, sparsely knit and loosely bounded, they are rarely local groupings of neighbors and kin. The residents of developed societies usually know few neighbors, and most members of their personal communities do not live in the same neighborhood (Wellman 1990b, 1992c). People easily maintain far-flung ties by telecommunications (with telephones recently being joined by faxes, electronic mail, and the Web) and transportation (based on cars, expressways, and airplanes). In Toronto, being within one hour's drive or within the local telephone zone—not being in the same neighborhood—is the effective boundary for high levels of face-to-face contact and social support (Wellman, Carrington, and Hall 1988; Wellman and Tindall 1993). Many ties stretch even farther than the metropolitan area, with an appreciable number spanning the continent or the ocean. This lack of local ties and the presence of community members living elsewhere weakens local commitment and encourages people to vote with their feet, leaving when conditions are bad rather than staying to improve things.[10] For example, the Hong Kong emigrants studied by Salaff, Fong, and Wong (Chapter 9) rely heavily on trans-Pacific ties to make their moves to Canada.

However, communities have not totally lost their domestic roots. Although the community networks of Torontonians are far-flung, most of Torontonians' face-to-face interactions are with people who live or work near them. Torontonians even have much of their telephone contact with neighbors (Wellman 1996). Thus, even spatially liberated people cannot avoid neighbors. Local relationships are necessary for domestic safety, controlling actual land-use, and quickly getting goods and services, as Jane Jacobs (1961) has pointed out for North America in the 1950s and Lee and Campbell (Chapter 3) and Wellman and Gulia (Chapter 2) reaffirm. Moreover, when transportation and communication resources are scarce, local ties assume more importance as Charles Tilly (1973) has argued for portions of preindustrial Europe and Vicente Espinoza (Chapter 4) shows for impoverished Chileans.

In saying that communities are not as local as they used to be, we need to avoid committing the pastoralist fallacy of thinking that our cities and suburbs are inferior to the pestilent, crime-ridden, and insecure villages or cities of yore. Preindustrial communities may never have been as locally bounded as tradition has maintained. Whenever scholars have looked for nonlocal ties, they have found far-ranging networks. As noted above, radioactive analyses of obsidian have found Neolithic spear points and choppers more than one thousand miles from their origin (Dixon, Cann, and Renfrew 1968). Moreover, Le Roy Ladurie (1975, 1997), Natalie Davis (1983), among others, have described far-flung, mobile networks in Medieval and Renaissance Europe.

Consider, also, the fruits of the unlikely comparison of communities in twentieth-century Toronto and eighteenth-century rural Latvia (Wetherell, Plakans, and Wellman 1994). By contrast to the mythical kinship-ridden past, we found that this rural Latvian community did not have enough kin to construct the kinds of social networks that exist today. As these farmers do not appear to have had many friends living beyond the local area, it seems that half the myth was true: Although these groups were local, they only had small clusters of kin at their core. Closer to home, many guests at mid-nineteenth century New York City weddings—presumably the heart of the marital family's social networks—came from other parts of the city, and often from other counties or states (Scherzer 1992).

4. **Private Intimacy Has Replaced Public Sociability.**

Rather than operating out of public neighborhood spaces, contemporary communities usually operate out of private homes. Yet until well into this century, men customarily gathered in communal, quasipublic milieus, such as pubs, cafés, parks, and village greens. Take for example this description of eighteenth century Paris:

> The whole neighborhood overflowed into the street from nearby houses, workshops, shops and taverns. Around every inhabitant in a *quartier* took on its shape, made up of daily contacts and changing reputations. Individuals worked round the corner from where they lived. (Roche 1981, p. 246)

More accessible than private homes, such places drew their clienteles from fluid networks of regular habitués. Men could drop into such places to talk and to escape domestic boredom. The high density of the city meant that they were likely to find others to talk with. This density, combined with the permeability of the public spaces, provided many opportunities for chance encounters with friends of their friends, and to form new ties.

Although the men generally went out to enjoy themselves, they also used these public communities to organize politically, to accomplish collective tasks, and to deal with larger organizations. In colonial New England, "neighbors assumed not only the right but the duty to supervise one another's lives" (Wall 1990). This public community was largely a man's game. A woman who went alone to a Parisian wine shop risked being mistaken for a prostitute (Garrioch 1986).

Community has moved inside now, into private homes. The separation of work from residential localities means that coworkers commute from different neighborhoods and no longer come home from work in solidary sociable groups. While men now spend more time at home instead of at bars or cafés, the high percentage of women engaged in paid work outside their homes means that women spend less time at home. Thus husbands and wives are now apt to be at home when both are available to each other. They stay home too, for they are in no mood to go out and socialize after their weary trip home from work. In any event, zoning regulations in North America often place commercial areas for recreation far from home. Domestic pursuits dominate, with husbands and wives spending evenings and weekends together instead of the men going off to pubs and street corners, and few women being home during the day. Workaholics bring their computer disks home; couch potatoes rent videos; teleworkers stay home day and night.

Rather than being accessible to others in public places, people now overcome their isolation by getting together in each other's homes or by telephone and electronic mail (Chapter 10). Most members of Torontonians' personal communities do not live nearby but a median distance of nine miles apart (Wellman, Carrington, and Hall 1988). The absence of well-used public spaces and nearby community members means that people cannot go out into the neighborhood to find much community. Instead, they have selective encounters, singly or in couples, with dispersed community network members.

Yet the easy accessibility of local relationships means that those local ties that do exist are significant. Although neighbors (living within one mile) comprise only 22% of the Torontonians' active ties, these neighbors engage in fully 42% of all interactions with active network members (Wellman 1996).

The neoconservative privatization of Western societies, with its withering of collective public services for general well-being, is reflected in the movement indoors of community life. Even in Toronto, the safest North American metropolis, 36% of the residents report that they feel unsafe walking alone in their neighborhoods at night (Duffy 1991). Yet the usual flight to safety—driving a car or staying home and using the telephone or e-mail—offers little opportunity en route for the casual contact and new encounters that can diversify lives. Cars leave garages as sealed units, opened only on reaching the other's home; telephones and modems stay indoors, sustaining closed duets with already known others.

North Americans go out to be private—in streets where no one greets each another—but they stay inside to be public—to meet their friends and relatives. Where a generation ago North Americans often spent Saturday night going out for pizza and a movie, they now invite a few friends over to their homes to watch videos and order a pizza to be delivered. In 1992, the average Canadian household spent $101 for buying and renting videos compared with $99 for going to live theatre, concerts, and movies. It costs $3 *per household* to rent a video in Toronto, but $8 *per person* to go to the movies and about $30 to attend a play or concert (Film Canada 1990; Strike 1990). This means that people watch videos at home an average of thirty times per year but go out for entertainment only three or four times a year. The telephone number for Toronto's largest pizza delivery service, 967–11–11, has become so well known that Canadian immigration officers use it as a test to see if border crossers are bona fide Canadian residents.

Public spaces have become residual places to pass through or to shop in. Rather than participating in clubs or organizations, when they do go out, North Americans usually go out alone, in couples or in small, informal groups (Putnam 1995). North American church attendance is declining, and Canadian movie attendance declined from eighteen times per year in 1952 to three times per year in 1993. When Torontonians do go out to the movies, most (55%) go alone or in pairs (Oh 1991). The community of the pub in the recent television show, *Cheers,* was appealing because it is rare. In reality, only 10% of adult Canadians go to a pub once a week or more.[11] The more common experience is reflected in the *Seinfeld* television show: One or a few close ties casually getting together in each other's private homes.

Suburban shopping malls have become residual agoras—for consumption purposes only but not for discussion. Their cafés mock the name, deliberately using tiny tables and uncomfortable chairs to discourage lingering sociability. They provide little opportunity for casual contact or the expansion of networks. This trend is most marked in North America, where "fast food" restaurants tell their patrons to "have a nice day" and expect them to stay less than a half-hour.

As community has become private, people feel responsible for their "own"—the members of their community networks with whom they have strong ties—but not for the many acquaintances and strangers with whom they rub shoulders but are not otherwise connected. Private contact with familiar friends and relatives has so replaced public gregariousness that people pass each other unsmiling on streets. This privatization may be responsible for the lack of informal help for strangers who are in trouble in public spaces (Latané and Darley 1976). It is probably also a reason that people feel they lack friends and are surrounded by strangers even when their networks are abundantly supportive (Lofland 1973).

Unfortunately, social network analysis has been better at studying the strong ties of personal, private community than at studying the weak ties and ecological juxtapositions of public community. Analysts have only investigated strong ties (Campbell and Lee 1991; Marsden and Campbell 1984) by asking people who they feel close to—as I did (Wellman 1979, 1982) and as the U.S. General Social Survey did in 1985 (Burt 1984; Marsden 1987) and the Canadian equivalent did in 1985 (Statistics Canada 1987, Stone 1988)—or by asking who they get various kinds of social support from, as American (e.g., Fischer 1982b), British (e.g., Wenger 1992), and Dutch social scientists have done (e.g., Knipscheer and Antonucci 1990; Thomése and van Tilburg 1998). Network analysts have been useful and accurate in saying that strong personal communities continue to exist, but they have neglected to look at what is happening all around these networks.

5. **Communities Have Become Domesticated and Feminized.**

Home is now the base for relationships that are more voluntary and se-lective than the public communities of the past. Despite the importance of neighborhood ties portrayed by Lee and Campbell (Chapter 3) and by Espinoza (Chapter 4), only a minority of community ties in the Western world operates in the public contexts of the neighborhood, formal orga-nizations, or work. Community networks now contain high proportions of people who enjoy each other and low proportions of people who are forced to interact with each other because they are juxtaposed in the same neighborhood, kinship group, organization, or workplace (Feld 1981). Friends and relatives get together as small sets of singles or cou-ples, but rarely as communal groups (Wellman 1992b). This voluntary se-lectivity means that communities have become homogeneous networks of people with similar attitudes and lifestyles. Wellman and Gulia (Chap-ter 10) suggest that the proliferation of computer-mediated communica-tion will only accelerate this trend.

Where once-public communities had been men's worlds, now home-based community networks bring husbands and wives together. Men's community ties are tucked away in homes just as women's ties have usu-ally been. As community has moved into the home, homes have become less private. Previous generations had confined visitors to ground-floor parlors and dining rooms, but network members now roam all floors.

In their domestic headquarters, Toronto couples operate their net-works jointly (Wellman and Wellman 1992). It is a far different scene from the segregated networks that Elizabeth Bott (1957) described in the 1950s for England, where husband and wife each had their separate circles of kin and friends. Usually it is the household that exchanges support rather than the person: for example, our Toronto research found in-laws to be as supportive as blood relatives (Wellman and Wortley 1989). In contrast to the specialized support that community members exchange, spouses supply each other with almost all types of social support (Well-man and Wellman 1992). Hence unmarried adults obtain much less social support domestically and do not have access to the networks (and their resources) that accompany spouses to marriage.

In the current situation, married women not only participate in com-munity, they are central in it. Women have historically been the "kin-keepers" of Western society: mothers and sisters keeping relatives con-nected for themselves, their husbands, and their children. They continue to be the pre-eminent suppliers of emotional support in community net-works as well as the major suppliers of domestic services to households (Wellman 1992b; Wright 1989). With the privatization and domestication of community, community-keeping has become an extension of kinkeep-ing, with both linked to domestic management. No longer do husbands and wives have many separate friendships. As men now usually stay at home during their leisure time, the informal ties of their wives form the basis for relations between married couples. Women define the nature of friendship and help maintain many of their husbands' friendships. Women bear more than the "double load" of domestic work and paid work; their "triple load" now includes community "net work."

Seen in one way, women now dominate the practice of community in their households. Seen in another way, women now assist their husbands even in maintaining community ties. Seen more neutrally, community-keeping has become women's concern in the often-ambiguous marital division of labor.

Thus the privatization and domestication of ties have transformed the nature of community. The domesticated community ties interact in small groups in private homes rather than in larger groups in public spaces. This makes it more difficult for people to form new community ties with friends of their friends, and it focuses the concerns of relationships on dealing with household problems (Wellman 1992b). Women's ties, which dominate community networks, provide important support for dealing with domestic work. Community members help with daily hassles and crises; neighbors mind each other's children; sisters and friends provide emotional support for child, husband, and elder care. Because women are the community-keepers and are pressed for time caring for homes and doing paid work, men have become even more cut off from male friendship groups (Wellman 1992b). North American men rarely use their community ties to accomplish collective projects of work, politics, or leisure. Their ties have largely become sociable relationships, either as part of the link between two married couples or as disconnected ties with a few male "buddies."

This domestication helps explain the contemporary intellectual shift to seeing community and friendship as something that women do better than men. Just as husbands and wives are more involved with each other at home, the focus of couples and male friends is on private, domestic ties. Men's ties have come to be defined as women's have been: relations of emotional support, companionship, and domestic aid. Thus the nature and success of community are now being defined in domestic, "women's" terms. Concurrently, the growing dominance of the service sector in the economy means that the manipulation of people and ideas has acquired more cultural importance than the industrial and resource-extraction sectors' manipulation of material goods. With developed economies having more managers and professionals than blue-collar workers (Statistics Canada and Status of Women 1993), the workplace has shifted to the very emphasis on social relationships that women have traditionally practiced at home.

At the same time, the material comfort of most North Americans means that they no longer need to rely on maintaining good relations with community members to get the necessities for material survival. The goods and services that community members exchange are usually matters of convenience, rarely of necessity, and hardly ever of life and death. Community ties have become ends in themselves, to be enjoyed in their own right and used for emotional adjustment in a society that puts a premium on feeling good about oneself and others. This resonates with contemporary feminist celebration of women for being more qualified in the socioemotional skills that are the basis of contemporary communities—and the downgrading of the allegedly masculine qualities of instrumentalism and materialism. Community is no longer about men fixing cars together; it is about couples chatting about domestic problems.

Contemporary discussions of community often reverse the traditional sexist discourse that has seen women as inadequate men. Now it is men who are seen as unable to sustain meaningful community ties, especially when such ties are defined only in terms of socioemotional support. This socioemotional definition has almost totally replaced the traditional definition of community as also including instrumental aid. Patriarchical arguments for male superiority in getting things done are being replaced by celebrations of female superiority in knitting together social networks. As "feminist author" Maggie Scarf (Scarf 1987) said on Oprah Winfrey's television show, "Men just don't have friends the way women have friends. Men just don't like to make themselves vulnerable to other men." Clitoris-envy, the alleged longing for empathy among men, has become the new-age replacement for penis-envy among the not-so Iron Johns (Bly 1990).

Seeing Community Networks in Context

Although the assertion that women have a greater capacity for community has raised much consciousness, it is an idea that is time-bound, culture-bound, and empirically unsound. It ignores the thousands of years during which men's bonds largely defined community in public discourse. By reducing the definition of community to socioemotional support, it assumes that the world is as materially comfortable as are North American intellectuals.

In less materially comfortable parts of the world, community members do more for each other than being privately sociable and emotionally supportive. Consider how people elsewhere use friends for economic, political, and social survival. Greek men argue and plan projects in cafés, poor Chileans help barrio neighbors to survive and find jobs for kin (Chapter 4), Chinese job-seekers rely heavily on networks (Chapter 7; Lin, Ye, and Chen 1997), Hungarians help each other build new homes

(Chapter 6), and Hong Kong networks help people to leave their homes (Chapter 9). Even in more affluent Britain, people value getting services and information from community members as much as they value getting esteem and affection (Argyle 1990). To put matters more broadly, communities do not function in isolation but in political, economic, and social milieus that affect their composition, structure, and operations. The nature of different societies strongly affects the opportunities and insecurities with which individuals and households must deal, the supportive resources they seek, and the ways in which markets, institutions, and networks structure access to these resources.

In many societies, communities are not just ways in which people spend some of their leisure time but key mechanisms by which people and households obtain resources. Yet most North American research has ignored the broader implications of community ties and looked only at "social support": the effects of community ties on maintaining physical and mental health. Although this is an important matter, it is unfortunate how the high level of funding for health-care research has focused attention so narrowly. A broader view would see community as an essential component of society, one of the five principal ways by which people gain access to resources:[12]

- *Market exchanges* as purchases, barter, or informal exchanges. Seeing this as the only means of access to resources is in line with the neoconservative belief in the loss of community. (*Liberty*)
- *Institutional distributions* by the state or other bureaucracies as citizenship rights, organizational benefits, or charitable aid. Such access to resources is in line with those who have traditionally seen society as a moral community writ large, as in the current American debate about whether health care is a community obligation or a market decision. However, the use of the term "community" to describe such institutional distributions can be a subterfuge for bureaucratic privilege, as was the case in communist eastern Europe. (*Equality*)
- *Community exchanges* If informal, interpersonal access to resources occurs within neighborhood or kinship solidarities, then it fits traditional notions of community. However, the two chapters that portray this pattern describe community among impoverished, new in-migrants (see Chapter 4 describing social support among poor Chileans) and among segregated, low-income African-Americans (see Chapter 3 describing neighboring in Nashville). If the exchanges are less-bounded (and so less normatively-enforceable), then it fits the ramified

networks that Wellman and Gulia (Chapter 2) describe among materially comfortable Canadians. *(Fraternity)*

- **Coercive appropriations** Direct predatory behavior by interpersonal (robbery) or institutional bullies (expropriation). Involuntary appropriations usually occur under the legitimating guise of imbalanced market exchanges or state extractions for unequal institutional distributions (as in governments forcing farmers to sell produce to urbanites at low prices (Tilly 1975)). More extreme instances of the loss of community are common in societies where institutional and communal mechanisms of social control have broken down, such as in Bosnia or Rwanda. *(Robbery)*
- **Self-provisioning** Making and growing things in one's household. Self-provisioning is used even in market societies (see Pahl's [1984] discussion of growing food in England) and in socialist-institutional ones (see Sik's [1988] discussion of Hungarian home-building). Such self-provisioning rests on an infrastructure of market and community exchanges that provide advice, skills, and materials. *(Peasantry)*

Although all types of resource access can be found in all societies:

- market exchanges are especially characteristic of Western societies;
- institutional distributions are characteristic of centrally planned statist societies;
- community exchanges are characteristic of third-world societies with weak states and few formal organizations (see also Wolf 1966).

While personal communities are important in Western, statist, and third-world societies, communities are differently composed, structured, and used in each type of society. For example, the insecurities of members of Western societies largely come from physical and emotional stresses in their personal lives and social relations. Hence people seek support from community members for emotional problems, homemaking chores, and domestic crises, and they look to markets and institutions to deal with their economic and political problems.

The comparatively low importance of economic and political concerns in Western societies distinguishes the communities in them from those in societies that are less economically or politically secure. Most Westerners rely on market exchanges for almost all of their production and much of their consumption. Institutional benefits such as schooling and medical care are abundantly available as citizenship rights. Westerners do not pay as much attention as the inhabitants of statist societies (such as the former East European socialist states) to having community members who can make and fix things (such as home-building) or who have connections to strategic institutional circles (see Chapter 6). To make another contrast, because westerners rarely have urgent cares about daily survival, they can manage domestic resources with less apprehension than third-worlders living on the margins.

Networks in the Global Village

Malvina Reynolds (1963) sang satirically a generation ago about supposedly buttoned-up, carefree North American life. She described it as:

> *Little boxes made of ticky-tacky*
> *Little boxes, little boxes, little boxes*
> *All the same.*
> *There's a green one, and a pink one, and a blue one, and a yellow one.*
> *And they're all made out of ticky-tacky*
> *And they all look just the same.*

Although Ms. Reynolds was giving her dystopian vision of American suburban homes, she also was critiquing American society as a set of little boxes. The chapters in this book show, fortunately, that the little boxes are only the homes and not the social reality. Wherever possible—across the global village—people have reached out and transcended their little neighborhood and kinship boxes. They are involved in complex community networks stretching across their cities, regions, nations, and even the oceans. The multiple clusters and limited social control in these networks give people room to maneuver, even if the cost is that they must actively maintain their ties and scan their networks for help. The cost of escaping these little boxes is that people think that they and the world are not well connected. The advantage is that they have much autonomy to connect where they will.

In the bad old days, before the 1960s, people feared that community had disappeared.

In the good old days of the 1960s and 1970s, people thought community was thriving naturally, as a combined group love-in and support-in.

In the entrepreneurial days of the present, the product of a neoconservative zeitgeist, people think that community flourishes only if they go out and pull its strings.

Yet community is not alienated chaos, it is not a solidary, all-loving group, and it is not a set of exchange freaks playing "Let's Make a Deal!"

It is a network—nebulous, far-flung and sparsely knit, but real and supportive.

Notes

1. I thank Mark Chapman and Reena Zeidman for advice in Biblical matters, and Abraham Friedman who gave Bev Wellman and me the Bible used here ("translated in accordance with Jewish tradition," 1947) upon our marriage in 1965, inscribed with the blessing, "May you be blessed with Love, Contentment and Devotion for each other").

2. For further details of this paragraph's argument, see Wellman and Wetherell (1996).

3. For a summary of mass society fears, see Kornhauser (1968). Key third world community studies from this period include Mayer (India, 1966), Cohen (Nigeria, 1969), Mayer and Mayer (South Africa, 1974), Mitchell (Rhodesia, 1956), and Peattie (Venezuela, 1968).

4. During the communist era, there were rural village studies, such as Hinton's study of *Fanshen* in China (1967), and also studies of work organizations as intermediary units, such as Burawoy's study of a Hungarian factory (1985). See also Kennedy and Galtz's review (1996). With the exception of Radoeva's Bulgarian analysis (1988), I confine myself to works in English.

5. Similar rural-urban mobility often occurs in contemporary third world societies, with low-cost buses, and letter-writers helping to maintain connectivity. (See Chapter 4 in this volume; also see, for example, Mayer and Mayer 1974; Doudou 1967; Roberts 1973, 1978).

6. The network members in community studies are persons but in other network analyses they could be larger units, such as organizations or states.

7. In addition to the discussion below, see also Fischer 1982a; Wellman 1988a; Wellman and Leighton 1979.

8. The specifics are drawn from the Toronto studies described in this book; see also Wellman, Carrington, and Hall 1988.

9. Haythornthwaite and Wellman (1996) have created a procedure using SAS software for decomposing whole networks into ego-centered networks so that each network member's world can be analyzed separately.

10. I am *not* arguing that local ties are unimportant, only that they usually comprise a minority of important community ties.

11. Special analysis by Scot Wortley of the 1989 Canadian *National Alcohol and Other Drug Survey.*

12. French revolutionaries may have realized three-fifths of this with their demand for Liberty, Equality, and Fraternity. Perhaps their revolutionary sentiments for a new order led them to deny both Robbery and Peasantry.

References

Abu-Lughod, Janet. 1991. *Changing Cities.* New York: HarperCollins.

Aminzade, Ronald and Randy Hodson. 1982. "Social Mobility in a Mid-Nineteenth Century French City." *American Sociological Review* 47:441–457.

Anderson, Elijah. 1990. *Streetwise*. Chicago: University of Chicago Press.

Anderson, Michael. 1971. *Family Structure in Nineteenth Century Lancashire*. Cambridge: Cambridge University Press.

Argyle, Michael. 1990. "An Exploration of the Effects of Different Relationships on Health, Mental Health and Happiness." Working Paper. Oxford, July.

Ariès, Phillipe. 1962. *Centuries of Childhood: A Social History of Family Life*. Translated by Robert Baldick. New York: Knopf.

Atwood, Margaret. 1985. *The Handmaid's Tale*. Toronto: McClelland and Stewart.

Austen, Jane. 1811 [1969]. *Sense and Sensibility*. Harmondsworth, UK: Penguin.

Ballard, J. G. 1975. *High-rise*. London: Jonathan Cape.

Bell, Wendell. 1968. "The City, The Suburb, and a Theory of Social Choice." Pp. 132–178 in *The New Urbanization*, edited by Scott Green. New York: St. Martin's Press.

Bender, Thomas. 1978. *Community and Social Change in America*. New Brunswick, NJ: Rutgers University Press.

Berger, Bennett. 1960. *Working Class Suburb*. Berkeley: University of California Press.

Bernard, H. Russell, Peter Killworth, David Kronenfield, and Lee Sailer. 1984. "The Problem of Informant Accuracy: The Validity of Retrospective Data." *Annual Review of Anthropology* 13:495–517.

Bible, Holy. 1947. New York: B & S Publishing House.

Bly, Robert. 1990. *Iron John: A Book About Men*. Reading, MA: Addison-Wesley.

Boissevain, Jeremy. 1974. *Friends of Friends: Networks, Manipulators, and Coalitions*. Oxford: Blackwell.

Bott, Elizabeth. 1957. *Family and Social Network*. London: Tavistock.

Bourdieu, Pierre. 1984. Distinction. Cambridge, MA: Harvard University Press.

Brunner, John. 1968. *Stand on Zanzibar*. Garden City, NY: Doubleday.

Brunner, John. 1975. *The Shockwave Rider*. New York: Harper and Row.

Buccellati, Giorgio. 1967. *Cities and Nations of Ancient Syria*. Rome: Istituto di Studi del Vicino Oriente, Università di Roma.

Burawoy, Michael. 1976. "Functions and Reproduction of Migrant Labour." *American Journal of Sociology* 81:1050–1086.

Burawoy, Michael. 1985. *The Politics of Production: Factory Regimes under Capitalism and Socialism*. London: Verso.

Burt, Ronald. 1984. "Network Items and the General Social Survey." *Social Networks* 6:293–339.

Burt, Ronald. 1986. "A Note on Sociometric Order in the General Social Survey Network Data." *Social Networks* 8:149–174.

Burt, Ronald. 1992. *Structural Holes*. Chicago: University of Chicago Press.

Burt, Ronald. 1997. "The Contingent Value of Social Capital." *Administrative Science Quarterly* 42:339–65.

Campbell, Karen, and Barrett Lee. 1991. "Name Generators in Surveys of Personal Networks." *Social Networks* 13:203–221.

Carrière, Jean-Claude [writer]. 1982. *La Retour de Martin Guerre* [The Return of Martin Guerre]. Film Director: Daniel Vigne.

Casey, Chris. 1995. "The Senate's New Online Majority". *CMC Magazine*, October 1, website: http://www.december.com/cmc/mag/1995/oct/toc.html

Castells, Manuel. 1972. *The Urban Question*. London: Edward Arnold.

Castells, Manuel. 1996. *The Rise of the Network Society*. Malden, MA: Blackwell.

Choldin, Harvey. 1985. *Cities and Suburbs*. New York: McGraw-Hill.

Chudacoff, Howard P. 1972. *Mobile Americans: Residential and Social Mobility in the United States*. New York: Oxford University Press.

Clark, Samuel D. 1966. *The Suburban Society*. Toronto: University of Toronto Press.

Coates, D[onald] B. 1966. "Proposal for a Community Study Project Yorklea Project." Report to Clarke Institute of Psychiatry.

Coates, D[onald] B., Sharon Moyer, and Barry Wellman. 1969. "Yorklea Study: Symptoms, Problems and Life Events." *Canadian Journal of Public Health* 60(12):471–481.

Cohen, Abner. 1969. *Custom and Politics in Urban Africa*. London: Routledge and Kegan Paul.

Cohen, Sheldon, William Doyle, David Skoner, Bruce Rabin, and Jack Gwaltney, Jr. 1997. "Social Ties and Susceptibility to the Common Cold." *Journal of the American Medical Association* 227 (June 25):1940–1944.

Coleman, James S. 1990. *Foundations of Social Theory*. Cambridge, MA: Harvard University Press.

Craven, Paul, and Barry Wellman. 1973. "The Network City." *Sociological Inquiry* 43:57–88.

Darroch, A. Gordon, and Michael Ornstein. 1983. "Family Co-residence in Canada in 1871: Family Life Cycles, Occupations and Networks of Mutual Aid." Report to Institute for Behavioural Research and Department of Sociology, York University.

Davis, Natalie Zemon. 1975. *Society and Culture in Early Modern France*. Stanford, CA: Stanford University Press.

Davis, Natalie Zemon. 1983. *The Return of Martin Guerre*. Cambridge, MA: Harvard University Press.

Delaney, Samuel. 1976. *Triton*. New York: Bantam.

Dixon, J. E., J. R. Cann, and Colin Renfrew. 1968. "Obsidian and the Origins of Trade." *Scientific American* (March):80–88.

Doudou, Cameron. 1967. *The Gab Boys*. London: Deutsch.

Duffy, Andrew. 1991. "Fear on Streets of Metro is Increasing, Poll Shows." *Toronto Star*, June 7.

Durkheim, Émile. 1893 [1984]. *The Division of Labor in Society*. New York: Free Press.

Durkheim, Émile. 1897 [1951]. *Suicide*. Glencoe, IL: Free Press.

Engels, Friedrich. 1885 [1970]. *The Housing Question*. Moscow: Progress Publishers.

Etzioni, Amitai. 1991. "Liberals and Communitarians." Pp. 127–152 in Amitai Etzioni, *A Responsive Society: Collected Essays on Guiding Deliberate Social Change*. San Francisco: Jossey-Bass.

Feagin, Joe. 1973. "Community Disorganization." *Sociological Inquiry* 43:123–146.

Feagin, Joe, and Harlan Hahn. 1973. *Ghetto Revolt: The Politics of Violence in American Cities*. New York: Macmillan.

Feld, Scott. 1981. "The Focused Organization of Social Ties." *American Journal of Sociology* 86:1015–1035.

Film Canada. 1990. *Film Canada Yearbook*. Toronto: Telefilm Canada.

Fischer, Claude. 1976. *The Urban Experience*. New York: Harcourt Brace Jovanovich.

Fischer, Claude. 1978. "On the Marxian Challenge to Urban Sociology." *Comparative Urban Research* 6(2–3):10–19.

Fischer, Claude. 1982a. "The Dispersion of Kinship Ties in Modern Society." *Journal of Family History* 7:353–375.

Fischer, Claude. 1982b. *To Dwell Among Friends*. Berkeley: University of California Press.

Fischer, Claude. 1984. *The Urban Experience*, 2nd ed. Orlando, FL: Harcourt Brace Jovanovich.

Fischer, Claude, Robert Max Jackson, C. Ann Steuve, Kathleen Gerson, Lynne McCallister Jones, and Mark Baldassare. 1977. *Networks and Places*. New York: Free Press.

Flap, Henk. 1995. "No Man is an Island: The Research Program of a Social Capital Theory." Presented at International Social Network Conference, London, July.

Freeman, Linton, and Danching Ruan. 1997. "An International Comparative Study of Interpersonal Behavior and Role Relationships." *L'Année Sociologique* 47:89–115.

Frommer, Arthur. 1967. *Europe on $5 a Day*. New York: Arthur Frommer Publications.

Gans, Herbert. 1962. *The Urban Villagers*. New York: Free Press.

Gans, Herbert. 1967. *The Levittowners*. New York: Pantheon.

Garrioch, David. 1986. *Neighbourhood and Community in Paris, 1740–1790*. Cambridge: Cambridge University Press.

Gibson, William. 1986. *Count Zero*. New York: Arbor House.

Gillis, A. R., and John Hagan. 1982. "Bystander Apathy and the Territorial Imperative." *Sociological Inquiry* 53(4):448–60.

Gordon, Michael. 1978. *The American Family*. New York: Random House.

Granovetter, Mark. 1973. "The Strength of Weak Ties." *American Journal of Sociology* 78:1360–1380.

Granovetter, Mark. 1982. "The Strength of Weak Ties: A Network Theory Revisited." Pp. 105–130 in *Social Structure and Network Analysis*, edited by Peter Marsden and Nan Lin. Beverly Hills, CA: Sage.

Granovetter, Mark. 1985. "Economic Action and Social Structure: The Problem of Embeddedness." *American Journal of Sociology* 91:481–510.

Granovetter, Mark. 1995. *Getting a Job: A Study of Contacts and Careers*. Chicago: University of Chicago Press.

Grant, George. 1969. *Technology and Empire: Perspectives on North America*. Toronto: Anansi.

Guare, John. 1990. *Six Degrees of Separation*. New York: Lincoln Center.

Gurr, Ted Robert. 1981. "Historical Trends in Violent Crimes." *Crime and Justice: Annual Review of Research* 3:295–53.

Hall, Alan, and Barry Wellman. 1985. "Social Networks and Social Support." Pp. 23–41 in *Social Support and Health*, edited by Sheldon Cohen and S. Leonard Syme. New York: Academic Press.

Haythornthwaite, Caroline, and Barry Wellman. 1996. "Using SAS to Convert Ego-Centered Networks to Whole Networks." *Bulletin de Methode Sociologique* 50:71–84.

Herting, Gerald, David Grusky, and Stephen Van Rompaey. 1997. "The Social Geography of Interstate Mobility and Persistence." *American Sociological Review* 62 (April):267–87.

Hillery, George, Jr. 1955. "Definitions of Community: Areas of Agreement." *Rural Sociology* 20:111–122.

Hiltz, S. Roxanne, and Murray Turoff. 1978. *The Network Nation*. Reading, MA: Addison-Wesley.

Hinton, William. 1967. *Fanshen: A Documentary of Revolution in a Chinese Village*. New York: Monthly Review Press.

Hobbes, Thomas. 1651 [1982]. *Leviathan*. New York: Penguin Books.

Howard, Leslie. 1988. "Work and Community in Industrializing India." Pp. 185–197 in *Social Structures: A Network Approach*, edited by Barry Wellman and S. D. Berkowitz. Cambridge: Cambridge University Press.

Hufton, Olwen. 1974. *The Poor of Eighteenth-Century France: 1750–1789*. Oxford: Clarendon Press.

Jacobs, Jane. 1961. *The Death and Life of Great American Cities*. New York: Random House.

Jefferson, Thomas. 1784 [1972]. *Notes on the State of Virginia*. Edited by William Peden. New York: Norton.

Kadushin, Charles. 1981. "Notes on Expectations of Rewards in N-Person Networks." Pp. 235–254 in *Continuities in Structural Inquiry*, edited by Peter Blau and Robert Merton. Beverly Hills, CA: Sage.

Katz, Michael. 1975. *The People of Hamilton, Canada West*. Cambridge, MA: Harvard University Press.

Katz, Michael, Michael Doucet, and Mark Stern. 1982. *The Social Organization of Early Industrial Capitalism*. Cambridge, MA: Harvard University Press.

Keller, Suzanne. 1968. *The Urban Neighborhood*. New York: Random House.

Kennedy, Michael, and Naomi Galtz. 1996. "From Marxism to Postcommunism: Socialist Desires and East European Rejections." *Annual Review of Sociology* 22:437–458.

Knipscheer, C. P. M., and Toni Antonucci, eds. 1990. *Social Network Research*. Amsterdam: Swets and Zeitlinger.

Kochen, Manfred, ed. 1989. *The Small World*. Norwood, NJ: Ablex.

Kornhauser, William. 1959. *The Politics of Mass Society*. New York: Free Press.

Kornhauser, William. 1968. "Mass Society." *International Encyclopedia of the Social Sciences*. New York: Macmillan.

Laslett, Peter. 1965. *The World We Have Lost*. London: Metheun.

Laslett, Peter, ed. 1972. *Household and Family in Past Time: Comparative Studies in the Size and Structure of the Domestic Group Over the Last Three Centuries*. Cambridge: Cambridge University Press.

Latané, Bibb, and John Darley. 1976. *Help in a Crisis: Bystander Response to an Emergency*. Morristown, NJ: General Learning Press.

Laumann, Edward. 1966. *Prestige and Association in an Urban Community*. Indianapolis: Bobbs-Merrill.

Laumann, Edward. 1969a. "Friends of Urban Men." *Sociometry* 32:54–69.

Laumann, Edward. 1969b. "The Social Structure of Religious and Ethnoreligious Groups in a Metropolitan Community." *American Sociological Review* 43:182–197.

Laumann, Edward. 1973. *Bonds of Pluralism: The Forms and Substance of Urban Social Networks.* New York: Wiley.

Leach, Edmund. 1966. "The Legitimacy of Solomon: Some Structural Aspects of Old Testament History." *Archives of European Sociology* 7:58–101.

Le Roy Ladurie, Emmanuel. 1975 [1978]. *Montaillou : The Promised Land of Error [Montaillou, Village Occitan de 1294 à 1324].* Translated by Barbara Bray. New York: Braziller.

Le Roy Ladurie, Emmanuel. 1997. *The Beggar and the Professor: A Sixteenth-Century Saga.* Translated by Arthur Goldhammer. Chicago: University of Chicago Press.

Lessing, Doris. 1974. *Memoirs of a Survivor.* London: Octagon Press.

Liebow, Elliot. 1967. *Tally's Corner.* Boston: Little Brown.

Lin, Nan. 1997. "Guanxi: A Conceptual Analysis." Presented at Conference on the Chinese Triangle of Mainland-Taiwan-Hong Kong, Toronto, August.

Lin, Nan, Xialolan Ye, and Yu-shu Chen. 1997. "Human Capital, Social Resources and Social Capital: Their Contributions to Socioeconomic Attainment in Taiwan". Working Paper. Department of Sociology, Duke University, August.

Lofland, Lyn. 1973. *A World of Strangers.* New York: Basic.

Machiavelli, Niccolo. 1532 [1979]. *The Prince.* New York: Penguin.

Marsden, Peter. 1987. "Core Discussion Networks of Americans." *American Sociological Review* 52:122–131.

Marsden, Peter, and Karen E Campbell. 1984. "Measuring Tie Strength." *Social Forces* 63:482–501.

Marx, Karl. 1852 [1926]. *The Eighteenth Brumaire of Louis Bonaparte.* Translated by Eden and Cedar Paul. London: Allen and Unwin.

Marx, Leo. 1964. *The Machine in the Garden.* New York: Oxford University Press.

Mayer, Philip, and Iona Mayer. 1974. *Townsmen or Tribesmen.* Capetown: Oxford University Press.

McLuhan, Marshall. 1973. "Liturgy and the Media." *The Critic* (February): 15–23.

Meier, Richard. 1962. *A Communications Theory of Urban Growth.* Cambridge, MA: MIT Press.

Merton, Robert. 1957. "Patterns of Influence: Cosmopolitans and Locals." Pp. 387–420 in *Social Theory and Social Structure,* edited by Robert Merton. Glencoe, IL: Free Press.

Michelson, William. "Municipal Boundaries and Prospective LULU Impacts." *Research in Community Sociology* 7:117–40.

Milgram, Stanley. 1967. "The Small-World Problem." *Psychology Today* 1:62–67.

Mitchell, J. Clyde. 1956. *The Kalela Dance.* Manchester: Manchester University Press.

Monkkonen, Eric. 1995. "New York City Homicides: A Research Note." *Social Science History* 19(2):201–214.

Nisbet, Robert. 1962. *Community and Power.* New York: Oxford University Press.

Nozawa, Shinji. 1997. "Marital Relations and Personal Networks in Urban Japan." Working Paper. Department of Sociology, Shizouka University, May.

Oh, Sandy. 1991. "A Study of Urban and Suburban Movie Audiences and Their Patterns." Urban Sociology Term Paper, University of Toronto.

Oliver, Melvin. 1988. "The Urban Black Community as Network." *Sociological Quarterly* 29(4):623–645.

Pahl, Ray 1984. *Divisions of Labour*. Oxford: Basil Blackwell.

Park, Robert. 1925 [1967]. "The Urban Community as a Spatial Pattern and a Moral Order." Pp. 55–68 in *Robert E. Park on Social Control and Collective Behavior*, edited by Ralph Turner. Chicago: University of Chicago Press.

Parsons, Talcott. 1943. "The Kinship System of the Contemporary United States." *American Anthropologist* 45:22–38.

Peattie, Lisa. 1968. *The View From the Barrio*. Ann Arbor: University of Michigan Press.

Poggioli, Renato. 1975. "The Oaten Flute." Pp. 1–41 in Renato Poggioli, *The Oaten Flute: Essays on Poetry and the Pastoral Ideal*. Cambridge, MA: Harvard University Press.

Putnam, Robert. 1995. "Bowling Alone: America's Declining Social Capital." *Journal of Democracy* 6(1):65–78.

Radoeva, Detelina. 1988. "Old Bulgarians: Value Aspects of their Attitude towards Children as a Part of the Family." Balatonzamardi, Hungary: International Sociological Association Conference on Kinship and Aging.

Redfield, Robert. 1947. "The Folk Society." *American Journal of Sociology* 52:293–308.

Reynolds, Malvina. 1963. "Little Boxes." New York: Schroeder Music/ASCAP.

Roberts, Bryan. 1973. *Organizing Strangers: Poor Families in Guatemala City*. Austin: University of Texas Press.

Roberts, Bryan. 1978. *Cities of Peasants*. London: Edward Arnold.

Roche, Daniel. 1981. *The People of Paris: An Essay in Popular Culture in the 18th Century*. Berkeley: University of California Press.

Ruan, Danching, Linton Freeman, Xinyuan Dai, Yunkang Pan, and Wenhong Zhang. 1997. "On the Changing Structure of Social Networks in Urban China." *Social Networks* 19:75–89.

Salaff, Janet, and Siu-lun Wong. 1995. "Exiting Hong Kong: Social Class Experiences and the Adjustment to 1997." Pp. 176–233 in *Emigrating From Hong Kong*, edited by Ronald Skeldon. Hong Kong: Chinese University Press.

Scarf, Maggie. 1987. *Intimate Partners: Patterns in Love and Marriage*. New York: Random House.

Scherzer, Kenneth. 1992. *The Unbounded Community: Neighborhood Life and Social Structure in New York City, 1830–1875*. Durham, NC: Duke University Press.

Schweizer, Thomas, Michael Schnegg, and Susanne Berzborn. 1998. "Personal Networks and Social Support in a Multiethnic Community of Southern California." *Social Networks* 20:1–21.

Schwirian, Kent, and Gustavo Mesch. 1993. "Embattled Neighborhoods: The Political Ecology of Neighborhood Change." *Research in Urban Sociology* 3:83–110.

Scott, John. 1991. *Social Network Analysis*. London: Sage.

Shorter, Edward. 1975. *The Making of the Modern Family*. New York: Basic Books.

Sik, Endre. 1988. "Reciprocal Exchange of Labour in Hungary." Pp. 527–547 in *On Work*, edited by Raymond Pahl. Oxford: Basil Blackwell.

Simmel, Georg. 1903 [1950]. "The Metropolis and Mental Life." Pp. 409–424 in *The Sociology of Georg Simmel,* translated and edited by Kurt Wolff. Glencoe, IL: Free Press.

Slater, Philip. 1970. *The Pursuit of Loneliness.* Boston: Beacon Press.

Smith, Michael Peter. 1979. *The City and Social Theory.* New York: St. Martins.

Stack, Carol. 1974. *All Our Kin.* New York: Harper and Row.

Starr, Kevin. 1985. *Inventing the Dream: California through the Progressive Era.* New York: Oxford University Press.

Starr, Kevin. 1990. *Material Dreams: Southern California Through the 1920s.* New York: Oxford University Press.

Statistics Canada. 1987. *Health and Social Support, 1985.* Ottawa: Ministry of Supplies and Services. General Social Survey Analysis Series.

Statistics Canada and Status of Women Canada. 1993. Summary Proceedings of International Conference on the Measurement and Valuation of Unpaid Work. Ottawa: Ministry of Supplies and Services.

Stein, Maurice. 1960. *The Eclipse of Community.* Princeton, NJ: Princeton University Press.

Stephenson, Neal. 1992. *Snow Crash.* New York: Bantam.

Stone, Lawrence. 1977. *The Family, Sex, and Marriage in England, 1500–1800.* New York: Harper and Row.

Stone, Leroy. 1988. *Family and Friendship Ties among Canada's Seniors.* Ottawa: Statistics Canada.

Strike, Carol. 1990. "The Film Industry in Canada." Pp. 255–257 in *Canadian Social Trends,* edited by Craig McKie and Keith Thompson. Toronto: Thompson Educational Publishing.

Taub, Richard, George Surgeon, Sara Lindholm, Phyllis Betts Otti, and Amy Bridges. 1977. "Urban Voluntary Associations: Locality Based and Externally Induced." *American Journal of Sociology* 83(2):425–442.

Thernstrom, Stephan. 1964. *Poverty and Progress: Social Mobility in a Nineteenth-Century City.* Cambridge, MA: Harvard University Press.

Thernstrom, Stephan. 1973. *The Other Bostonians: Poverty and Progress in the American Metropolis, 1880–1970.* Cambridge, MA: Harvard University Press.

Thomése, G. C. Fleur, and Theo van Tilburg. 1998. "Neighborhood Networks of Older Adults: A Social Scientific Study among Independently Living Older Adults in the Netherlands." World Congress of Sociology, Montreal, July.

Tilly, Charles. 1964. *The Vendée: A Sociological Analysis of the Counter-revolution of 1793.* Cambridge, MA: Harvard University Press.

Tilly, Charles. 1973. "Do Communities Act?" *Sociological Inquiry* 43:209–240.

Tilly, Charles. 1975. "Food Supply and Public Order in Modern Europe." Pp. 380–455 in *The Formation of National States in Western Europe,* edited by Charles Tilly. Princeton, NJ: Princeton University Press.

Tilly, Charles. 1979. "Collective Violence in European Perspective." Pp. 83–118 in *Violence in America: Historical and Comparative Perspectives,* edited by Hugh Davis Graham and Ted Robert Gurr. Beverly Hills, CA: Sage.

Tilly, Charles. 1984a. *Big Structures, Large Processes, Huge Comparisons.* New York: Russell Sage Foundation.

Tilly, Charles. 1984b. "The Old New Social History and the New Old Social History." *Review* 7:363–406.

Tocqueville, Alexis de. 1835 [1945]. *Democracy in America*. New York: Knopf.

Tönnies, Ferdinand. 1887 [1955]. *Community and Organization*. London: Routledge and Kegan Paul.

Turner, Frederick Jackson. 1893 [1992]. "The Significance of the Frontier in American History." Pp. 1–38 in Frederick Jackson Turner, *The Frontier in American History*. Tucson: University of Arizona Press.

Wall, Helena. 1990. *Fierce Communion: Family and Community in North America*. Cambridge, MA: Harvard University Press.

Warren, Rolland. 1978. *The Community in America*. Chicago: Rand McNally.

Wasserman, Stanley, and Katherine Faust. 1993. *Social Network Analysis: Methods and Applications*. Cambridge: Cambridge University Press.

Weber, Max. 1946. *From Max Weber: Essays in Sociology*. New York: Oxford University Press.

Weber, Max. 1958. *The City*. Glencoe, IL: Free Press.

Wellman, Barry. 1968. *Community Ties and Mental Health*. Toronto: Clarke Institute of Psychiatry, August.

Wellman, Barry. 1979. "The Community Question." *American Journal of Sociology* 84:1201–1231.

Wellman, Barry. 1982. "Studying Personal Communities." Pp. 61–80 in *Social Structure and Network Analysis*, edited by Peter Marsden and Nan Lin. Beverly Hills, CA: Sage.

Wellman, Barry. 1988a. "The Community Question Re-evaluated." Pp. 81–107 in *Power, Community and the City*, edited by Michael Peter Smith. New Brunswick, NJ: Transaction Books.

Wellman, Barry. 1988b. "Structural Analysis: From Method and Metaphor to Theory and Substance." Pp. 19–61 in *Social Structures: A Network Approach*, edited by Barry Wellman and S. D. Berkowitz. Cambridge: Cambridge University Press.

Wellman, Barry. 1990a. "The Place of Kinfolk in Community Networks." *Marriage and Family Review* 15(1/2):195–228.

Wellman, Barry. 1990b. "Where Have All the Friends Gone: Re-Assessing Liberated Communities." Working Paper. Centre for Urban and Community Studies, University of Toronto, August.

Wellman, Barry. 1992a. "How to Use SAS to Study Egocentric Networks." *Cultural Analysis Methods* 4(2):6–12.

Wellman, Barry. 1992b. "Men in Networks: Private Communities, Domestic Friendships." Pp. 74–114 in *Men's Friendships*, edited by Peter Nardi. Newbury Park, CA: Sage.

Wellman, Barry. 1992c. "Which Types of Ties and Networks Give What Kinds of Social Support?" *Advances in Group Processes* 9:207–235.

Wellman, Barry. 1993. "An Egocentric Network Tale." *Social Networks* 17(2):423–436.

Wellman, Barry. 1996. "Are Personal Communities Local? A Dumptarian Reconsideration." *Social Networks* 18:347–354.

Wellman, Barry, Peter Carrington, and Alan Hall. 1988. "Networks as Personal Communities." Pp. 130–84 in *Social Structures: A Network Approach*, edited by Barry Wellman and S. D. Berkowitz. Cambridge: Cambridge University Press.

Wellman, Barry, Ove Frank, Vicente Espinoza, Staffan Lundquist, and Craig Wilson. 1991. "Integrating Individual, Relational and Structural Analysis." *Social Networks* 13:223–250.

Wellman, Barry, and Barry Leighton. 1979. "Networks, Neighborhoods and Communities." *Urban Affairs Quarterly* 14:363–390.

Wellman, Barry, and David Tindall. 1993. "Reach Out and Touch Some Bodies: How Social Networks Connect Telephone Networks." Pp. 63–93 in *Progress in Communication Sciences*, edited by William Richards, Jr., and George Barnett. Norwood, NJ: Ablex.

Wellman, Barry, and Charles Wetherell. 1996. "Social Network Analysis of Historical Communities: Some Questions from the Present for the Past." *History of the Family* 1(1):97–121.

Wellman, Barry, Renita Wong, David Tindall, and Nancy Nazer. 1997. "A Decade of Network Change: Turnover, Mobility and Stability." *Social Networks* 19(1):27–51.

Wellman, Barry, and Scot Wortley. 1989. "Brothers' Keepers: Situating Kinship Relations in Broader Networks of Social Support." *Sociological Perspectives* 32:273–306.

Wellman, Barry, and Scot Wortley. 1990. "Different Strokes From Different Folks: Community Ties and Social Support." *American Journal of Sociology* 96:558–588.

Wellman, Beverly, and Barry Wellman. 1992. "Domestic Affairs and Network Relations." *Journal of Social and Personal Relationships* 9:385–409.

Wenger, G. Clare. 1992. *Help in Old Age—Facing Up to Change: A Longitudinal Network Study*. Liverpool: Liverpool University Press.

Wetherell, Charles, Andrejs Plakans, and Barry Wellman. 1994. "Social Networks, Kinship and Community in Eastern Europe." *Journal of Interdisciplinary History* 24(4, Spring):639–663.

White, Harrison. 1970. "Search Parameters for the Small World Problem." *Social Forces* 49:259–264.

White, Morton, and Lucia White. 1962. *The Intellectual Versus the City*. Cambridge, MA: Harvard University Press.

Whitfield, Stephen, and Gene Roddenbery. *The Making of Star Trek.* New York: Ballantine.

Whyte, William Foote. 1943. *Street Corner Society*. Chicago: University of Chicago Press.

Williams, Raymond. 1973. *The Country and the City*. London: Chatto and Windus.

Wills, Gary. 1978. *Inventing America: Jefferson's Declaration of Independence*. Garden City, NY: Doubleday.

Wirth, Louis. 1938. "Urbanism as a Way of Life." *American Journal of Sociology* 44:3–24.

Wolf, Eric. 1966. "Kinship, Friendship and Patron-Client Relations." in *The Social Anthropology of Complex Societies*, edited by Michael Banton. London: Tavistock.

Wright, Paul. 1989. "Gender Differences in Adults' Same- and Cross-Gender Friendships." Pp. 197–221 in *Older Adult Friendship,* edited by Rebecca Adams and Rosemary Blieszner. Newbury Park, CA: Sage.

Young, Michael, and Peter Willmott. 1957. *Family and Kinship in East London.* Harmondsworth, UK: Penguin.

Zeidman, Reena. 1985. "Integration or Alienation: A Case Study of the Twelve Tribes." Working Paper. University of Toronto, Department of Sociology, April.

1

The Elements of
Personal Communities

Barry Wellman and Stephanie Potter

From Societal Typologies to
Ego-Centered Elements

Beyond Gemeinschaft

Since the start of systematic sociological thinking in the 1800s, analysts have worked to develop typologies that would organize the surface confusion of the real world into a coherent set of simpler terms. For example, analysts of nation-states have used economic relationships to distinguish between first (capitalist), second (state socialist), and third world developing societies, while world systems analysts have used international political and trading relationships to distinguish between core, semiperiphery, and periphery states. Such typologies claim that clusters of variables form coherent sets so that, if we can say whether a nation is first world or core state, we have some notion of such matters as its level of industrialization, trading patterns, and social-class organization.

Typological thinking has influenced urban and community studies for more than one hundred years (discussed in somewhat more detail in the introductory chapter). The starting point was Ferdinand Tönnies's typological contrast (1887) between:

1. Rural, preindustrial societies based on densely knit networks of kin and neighbors who have broadly based supportive relations (*gemeinschaft*); and
2. Urban, industrial societies based on sparsely knit networks of friends and acquaintances that have more specialized, almost contractual, exchanges of support (*gesellschaft*).

Although Tönnies's typology compared entire societies, analysts soon began using his approach to compare social systems within societies.

They searched for differences between rural and urban societies, such as Robert Redfield's assertion of a *folk-urban* societal continuum (1947). Many analysts nostalgically lamented the loss of community that they believed had occurred when social systems changed from gemeinschaft to gesellschaft (Nisbet 1962; Slater 1970; Stein 1960). Some analysts also developed typologies to compare areas within cities, asking, for example, if poor inner-city areas have more communal gemeinschaft than suburban ones (e.g., Gans 1962, 1967; Berger 1960: Liebow 1967).

The development of the notion of *personal communities* shifted the unit of analysis from the society and the social area to interpersonal ties and networks (Wellman and Leighton 1979; Wellman 1988, 1993). Following Talcott Parsons's (1951) suggestion that social scientists can use the same grammar to analyze interpersonal and societal relationships, analysts began to wonder if there were systematic differences in personal communities. For example, our research group has investigated if Torontonians are principally immersed in densely knit, tightly bounded personal communities of kin and neighbors—a gemeinschaft-like "community saved"— or in sparsely knit, loosely bounded, heterogeneous communities—a gesellschaft-like "community liberated." This research has moved us from studying traditional neighborhood-bound communities to studying the personal community networks of each individual. In our work, we have assumed that we could typologize such personal communities in a manner similar to neighborhood communities. For example, we have wondered if people doing paid work outside their homes would have more "liberated" communities than those who stayed home and did not do paid work. We have suggested that many personal community networks might consist of a "saved" core and a "liberated" periphery (Craven and Wellman 1973; Wellman 1979; Wellman, Carrington, and Hall 1988).

All such typologies assume that because several variables vary together, reducing the observed variety of communities to a few types is possible. Despite widely differing variation in their depictions of contemporary urban communities, all these typologizing accounts have some common characteristics:

• They define community in terms of interpersonal relations of sociability and support between residents of different households. These definitions are based on *behavior* (what community members are linked to each other in what ways), and they treat *attitudes* (a sense of belonging) as a product of behavior. The definitions focus on ties with nonresident neighbors, friends, and (sometimes) kin. They exclude almost all relations with coworkers and household members.

- They assume that the variables describing the behavior of community members are only manifestations of a smaller set of factors, and that each variable loads highly on only one factor. In other words, communities form coherent types.
- They often assume that the typologies form a single dimension. For example, gemeinschaft-gesellschaft is either a unidimensional dichotomy or a single continuous dimension in which several variables are assumed to have one set of values in rural areas (high density, percent kin, etc.) and the opposite set of values in urban areas (low density, percent kin, etc.).

Until recently, analysts have usually derived their assertions about the existence and composition of these typologies from theoretical assumptions rather than from the many empirical studies of community. Of course, there have been many empirical studies of community, but the typologies themselves have largely been induced from theory.[1] Moreover, the typologies have come from traditional community sociology that assumes that neighborhoods are the only basis of community. Yet since the 1970s, research has shown that most community ties stretch well beyond neighborhoods. Such community ties are ramified social networks, and not local groups. Analyzing these social networks can provide a basis for the analysis of personal communities that focuses on relations between community members rather than on the characteristics of neighborhoods or societies (Introduction; Berkowitz 1982; Wellman 1988).

A Social Network Approach

Social network analysis enables us to evaluate typologies such as the Tönniesian belief that densely knit networks have frequent face-to-face contact and high percentages of kin and neighbors. Combined with multivariate analysis, it allows us to consider factors that may make up the elements of communities in various combinations. Such a multiple-factor approach means that we are not confined to finding that communities are either gemeinschaft-saved or gesellschaft-liberated. We can investigate the extent to which communities are complexly, but systematically, formed.

A battery of concepts and techniques has helped community network analysts to move from speculation to systematic analysis. Where traditional community studies had implicitly been concerned with *whole networks*—all the ties in a bounded area such as a neighborhood—community network analysts began studying personal communities, *ego-centered social networks*, defined from the standpoint of the *focal persons* at their centers (see the Introduction to this volume). An ego-centered network is like a planetary system in which a host of *network members* surrounds a

TABLE 1.1   Bott's Family Network Typology

	Conjugal Network Types		
Variables	*Segregated*	*Intermediate*	*Joint*
Network size	large	variable	small
% Kin	high	moderate	low
Multiplexity	high	variable	low
Density	high	moderate	low
Heterogeneity	low	moderate	high

focal person. Membership in such a network is defined by the *ties* of interest that each has with the focal person, be they relations of kinship, social closeness, or frequent contact. As North Americans usually have informal ties with about 1,000 others (Kochen 1989), almost all ego-centered network analyses impose stringent selection criteria on the ties that they take into account. Most studies, including the one we present here, examine between six and twenty of the most *active ties*; some also examine the *links* that these *network members* have with each other (Wellman 1990, 1992c; Walker, Wasserman and Wellman 1993).

The first typology of ego-centered networks (i.e., personal communities) was Elizabeth Bott's (1957, 1971). It was pioneering and influential, although confined to the ties of married couples with their *immediate kin.* Based on detailed interviews with a small English sample, Bott suggested that situations where husbands and wives lived independent lives were largely a result of the wives being immersed in large, densely knit networks of kin dominated by sisters and Mum. By contrast, where husbands and wives acted jointly, they usually had smaller, more sparsely knit networks that were mostly composed of friends (Table 1.1).

Our group's work has expanded Bott's focus on kinship to analyze all active community ties: friends, relatives, neighbors, and workmates. As the introductory chapter recounts, our research group has linked our work to the continuing debate about the existence and nature of community. We have developed a "community lost/community saved/community liberated" typology that integrated the ideas of Tönnies, Bott, and their successors (see also Wellman 1979, 1982, 1988, 1993; Wellman and Leighton 1979). We have argued that what we have called the Community Question" is really tripartite: Have communities atrophied in modern times (community lost); maintained their traditional density, homogeneity, and solidarity (community saved); or been transformed into less local, more sparsely knit, more heterogeneous, and less solidary networks (community liberated) (Table 1.2)?

Typologies have continued to emerge. Although Mark Granovetter (1973, 1982) did not study community networks, he influentially conjec-

TABLE 1.2   Wellman's Community Typology

Variables	Community Lost	Community Saved	Community Liberated
Network size	small	large	large
Tie strength	weak	strong	strong
% Kin	low	high	low
% Neighbors	low	high	low
% Friends	high	low	high
Multiplexity	low	high	low
% Voluntary ties	high	low	high
Network density	low	high	moderate
Face-to-face contact	low	high	low
Phone contact	low	moderate	high
Heterogeneity	heterogeneous	homogeneous	heterogeneous
Group contact	dyads	group	couples, dyads
Social support	low	high	moderate

tured that intimacy, multiplexity, and frequent contact occur together in *strong ties*. He also suggested that communities with high proportions of weak ties will be heterogeneous and sparsely knit (Table 1.3). More recently, Clare Wenger (1991, 1992) has derived a list of personal community types from her field study of Welsh caregiving networks (with the defined characteristics of these types in parentheses): *local family dependent* (small, kin, multiplex, dense, homogeneous); *local integrated* (large, neighbors and friends, multiplex, sparsely knit, moderately heterogeneous); *local self-contained* (small, neighbors, specialized roles, sparsely knit, moderately heterogeneous); *wider community-focused* (large, specialized roles, sparsely knit, heterogeneous); and *private restricted* (small, specialized roles, sparsely knit, heterogeneous) (see Table 1.4). With a typology derived from empirical analysis, Wenger's *local family dependent* type is similar to Bott's *independent* family network. Moreover, the *local family dependent* and *local self-contained* types are similar to Wellman's *community saved*, Wenger's *wider community focused* is similar to Bott's *joint family network* and Wellman's

TABLE 1.3   Granovetter's Strong-Ties Conjecture

Variables	Strong Ties	Weak Ties
Network size	small	large
% Kin	high	low
Multiplexity	high	low
Density	high	low
Heterogeneity	low	high
Frequency of contact	high	low
Intimacy	high	low

TABLE 1.4   Wenger's Support Network Typology

| | *Type of Support Network* | | | | |
| | | | | | |
Variables	*Local Family Dependent*	*Local Integrated*	*Local Self-contained*	*Wider Community-focused*	*Private Restricted*
Network size	small	large	small	large	small
% Kin	high	low	low	moderate	low
% Neighbors	low	high	high	high	low
% Friends	low	high	low	high	low
Multiplexity	high	high	low	low	low
Network density	high	low	low	low	low
Heterogeneity	low	moderate	moderate	high	high
Proximity of supportive tie	near	near	near	variable	far
Level of support	high	high	low	high	variable
Access to scarce resources	low	high	low	high	low

community liberated, while Wenger's *private restricted* resembles Wellman's *community lost.*

In order to go beyond conjecture and ad hoc typologizing, our data analysis in this chapter does not assume that there can be only two or three types of personal communities. That would be unlikely because of the multiple, diverse circles in which people in the first world now travel (see the Introduction). However it is just as unlikely that each person's community has unique characteristics, given the tendency for community variables to covary. So we are looking for a reasonably small, but multidimensional, set of the basic building blocks of community

In this chapter, we describe what our data suggest are elements of personal communities, with each element composed of one or more community variables. For example, personal communities with a high proportion of immediate kin will probably also be densely knit. Under such circumstances, density and percent kin would be components of the same element in the constitution of personal communities.[2] Yet if network size varies independently from network density, they would be components of different elements. A small set of elements—in different combinations—may summarize variations in personal communities while preserving their empirical complexity. For example, a simple dichotomization of four elements yields sixteen different combinations.

Factor analysis is a straightforward way to discover how variables combine into the elements of personal communities. We use it here to identify the basic building blocks of the Torontonians' personal communities.[3] We supplement this statistical analysis with the study participants' accounts of their community life.

Analyzing Personal Communities

Milieu

As in Chapter 2, our information comes from a large closed-ended survey and a small set of detailed interviews collected from one-time residents of the Toronto (Canada) Borough of East York.[4] The two data-sets complement each other. The survey provides a large set of reliable information without much detail. By contrast, the interviews provide much detail, but only for a small subsample of the original participants.

Densely settled East York, with a population of about 100,000, is an integral part of the transportation and communication networks of metropolitan Toronto (population = 4 million +). East York's center is about six miles (ten kilometers) east of Toronto's central business district, a half-hour subway ride or drive. When our survey and interviews were conducted, East York's small private homes and apartments housed a settled, predominantly British-Canadian working- to middle-class population (for details see Chapter 2, Gillies and Wellman 1968; Wellman, Carrington, and Hall 1988). The men we interviewed held jobs such as electrician, laboratory technician, and truck driver, and the women held jobs such as secretary, insurance claims examiner, and waitress. All but two of the study participants were employed by others.

The Survey Data-set

The large data-set derives from a closed-ended, in-person survey, conducted in 1968 with a random sample of 845 adult (aged eighteen and over) residents of East York. Survey participants reported about their relationships with a total of 3,930 network members, a mean of about 5 ties each. About half the intimates were kin, especially immediate kin (parents, siblings, and adult children). Most of the nonkin were friends; there were few intimate ties with neighbors and coworkers. Although most intimates lived in metropolitan Toronto, only about an eighth lived in the same neighborhoods as the focal persons. Intimates used the telephone as much as in-person contact to stay in touch.

The virtues of this data-set are its large sample size, systematic information about each intimate, information about each network's social density, and its fit with the subsequent interviews. Although this data-set is older than one of the coauthors, we are not very concerned about its age. We are using it to explore the basic elements of community, and earlier findings based on this data-set have been useful and consistent with other studies (for details see Wellman et al. 1971, 1973; Wellman 1979, 1988, 1993). We do note that both the survey and the interviews contain a higher percentage of two-parent households than a current study would.

Because of its pioneering quality, this data-set has several limitations:

1. In asking only about the strongest intimate ties in each focal person's community, it does not provide information about weaker, but still active, relationships.
2. Brief answers to the short, closed-ended survey questions reveal little about the subtleties and details of interaction.

The Interview Data-sets

To deal with some limitations of the survey, we conducted thirty-three indepth interviews in 1977–78 with a subsample of the 845 originally surveyed East Yorkers (Wellman 1982; Wellman, Carrington, and Hall 1988).[5] The depth of these interviews complemented the breadth of the original survey, providing more information about more ties in each personal community. We held several open-ended discussions with each of the participants lasting about fifteen hours, asking them about each network member with whom they were significantly "in touch." The participants told us how they first met, the ways in which they are linked in network structures, and what network members do for each other. We wound up with both qualitative (full interview transcripts and online text bases) and quantitative information stored in data-sets that could be statistically analyzed.

The 33 personal communities contain a total of 412 "active" ties, with a mean of 5 "intimate" ties and 7 somewhat weaker (but still relatively active) "significant" ties.[6] Kin play an important role in most East Yorkers' lives, comprising 45% of all active ties. Immediate kin (parents, adult children, siblings) are especially important. Friends are the second most prevalent type of active tie (25%). They are especially apt to be intimate, comprising 39% of all intimate ties. Neighbors, coworkers, and fellow members of formal organizations are active community members in lesser proportions; their ties are rarely intimate (for details see Wellman, Carrington, and Hall 1988). Many ties have been long-standing: The median relationship had lasted nineteen years for all community members and nine years for those who are not kin.

The networks of these active ties are more structurally complex than the densely knit local and kinship solidarities which gemeinschaft thought implicitly uses as a normative criterion. For example, the average East Yorker deals with three otherwise unconnected pieces of his/her network: one isolate, one dyad, and one larger, internally connected, component. Moreover, the components themselves are often composed of several clusters—densely knit internally but only thinly connected with each other. Although only one-third of all ties are directly linked in the median network (density = 0.33), the higher densities (median = 0.67) of the networks' largest components help coordinate the provision of support and social control. The many links between community members mean that East Yorkers must deal with network structures and not just juggle sets of disconnected ties.

Choice of Variables

Our first task was to choose a reasonable set of variables to analyze. Because of the small sample size of the interview data-sets, we did not want to throw a large, unwashed set of variables into the kitchen sink of factor analysis. As we did not see the intellectual or practical point of pruning a single large correlation matrix of more than one hundred candidate variables, we selected variables from six separate correlation matrices, each measuring aspects of ego-centered networks: their size, pattern, contact, strength, context, and heterogeneity. If the variables in a matrix were highly correlated ($r > 0.5$), we selected for the factor analysis the one that was most central to theory and provided the most information (e.g., a continuous rather than a categorical variable). When the correlations were low, more than one variable was selected, e.g., both the *proportion of ties living in metro* and the *rate of phone contact* were used to measure *contact*.[7] Although the survey and interview data-sets contain different questions and variables, we attempted to retain as much comparability as possible in the selection of the variables that we retained for analysis. Table 1.5 presents the variables and their summary statistics.

Factor Analysis

The survey data-set only contains information about intimate ties while the interview data-set contains information about both intimate and significant ties. To improve the comparability of the interview data-set with the intimate-only survey data-set, we conducted two separate factor analyses of the interview data-set: one of only the intimate ties, and one of both the intimate and significant ties.

We used oblique promax factor analyses to determine what characteristics of personal communities are related.[8] The oblique rotation pre-

TABLE 1.5   Variables Used in the Analysis

| Original Constructs | Variables: Mean Statistics for Data-sets | | | |
	Survey Data-set		Interview Data-set (All active ties)	
Size	Mean number of intimates	4.8	Mean number of intimates	4.7
	Mean number of significants	N.A.	Mean number of significants	7.1
Pattern	Mean network density	.33	Mean network density	.42
Strength	% Immediate kin	30	% Immediate kin	35
	% Extended kin	19	% Extended kin	11
	% Friends	38	% Intimates	43
	Mean multiplicity of ties	N.A.	Mean multiplicity of ties	3.1
Contact	Mean rate of phone contact (times per year)	79	Median annual rate of phone contact with an intimate (times per year)	24
	% Ties living in Metropolitan Toronto	76	Mean residential distance (miles)	34
	% Ties informally visited	76	Median annual rate of in-person contact with an intimate (times per year)	24
Context	% Neighbors	7	% Neighbors	18
	% Workmates	5	% Workmates	7
	Mean % contact is in groups	N.A.	Mean % contact is in groups	.39
Heterogeneity	Standard deviation of SES score (Blishen)	21.3	Heterogeneity of ties— composite measure	100

serves the possibility that the factors could be correlated, as there is no theoretical reason to assume a priori that they would be independent. In fact, as the highest interfactor correlation is a low 0.22, the factors are substantially independent. We did three factor analyses:

1. intimates only for the survey data (Table 1.6)
2. intimates only for the interview data (Table 1.7)
3. all active ties (intimate + significant ties) for the interview data (Table 1.8).

The three analyses produce broadly comparable results, indicating that four elements shape the types of personal communities:

1. A predominance in the community of *immediate kin* or *friends,*
2. the frequency of *contact* with community members,

TABLE 1.6   Factor Pattern of the Survey Data-set: Intimates Only

Variables	Immediate Kinship	Contact	Extended Kinship	Neighboring	Coworking	Range
% Immediate kin	.88	–.19	–.21	–.10	.06	.11
Network density	.63	.07	.13	–.12	–.15	–.28
% Friends	–.78	–.02	–.47	–.28	–.19	–.07
Mean face-to-face contact	.01	.85	.00	.16	.21	–.08
% Metro	–.22	.79	–.01	.14	.04	–.01
Mean phone contact	.30	.57	–.04	–.34	–.46	–.10
% Extended kin	.07	–.02	.95	–.05	–.11	.01
% Neighbors	–.02	.20	–.03	.90	–.07	.00
% Informal visits	.02	.38	.23	–.34	–.46	–.10
% Coworkers	–.05	.24	–.04	–.10	.87	–.07
Heterogeneity—SES	.08	.05	–.14	–.10	–.23	.78
Size of intimate network	–.17	–.12	.24	–.15	.24	.66
Eigenvalue	2.17	1.96	1.33	1.22	1.14	1.10
% Variance explained	18.08	16.33	11.08	10.17	9.50	9.17

NOTE: Only loadings > |0.5| are considered part of a factor.

TABLE 1.7   Factor Pattern of the Interview Data-set: Intimates Only

Variables	Contact	Range	Group	Immediate Kinship
Mean face-to-face contact	.87	–.06	.20	.02
Mean residential distance	–.84	.04	.12	.19
Mean phone contact	.66	–.24	–.11	.52
Mean multiplexity	.61	–.24	.51	–.33
Number of intimates	–.09	.94	–.09	–.09
Heterogeneity	–.14	.91	.15	–.05
% Extended kin	–.04	.48	–.15	.19
Network density	–.04	–.23	.80	–.06
% Group contact	.10	.19	.65	.25
% Immediate kin	–.13	.06	.13	.87
Eigenvalue	2.93	1.65	1.37	1.27
% Variance explained	40.58	22.85	18.98	17.59

NOTE: Only loadings > |0.5| are considered part of a factor.

TABLE 1.8   Factor Pattern of the Interview Data-set: All Active Ties

Variables	Range	Intimacy	Contact	Immediate Kinship	Dyads
Heterogeneity	.90	.12	−.01	−.20	−.08
Number of significants	.87	−.39	−.06	−.19	−.03
Network density	−.69	−.19	−.13	−.31	−.09
Number of intimates	.29	.88	.08	−.06	.03
% Intimates	−.50	.81	.07	.09	.04
Mean face-to-face contact	−.00	−.29	−.75	−.05	.12
Mean residential distance	−.29	.06	.71	.41	−.06
% Extended kin	.23	−.18	.60	−.22	.17
% Immediate kin	−.31	.07	−.16	.83	−.05
Mean multiplexity	−.37	.12	−.39	−.74	−.08
Mean phone contact	−.12	−.16	−.32	.10	.81
% Group contact	−.01	−.23	−.27	.09	−.71
Eigenvalue	3.00	2.31	1.62	1.27	1.15
% Variance explained	32.09	24.70	17.33	13.58	12.30

NOTE: Only loadings > | 0.5 | are considered part of a factor.

3. the *range* (size, density, and heterogeneity) of the community,
4. the number and proportion of close *intimate relationships* in the community.

Elements of Torontonians' Personal Communities

Immediate Kinship/Friendship

Personal communities that load highly on this element have a high proportion of immediate kin, are densely knit, and consist of specialized ties that only interact in a few contexts.[9] The ties that load highly on this element are predominantly those of *immediate kinship* (parents, adult children, siblings), rather than all kin (aunts, grandparents, cousins, etc.). This difference between immediate kin and other, *extended kin* is consistent with previous research showing that, whereas immediate kin are highly supportive, extended kin are rarely supportive (Wellman 1990; Wellman and Wortley 1989, 1990; Chapter 2 this volume). The presence of this immediate kinship element shows that many people continue to retain immediate kin as vital members of their personal communities even as people's networks are expanding and they live largely surrounded by strangers.

Personal communities with a high percentage of immediate kin are usually densely knit. This is not surprising because kinship, unlike friendship, is a *system* with built-in connectivity. To be sure, one's own kin and in-laws are often not closely connected, and there are often family quarrels. Still, connections among immediate kin are longstanding, and one mother or sister is usually a "kinkeeper" who arranges family get-togethers and transmits family news. Yet there are limits to kinship: They have specialized relationships of emotional support, services, and financial exchange rather than the broadly based ties that Tönnies's gemeinschaft celebrated.

By contrast to those networks that have many immediate kin, others have a high proportion of friends, are sparsely knit, and have broadly based ("multiplex") relationships.[10] Torontonians are rarely members of large friendship groups. Rather, they are partners in a series of two-person or two-couple duets. As a result, they must laboriously and repeatedly work to maintain their friendship ties through frequent contact and mutual aid. Yet these friendship-based communities are not filled with souls who have Lost communities. These are not the tiny networks of weak ties that Tönnies feared. They are filled with friends, resembling Georg Simmel's depiction of Liberated urbanites (1902–1903). Moreover, the multiplexity of many friendship ties means that community members meet each other in a variety of situations.[11]

Survey Data-set—Intimates. The *kinship/friendship factor* explains 18% of the variance in this data-set, the most of any factor. The variables loading highly on this factor (Table 1.6) are the percentage of immediate kin in the networks (0.88), the percentage of friends (–0.78), and network density (0.63).[12] Thus a network with a high proportion of immediate kin usually has a low proportion of friends. As immediate kin and friends together comprise the bulk of intimates (and even of all active ties), their percentages usually vary inversely in a zero-sum fashion.

Interview Data-set—Intimates. The immediate kinship/friendship factor is present here too. Although it explains as much of the explained variance (18%) as the immediate kinship/friendship factor did in the survey data-set discussed just above, other factors explain more variance in the interview-intimate data-set (Table 1.7). The defining characteristic of this factor is the percentage of immediate kin (.87). The appreciable loading of the frequency of telephone contact (.52) reflects the tendency of network members to call distant immediate kin (Wellman and Tindall 1993).

Interview Data-set—All Active Ties. The immediate kinship/friendship factor appearing in this analysis explains somewhat less of the variance (14%). As in the survey data-set, multiplexity has a high negative loading (–0.74) showing that members of communities with a high proportion of immediate kin usually interact in only a few contexts (Table 1.8). One puzzling matter is that the sign of the density variable is reversed (–0.31) compared with the immediate kin element from the survey data-set. Here, a high percentage of kin is associated with lower network density. We suspect that this reflects a difference in the nature of this data-set, the only one to analyze all active ties and not just intimate ties. Non-intimate active ties are more apt to be with in-laws, and in-laws do not have many connections with a focal person's own kin or with friends, neighbors, and coworkers. Even though one's own kin form densely knit clusters, the lack of active ties between the non-intimate kin of each spouse lowers the overall density of the network (Wellman et al. 1991).

For example, study participant John Williams[13] is a forty-four-year-old upholsterer with three children. He has a kin-centered, densely knit personal community. He believes that the household and immediate kin are the most important aspects of a person's life, and that friends exist only to compensate for a lack of kin. "We are very close, we are very private people, we don't interfere with anybody. We are strictly with relatives: I have sisters, my wife has sisters and a brother. I can't say I have any outside friends really."

Yet John's ties are stressful as well as supportive for he feels imposed upon by the kin he holds so dear. Our interviewer noted that John

> seems to be a very lonely, unhappy man, "strung out" with obligation and guilt revolving around his mother and his job—he is always pleasing the customer as he is at home. . . . He feels persecuted in the sense that his friends and relatives only use him and telephone him because of his mother, and not because they are interested in him, while friends only come to the cottage for something to eat.

Contact

The variables in the *contact* element measure the level of interaction in a personal community: how accessible community members are for contact and how much contact they actually have. Some scholars have argued that the more contact among network members, the more supportive the relationship. This is because frequent contact fosters shared values, increases mutual awareness of needs and resources, mitigates feelings of loneliness, encourages reciprocal exchanges, and facilitates the delivery of aid (Homans 1961; Galaskiewicz 1985).[14]

Even with the widespread use of automobiles and airplanes,[15] those Torontonians who live relatively near each another usually have more frequent face-to-face contact. But "relatively near" means within the metropolitan area and not only the same neighborhood. Community members who live thirty miles apart have almost as much contact and support as those who live a block away. These are not the neighborhood-bound "urban villagers" that Herbert Gans found in the 1950s in a Boston Italian-American enclave (1962).

Participants in the survey and interviews report being in contact with the average member of their community about once every two weeks. Face-to-face contact is more frequent than telephone contact. Moreover, face-to-face contact has a greater bandwidth of communication than telephone contact, and it is more strongly associated with the provision of supportive services by community members. The telephone (and now, electronic mail) is often a complement to face-to-face contact rather than a replacement for it. Frequent telephone contact is positively associated with frequent face-to-face contact because telephone calls are often used to arrange face-to-face get-togethers or to sustain relationships between meetings. Those who see each other often and live within a short drive usually talk on the telephone more often. Those who live farther away have less contact (Wellman and Wortley 1990; Wellman and Tindall 1993; Wellman 1996; see also Chapter 10, this volume).

Survey Data-set—Intimates. In the survey data-set, contact is second only to the immediate kinship factor in the variance it explains (16%; Table 1.6). Variables loading highly on contact measure frequency of face-to-face contact (0.85), frequency of telephone and letter contact (.57), the percentage of ties within metropolitan Toronto (0.79), and, to some extent, the frequency of informal visits (0.38). Because coworkers are seen daily by many focal persons, the percentage of workmates also loads on the contact factor to some extent (0.24).

Interview Data-set—Intimates. The contact factor explains the most variance of all factors in this data-set, 41% (Table 1.7). Four variables load highly on this factor: the frequency of face-to-face contact (0.87), residential distance (−0.84), frequency of telephone contact (0.66), and the mean multiplexity of the relationships (0.61). As was the case for the contact factor in the survey data-set, residential proximity and frequent face-to-face and phone contact usually occur together. In this data-set, frequent contact with intimates is associated with multiplexity, that is, people with much contact interact in a greater variety of contexts. This association provides limited support for Granovetter's (1973) typological conjecture that strong ties are both multiplex and in frequent contact (see Table 1.3 above).

Interview Data-set—All Active Ties.   The contact factor explains 17% of the variance in this data-set (Table 1.8). It is the least clearly defined of the three contact factors. Although face-to-face contact (–0.75), telephone contact (–0.32), and multiplexity (–0.39) again load together, residential distance has the opposite sign (0.71). As with the immediate kinship factor from the same data-set, this is the result of the inclusion of significant (i.e., active, but not intimate) ties in this analysis. As geographically distant, nonintimate ties only remain active with frequent contact, there is a negative association between distance and frequency of contact.

In sum, our data show that people who live near each other continue to have more frequent contact despite the opportunities for longer distance ties afforded by phones, cars, and planes. Yet this is not the villagelike milieu to which the Community Saved argument looks back nostalgically because the bound is the metropolitan area and not the neighborhood. At the other end of the spectrum are those Torontonians who have a preponderance of distant ties in their networks and have little contact with their network members.

Eve Spencer's personal community is a good example of a network with much contact. Eve is thirty-one years old, married with two children, and without paid employment. She feels close to her immediate kin and also to two friends that she knew before she moved. Eve's network shows that contact and residential distance are clearly related, and that more frequent telephone contact is positively related to phone contact. She had just recently moved when the interview was conducted. Although Eve feels closest to her friend Roberta from her old neighborhood, they see each other less often since Eve moved a half-hour away. They now see each other only at planned monthly dinners that also include their husbands. However, Eve and Roberta talk frequently on the phone, and they exchange cards on special occasions.

By contrast to her tie with Roberta, Eve sees her friend Carol about once a week because they live only ten minutes apart. They also talk on the phone "pretty well every day." Their friendship retains its informal nature due to their proximity; Eve explains that her meetings with Carol are casual "drop-ins" compared with the monthly planned dinner with Roberta. Eve says that although Roberta is a closer friend, she sees more of Carol. Although she has no difficulty keeping in touch with Carol, Eve has difficulty seeing Roberta "out of laziness" because of the distance. Interestingly, Eve's move did not affect her contact with her kin, with whom she is often in touch. This lends support to the argument that the structurally embedded nature of kinship ties makes them qualitatively different from other intimate ties.

Range

Range is the combination of network size and heterogeneity that jointly increases the ability of personal communities to provide a variety of resources (social support, social capital) and to provide access to other social milieus (Craven and Wellman 1973; Burt 1992; Haines and Hurlbert 1992). The *heterogeneity* aspect of range measures the extent to which the social characteristics of network members vary (such as their gender and socioeconomic status). Some analysts have shown that network members are likely to have relatively homogeneous social characteristics: Friends are apt to be more like each other than a random sample of people (Lazarsfeld and Merton 1954; Feld 1982). Birds of a feather flock together. Moreover, people with relatively homogeneous characteristics usually have more similar interests, and such shared interests can foster empathetic understanding and mutual support (Marsden 1988).

However, other analysts have argued that heterogeneous networks may provide a greater variety of social support. Their argument reflects Durkheimian (1893) and Simmelian (1922) conjectures that ties that cut across social categories satisfy mutual needs (Kemper 1972; Blau and Schwartz 1984; Blau 1993). Thus Granovetter's "strength of weak ties" (1973, 1982) argument contends that weak ties provide better connections to different social milieus because they usually connect socially dissimilar people (see also Table 1.3 above). Hence heterogeneous networks should provide good access to information and services and also make for more varied lives.

Having higher-status people in one's personal community may be important. Lin and Dumin's research (1986) shows that people often prefer ties with higher-status network members who have more resources, while patron-client research shows that high-status people command resources from their low-status clients (Bodemann 1988).

Our data-sets show that large personal communities with a high proportion of *significant* ties (i.e., active, but *non*intimate ties) are usually sparsely knit, socially heterogeneous networks.[16] In short, they have much *range.* This is because the larger the personal community, the less likely it is to be densely knit, since links among community members must expand geometrically to maintain the same social density when the number of members increases arithmetically. Moreover, the larger the community and the more weak ties it contains, the more heterogeneous it is likely to be. In such situations, socially distant people will have less resemblance to the focal persons at the centers of these networks (Feld 1982).

The presence of a range element in the Toronto data fits Wellman's (1979) community liberated argument and Granovetter's (1973, 1982) weak-tie hypothesis. The number of significant ties in networks varies more than the number of intimate ties, showing that most people have similar-sized cores of intimates but differ in the extent to which this core is surrounded by less intimate, but still significant, ties.

People whose personal communities have much range are structurally able to tap many diverse resources for social support, companionship, and information. They have many significant ties, their sparsely knit networks connect with more social circles, and their heterogeneous communities give access to people in a wider range of positions in society. Because larger personal communities usually provide more social support (Chapter 2), people with good social skills or in favorable situations benefit doubly by having many ties and more social support provided by each tie. Beyond the sheer numbers, such people also benefit by the Granovetterian connections that heterogeneous networks provide to the resources of other social milieus. Yet the sparse density of these large personal communities means that people must actively navigate among poorly connected clusters and dyads in their networks and be in structural positions to reap the rewards and burdens of being the bridges between disparate groups.

By contrast, small personal communities are more homogeneous and densely knit. The ties in such networks are more apt to be densely knit because it is easy for everybody to know everybody else. Yet our interviews reveal that many members of small personal communities do not get along. They are tied with each other not out of liking but because they have ties to the same third parties that structurally embed their relationship. In married couples, wives usually make special efforts to keep their households' personal communities going. Although we studied *individuals,* we found that *married couples* are usually jointly involved in their personal communities (Wellman 1985; Wellman and Wellman 1992).

Insular and isolated, these small homogeneous personal communities are usually composed of only close friends and immediate kin. There are few ties with neighbors and coworkers, and there is little trust of anyone outside the immediate circle of intimates. Although those Torontonians in communities with little range are less structurally able to gain access to new resources, they are better able to control and coordinate their existing resources (Wolf 1966; Wellman and Leighton 1979). They are tight little knots of similar people who deal mostly with themselves. Such an arrangement is not conducive for obtaining much social support from other milieus, and the members of such personal communities provide comparatively little support to each other (Chapter 2).

Survey Data-set—Intimates. Although it is the least significant factor obtained from the analysis of this data-set (explaining 9% of the variance), the range factor does appear (Table 1.6). Socioeconomic heterogeneity (.78) and a larger number of intimates (.66) load highly on it.

Interview Data-set—Intimates. The range factor is the second most significant one in this data-set, explaining 23% of the variance (Table 1.7). As with the survey data-set, two variables load highly on this factor: the number of intimates (0.94) and the heterogeneity of the network (0.91). The percentage of extended kin (0.48) also loads highly on the range factor because extended kin (usually the weakest of all intimate ties) rarely appear when there are only a few intimates.

Interview Data-set—All Active Ties. This data-set provides the most interesting example of the range factor because it is the only one that affords the study of significant as well as intimate ties. Reflecting the greater variability in the size of networks that include significant ties, the range factor explains the most variance of all factors in this data-set (32%). It displays the same characteristics as in the other data-sets (Table 1.8). Heterogeneous networks (0.90) usually occur when there are a high number of significant network members (0.87), low network density (–0.69), a low percentage of intimates (0.50), and ties that are less multiplex (–0.37).

Diane Creasey's high-range personal community illustrates what a large, sparsely knit network is like. Diane is thirty-four, separated, and has two children. She works part time as an actress, teaching and performing in a small company. She has many significant, but nonintimate, ties. Diane draws her ties from a variety of contexts, demonstrating the relationship between large network size and network heterogeneity. Her network comprises kin, actors, neighbors, and members of her sports club. There is little overlap between the clusters of her network, low multiplexity in her ties, and infrequent contact with network members. Diane articulates her own attitude toward social relationships as: "People don't have friends, they have acquaintances. I have very few friends. I like to be alone. I don't like people bugging me. I don't have enough contact with people nor do I want any."

Intimacy

Intimate ties combine three characteristics (Duck 1983; Perlman and Fehr 1987; Blumstein and Kollock 1988):

- A sense of the relationship being intimate and special, with a voluntary investment in the tie and a desire for companionship with the tie partner.

- An interest in being together as much as possible through interactions in multiple social contexts over a long period.
- A sense of mutuality in the relationship, with the partner's needs known and supported.[17]

Community theory has traditionally seen ties between two persons (or two couples) who interact privately and voluntarily as different from ties that only operate because social structural auspices hold the people together. Although there is a North American myth that people freely choose their communities (Webber 1963), many nonintimate ties are actually created when outside situations bring people into juxtaposition (Feld 1981, 1982). The neighborhood, the traditional locus of community, is one such milieu. Yet our Toronto research has shown that many of the women who stay home during the day to care for young children do not like each other, even though they have active relationships (Wellman 1985, 1993). Like those in paid workplaces, they have no choice but to interact in order to accomplish their jobs.

Although all of the Torontonians' ties that we are studying are strong ties when compared with their 1,000 or so other ties (Wellman 1990), some ties are stronger than the others. There are several ways to measure the strength of ties in networks, even when we are confined to making distinctions among a person's half-dozen intimate ties or dozen most active ties. Unfortunately, the most straightforward measure, *the percentage of intimates* (0.81), is only available for the interview data-set that contains information about nonintimate (significant) ties and about intimate ties (Table 1.8). Here, Torontonians report that 40% of their active ties are ones of socially close intimacy. The *number of intimates* in a network also loads highly on this factor (0.88). This suggests that personal communities tend to contain either a high percentage and high number of intimates or a low proportion and low number of intimates. They rarely have the mixed situation of small communities that are heavily composed of intimates or large communities that only contain a few intimates. It appears that the conditions that enable some people to attract many intimates to their personal communities are similar to those that make a high percentage of the ties intimate. Moreover, the negative loading of face-to-face contact and network density on this factor suggest that the intimacy it represents is not the traditional gemeinschaft of small, localized, kin-based societies.

For example, Chris Armstrong's large network is structured significantly by the presence of intimates in it. Chris is thirty-one, married, and has two children; he works as a firefighter. His network includes intimate friends and intimate and nonintimate kin, several of whom are intimates. The high density of his intimate network is partially explained by the fact that three of his six intimates are also relatives. They provide a bridge to a larger kinship group, many of whom are directly linked with each other.

Chris's ties illustrate the three bases for intimacy enumerated above: They voluntarily interact in many contexts, and they have a sense of mutuality and shared interests and liking. Chris thinks of his intimate friends as family members. "I enjoy people here, and they know any time they come over to my house that they are welcome. They can come over any time, they don't have to phone. There are always people dropping in—it's great."

Other Factors

Several other factors that appear in Tables 1.6, 1.7, and 1.8 are more marginal to analysis because: they do not explain much variance; only one or two variables load highly on them; or they are products of peripheral situational contexts. Thus the *neighboring* and *coworking* factors that emerge in the intimate-only survey data-set (Table 1.6) have only one variable respectively loading heavily on them: the percentage of neighbors and the percentage of coworkers in the intimate networks. Yet the percentage of neighbors and coworkers are small in almost all personal communities. Similarly, the single-variable *extended kinship* factor is not interesting because (1) extended kin are less active and supportive than other intimates (Wellman 1979; Wellman and Wortley 1989), and (2) when there are many extended kin in the community, this is largely a situational product of one's parents having an unusually high number of siblings.

We measured in all data-sets the percentage of personal community members who are *neighbors, coworkers,* and *extended kin.* Only a small minority of intimates—but a larger minority of active ties—are in these situations. We also use another piece of information available only in the interview data-sets: the percentage of personal community members who normally interact in *groups* rather than in couples or in two-person dyads.

Remarkably, the intimate networks in the survey data-set (Table 1.6) that have a high percentage of neighbors have relatively low levels of telephone contact and informal visiting. Although informal visits would seem to be a natural component of a person's relationship with neighbors, this is not often the case. Neighboring has been replaced by friends and immediate kin who do not live next door, but "within reach," and by telephone and in-person visits within the metropolitan area. Similarly, in the survey data-set, a high percentage of coworkers in a network, low telephone contact with network members, and few informal visits load highly on the *coworker* factor (Table 1.6). Even the few intimate ties that

TABLE 1.9   Comparing the Factors of the Two Data-sets

	Data-set		
Elements	Survey Intimates Only	Interviews All Active Ties	Interviews Intimates Only
Immediate kinship	yes	yes	yes
Range	yes	yes	yes
Contact	yes	yes	yes
Intimacy	not applicable	yes	not applicable
Extended kinship	yes	no	no
Neighboring	yes	no	no
Coworking	yes	no	no
Dyads	no	yes	no
Group	no	no	yes

are with coworkers are largely confined to the workplace, with few meetings or phone calls after work.

The *dyad* factor in the active ties, interview data-set captures the potentially fragmenting nature of telephone contact. Its two heavily loading variables (Table 1.8) are frequency of telephone contact (.81) and (low) group contact (–.71). Their co-occurrence poignantly shows that in some networks a high level of telephone contact—usually a two-person affair—is associated with little interaction among community members as a group (Wellman 1992b; Wellman and Tindall 1993).

The Elementary Building Blocks of Personal Communities

Abstract Building Blocks and Concrete Personal Communities

The multiple elements we have found show the inadequacy of a simple, unidimensional typology of community. The personal communities of Torontonians do not fall along one gemeinschaft-gesellschaft dimension; they are varying combinations of elements. Four elements largely describe the structure and composition of these personal communities: *immediate kinship/friendship, contact, range,* and *intimacy* (Table 1.9). These types can be combined to fit the typologies discussed at the beginning of this chapter. For example, a gemeinschaft personal community is predominantly composed of kin, in frequent contact, with little range but much intimacy. By contrast, a gesellschaft personal community is predominantly composed of friends with little contact and intimacy, but with much range.[18]

TABLE 1.10   Percentage Distribution of Personal Community Types

Type	Range	Intimacy	Contact	Immed. Kin	Percentage
1	High	High	High	High	7
2	High	High	High	Low	14
3	High	High	Low	Low	7
4	High	Low	Low	Low	7
5	High	Low	High	High	3
6	High	High	Low	High	0
7	High	Low	High	Low	3
8	Low	High	Low	High	10
9	Low	Low	Low	Low	10
10	Low	High	High	High	7
11	Low	Low	High	High	10
12	Low	Low	Low	High	3
13	Low	High	High	Low	3
14	High	Low	Low	High	7
15	Low	Low	High	Low	7
16	Low	High	Low	Low	0

NOTE: N = 33 personal communities.   98

Our data show four *elements* of communities, not four *types* of communities. Indeed, simply dichotomizing and combining each element produces sixteen types (see Table 1.10). There is no theoretical or empirical reason to assume that only one—or a few—types of combinations are present in these personal communities. Indeed, there is an uneven distribution of types in the active interview data-set (the only one that contains information about the percentage of intimates, Table 1.10). Four types are relatively numerous:

- *Type 2: High intimacy, range, contact, and friendship (or low immediate kin).* A large, heterogeneous set of friends who have much contact. This is reminiscent of Wellman's (1979) community liberated. For example, one study participant, forty-nine-year-old single accountant Henry Harrison, is intensely involved with a large, diverse, sparsely knit network of male friends. As he interacts with each man separately, he is linked to many social worlds.
- *Type 8: High intimacy and immediate kinship; low range and contact.* A small, homogeneous, intimate set of kin who do not have much contact with the focal person. John Williams's personal community is an example of this.
- *Type 9: High friendship (low immediate kin); low intimacy, range, and contact.* A small, homogeneous network built around

nonintimate friends who are not in frequent contact. This is congruent with the loss of community type depicted by Tönnies's gesellschaft (1887), Wirth (1938), and Wellman's community lost (1979). An example of this is Penny Crawford's personal community, which is described in detail below.

- *Type 11: High contact and immediate kinship; low intimacy and range.* A small, homogeneous network built around non-intimate immediate kin who are in frequent contact. Thus divorced study participant Maureen O'Sullivan (forty-nine, two children, executive secretary) is intimate only with her sister but speaks often with other kin at family gatherings. This type of personal community is somewhat congruent with Tönnies's gemeinschaft, Redfield's folk society (1947), Bott's independent family network (1957), and Wellman's community saved (1979). Such societies may contain many communities without much intimacy because kinship and propinquity constrain people to be network members whether they want to be or not.

Penny Crawford's *Type 9* situation—low intimacy, range, contact, and immediate kin—illustrates how the elements of personal community intertwine. A thirty-five-year-old married mother of three and clerk in a small store, Penny came to Canada thirteen years ago when she married a Toronto man. Most of her kin remain in Europe, and she keeps in touch with a few by calling one once or twice a month. Her only intimates are her father, her boss, and a neighbor. They do not know each other. Although Penny's father and brother live an hour's drive from her, she dislikes her sister-in-law so she has not contacted her brother for a year or her sister-in-law for more than three years. Penny does talk on the phone with her father twice a week, they occasionally go to the horse races together, and he once lent her money to fly to Europe to visit an ailing relative.

Proximity is the key to Penny's ties and contact. Her emigration means that she has few kin nearby. She dislikes telephone calls and restricts the length of her conversations. "I like to talk in person, see people's faces." Her boss is a former neighbor and current coworker. Her current intimate neighbor is "kind of a sister" with whom she is "able to talk about personal things, about marriage, that my husband would kill me if he knew." In short, Penny has a small, homogeneous, and sparsely knit network. Her low level of contact is mainly due to the proximity of a neighbor and a coworker, as well as to a desire to maintain some connections with distant kin.

Two of the sixteen types of personal communities—combinations of elements—just do not occur in this small data-set:

- *Type 6: High intimacy, range, and immediate kin, but low contact.* This combination would be difficult to find in real life. Large intimate networks usually have high—not low—contact.
- *Type 16: Low range, immediate kin, and contact, but high intimacy.* This combination would also be difficult to find in real life, although it might occur when a focal person has separate intimate relations with a small, homogenous, but physically dispersed set of friends who have few links with each other.

Are There Elementary Forms of Community?

The largely independent nature of the four elements only partially sustain earlier typologies. The data show that although many combinations of elements fit earlier typologies, many combinations do not. There is a more complicated pattern than the uniform urban gesellschaft imagined by Tönnies. There is also little basis for assuming that kinship-based networks will be as actively in contact or as constricted as either Bott's independent family network or Wellman's community saved types would have it. To the contrary, the essential independence of the four elements suggests that kinship networks can have a wide range and less contact while friendship networks can have much contact and a narrow range. Only to some extent does the Range element's combination of network size and heterogeneity support Wellman's threefold typology: Yet, contrary to the community saved argument, personal communities with little range are not always multiplex nor heavily composed of kin or neighbors. Indeed, friends have more multiplex ties than kin. Friends interact in more milieus than do even immediate kin.[19]

The question remains: Are the four elements we have "discovered" fundamental building blocks of personal communities—and perhaps of other kinds of ego-centered networks—or are they only idiosyncratic manifestations of a local Toronto reality? Personal community networks are little Ptolemaic social systems in which the focal person is the sun and the network members are the planets. There are bonds of attraction and repulsion among them as well as forces exerted from outside. As in all social systems, the composition and structure of its constituents affect the ways in which the system can function. In part, people construct their personal community networks based on their personality and through the relationships they form. In part, as with Penny Crawford, social structures create networks by putting people into social positions that juxtapose them with potential community members: work, neighborhood, kinship, friendship circles, and the like (see Howard's 1988 discussion). Yet similar elements of community may arise in a society in which networks are organized along different principles. For example, in poor Chilean barrios, social networks have been crucial for getting access to scarce food, housing, and jobs (Chapter 4). Where people in North America usually use networks to gain additional resources, in Chile they often use their networks to preserve what they have.

Although our research can only be suggestive, we wonder if the four elements we have identified tap four fundamental ways in which interpersonal, ego-centered networks can vary. The four elements lead to different questions:

1. *(Immediate) kinship/friendship:* This element describes how much of a group is a network. Is it composed of densely knit (immediate) kin or separate duets of friends? How solidary is it? Does it have continuity or transiency? The important role that immediate kin play as the preeminent carriers of a network's norms and values should be stressed.

2. *Contact:* This element describes the extent to which people access the social capital that their ties represent, or leave them untapped and stagnant. Is a network awake or asleep? How active are the relationships in it? To what extent do the members of a social network work together, support each other, and exchange services?

3. *Range:* How open or constricted is a personal community? This element describes the extent to which a social system has the large size and heterogeneity that enable it to reach out to other social milieus or remain a small, insular world. How diverse are the potential resources of the network?

4. *Intimacy:* This element describes the extent to which members of a social system are strongly connected to each other. How strong or weak are the ties? Are these valued ties with socially close people or are they the fragile and weak relationships which pastoralists always feared would engulf cities (Jefferson 1784; Marx 1964)?

Readers with an interest in sociological theory may recall that we have independently produced a fourfold scheme reminiscent of Talcott Parsons's *AGIL* formulation (1951): Adaptation (range), Goal-orientation (contact), Integration (intimacy), and Latent pattern maintenance (kinship). We are not sure whether this is just happenstance or a demonstration that any determined analyst can match one typology with another. Yet Parsons proposed AGIL as an exposition of the fundamental ways in which social systems could vary, and he believed his formulation would hold true at all analytic levels, from interpersonal to global. Personal communities are interpersonal social systems. Thinking about Parsons's formulation leads us to wonder if range, contact, intimacy, and kinship/friendship represent basic structural building blocks of interpersonal life, the combinations of which affect—and are affected by—the opportunities, constraints, and choices that people make in engaging with the networks and worlds around them. For example, those with low range and contact but high intimacy and kinship may have a relatively stable protective shell of network members around them. By contrast, those with high range and contact but low intimacy and kinship (e.g., high friendship) may live in a more unstable world reaching out—and buffeted by—the multiple social circles with which they are engaged.

Notes

We appreciate the assistance and advice of Nadia Bello, Bonnie Erickson, Milena Gulia, Charles Jones, Thy Phu, Beverly Wellman, Renita Wong, and Scot Wortley. We are grateful for financial support from the Social Sciences and Humanities Research Council of Canada and the National Welfare Grants program of Health and Welfare Canada. As always, the Centre for Urban and Community Studies, University of Toronto, has been our supportive home. This paper is dedicated to the memory of Talcott Parsons.

1. This is analogous to the shift in urban studies from *social area analysis*, which used a priori typologies of census tracts (e.g., Shevky and Bell 1955) to *factorial ecology* which derived its typologies more inductively (e.g., Murdie 1969).

2. In statistical language they both would load highly on the same factor or be located in the same cluster of variables.

3. Haslam's (1995) study of the "elementary relational forms" of American undergraduates is the only other research that we have seen to take a similar approach.

4. The Borough of East York disappeared as a separate municipality on January 1, 1998, when all six entities previously federated as the Municipality of Metro Toronto merged into a unified City of Toronto. An East York "community council" still attempts to preserve some local discussion.

5. Our sampling criteria for the interviews differed from that of the survey. We wanted to preserve a 1968–1978 longitudinal sample, but we did not see the point in preserving an ability to generalize to the East York population of 1968. We randomly selected roughly equal numbers of participants who had remained in their 1968 East York home, had moved elsewhere in East York, had moved elsewhere in metropolitan Toronto, and had moved farther away in south central Ontario. We were able to trace the addresses of 82% of the original survey sample and to interview 77% of them (Wellman 1982; Wellman, Carrington, and Hall 1988).

6. Our analyses count ties to a couple as one relationship in the majority of cases where a couple functions as a joint unit vis-à-vis the focal person. In other words, we take seriously Bott's (1957) distinction between independent and joint marriages. Moreover, most of the Torontonians report that their households operate jointly, as do most of their network members (Wellman and Wellman 1992). If we had always treated the joint relationship as ties to two persons, this would

have increased the average number of ties in a network by about one-third to a mean of seventeen (Wellman, Carrington, and Hall 1988; Wellman and Wortley 1989).

7. Despite their importance (to people and typologies), social support variables were excluded from the analysis in order to be able to relate our typology to the availability of social support in future analyses.

8. We used hierarchical cluster analysis and multidimensional scaling to verify our findings and obtained similar results. We note that Kaiser's Measure of Sampling Adequacy was slightly below a desirable 0.5 criterion for the two factor analyses of the small interview data-set. As the communality estimates of all the factors point to considerable interrelation between the variables, all were retained in the final rotation.

9. Network structure variables indicate the capacity of social networks to channel flows of resources to network members, integrating and decoupling them. There are high correlations among many of these variables. We chose *network density* from several correlated variables because it has been the most central in theory and research, and because it is the only measure available from both the survey and the interviews. Density is calculated as the ratio of the number of actually existing links between network members to the number of links that are theoretically possible. As this is information reported by the focal persons about their network members, we treat links as symmetrical, i.e., an A > B link assumes a B > A link. We exclude in our calculations the ties between network members and the focal persons at the centers of the networks. Although including such ties would inflate the network density measure, such ties are unnecessary for analysis because all network members are tied to their focal persons by definition. Both the survey (33%) and the interviews (42%) show moderate density among network members; i.e., a substantial minority of the members of personal communities tend to be linked with each other (see also Wellman et al. 1991).

10. Multiplexity is operationally defined here as the mean number of nine social contexts in which the focal person and network members might interact: at each others' homes, in the neighborhood, at work, etc. This measure is only available for the interviews.

11. Network size varies independently of the kinship/friendship factor. It is subsumed in another element (Range), while network strength, intimacy, and frequent contact also vary independently and are parts of other elements.

12. Factor loadings are indicated in parentheses.

13. All names are pseudonyms. Where necessary we have changed other identifying details.

14. We use in all data-sets the logged *mean frequency of face-to-face contact* and of *telephone contact*. We also use logged *residential distance*: the interview data-sets show that network members live a median of nine miles apart, although a significant minority live in the same neighborhood and a handful live in Europe. The survey data-set does not have such a nice, continuous residential distance; we make do with calculating the *percentage of network members who live in metropolitan Toronto* (76%). We use this statistic, rather than the percentage of network members living in the same neighborhood, because network members living outside of the neighborhood but within metropolitan Toronto give as much social sup-

port as those living in the same neighborhood (Wellman and Wortley 1990; Wellman and Tindall 1993). We use logged statistics (base 10) for the contact variables to normalize the distributions. Logging also makes intellectual sense because a one-unit increase at the lower end of each scale (residential distance and frequency of contact) has a greater statistical impact than at the upper end. That is, an increase in mean face-to-face contact from 1 to 2 times a year makes more of a substantive difference than a mean increase from 364 to 365 times a year.

15. Our data were collected when electronic mail was hardly ever used.

16. Creating *heterogeneity* measures in our data-sets is difficult because simple measures of heterogeneity are strongly correlated with network size: The larger the network, the more socially heterogeneous. In effect, size and heterogeneity are part of the same network element. However, because of our interest in patron-clientage, we measured the *standard deviation of socioeconomic status* in the survey data-set, using the Blishen (1967) scale for Canadian occupations. The most feasible measure for the interview data-set is a composite one, combining seven specific indicators of network heterogeneity: marital status, employment status, religious affiliation, ethnicity, age of network members, educational similarity of network members to focal persons, and socioeconomic status. The *composite heterogeneity* measure is standardized. The higher the heterogeneity score (ranging from 0 to 4), the more heterogeneous the network.

17. This definition does not include Granovetter's (1973) conjecture that frequently contacted ties are strong ties, for most of the people with whom Torontonians feel close are not those whom they frequently contact. As discussed above in the Access section, frequently contacted network members tend to be people who live or work relatively nearby. Many are neighbors and coworkers whom geography or institutions have brought together rather than those with especially close feelings (Wellman, Carrington, and Hall 1988). Nor do the data support Granovetter's conjecture (1973) that weaker ties support network diversity. Networks with a larger percentage of non-intimate, significant ties tend to be homogeneous—not heterogeneous.

18. The other factors that appear in Table 1.9 refer to peripheral, less consequential aspects of personal communities such as the presence of coworkers or extended kin. As neither coworkers nor extended kin play important roles in most personal communities, these other factors are better seen as minor elements of community rather than as their basic building blocks.

19. Wenger's (1992) typological concentration on locally based personal communities differs markedly from the essentially nonlocal Torontonians. This may reflect her elderly rural sample. Yet her two types of *Wider Community Focused* and *Private Restricted* communities reflect two ends of a Range continuum.

References

Berger, Bennett. 1960. *Working Class Suburb.* Berkeley: University of California Press.

Berkowitz, S. D. 1982. *An Introduction to Structural Analysis.* Toronto: Butterworth.

Blau, Peter. 1993. "Multilevel Structural Analysis." *Social Networks* 15 (June):201–215.

Blau, Peter, and Joseph Schwartz. 1984. *Crosscutting Social Circles*. Orlando, FL: Academic Press.

Blishen, Bernard. 1967. "A Socio-Economic Index for Occupations in Canada." *Canadian Review of Sociology and Anthropology* 4:41–53.

Blumstein, Philip, and Peter Kollock. 1988. "Personal Relationships." *Annual Review of Sociology* 14:467–90.

Bodemann, Y. Michal. 1988. "Relations of Production and Class Rule: The Hidden Basis of Patron-Clientage." Pp. 198–220 in *Social Structures: A Network Approach*, edited by Barry Wellman and S. D. Berkowitz. Cambridge: Cambridge University Press.

Bott, Elizabeth. 1957. *Family and Social Network*. London: Tavistock.

Bott, Elizabeth. 1971. *Family and Social Network*. 2d ed. London: Tavistock.

Burt, Ronald. 1992. *Structural Holes: The Social Structure of Competition*. Cambridge, MA: Harvard University Press.

Craven, Paul and Barry Wellman. 1973. "The Network City." *Sociological Inquiry* 43:57–88.

Duck, Steve. 1983. *Friends for Life*. Brighton, UK: Harvester.

Durkheim, Émile. 1893 [1984]. *The Division of Labor in Society*. New York: Free Press.

Feld, Scott. 1981. "The Focused Organization of Social Ties." *American Journal of Sociology* 86:1015–35.

Feld, Scott. 1982. "Social Structural Determinants of Similarity Among Associates." *American Sociological Review* 47 (December):797–801.

Fischer, Claude. 1975. "Toward a Subcultural Theory of Urbanism." *American Journal of Sociology* 80:1319–41.

Galaskiewicz, Joseph. 1985. *Social Organization of an Urban Grants Economy: A Study of Business Philanthropy and Nonprofit Organizations*. Orlando, FL: Academic Press.

Gans, Herbert. 1962. *The Urban Villagers*. New York: Free Press.

Gans, Herbert. 1967. *The Levittowners*. New York: Pantheon.

Garton, Laura, and Barry Wellman. 1995. "Social Impacts of Electronic Mail in Organizations: A Review of the Research Literature." *Communication Yearbook* 18:434–453.

Gillies, Marion, and Barry Wellman. 1968. "East York: A Profile." Toronto: Community Studies Section, Clarke Institute of Psychiatry.

Granovetter, Mark. 1973. "The Strength of Weak Ties." *American Journal of Sociology* 78:1360–80.

Granovetter, Mark. 1982. "The Strength of Weak Ties: A Network Theory Revisited." Pp. 105–130 in *Social Structure and Network Analysis*, edited by Peter Marsden and Nan Lin. Beverly Hills, CA: Sage.

Haines, Valerie, and Jeanne Hurlbert. 1992. "Network Range and Health." *Journal of Health and Social Behavior* 33 (Sept.): 254–266.

Haslam, Nick. 1995. "Factor Structure of Social Relationships: An Examination of Relational Models and Resource Exchange Theories." *Journal of Social and Personal Relationships* 12 (2): 217–227.

Homans, George. 1961. *Social Behavior: Its Elementary Forms*. New York: Harcourt Brace Jovanovich.

Howard, Leslie. 1988. "Work and Community in Industrializing India." Pp. 185–197 in *Social Structures: A Network Approach*, edited by Barry Wellman and S. D. Berkowitz. Cambridge: Cambridge University Press.

Jefferson, Thomas. 1784 [1972]. *Notes on the State of Virginia*. Edited by William Peden. New York: Norton.

Kemper, Theodore D. 1972. "The Division of Labor: A Post-Durkheimian Analytical View." *American Sociological Review* 37 (Dec.):739–753.

Kochen, Manfred, ed. 1989. *The Small World*. Norwood, NJ: Ablex.

Lazarsfeld, Paul, and Robert Merton. 1954. "Friendship as Social Process." Pp. 18–66 in *Freedom and Control in Modern Society*, edited by Morroe Berger, Theodore Abel, and Charles Page. New York: Octagon.

Liebow, Elliot. 1967. *Tally's Corner*. Boston: Little, Brown.

Lin, Nan, and Mary Dumin. 1986. "Access to Occupations through Social Ties." *Social Networks* 8 (December):365–386.

Marsden, Peter. 1988. "Homogeneity in Confiding Relations." *Social Networks* 10:57–76.

Marx, Leo. 1964. *The Machine in the Garden*. New York: Oxford University Press.

Murdie, Robert. 1969. *A Factorial Ecology of Toronto*. Department of Geography, University of Chicago.

Nisbet, Robert. 1962. *Community and Power*. New York: Oxford University Press.

Parsons, Talcott. 1951. *The Social System*. Glencoe, IL: Free Press.

Perlman, Daniel, and Beverley Fehr. 1987. "The Development of Intimate Relationships." Pp. 13–42 in *Intimate Relationships*, edited by Daniel Perlman and Steve Duck. Newbury Park, CA: Sage.

Redfield, Robert. 1947. "The Folk Society." *American Journal of Sociology* 52:293–308.

Shevky, Eshrev, and Wendell Bell. 1955. *Social Area Analysis*. Stanford, CA: Stanford University Press.

Simmel, Georg. 1902–1903 [1950]. "The Metropolis and Mental Life." Pp. 409–424 in *The Sociology of Georg Simmel*, edited and translated by Kurt Wolff. Glencoe, IL: Free Press.

Simmel, Georg. 1922 [1955]. "The Web of Group Affiliations." Pp. 125–195 in *Conflict and the Web of Group Affiliations*. Glencoe, IL: Free Press.

Slater, Philip. 1970. *The Pursuit of Loneliness*. Boston: Beacon Press.

Stein, Maurice. 1960. *The Eclipse of Community*. Princeton, NJ: Princeton University Press.

Tönnies, Ferdinand. 1887 [1955]. *Community and Organization*. London: Routledge & Kegan Paul.

Walker, Michael, Stanley Wasserman, and Barry Wellman. 1993. "Statistical Models for Social Support Networks." *Sociological Methods and Research* 22 (August):71–98.

Webber, Melvin. 1963. "Order in Diversity: Community without Propinquity." Pp. 23–54 in *Cities and Space*, edited by Lowdon Wingo, Jr. Baltimore: Johns Hopkins Press.

Wellman, Barry. 1979. "The Community Question." *American Journal of Sociology* 84 (March): 1201–1231.

Wellman, Barry. 1982. "Studying Personal Communities." Pp. 61–80 in *Social Structure and Network Analysis*, edited by Peter Marsden and Nan Lin. Beverly Hills, CA: Sage.

Wellman, Barry. 1985. "Domestic Work, Paid Work and Net Work." Pp. 159–191 in *Understanding Personal Relationships*, edited by Steve Duck and Daniel Perlman. London: Sage.

Wellman, Barry. 1988. "The Community Question Re-evaluated." Pp. 81–107 in *Power, Community and the City*, edited by Michael Peter Smith. New Brunswick, NJ: Transaction Books.

Wellman, Barry. 1990. "The Place of Kinfolk in Community Networks." *Marriage and Family Review* 15(1/2):195–228.

Wellman, Barry, 1992a. "How to Use SAS to Study Egocentric Networks." *Cultural Anthropology Methods Bulletin* 4 (June):6–12.

Wellman, Barry. 1992b. "Men in Networks: Private Communities, Domestic Friendships." Pp. 74–114 in *Men's Friendships*, edited by Peter Nardi. Newbury Park, CA: Sage.

Wellman, Barry. 1992c. "Which Types of Ties and Networks Give What Kinds of Social Support?" *Advances in Group Processes* 9:207–235.

Wellman, Barry. 1993. "An Egocentric Network Tale." *Social Networks* 15, 4 (Dec.): 423–436.

Wellman, Barry. 1996. "Are Personal Communities Local? A Dumptarian Reconsideration." *Social Networks* 18, 3 (Sept.): 347–354.

Wellman, Barry, Peter Carrington, and Alan Hall. 1988. "Networks as Personal Communities." Pp. 130–184 in *Social Structures: A Network Approach*, edited by Barry Wellman and S. D. Berkowitz. Cambridge: Cambridge University Press.

Wellman, Barry, with Paul Craven, Marilyn Whitaker, Sheila du Toit, and Harvey Stevens. 1971. "The Uses of Community." Working Paper No. 47. Toronto: Centre for Urban and Community Studies, University of Toronto.

Wellman, Barry, with Paul Craven, Marilyn Whitaker, Sheila du Toit, Harvey Stevens, and Hans Bakker. 1973. "Community Ties and Support Systems." Pp. 152–67 in *The Form of Cities in Central Canada*, edited by Larry Bourne, Ross MacKinnon, and James Simmons. Toronto: University of Toronto Press.

Wellman, Barry, Ove Frank, Vicente Espinoza, Staffan Lundquist, and Craig Wilson. 1991. "Integrating Individual, Relational and Structural Analysis." *Social Networks* 13 (Sept.):223–250.

Wellman, Barry, and Barry Leighton. 1979. "Networks, Neighborhoods and Communities." *Urban Affairs Quarterly* 14 (March):363–390.

Wellman, Barry, and David Tindall. 1993. "Reach Out and Touch Some Bodies: How Social Networks Connect Telephone Networks." Pp. 63–93 in *Progress in Communication* Sciences, Vol. 12, edited by William Richards, Jr. and George Barnett. Norwood, NJ: Ablex.

Wellman, Barry, and Scot Wortley. 1989. "Brothers' Keepers: Situating Kinship Relations in Broader Networks of Social Support." *Sociological Perspectives* 32 (Fall):273–306.

Wellman, Barry, and Scot Wortley. 1990. "Different Strokes from Different Folks: Community Ties and Social Support." *American Journal of Sociology* 96 (November):558–588.

Wellman, Beverly, and Barry Wellman. 1992. "Domestic Affairs and Network Relations." *Journal of Social and Personal Relationships* 9 (August):385–409.

Wenger, G. Clare. 1991. "A Network Typology: From Theory to Practice." *Journal of Aging Studies* 5 (2):147–162.

Wenger, G. Clare. 1992. *Help in Old Age–Facing Up to Change: A Longitudinal Network Study.* Liverpool: Liverpool University Press.

Wirth, Louis. 1938. "Urbanism as a Way of Life." *American Journal of Sociology* 44:3–24.

Wolf, Eric. 1966. "Kinship, Friendship and Patron-Client Relations." Pp. 1–22 in *The Social Anthropology of Complex Societies*, edited by Michael Banton. London: Tavistock.

2

The Network Basis
of Social Support:
A Network Is More Than
the Sum of Its Ties

Barry Wellman and Milena Gulia

Personal Community Networks of Social Support

The Persistence of Interpersonal Support

When North Americans need help, where do they turn? They buy many kinds of help in *the marketplace*, but the cost might be too expensive and not be sensitively suited to their needs. They obtain help from governments and other organizations—that is how most people obtain education and formal health care—but *such institutional distributions* are often in short supply and may require difficult dealings with complex bureaucracies. If they are uncivilized, they might *coercively appropriate* helpful resources through theft or force, but this is only possible for unskilled services, material goods, and information, and the social control of such deviant behavior may cause more stress than the coercion alleviates. If they are handy, they can help themselves as peasants have historically done by making things (e.g., sewing clothes) or doing things (fixing cars and homes), but such *self-provisioning* cannot provide many of the complex goods and services that people need.

Hence North Americans obtain many helpful resources by means of the *social support* that members of their social networks provide. *Interpersonal* relations—with relatives, friends, neighbors, and workmates—meet a wide variety of people's needs: emotional aid; material aid (goods, services, and money); information; companionship. Yet not all networks are likely to provide the same amount or kind of support. Our concern in this chapter is how different kinds of networks tend to provide different kinds of support. It builds on and complements earlier work done by our research group and others about how different kinds of *ties* provide different kinds of support and the importance of such support for health and well-being.[1]

Supportive Communities Are Personal Networks

Although scholars used to think that a (post)industrial loss of community had dried up interpersonal sources of support, the Introduction showed that scholars now know that community has stood up well to the large-scale social transformations of urbanization, industrialization, bureaucratization, technological change, capitalism, and socialism.[2] Although few North Americans are embedded in densely knit, tightly bounded villages, urban or rural—most are enmeshed in ramified, supportive *personal communities*—analysts have learned that kith and kin are not relics from a pastoral past, but are active arrangements for helping individuals and households deal with stresses and opportunities (Willmott 1987; Wellman 1988, 1990, 1992b; Schweizer, Schnegg, and Berzborn 1998).

The residents of Western societies usually know only a few neighbors. Most members of their personal communities do not live nearby; many live far away. People maintain their far-flung relationships by telecommunications—with telephones now being supplemented by faxes and electronic mail—and transportation based on cars, public transit, and airplanes. In Toronto, the neighborhood is no longer the effective boundary for frequent face-to-face contact and delivering supportive goods and services. Interaction and support does not start decreasing until network members live more than thirty miles away. In Toronto, this means that those living within an hour's drive or being in the local flat-rate telephone calling zone provide as much companionship and support as those living next door (Wellman, Carrington, and Hall 1988; Wellman and Wortley 1990). Friends comprise the largest segment of the active ties in these networks, but neighbors and coworkers dominate daily meetings (Wellman 1996), and many kin are important network members.

As the Introduction described, since the early 1970s, social network analysis has led sociology away from sterile polemics about whether modern times have destroyed community (Wellman and Leighton 1979). The organizing concept of the *personal community network* has led analysts to study the composition, structure and contents of people's ties with friends, kin, neighbors, workmates, and acquaintances, wherever located and whomever with. Analysts no longer start with the a priori assumption that communities must be tightly bounded, densely knit, broadly supportive solidarities. Analysts no longer limit their searches for community to neighborhoods, work places, and kinship groups. Most people have sizeable personal community networks with complex structures and variegated compositions. These networks provide a wide range of supportive resources that are important to the lives of both the recipients and the providers.

Communities operate now as private personal communities rather than as public collectivities, and people have come to rely heavily on their active community ties for informal help (Wellman 1992a). Ties in these communities vary markedly in strength, typically consisting of 3 to 6 socially close intimate ties, 5 to 15 less strong but still significant ties, and approximately 1,000 acquaintances and latent (but often still mobilizable) relationships. Although not all ties and networks are supportive, most ties do provide some kind of support and most networks provide a range of assistance that is often low-cost, flexible, effective, and quickly available (Wellman 1992b).

One type of social network analysis studies personal networks whose composition, structure, and contents are defined from the standpoint of a (usually large) sample of focal individuals at their centers (see Laumann, Marsden, and Prensky's 1983 discussion on realism and nominalism in such studies). They are centrally concerned with questions of social structural form originally raised by Georg Simmel (e.g., 1922): How do patterns of relations in networks affect the ways in which resources flow to their members?

This network approach to community makes analysis complex. Personal community networks come in all shapes, sizes, and flavors: large and densely knit extended families, sparsely connected and fragmented sets of friends, small self-reliant clusters, and so on. Even if we restrict our attention to a person's most active ties (those that are intimate or significant), these 10 to 20 ties usually provide network members with an important share of their resources. Active network members get a good deal (pun intended) from their friends and relatives, receiving quickly available, low-cost, flexible and effective "social support." A key question for us is how the complex variation in the size, composition, and structure of these networks is related to the quantity and quality of the social support they deliver.

Such personal community networks are not simple, homogeneous structures, but have complex patterns and compositions, such as large and densely knit extended families, sparsely connected and fragmented sets of friends, or small self-reliant clusters. Our group's research suggests that personal community networks basically vary along four dimensions:[3]

- *Range:* How large and heterogeneous are these networks? Does high range mean that networks have more resources—and more diverse resources—available?

- _Availability:_ How available for contact are network members so that they can easily receive information about each other's needs? Does high availability mean that they can conveniently deliver instrumental aid?
- _Densely knit kin/sparsely knit friends:_ Are network members bound by densely knit, normative ties of obligation and social control or sparsely knit voluntary ties of companionable shared interests?
- _Composition:_ To what extent are these networks composed of women, who usually offer more emotional support, or people of high socioeconomic status, who may have more material resources available?

This chapter's main thrust is to see how these different dimensions of personal community networks are associated with the networks' provision of various kinds of social support.

Stress, Support, and Well-being

Until recently, the nature of support itself has largely remained an unanalyzed, antecedent "black box." Most scholars originally treated it as a single, unidimensional phenomenon. They viewed it as a generalized resource (whose precise manifestations might vary by circumstances) available from "supportive" members of social networks (e.g., Wellman 1979). In recent years analysts have developed more differentiated typologies, distinguishing among such types of support as empathetic understanding, emotional support, material aid (goods, money, and services), and providing information (Barrera and Ainlay 1983; Tardy 1985; Israel and Rounds 1987). They have come to look more at the specific resources flowing through networks than at the general potential for network members to be supportive.

Since the late 1970s, researchers have been interested in the relationship between the social support found in personal communities and physiological and psychological well-being (Cobb 1976; Cassel 1976). Researchers have generally been more interested in the outcomes of support—its implications for well-being—than its causes. They have focused on the _effects_ of support on health and not, as we do here, on the interpersonal phenomena that foster social support. Analysts have worked hard to document the consequences of support: It appears to make individuals healthier, feel better, cope better with chronic and acute difficulties, and live longer.

Concerned with demonstrating the therapeutic effects of support, researchers have refined concepts and measures of acute stress, chronic strain, consequent physical and mental distress, and compensatory coping behavior (Berkman 1984; Dohrenwend and Dohrenwend 1984; Lazarus and Folkman 1984).[4] They have claimed that the evidence indicates a process in which social support may be a protective factor in alleviating the physiological and psychological consequences of exposure to stressors. They have argued that support prevents people from encountering stress, "buffers" them from experiencing the full brunt of the stresses encountered, and steers them toward help from formal and informal caregivers. Thus, social support is seen as one among many factors that can affect a person's ability to resist disease in the face of acute and chronic stress (more recently, see Pearlin 1989).

Fueled by comparatively large funding by health-care agencies, social scientists have launched many studies of how such support promotes physical and mental health. Until about a decade ago, such research had several unfortunate characteristics:

- It implicitly assumed that social support itself was a unidimensional phenomenon, a broad array of informally provided emotional aid, material aid, and companionship, largely provided by the active members of personal community networks;
- it assumed that just about all active ties were broadly supportive;
- it analyzed social support as an interpersonal duet between sender and receiver, without taking into account the networks in which such relationships are embedded;
- it concentrated on the funding agencies' chief preoccupation: the health-maintaining *consequences* of social support. It took for granted the factors that led to the provision of social support.

We now know that the first two assumptions are not true. Analysts have shown that network members specialize in the kinds of support they provide. Some mostly provide emotional aid or material aid or only companionship. Some provide little or no social support.

Recent work has gone from sensitizing statements to more rigorous formulations of support and analyses of its consequences. For example, Lin, Dean, and Ensel (1986) used a battery of measures to show the relationship of emotional support to depression, and other researchers have linked stress and support (see the reviews in Berkman 1984; House, Landis, and Umberson 1988; Lin and Ensel 1989; Gottlieb and Selby 1990; Wellman 1992b; Tijhuis 1994). Although results are mixed, on balance there is a positive relationship between receiving higher levels of social support and having better physical health.

Some work has integrated studies of support with studies of stress and immune function (e.g., Woolfolk and Lehrer 1995). Social support can mitigate the harmful effects of stressful stimuli on cholesterol level, uric acid level, and immune function (e.g., Thomas and Goodwin 1985, Dorian 1985). Such studies suggest that links between stress, social support, and coping strategies can result in a specific immune response. The two systems most closely associated with maintaining homeostasis of the organism, the neuroendocrine system and the immune system, are more effective adaptive systems under the influence of social support. Stress exerts a negative influence on both systems, while support mediates the effects of stress on the central nervous system and ultimately on the immune system. Moreover, more heterogeneous networks lessen susceptibility to common colds, probably by causing focal persons to develop more diverse immune systems (Cohen et al. 1997).

With respect to psychological health, a person's receipt of social support may help moderate the effects of stressful life events on his or her psychological state.[5] For example, Brown et al. (1977) found that among two small samples of working-class London women, those who were more socially "integrated" (i.e., more social support) tended to have lower rates of depression. Support affects health independently of stress, or the extent to which support "buffers" people from experiencing the full brunt of stress when it is encountered. Both processes appear to be operative (Lin, Dean, and Ensel 1986). *Affective support* (emotional aid, companionship) appears to be a better predictor than *instrumental support* (goods, services, money, information) of psychological well-being and physical health (Abbey, Abramis, and Caplan 1985; Israel and Rounds 1987; Kessler and McLeod 1984).

The distinction between affective and instrumental support indicates that "support" is as vaguely a metaphorical concept as "disease." It is a global, unidimensional, sensitizing concept rather than a variable to be analyzed. Support needs to be deconstructed into its constituents, operationalized for measurement, and studied for its functionality. In addition to analyzing the consequences of social support for health, investigators need to consider its etiology and understand what kinds of personal communities and community ties produce which kinds of social support. When applied to the study of social support, the social network approach engenders a more fine-grained attention to how the composition and structure of personal networks affect the quantity and quality of support available through them.

Fostering Social Support

The discovery that one could not just assume the existence of a broad spectrum of social support in all interpersonal ties led analysts to start investigating the *causes and correlates* of social support as well as its consequences. Support analysts have become more interested in extending the analytic chain backwards to discover social factors associated with the provision of support. They acknowledge that "research on the relationship of social networks to health care use has been retarded by imprecise definitions of social network characteristics, nonspecific hypotheses concerning their relationships to utilization, [and] a confusion of social support and social networks . . . " (Horwitz, Morgenstern, and Berkman 1985, p. 947). Current work is now more likely to distinguish between supportive and unsupportive ties and to recognize that different types of ties and networks may provide different kinds and amounts of support.

If one cannot assume the universal existence of broadly supportive relationships, then it becomes important to understand the circumstances under which particular kinds of social support will be available to maintain health. By contrast to the emphasis on the health-giving effects of social support, fewer studies have looked at the social causes of social support. What social factors are associated with the production of social support in community ties and networks? This is an important practical as well as intellectual question, for people want to know which types of network members are apt to help their various needs. Most research into this question has concentrated on identifying the types of ties that provide different kinds of support. Thus our research group has found that people tend to receive different kinds of social support through different types of relationships. Parents and adult children are preeminent sources of emotional support and large services. Available relationships (living or working nearby, or otherwise in frequent contact) provide many small services. Friends and siblings are preferred sociable companions. Women provide much emotional support, especially to other women (Wellman and Wortley 1990). The specialized nature of these supportive ties and the fragmented nature of the networks means that people must actively work to maintain each supportive relationship rather than relying on solidary communities to do their maintenance work.

Initially most studies of social support have treated community ties as discrete dyads, using exchange theory as an underlying perspective. While they often termed the aggregate of these dyadic ties a "social network," their loose, metaphoric formulation did not allow them to analyze the characteristics of these networks. Their work implicitly assumed that networks are homogeneous in their structure and composition, and that variations in structure and composition are largely irrelevant to the provision of support. Such assumptions led to a focus on network size as the only important precursor variable, for if all relationships are treated as the same, then the greater the body count, the more support available. Yet the essence of community ties is that they are parts of social systems: Each tie is structurally embedded in larger social networks, and the form of these networks can markedly affect the kinds of resources that flow through any specific tie.

Our research builds on existing work by considering how the characteristics of personal community networks affect the supportiveness of these networks. Social support has a social network as well as a relational basis. Not only do people need—and want to know—which of their relationships are apt to provide different kinds of support, they also have a need and desire to know the number and percentage of the members of their social networks who provide different kinds of support. Thus the flow of supportive resources through a network is inherently a social network phenomenon, shaped by the characteristics of the networks themselves as well as by the characteristics of the persons and ties of which these networks are composed.

In this chapter we investigate the extent to which the properties of personal community networks—their range, availability, kin dominance, and composition—shape the kinds and amount of resources that flow through these networks. Using evidence from the Toronto area, we examine the extent to which different types of personal community networks provide high aggregate volumes and per capita rates of social support. We relate structural and compositional properties of these networks to the occurrence of four distinct types of social support: empathetic companionship, emotional aid, supportive services, and financial aid. We investigate which network characteristics better facilitate the delivery of different kinds of social support.

Studying Networks of Social Support

The Context

As in Chapter 1, our information comes from two linked data sources: a large survey conducted in 1968 and a small set of interviews conducted a decade later. This information was collected from one-time residents of the Toronto borough of East York. Densely settled East York, with a population of about 100,000, is an integral part of the transportation and communication networks of metropolitan Toronto (population = 3 million+). It is located about six miles east of Toronto's central business district, a half-hour subway ride or drive. When the survey and interviews were conducted, its small private homes and apartments housed a settled, predominantly British-Canadian working- to middle-class population (for details see Gillies and Wellman 1968; Wellman 1982). East York has had a long tradition of communal aid and active social service agencies. Medical services are "free" for Canadians, paid for by taxes. Hence social support among East Yorkers (and Torontonians in general) is often intertwined with and complementary to formally mandated care.

The Large Survey

As was described in Chapter 1, the large in-person survey was closed-ended, conducted in 1968 with a random sample of 845 adult (aged eighteen and over) East Yorkers. Respondents reported about their relationships with each of a maximum of 6 intimates (mean = 5), a total of 3,930 relationships. The virtues of this data-set are its large sample size, systematic information about each intimate, information about each network's social density, and its fit with the subsequent interviews. Its findings have proven to be useful and consistent with other studies (for details see Wellman 1979, 1988, 1993).

This was one of the first two surveys to ask about social support (Wellman 1993), and at that time we did not appreciate its differentiated nature. Therefore, we asked only two broad questions about whether each intimate provides social support:

"Which of these [intimates] do you rely on for help in everyday matters?" The respondents reported that 22% of their intimates provide such everyday support. However, 60% of the respondents report that they have such everyday help available from at least one intimate.

"Which of these [intimates] do you rely on for help in an emergency?" The respondents reported that 30% of their intimates provide such emergency support. However, 81% of the respondents report that they have such emergency help available from at least one intimate.

The overly broad questions about "everyday" and "emergency" social support reduce our ability to understand the kinds of support that different types of ties and networks may provide, and it also probably led to the underreporting of the support provided by intimates. Moreover, in asking only about the strongest intimate ties in each focal person's network, the survey ignored the support that could be provided by weaker, but still active, relationships.

The In-depth Interviews

To deal with these limitations, we conducted thirty-three in-depth interviews in 1977–78, with a subsample of the 845 originally surveyed respondents. Twenty-nine of these respondents discussed their exchange of social support. These detailed interviews complemented the breadth of the original survey, gaining much more information about many more ties in each network. We elicited the kinds of support exchanged with each network member by asking each respondent to complete a questionnaire reporting "Yes/No" about each of 18 kinds of help the respondent had ever given to/received from each network member.[6]

The 29 networks contain a total of 343 "active" ties, with a mean of 5 "intimate" ties and 7 somewhat weaker "significant" ties per network. By revealing that most ties (both intimate and significant nonintimate) provide some kind of support, these detailed data correct the impression left by the large survey that only a minority of intimate ties are supportive. Eight specific types of support dominate the contents of these networks, each present in at least one-third of the ties and two-thirds of the networks: minor emotional aid (provided by 47% of network members), advice about family problems (39%), major emotional aid (33%), minor services (40%), lending household items (38%), minor household services (35%), sharing ideas (47%), and doing things together (39%). Thus active network members are most apt to provide intangibles—emotional support and companionship—along with minor goods and services. Note that no specific type of support is given by most of these active network members, and presumably the 1,000 or so weaker ties in a person's network are even less apt to be supportive.

The other specific types of support are each present in less than one-fifth of the ties: aid in dealing with organizations (10%), major household services (16%), regular help with housework (16%), major services such as children's day care and long-term health care (7%), small (13%) and large (4%) loans and gifts, financial aid for housing (4%), participating together in an organization (19%). Only a small minority of network members provide financial aid, or major goods and services.

Grouping the 18 specific types of support into six basic support dimensions is possible (using oblique promax factor analysis) because certain types of support are usually provided in the same relationships. For example, relationships that provide minor emotional support tend to provide major emotional support. Three dimensions are provided by most active network members and are present to some extent in almost all networks: emotional aid (provided by 62% of all network members), minor services (61%), and companionship (59%). Three dimensions are much more rarely provided by network members but are available from at least one person in most networks: major services (16%), financial aid (16%), and job information (10%).[7]

These dimensions are congruent with other studies of social support (see the reviews in Gottlieb and Selby 1990; Wellman 1992b). Moreover, the grouping of specific kinds of support into substantively different dimensions has its own interest. By contrast to the broadly supportive relationships of the East Yorkers' husbands and wives (Wellman and Wellman 1992), the members of their personal community networks specialize in the dimensions of support they provide. To be sure, 87% of the ties provide at least one dimension of support. However, only 39% of the ties provide at least three dimensions. To obtain a wide range of support, people must actively shop within their networks for those who specialize in giving this sort of help to them. They cannot count on most ties within their networks to give them the kinds of support they might need.

Measuring the Number and Percentage of Social Supporters

Moving from relationships to networks is not necessarily a matter of simple aggregation. If this were the case, then all we would have to do is multiply the number of network ties by the probability that each type of tie is likely to provide a specific kind of support. Let us take a simple example, using information about active network members from the East York data-sets that show that 68% of women and 49% of men are likely to provide emotional support. Then simple aggregation would suggest that 9 network members (63%) would provide emotional support in a 14-person network containing 10 women and 4 men:

$$((68\% \times 10) + (49\% \times 4)) / 14 = 63\%$$
[percentage of network members providing support]

$$(63\% / 100) \times 14 = 9 \text{ [number of network members providing support]}$$

It is unlikely that simple aggregation will take place even if we refine our percentages to be more multivariate: e.g., the percentage of women who are parents, who are intimate friends, who are extended kin living far away, etc. For one thing, there are compositional ceiling effects. Just to know that parents tend to provide emotional support does not tell us which types of networks are especially apt to be emotionally supportive. For example, most people can have a maximum of four parents in their networks (including in-laws, but excluding remarried parents). More generally, we must take into account matters of network connectivity, heterogeneity, and similarity. For example, does more support flow through densely knit networks because of their putatively greater ability to convey information and control members' behavior?

Hence our principal analytic task in this chapter is to ask what variations in personal community networks are associated with the availability through these networks of various amounts and kinds of social support. If availability principally depends on network size and composition, then simple aggregation from relational analyses may suffice. If availability also depends on a network's structure and heterogeneity, then the network basis of support is more than the sum of its constituent relationships.

To study network support, we must transform tie-level data into network-level data. This is information about the types of ties that provide different kinds of support: social visits, everyday support, and emergency support in the survey data-set; and companionship, emotional aid, minor services, and major services in the interview data-sets. To complicate matters further, we have information in the survey *only about intimates*, but we have information in the interviews about *both intimates and significant ties*, that is, ties that are quite active but not intimate. Keeping information separate about intimate and significant ties allows us to see whether different phenomena affect the provision of support from intimates and less-intimate ties, and it aids comparison between the intimates in the original survey and in the later interviews. In short, we use data from both the large survey and the detailed interviews to study support from intimates, while we also use the interviews to compare support from intimate and significant ties. For each dimension of support, our two measures are the number of network members providing support, and the percentage of network members providing support.

Number of Supporters.   When people need support, it is often important to people to know how many network members are supportive. The *number* measures report how many members of each network provide everyday or emergency aid (from the survey) or companionship, emotional aid, services, or financial aid (from the interviews). For example, a 10-person network could provide a maximum of 10 strands of emotional support.

Percentage of Supporters.   People who need a particular dimension of support also take into account the percentage of network members who provide that support. The *percentage* measures report how likely a person is to receive support from an average network member. The percentage variables automatically control for network size in the way that the number variables do not. For example, we can easily find that 50% of network members provide emotional support in networks of 5 and 10 members, even though there are twice the number of supporters in the 10-person network.

We organize the next section somewhat unusually to deal with the complexities of evaluating the potential of five types of network characteristics to explain the number and percentage of intimate and significant network members who provide everyday and emergency support (survey data) and each of four dimensions of social support (interview data). Even though we analyze only selected network characteristics and we

TABLE 2.1 1968 Survey Data: Multiple Regression Statistics of Variables Predicting the Number and Percentage of Intimate Ties Providing Support

Dimensions of Support: Number and percentage providing support	*Visitation*		*Everyday Support*		*Emergency Support*	
	#	%	#	%	#	%
Range	.42	(−.03)	.16	−.08	.17	−.19
Availability	.14	.21	.18	.22	.13	.16
Kin/density	(.01)	.08	(.02)	(.05)	(.03)	.08
SES	(.06)	(.04)	(.06)	(.05)	.10	(.06)
Percent women	(.03)	(.01)	−.09	−.11	−.12	−.12
Adjusted R^2	.19	.05	.06	.07	.07	.09

NOTE: Standardized regression coefficients and adjusted R^2 are significant where $p \le .05$

Numbers in parentheses indicate regression coefficients that are significant where $p > .05$

have reduced the number of support variables in the survey data-set to 4 from 18, this is still 100 combinations of variables.

Survey data: 5 network characteristics x 2 types of support x 2 measures *(number, percent)* = 20

Interview data: 5 network characteristics x 2 types of ties *(intimates, significants)* x 4 support dimensions x 2 measures *(number, percent)* = 80

To handle this formidable number of combinations, we organize our writing into subsections. The first subsection discusses the overall regression models. Each of the next four subsections discusses a particular network dimension, stating its rationale, operationalizing it, and discussing the kinds of social support that are associated with it.

The Relationship of Network Characteristics to Social Support

Overall Effects

The interviews provide information about both intimate networks and significant networks (less intimate but still relatively strong active ties).[8] In both intimate and significant networks, the *number* of providers of all four types of support are significantly associated. For example, networks that have a high number of members providing companionship usually have a high number providing emotional support and services (Tables 2.2 and 2.3).

There are more complex results in these data for the *percentage* of network members who provide support. None of the regressions are significant, either for the intimate or significant networks (Tables 2.2 and 2.3). However, for the intimate networks, the percentage of network members providing support is weakly associated with companionship and emotional aid, although for significant networks the adjusted R^2s hover around zero.

We suspect that the lack of statistical significance in the interview data is due to its small sample size, for the large-sample survey network dimensions are significantly associated with both the number and percentage of all three types of support measured: visiting, everyday support, and emergency support (Table 2.1). However, compared with the more finely measured interview data, the regression coefficients are low.

Range

Rationale. The range of a network refers to a mix of structural characteristics that collectively heighten a network's capacity to provide diverse resources and to provide access to other social milieus (Burt 1983; Haines and Hurlbert 1992; Marsden 1987). A network with a high degree of range is one that is *large* and contains socially *heterogeneous* network members. This is not a theoretical assumption: our data show that large personal communities with a high proportion of significant ties are usually heterogeneous and sparsely knit (see Chapter 1).

The connection between network range and social support rests primarily on standard sociological interpretations of network heterogeneity. Are networks with high range more cohesive and supportive than networks with low range? Arguments that high range breeds much support reflect Durkheimian (1893) and Simmelian (1922) conjectures that relationships that cut across social categories foster solidarity and satisfy mutual needs (see also Kemper 1972; Blau and Schwartz 1984; Blau 1993). Thus Granovetter's "strength of weak ties" (1973, 1982) argument contends that weak ties provide better connections to different social milieus because they usually connect socially dissimilar people (see also Burt 1987). Hence, the greater the range within a network (greater size and heterogeneity, lower density), the more access to diverse sources of support and thus the greater availability of support.

Network size enters into the equation with the standard expectation that as the number of network members increases, the relative heterogeneity of the network also increases (Haines and Hurlbert 1992). Under

TABLE 2.2 1978 Interview Data: Multiple Regression Statistics of Variables Predicting the Number and Percentage of Intimate Ties Providing Support

Dimensions of Support: Number and percentage providing support	Companionship		Minor Services		Major Services		Emotional Aid	
	#	%	#	%	#	%	#	%
Range	.58	(−.23)	.58	(−.08)	.46	(.18)	.66	(.20)
Availability	(.27)	(.28)	(.15)	(.18)	(.20)	(.22)	(.22)	(.38)
Kin/density	−.32	(−.28)	(−.02)	(.09)	(.12)	(.04)	(−.01)	(−.07)
SES	(.21)	(.08)	(−.15)	(−.20)	−.40	(−.40)	(−.05)	(−.06)
Percent women	(−.16)	(−.30)	(.07)	(−.22)	(.06)	(−.11)	.32	.38
Adjusted R²	.40	(.13)	(.20)	(−.06)	.23	(.003)	.39	(.11)

NOTE: Standardized regression coefficients and adjusted R² are significant where p ≤ .05
Numbers in parentheses indicate regression coefficients that are significant where p > .05

TABLE 2.3 1978 Interview Data: Multiple Regression Statistics of Variables Predicting the Number and Percentage of Significant Ties Providing Support

Dimensions of Support: Number and percentage providing support	Companionship		Minor Services		Major Services		Emotional Aid	
	#	%	#	%	#	%	#	%
Range	.60	(.24)	.69	(.36)	(.44)	(−.004)	.56	(.11)
Availability	(.04)	(.03)	(−.08)	(−.03)	(.10)	(.15)	(−.21)	(−.10)
Kin/density	(−.08)	(.002)	(.12)	(.11)	(.08)	(.20)	(.10)	(.07)
SES	(.10)	(.31)	(−.06)	(−.009)	(−.19)	(−.18)	(.10)	(.12)
Percent women	(−.02)	(−.12)	(.07)	(.15)	(.12)	(.34)	(.16)	(.33)
Adjusted R^2	.34	(.05)	.32	(−.03)	(.004)	(.02)	.33	(−.01)

NOTE: Standardized regression coefficients and adjusted R^2 are significant where $p \leq .05$. Numbers in parentheses indicate regression coefficients that are significant where $p > .05$

this assumption, greater size extends to a greater variety of potential sources of support. Accordingly, as the size of a network increases, so should the number of potential support givers. The relationship might be linear, so that as the number of network members increases, the number of persons providing support would increase at the same rate, while the percentage of network members providing support would remain constant. An even stronger relationship would be one where, as the number of network members increases, the number and percentages of network members providing support also increases. This curvilinear relationship fits research showing that people with more social skills usually have larger, more supportive networks (Parks and Eggert 1991; Riggio and Zimmerman 1991).

Hypothesis 1A: The higher the network range, the higher the number of network members who provide support.

Hypothesis 1B: The higher the network range, the higher the percentage of network members who provide support.

The contrasting hypothesis that low network range fosters supportiveness is based on the argument that network members with similar social characteristics often flock together in similar structural positions and become supportive friends (Lazarsfeld and Merton 1954; Marsden 1988). Thus the similar characteristics and interests of network members may foster cohesive networks, empathetic understanding, and mutual support. Under this argument, we would hypothesize that the greater the range (and hence, diversity) within a network, the less support one would find.

Bystander intervention research also suggests that networks with low range—especially networks that are small—would be more supportive (Latané and Darley 1976). Its findings suggest that network members would be reluctant to get involved when they think that others can provide support. A weaker form suggests that more network members are associated with having more supporters, but that the percentage of network members providing support is lower in larger networks (Van Tilburg 1990).

Smaller, low range, networks might be supportive if quality compensates for quantity: Persons with smaller networks might have more time to attend to each network member and so would be better at evoking reciprocal help from each of them. As the number of network members increases, the number of supporters stays the same, but the percentage of network members providing support decreases. An extreme expectation would be that as the number of network members increases, both the number *and* percentage of network members providing support decreases. Under each of these scenarios, low range is associated with significant amounts of support from the network. Thus they are in point-for-point opposition to the arguments outlined under the first hypothesis.

> *Hypothesis 2A: The higher the network range, the lower the number of network members who provide support.*
>
> *Hypothesis 2B: The higher the network range, the lower the percentage of network members who provide support.*

Operationalization. Network size may appear to be a straightforward structural characteristic, but social networks have fuzzy boundaries. Social networks are dynamic entities since network members come and go (Wellman et al. 1997). As there is no such thing as "the network," analysts must specify inclusion criteria. The 1968 survey focused on intimate ties, a mean of 5 in a network. Since the 1978 data allowed us to control for tie strength, we could analyze network size in terms of the number of active ties per network, including the number of intimate and significant ties per network. In 1978, the mean network size was 12 active ties (5 intimate ties and 7 significant ties). The mean number of intimate ties per network in both 1968 and 1978 is identical, giving us confidence in the comparability of the two intimate data-sets. Because intimate ties are more apt to give all kinds of support than significant ties, we analyze separately in the interview data, (a) relationships between the number of intimates and significants with (b) the number and percentage of network members providing each kind of support.

Measures of *network heterogeneity* and network size are usually correlated: the larger the network, the less homogeneous. For both data-sets, we used the standard deviation to measure the homogeneity of network characteristics that are continuous variables: age and socioeconomic status.[9] In the 1978 data-set, we could use Schuessler's Index of Qualitative Variation (IQV) (Mueller, Schuessler, and Costner 1970) to measure the heterogeneity of network characteristics that were nominal variables: ethnicity, role, sex, religion, employment status, and marital status. As preliminary work showed that almost all heterogeneity measures in the interview data formed one factor, we constructed a composite measure, combining all of the indicators of network homogeneity: marital status, employment status, religious affiliation, ethnicity, age of network members, similarity of education of network members with respondents, and socioeconomic status. This standardized, composite measure is based on a scale of 0 to 4: the higher the score, the more heterogeneous is the network.

As our research has shown a strong correlation between network size and heterogeneity (see Chapter 1), we constructed a single range variable. To simplify analysis and provide comparable measures between data-sets, we standardized the variables for size and heterogeneity in each data-set and combined them in a single range variable.

Findings. Our findings show the importance of high network range for the provision of social support. Large, heterogeneous networks have greater *numbers* of members who provide all kinds of support.[10] The interviews show that both intimate and significant networks with high range contain many members who provide companionship, minor services, major services, and emotional support; their quite large regression coefficients are far greater than any others in the models. In the survey data, the regression coefficient of range is quite strongly associated with the number of network (intimate) members engaging in social visits, and is significantly (although less strongly) associated with the number providing everyday and emergency support (Table 2.1). Thus these data support Hypothesis 1A and disconfirm Hypothesis 2A. However, high network range is not significantly associated with higher *percentages* of network members who are supportive, and there is no consistent pattern in the signs of the coefficients across the data-sets.

These findings give some credence to the supposition that networks with high range have both a larger number of support givers and a greater variety of support givers. Range (size and heterogeneity) is just as important in intimate networks as it is in less intimate, significant networks. So it is not only the strength of weak ties that is important but also the number and diversity of all active ties.

Network Availability

Rationale. Analysts have argued that the more contact there is among network members, the more supportive the relationship. They argue that frequent contact fosters shared values, increases mutual awareness of needs and resources, mitigates feelings of loneliness, encourages reciprocal exchanges, and facilities the delivery of aid (Homans 1950, 1961; Clark and Gordon 1979; Galaskiewicz 1985; Connidis 1989a, 1989b, 1989c; Bumpass 1990; Schweizer, Schnegg, and Berzborn 1998). Frequent contact, or even just being physically available for contact, provides an important basis for the delivery of goods and services. Our research group has found that available ties—those in frequent face-to-face or telephone contact or just living or working nearby—are more likely to provide small supportive services, such as child-minding or the lending of household goods (Wellman 1979; Wellman and Wortley 1989, 1990; see also Marsden and Campbell 1984). Such findings suggest that the effects of availability operate independently of the strength of the relationship, so that there is much material support provided in all highly available networks, regardless of whether they are composed of strong, *intimate ties* or are more broadly composed of all active ties.

> *Hypothesis 3A: The greater the availability of a network, the more social support in the network.*

Other scholars see an interaction between availability, the strength of relationships, and supportiveness. They argue that many routinely available ties (such as with coworkers or people living in the same neighborhood) are not likely to be supportive under any circumstances. This suggests that it is the availability of *strong* (intimate) ties, and not of all ties, that fosters support (Rook 1984; Israel and Antonucci 1987; Jones 1982; Kessler and McLeod 1984; Seeman and Berkman 1988).

> *Hypothesis 3B: The greater the availability of an intimate network, the more social support in the intimate network.*

Operationalization.   Our operationalization of network availability is a multistage process. To construct contact measures, we use in all data-sets the logged (base 10) *mean network frequency of face-to-face contact and telephone contact.* We also use (logged) *residential distance:* the 1978 data-sets show that network members live a median of nine miles apart, although a significant minority (22%) live in the same neighborhood and a handful live in Europe. As the 1968 data-set does not have a measure of continuous residential distance, we calculate the *percentage of network members who live in metropolitan Toronto* (75%). We use this measure, rather than the percentage living in the same neighborhood, because previous research has shown that network members living outside the neighborhood but elsewhere in metropolitan Toronto give about as much social support as those living locally. We use logged statistics because an increase of one day or mile at higher values (e.g., from 364 to 365 days or miles) is less socially meaningful than an increase at lower values (e.g., from one to two days or miles).

Similarly to the range variable examined earlier, our *availability* variable in all data-sets is based on Wellman and Potter's delineation (see Chapter 1) of the basic characteristics of personal communities, in this case the high loading on a single factor of frequency of face-to-face contact, telephone contact, and residential distance. To maintain comparability between data-sets, we do not use the factor loadings themselves. Instead, we combine into a composite measure of contact the standardized logged mean frequencies of telephone and face-to-face contact and the logged mean residential distance.

Findings.   Both the survey data and the in-depth interview data support Hypothesis 3B, the greater the availability of intimate networks, the greater their supportiveness. The large survey sample shows that highly available networks significantly have a higher number and a higher percentage of network members who provide all kinds of support: social visits, everyday aid, and emergency aid (Table 2.1). Indeed, these are consistently the strongest regression coefficients for the percentage of supportive network members, and, along with range, they are the only significant, positive coefficients for the number of network members. The pattern is similar for the intimate networks in the interview data-set, although the coefficients are not significant in this smaller sample (Table 2.2).

The pattern is different for the less-intimate, significant networks where network availability is not positively associated with any kind of network supportiveness (Table 2.3). Indeed, availability is negatively associated with the number (–0.21) and percentage (–0.10) of significant network members providing emotional support. In short, available networks are only more likely to be supportive when the strength of their ties can provide aid that may consume substantial time or money. Unlike the tie-level analysis of these data, availability fosters all kinds of network supportiveness, and not just the delivery of minor goods and services.

Densely Knit Kin/Sparsely Knit Friends

Rationale.   The saying that "blood is thicker than water" expresses the common understanding that kin are expected to be more supportive network members than others. There are both structural and normative reasons for this. The densely knit structure of most kinship ties intersects with the norm of encouraging supportive relations among kin. Such norms idealize the promotion of family welfare, encourage kin to share resources, urge them to give other kin privileged access to these resources, and cherish long-term reciprocity.[11]

Networks with a high percentage of kin tend to be densely knit. Standard sociological interpretations suggest that densely knit networks have stronger norms and better communication, control, and protection (Durkheim 1897; Bott 1957; Kadushin 1983; Fischer 1982; Marsden and Hurlbert 1988). Therefore, densely knit networks should lead to a higher number and percentage of network members providing support (Thoits 1982; Pescosolido and Georgiana 1989). This is especially likely to be true for the provision of material support that often requires more coordination than the provision of intangible support such as emotional aid and companionship. In practice, network density and the percentage of kin are so highly correlated that they must be analyzed jointly. Yet not all kin are equally supportive. Although immediate kin (parents, adult children, siblings) provide a wide range of support, other kin (aunts, cousins, grandparents) usually provide less support than friends, neighbors, or coworkers (Wellman and Wortley 1989, 1990). Therefore it is the percentage of immediate kin in these networks—and not of all kin—that may be the key to supportiveness.

Hypothesis 4A: The greater the proportion of immediate kinship ties per network (and the higher the density of these networks), the greater the availability of support.

An alternative hypothesis is also plausible, although less widely supported in the literature. Because there is more normative pressure to maintain kinship ties than friendship ties, kinship ties may be retained even if they are unsupportive, burdensome, and provide poor companionship (Stokowski and Lee 1991). Women with many kin in their networks can experience more stress in their lives (Haines and Hurlbert 1992). Moreover, the high density of kinship relations can lead to "inbreeding" (Burt 1992; Bienenstock, Bonacich, and Oliver 1990; Schweizer, Schnegg, and Berzborn 1998). Just as information flows rapidly between densely knit kin, such networks may be less apt to acquire new information from the outside, be it about politics (Gans 1962) or health care (Salloway and Dillon 1973; Pescolido 1991; Wellman 1995). Thus sparsely knit networks with few kin might have a high number and percentage of network members providing support because of the diversity of supportive resources that is made available.

Hypothesis 4B: The lower the proportion of immediate kinship ties per network (and the lower the density of these networks), the greater the availability of support.

Operationalization.   Because of the strong association between high percentages of kin and network density in all the data-sets, we create a single measure of kin/density. First we standardize the percentage of immediate kin, the percentage of friends, and network density. We then combine them into a composite measure for each data-set. Density is calculated as the ratio of the number of actually existing links between network members to the number of links that are theoretically possible.[12] Both the survey (33%) and the interviews (42%) show moderate density among network members; that is, a substantial minority of active network members are directly linked with each other and also indirectly linked (by a two-step path) through their respective ties to the respondents.

Findings. Kin/density is not an important factor in the provision of support. In the less intimate, significant networks, it is not related to the provision of any kind of support (Table 2.3). In the intimate networks, the few significant associations are congruent with how kinship ties affect support. In the interview data-set, intimate networks with high kin density are less likely to have high companionship (supporting Hypothesis 4B; see Table 2.2). This fits the tie-level data, including respondents' reports that they valued aid from parents and adult children but did not enjoy socializing with them. By contrast, the survey data fit Hypothesis 4A, showing that intimate networks with high kin density have larger percentages of social visitors and providers of emergency support (Table 2.1). Although the finding that dense kin networks have more social visitors is anomalous (and may be an artifact of a vague question), the profusion of emergency support in dense kin networks fits the tie-level finding that immediate kin help with major domestic needs and care for serious illness and infirmity.

Network Composition: Socioeconomic Status and Women

Rationale. Social characteristics are positional statuses that network members "possess" rather than qualities of network relationships. When people with certain social characteristics are likely to possess such resources as wealth, empathy, or skill, they may be especially useful sources of social support. For example, analysts have argued that because people with *high socioeconomic status* usually have more material resources and information available, they get more requests for instrumental support and companionship (Lin, Dayton, and Greenwald 1983; Lin, Dean and Ensel 1986; Lin and Dumin 1986; Lin 1997; Degraaf, Dirk, and Flap 1988; Campbell, Marsden, and Hurlbert 1986). Moreover, analysts have shown that North American women are more likely than men to provide emotional support, possibly because "women express, men repress" (Perlman and Fehr 1987, p. 21). Indeed, women are often the principal emotional supporters of men as well as of other women (Sapadin 1988; Wellman 1992a, 1992b). In addition, women provide many small services that are often taken for granted within the rubric of household chores (Fox 1980; Hammer, Gutwirth, and Phillips 1982; Gullestad 1984; Luxton 1980; Stack 1974).

Hypothesis 5: The higher the socioeconomic status of members of the network, the more supportive the network.

Hypothesis 6: The higher the proportion of women in a network, the more supportive the network.

Operationalization.   In all three data-sets the only decent indicator we have of *socioeconomic status* is the occupational status of the network members.[13] We use the Blishen scale to measure a network's mean occupational status (1978; mean = 55). For gender, we measure the *percentage of women* per network. Women are a majority in all three data-sets.

Findings.   Just as these data have shown no significant tie-level relationships between socioeconomic status (SES) and social support, there are few significant associations between a network's socioeconomic level and its provision of different types of support. Those significant associations that do exist for intimate networks are contradictory. Consistent with Hypothesis 5, in the survey data-set, high-SES intimate networks have more members who provide emergency support (0.10; Table 2.1). Yet in the interview data-set, high-SES intimate networks have fewer members who are providers of major services (–0.40; Table 2.2).

The *gender composition* of networks is not straightforwardly linked to the network provision of support as the survey and the interview data-sets show discrepant findings. The survey data-set shows that the percentage of women in networks is *negatively* associated with the number and percentage of the intimates in these networks who provide emergency and everyday support (Table 2.1). However, the survey did not ask specifically about emotional support, so the negative association does not clearly refute Hypothesis 6.

By contrast, the interview data have a *positive* association between the percentage of women in a network and the number of network members providing emotional support (Tables 2.2 and 2.3). This support of Hypothesis 6 is consistent with tie-level analyses of these data, which have shown women playing more active roles in the provision of emotional support. The discrepancy between the survey and interview data-sets leads us to question whether the role of men and women reversed between 1968 and 1978, or if the anomaly is an artifact of the different questions asked at each time. We are more comfortable with the more precise and more recent findings of the interview data that are consistent with tie-level analysis.

Summary and Conclusions

We have asked a basic question: What types of ties and networks provide what kinds of supportive resources to the persons at the centers of these personal communities? This question connects us with key social scientific concepts:

- The complex structure and composition of personal community networks;

- the multidimensional nature of social support;
- the interplay between the structure of social networks and the personal characteristics of network members in affecting the flow of resources through their networks;
- the longstanding, core sociological question of whether a social system is more than the sum of its constituent relationships.

Our data suggest that several network phenomena foster interpersonal supportiveness:

1. The *range* of a network—its size and heterogeneity—is generally the network characteristic that is the most closely associated with the supportiveness of a network. The more network members, and the more diverse their characteristics, the greater the number and percentage of support providers. Moreover, large networks are more apt to provide a wide range of support. Members of large networks clearly are not bystanders.
2. The *availability* of a network substantially fosters the provision of support. To an appreciable extent, the delivery of support depends on network members being in contact to learn of such needs and being physically accessible to provide assistance.
3. *Densely knit networks* with high percentages of immediate kin tend to provide more emotional and material support, although the effect of density is weaker than the effects of range and availability. The dense interconnections of kin networks help communication about needs, mobilization to deal with problems, and coordination of effective delivery of support. However, networks with many kin provide less companionship than do other networks.
4. The *composition* of networks affects the provision of support, but to a lesser extent than network structural properties (range, availability, and kin/density). There is no relationship between a network's socioeconomic level and its supportiveness. However, networks with a high percentage of *women* tend to provide more emotional support.

The supportiveness of networks is related to the aggregated characteristics of network members and relationships and to the emergent structural properties of networks.

- *Personal characteristics*: women are more emotionally supportive.

- *Relationships:* intimate ties (both kin and friends) and immediate kin (whether intimate or not) are especially supportive, although kinship usually does not extend to companionship. Tie-level dynamics are also apparent in another way. Networks with many available members or a high percentage of women members usually have a high number of members who provide support. However, such networks do not necessarily have a high *percentage* of members who provide support.
- *Network properties*: networks with high range (large size, high heterogeneity), more availability, and more density provide more of certain types of support. Such structural effects cannot be inferred from the aggregated characteristics of ties. When it comes to providing social support, a social network is more than the sum of its ties.

To our knowledge, this chapter is the first attempt to go beyond the dyadic, interpersonal level to study the supportiveness of the social networks in which these ties are embedded. Analyzing how each network characteristic is related to social support is in a sense testing theories about what aspects of social structure are apt to convey different kinds of resources. Our work therefore also addresses a key sociological question: Do structural properties of a social system affect processes beyond the aggregated sum of what happens in its two-person relationships? Is a social network more than the sum of its interpersonal duets?[14]

A Comparative Perspective

Unlike traditional conceptions of community and social support, personal community networks are not merely passive havens from large-scale social forces but active arrangements by which people and households reproduce and engage with the outside world. In North America (and elsewhere in the relatively comfortable Western world), supportive networks differ substantially from those of people in other circumstances. The low importance of the economic and political aspects of social support in the networks we have studied differs from those networks in the first, second, and third world that are less economically or politically secure. Most North Americans are not coping with shortages in consumer goods or with extensive bureaucratic regulation of their domestic affairs. They rely on market exchanges for most of their production and much of their consumption. Despite some variation, many institutional benefits such as schooling and medical care are available as citizenship rights. Hence members of developed societies do not pay as much attention as members of subsistence or central-bureaucratic societies to having network ties with persons skilled in making and fixing things (such as home-building) or with strong connections to strategic bureaucratic circles (Sik 1986; Walder 1986; also see Chapter 6). Having no urgent cares about daily survival, North Americans can manage domestic resources with less apprehension than, for example, Latin Americans living on the margins (Lomnitz 1977; Roberts 1978; also see Chapter 4).

The networks of North Americans are built around companionship, calming domestic stresses, and obtaining reliable, flexible, low-cost domestic services. These are not trivial pursuits as few people want to place themselves at the mercy of markets and institutions when they need to deal with their needs. Although analysts are just starting to calculate the costs and benefits of transactions in personal community networks, such networks clearly contribute important and central resources that enable people to go about their daily lives, handle chronic stresses, and cope with acute crises.

These are networks that support reproduction, not production. They center primarily on the household, secondarily on the neighborhood and active community network, and rarely concern earning a living. The networks provide *havens*, a sense of belonging and being helped. They provide *bandages*, routine emotional support and minor services to help people cope with the stresses and strains of their situations. They provide *safety nets* that lessen the impact of acute crises and chronic difficulties. Nor are they only passive reactors, because they provide *social capital:* to change situations—homes, jobs, spouses—or to change the world through interest group activity. These networks are important to the routine operations of households, crucial to the management of crises, and instrumental in helping people to change their situations. They are important for health: helping people to stay healthy and to get better when they are ill. But they are more than that: a core aspect of people's lives.

Notes

This work has been supported by the Social Science and Humanities Research Council of Canada and the (U.S.) National Institute of Mental Health. We appreciate the advice and comments of Bonnie Erickson, Leonard Pearlin, Stephanie Potter, Beverly Wellman, and Scot Wortley. We have benefited from the research assistance of Paula Goldman, Thy Phu, and Christine Wickens. The Centre for Urban and Community Studies, University of Toronto, has been our hospitable research home. This chapter is dedicated to Merrijoy Kelner, whose supportive networking is a model for us all.

1. See Wellman 1979; Wellman and Wortley 1989, 1990 for our group's research; see also the reviews in Gottlieb and Selby 1990; Cécora 1994; Wellman 1992b.

2. See the reviews in Fischer 1976, 1982; Wellman 1988, 1990, 1992b, 1994; Wellman and Leighton 1979; Sussman and Burchinal 1962; Mogey 1977; Lee 1980; Goldthorpe 1987.

3. We used orthogonal varimax factor analysis with data from the second East York (interview) study to develop these dimensions. The East York studies are described below and in Chapter 1, while the community dimensions are discussed in Chapter 1.

4. As such stresses were usually identified as related to health, psychological functioning, or interpersonal relations (e.g., Holmes and Rahe, 1967), it is not surprising that the proposed remedies fell into these domains. Yet significant gaps remained in these largely American formulations, such as stresses caused by the threat (or experiencing) of war, or by the lack of food, clothing, or shelter.

5. Kessler and McLeod 1984; Kessler, Price, and Wortman 1985; Vaux 1985; Abbey, Abramis, and Caplan 1985; Goldberg, Van Natta, and Comstock 1985; Hammer 1983; Thoits 1982; Turner 1981; Turner and Marino 1994.

6. Because of length constraints, we provide only quantitative data here, but qualitative evidence is available in other papers based on these interviews. For details, see Wellman 1982, 1992a; Wellman, Carrington and Hall 1988; Wellman and Tindall 1993; Wellman and Wortley 1989, 1990; Wellman et al. 1997.

7. One variable, information about housing vacancies, did not fall into any dimension. We exclude it, financial aid, and job information from our analyses because of their low prevalence and because they are usually provided only by network members in specialized roles: parents and coworkers respectively.

8. Combining intimate and significant networks into *active* networks provided results that were consistent with the separate intimate and significant analyses reported here. Numbers in parentheses are standardized regression coefficients that vary between 0 and ±1: the higher the number, the stronger the relationship.

9. We measured socioeconomic status using the Blishen (1967) scale for occupations, a Canadian adaptation of Duncan's (1961) U.S. scale.

10. Separate analyses for network size and network heterogeneity yield similar results as those obtained for the combined network range measure. This is to be expected, given the high correlation (and common factor location) of the size and heterogeneity variables. We found no association between network *similarity* and social support, where similarity is the extent to which the focal person at the center of a network is similar to network members. Other research has found that such structural similarity is less salient for the provision of support than "experiential" similarity between people who have experienced similar life events and traumas (Suitor, Pillemer, and Bohanon 1993).

11. Sussman and Burchinal 1962; Farber 1966; Nye 1976; Johnson 1977; Mogey 1977; Pitrou 1977; Horwitz 1978; Unger and Powell 1980; Fischer 1982; Hoyt and Babchuk 1983; Antonucci 1985; Litwak 1985; Riley and Cochran 1985; Taylor 1985, 1986; Arsenault 1986; Grieco 1987; Willmott 1987; Cheal 1988; Connidis 1989b; Retherford, Hildreth and Goldsmith 1988; Mancini and Blieszner 1989; Dykstra 1990; Allan 1979, 1989; Wellman 1990, 1992b; Wellman and Tindall 1993.

12. As this is information reported by the respondents about links between other members of their network, we treat links as symmetrical in our measurement of network density, so that a link from A to B assumes a link from B to A. We

exclude in our calculations the ties between network members and the focal persons at the centers of the networks. Although including such ties would increase the density statistic, such ties are unnecessary for analysis because each respondent is tied to all network members by definition. Moreover, it would confound the measure of network density with the measure of network size.

The percentage of friends (excluding neighbors and workmates) measures compositional information about sparsely knit network members whose ties are highly voluntary.

13. The respondents often did not know the network members' educational level or incomes.

14. Our next step is to use multilevel analysis to see the interplay between network, tie, and personal characteristics on the provision of support. Preliminary results are reported in Frank and Wellman (1998).

References

Abbey, Antonia, David Abramis, and Robert Caplan. 1985. "Effects of Different Sources of Social Support and Social Conflict on Emotional Well-being." *Basic and Applied Social Psychology* 6:111–129.

Allan, Graham. 1979. *A Sociology of Friendship and Kinship.* London: Allen and Unwin.

Allan, Graham. 1989. *Friendship.* London: Harvester Wheatsheaf.

Antonucci, Toni. 1985. "Personal Characteristics, Social Support, and Social Behavior." Pp. 94–128 in *Handbook of Aging and the Social Sciences,* edited by Ethel Shanas and Robert Binstock. New York: Van Nostrand Reinhold.

Arsenault, Anne-Marie. 1986. "Sources of Support of Elderly Acadian Women." *Health Care for Women International* 7(3):203–219.

Barrera, Manuel, Jr. 1986. "Distinctions between Social Support Concepts, Measures and Models." *American Journal of Community Psychology* 14:413–445.

Barrera, Manuel, Jr., and Sheila Ainley. 1983. "The Structure of Social Support." *Journal of Community Psychology.* 2:133–141.

Berkman, Lisa. 1984. "Assessing the Physical Health Effects of Social Networks and Social Support." *Annual Review of Public Health* 5:413–432.

Bienenstock, Elisa, Philip Bonacich, and Melvin Oliver. 1990. "The Effect of Network Density and Homogeneity on Attitude Polarization." *Social Networks* 12:153–172.

Blau, Peter. 1993. "Multilevel Structural Analysis." *Social Networks* 15:201–215.

Blau, Peter and Joseph Schwartz. 1984. *Crosscutting Social Circles.* Orlando, FL: Academic Press.

Blishen, Bernard. 1967. "A Socio-Economic Index for Occupations in Canada." *Canadian Review of Sociology and Anthropology* 4:41–53.

Bott, Elizabeth. 1957. *Family and Social Network.* London: Tavistock.

Brown, G[eorge], S. Davidson, T. Harris, U. Maclean, S. Pollack, and R. Prudo. 1977. "Psychiatric Disorder in London and North Uist." *Social Science and Medicine* 11:367–377.

Bumpass, Larry. 1990. "A Comparative Analysis of Coresidence and Contact with Parents in Japan and the United States." Working Paper No. 41, Madison: Center for Demography and Ecology, University of Wisconsin.

Burt, Ronald. 1983. "Range." Pp. 176–194 in *Applied Network Analysis,* edited by Ronald Burt and Michael Minor. Beverly Hills, CA: Sage.

Burt, Ronald. 1987. "A Note on Strangers, Friends and Happiness." *Social Networks* 9:311–331.

Burt, Ronald. 1992. *Structural Holes.* Chicago: University of Chicago Press.

Burt, Ronald, and Ilan Talmud. 1993. "Market Niche." *Social Networks* 15:133–149.

Campbell, Karen, Peter Marsden, and Jeanne Hurlbert. 1986. "Social Resources and Socioeconomic Status." Social Networks 8:97–117.

Cassel, John. 1976. "The Contribution of the Social Environment to Host Resistance." *American Journal of Epidemiology* 104:107–123.

Cécora, James, ed. 1994. *Changing Values and Attitudes in Family Households with Rural Peer Groups, Social Networks, and Action Spaces: Implications of Institutional Transition in East and West for Value Formation and Transmission.* Bonn: Society for Agricultural Policy Research and Rural Sociology.

Cheal, David. 1988. *The Gift Economy.* London: Routledge.

Clark, William, and Michael Gordon. 1979. "Distance, Closeness and Recency of Kin Contact in Urban Ireland." Journal *of Comparative Family Studies* 10:271–275.

Cobb, Sidney 1976. "Social Support as a Moderator of Life Stress." *Psychosomatic Medicine* 38:300–314.

Cohen, Sheldon, William Doyle, David Skoner, Bruce Rabin, and Jack Gwaltney, Jr. 1997. "Social Ties and Susceptibility to the Common Cold." *Journal of the American Medical Association* 277:1940–1944.

Cohen, Sheldon, and S. Leonard Syme, eds. 1985. *Social Support and Health.* New York: Academic Press.

Connidis, Ingrid. 1989a. "Contact between Siblings in Later Life." *Canadian Journal of Sociology* 14:429–442.

Connidis, Ingrid. 1989b. *Family Ties and Aging.* Toronto: Butterworth.

Connidis, Ingrid. 1989c. "Siblings as Friends in Later Life." *American Behavioral Scientist* 33:81–93.

Degraaf, Dirk, Nan Lin, and Henrik Flap. 1988. "With a Little Help from My Friends: Social Resources as an Explanation of Occupational Status in West Germany, The Netherlands, and the United States." *Social Forces* 62:454–472.

Dohrenwend, Barbara, and Bruce Dohrenwend. 1984. *Stressful Life Events and Their Contexts.* New Brunswick, NJ: Rutgers University Press.

Dorian, Barbara. 1985. "Psychoimmunology: A Current Perspective." *Perspectives in Psychiatry* 41:1–4.

Duncan, Otis Dudley. 1961. "A Socioeconomic Index for All Occupations, Properties and Characteristics of the Socioeconomic Index, Appendix B." Pp. 109–61, 263–95 in *Occupations and Social Status,* edited by Albert J. Reiss, Jr. New York: Free Press.

Durkheim, Émile. 1893 [1993]. *The Division of Labor in Society.* New York: Macmillan.

Durkheim, Émile. 1897 [1951]. *Suicide.* Glencoe, IL: Free Press.

Dykstra, Pearl. 1990. *Next of Nonkin: The Importance of Primary Relationships for Older Adults' Well-being.* Amsterdam: Swets and Zeitlinger.

Farber, Bernard, ed. 1966. *Kinship and Family Organization.* New York: Wiley.

Fischer, Claude. 1976. *The Urban Experience.* New York: Harcourt Brace Jovanovich.

Fischer, Claude. 1982. *To Dwell Among Friends.* Berkeley: University of California Press.

Fox, Bonnie. 1980. *Hidden in the Household.* Toronto: Women's Press.

Frank, Kenneth, and Barry Wellman. 1998. "Sources of Social Capital in Ties and Networks: A Multilevel Analysis of Social Support in Personal Communities." International Conference of Social Networks and Social Capital, Duke University, Durham, NC, October.

Gans, Herbert. 1962. *The Urban Villagers.* New York: Free Press.

Galaskiewicz, Joseph. 1985. *Social Organization of an Urban Grants Economy: A Study of Business Philanthropy and Nonprofit Organizations.* Orlando, FL: Academic Press.

Gillies, Marion, and Barry Wellman. 1968. "East York: A Profile." Report to Community Studies Section, Clarke Institute of Psychiatry, Toronto.

Goldberg, Evelyn, Pearl Van Natta, and George Comstock. 1985. "Depressive Symptoms, Social Networks and Social Support of Elderly Women." *American Journal of Epidemiology* 121:448–456.

Goldthorpe, John. 1987. *Family Life in Western Societies.* Cambridge: Cambridge University Press.

Gottlieb, Benjamin, and Peter Selby. 1990. *Social Support and Mental Health: A Review of the Literature.* Department of Psychology, University of Guelph, Canada.

Granovetter, Mark. 1973. "The Strength of Weak Ties." *American Journal of Sociology* 78:1360–1380.

Granovetter, Mark. 1982. "The Strength of Weak Ties: A Network Theory Revisited." Pp. 105–130 in *Social Structure and Network Analysis,* edited by Peter Marsden and Nan Lin. Beverly Hills, CA: Sage.

Grieco, Margaret. 1987. *Keeping it in the Family: Social Networks and Employment Chance.* London: Tavistock.

Gullestad, Marianne 1984. *Kitchen-Table Society.* Oslo: Universitetsforlaget.

Haines, Valerie, and Jeanne Hurlbert. 1992. "Network Range and Health." *Journal of Health and Social Behavior* 33:254–266.

Hammer, Muriel. 1983. "'Core' and 'Extended' Social Networks in Relation to Health and Illness." *Social Science and Medicine* 17:405–411.

Hammer, Muriel, Linda Gutwirth, and Susan Phillips. 1982. "Parenthood and Social Networks." *Social Science and Medicine* 16:2091–2100.

Holmes, Thomas, and Richard Rahe. 1967. "The Social Readjustment Rating Scale." *Journal of Psychosomatic Research* 11:213–218.

Homans, George. 1950. *The Human Group.* New York: Harcourt, Brace.

Homans, George. 1961. *Social Behavior: Its Elementary Forms.* New York: Harcourt Brace Jovanovich.

Horwitz, Allen. 1978. "Family, Kin, and Friend Networks in Psychiatric Help-Seeking." *Social Science and Medicine* 12:297–304.

Horwitz, Sarah, Hal Morgenstern, and Lisa Berkman. 1985. "The Impact of Social Stressors and Social Networks on Pediatric Medical Care Use." *Medical Care* 23:946–959.

House, James, Karl Landis, and Debra Umberson. 1988. "Social Relationships and Health." *Science* 241:540–545.

House, James, Debra Umberson, and Karl Landis. 1988. "Structures and Processes of Social Support." *Annual Review of Sociology* 14:293–318.

Hoyt, Danny, and Nicholas Babchuk. 1983. "Adult Kinship Networks: The Selective Formation of Intimate Ties with Kin." *Social Forces* 62:84–101.

Israel, Barbara, and Toni Antonucci. 1987. "Social Network Characteristics and Psychological Well-being." *Health Education Quarterly* 14:461–481.

Israel, Barbara, and Kathleen Rounds. 1987. "Social Networks and Social Support: A Synthesis for Health Educators." *Advances in Health Education and Promotion* 2:311–351.

Johnson, Laura Climenko. 1977. *Who Cares?* Toronto: Social Planning Council of Metropolitan Toronto.

Jones, Warren. 1982. "Loneliness and Social Behavior." Pp. 238–52 in *Loneliness*, edited by Letitia A. Peplau and Daniel Perlman. New York: Wiley.

Kadushin, Charles. 1983. "Mental Health and the Interpersonal Environment." *American Sociological Review* 48:199–210.

Kemper, Theodore D. 1972. "The Division of Labor: A Post-Durkheimian Analytical View." *American Sociological Review* 37:739–753.

Kessler, Ronald, and Jane McLeod. 1984. "Sex Differences in Vulnerability to Undesirable Life Events." *American Sociological Review* 49:620–631.

Kessler, Ronald, Richard Price, and Camille Wortman. 1985. "Social Factors in Psychopathology: Stress, Social Support and Coping Processes." *Annual Review of Psychology* 36:531–572.

Latané, Bibb, and John Darley. 1976. *Help in a Crisis: Bystander Response to an Emergency*. Morristown, NJ: General Learning Press.

Laumann, Edward, Peter Marsden, and David Prensky. 1983. "The Boundary Specification Problem in Network Analysis." Pp. 18–34 in *Applied Network Analysis*, edited by Ronald Burt and Michael Minor. Beverly Hills CA.: Sage.

Lazarsfeld, Paul, and Robert Merton. 1954. "Friendship as Social Process." Pp. 18–66 in *Freedom and Control in Modern Society*, edited by Morroe Berger, Theodore Abel, and Charles Page. New York: Octagon.

Lazarus, Richard, and Susan Folkman. 1984. *Stress, Appraisal and Coping*. New York: Springer.

Lee, Gary. 1980. "Kinship in the Seventies: A Decade Review of Research and Theory." *Journal of Marriage and the Family* 42:923–934.

Lin, Nan. 1997. "Social Resources and Social Capital." Working paper, Department of Sociology, Duke University, Durham, NC.

Lin, Nan, Paul Dayton, and Peter Greenwald. 1983. "Analyzing the Instrumental Use of Relations in the Context of Social Structure." Pp. 119–132 in *Applied Network Analysis*, edited by Ronald Burt and Michael Minor. Beverly Hills, CA.: Sage.

Lin, Nan, Alfred Dean, and Walter Ensel. 1986. *Social Support, Life Events and Depression*. Orlando FL: Academic Press.

Lin, Nan, and Mary Dumin. 1986. "Access to Occupations through Social Ties." *Social Networks* 8:365–386.

Lin, Nan, and Walter Ensel. 1989. "Life Stress and Health: Stressors and Resources." *American Sociological Review* 54:382–399.

Litwak, Eugene. 1985. *Helping the Elderly: The Complementary Roles of Informal Networks and Formal Systems.* New York: Guildford.

Lomnitz, Larissa Adler. 1977. *Networks and Marginality: Life in a Mexican Shantytown.* Translated by Cinna Lomnitz. New York: Academic Press.

Luxton, Meg. 1980. *More Than a Labour of Love.* Toronto: Women's Press.

Mancini, Jay, and Rosemary Blieszner. 1989. "Aging Parents and Adult Children." Journal *of Marriage and the Family* 51:275–290.

Marsden, Peter. 1987. "Core Discussions Networks of Americans." *American Sociological Review* 52:122–131.

Marsden, Peter. 1988. "Homogeneity in Confiding Relations." *Social Networks* 10:57–76.

Marsden, Peter, and Karen E Campbell. 1984. "Measuring Tie Strength." *Social Forces* 63:482–501.

Marsden, Peter, and Jeanne Hurlbert. 1988. "Social Resources and Mobility Outcomes." *Social Forces* 66:1038–1059.

Mogey, John. 1977. "Content of Relations with Relatives." Pp. 413–429 in *The Family Life Cycle in European Societies,* edited by Jeanne Cuisnier and Martine Segalen. Paris: Mouton.

Mueller, John, Karl Schuessler, and Herbert Costner. 1970. *Statistical Reasoning in Sociology.* 2d ed. Boston: Houghton Mifflin.

Nye, F. Ivan. 1976. *Role Structure and Analysis of the Family.* Beverly Hills, CA: Sage.

Parks, Malcolm, and Leona Eggert. 1991. "The Role of Social Context in the Dynamics of Personal Relationships." *Advances in Personal Relationships* 2:1–34.

Pearlin, Leonard. 1989. "The Sociological Study of Stress." *Journal of Health and Social Behavior* 30:241–256.

Perlman, Daniel, and Steve Duck, eds. 1987. *Intimate Relationships.* Newbury Park, CA.: Sage.

Perlman, Daniel, and Beverly Fehr. 1987. "The Development of Intimate Relationships." Pp. 13–42 in *Intimate Relationships,* edited by Daniel Perlman and Steve Duck. Newbury Park, CA: Sage.

Pescosolido, Bernice. 1991. "Illness Careers and Network Ties: A Conceptual Model of Utilization and Compliance." *Advances in Medical Sociology* 2:161–184.

Pescosolido, Bernice, and Sharon Georgianna. 1989. "Durkheim, Suicide, and Religion: Toward a Network Theory of Suicide." *American Sociological Review* 54:33–48.

Pitrou, Agnès. 1977. "Le Soutien Familial dans la Société Urbaine." *Revue Française de Sociologie* 18:47–84.

Retherford, Patricia, Gladys Hildreth, and Elizabeth Goldsmith. 1988. "Social Support and Resource Management of Unemployed Women." *Journal of Social Behavior and Personality* 3(4):191–204.

Riggio, Ronald, and Judy Zimmerman. 1991. "Social Skills and Interpersonal Relationships: Influences on Social Support and Support Seeking." *Advances in Personal Relationships* 2:133–155.

Riley, Dave, and Moncrieff Cochran. 1985. "Naturally Occurring Childrearing Advice for Fathers: Utilization of the Personal Social Network." *Journal of Marriage and the Family* 47:275–286.

Roberts, Bryan. 1978. *Cities of Peasants*. London: Edward Arnold.

Rook, Karen. 1984. "The Negative Side of Social Interaction: Impact on Psychological Well-being." *Journal of Personality and Social Psychology* 46:1097–1108.

Salloway, Jeffrey, and Patrick Dillon. 1973. "A Comparison of Family Networks and Friend Networks in Health Care Utilization." *Journal of Comparative Family Studies* 4:131–142.

Sapadin, Linda. 1988. "Friendship and Gender." *Journal of Social and Personal Relationships* 5:387–405.

Schweizer, Thomas, Michael Schnegg, and Susanne Berzborn. 1998. "Personal Networks and Social Support in a Multiethnic Community of Southern California." *Social Networks* 20:1–21.

Seeman, Teresa, and Lisa Berkman. 1988. "Structural Characteristics of Social Networks and Their Relationship with Social Support in the Elderly." *Social Science and Medicine* 26:737–749.

Sik, Endre. 1986. "Second Economy, Reciprocal Exchange of Labour and Social Stratification." Presented to the World Congress of Sociology, New Delhi, August.

Simmel, Georg. 1922. "The Web of Group Affiliations." Pp. 125–95 in *Conflict and the Web of Group Affiliations,* edited by Kurt Wolff. Glencoe, IL: Free Press.

Stack, Carol. 1974. *All Our Kin.* New York: Harper and Row.

Stokowski, Patricia, and Robert Lee. 1991. "The Influence of Social Network Ties on Recreation and Leisure." *Journal of Leisure Research* 2:95–113.

Suitor, J. Jill, Karl Pillemer, and Shirley Keeton Bohanon. 1993. "Sources of Support and Interpersonal Stress for Women's Midlife Transitions: The Case of Returning Students and Family Caregivers." Presented at the International Sunbelt Social Networks Conference, Tampa, February.

Sussman, Marvin, and Lee Burchinal. 1962. "Kin Family Network: Unheralded Structure in Current Conceptualizations of Family Functioning." *Marriage and Family Living* 24:231–240.

Tardy, Charles. 1985. "Social Support Measurement." *American Journal of Community Psychology* 13:187–202.

Taylor, Robert. 1985. "The Extended Family as a Source of Support to Elderly Blacks." *Gerontologist* 25:488–495.

Taylor, Robert. 1986. "Receipt of Support from Family among Black Americans." *Journal of Marriage and the Family* 48:67–77.

Thoits, Peggy. 1982. "Life Stress, Social Support, and Psychological Vulnerability." *Journal of Community Psychology* 10:341–362.

Thomas, Paula, and Jean Goodwin. 1985. "Effect of Social Support on Stress-Related Changes in Cholesterol Level, Uric Acid Level and Immune Function in an Elderly Sample." *American Journal of Psychiatry* 142:735–737.

Tijhuis, Marja. 1994. *Social Networks and Health.*" Utrecht, Neth.: Nivel.

Turner, R. Jay. 1981. "Social Support as a Contingency in Psychological Well-being." *Journal of Health and Social Behavior* 22:357–367.

Turner, R. Jay, and Franco Marino. 1994. "Social Support and Social Structure: A Descriptive Epidemiology." *Journal of Health and Social Behavior* 35:193–212.

Unger, Donald, and Douglas Powell. 1980. "Supporting Families Under Stress: The Role of Social Networks." *Family Relations* 29:566–574.

Van Tilburg, Theo. 1990. "The Size of the Supportive Network in Association with the Degree of Loneliness." Pp. 137–51 in *Social Network Research*, edited by Kees Knipscheer and Toni Antonucci. Amsterdam: Swets and Zeitlinger.

Vaux, Alan. 1985. "Variations in Social Support Associated with Gender, Ethnicity and Age." *Social Issues* 41:89–110.

Walder, Andrew. 1986. *Communist Neo-Traditionalism: Work and Authority in Chinese Industry.* Berkeley: University of California Press.

Wellman, Barry. 1979. "The Community Question." *American Journal of Sociology* 84:1201–1231.

Wellman, Barry. 1982. "Studying Personal Communities." Pp. 61–80 in *Social Structure and Network Analysis*, edited by Peter Marsden and Nan Lin. Beverly Hills, CA: Sage.

Wellman, Barry. 1988. "The Community Question Re-evaluated." Pp. 81–107 in *Power, Community and the City*, edited by Michael Peter Smith. New Brunswick, NJ: Transaction Books.

Wellman, Barry. 1990. "The Place of Kinfolk in Community Networks." *Marriage and Family Review* 15:195–228.

Wellman, Barry. 1992a. "Men in Networks: Private Communities, Domestic Friendships." Pp. 74–114 in *Men's Friendships*, edited by Peter Nardi. Newbury Park, CA: Sage.

Wellman, Barry. 1992b. "Which Types of Ties and Networks Give What Kinds of Social Support?" *Advances in Group Processes* 9:207–235.

Wellman, Barry. 1993. "An Egocentric Network Tale." *Social Networks* 17:423–436.

Wellman, Barry. 1994. "I was a Teenage Network Analyst: The Route from The Bronx to the Information Highway." *Connections* 17(2):28–45.

Wellman, Barry. 1996. "Are Personal Communities Local? A Dumptarian Reconsideration." *Social Networks* 18:347–354.

Wellman, Barry, Peter Carrington, and Alan Hall. 1988. "Networks as Personal Communities." Pp. 130–84 in *Social Structures: A Network Approach*, edited by Barry Wellman and S. D. Berkowitz. Cambridge: Cambridge University Press.

Wellman, Barry, and Barry Leighton. 1979. "Networks, Neighborhoods and Communities." *Urban Affairs Quarterly* 14:363–390.

Wellman, Barry, and David Tindall. 1993. "Reach Out and Touch Some Bodies: How Social Networks Connect Telephone Networks." Pp. 63–93 in *Progress in Communication Sciences*, edited by William Richards, Jr. and George Barnett. Norwood, NJ: Ablex.

Wellman, Barry, Renita Wong, David Tindall, and Nancy Nazer. 1997. "A Decade of Network Change: Turnover, Mobility and Stability." *Social Networks* 19:27–51.

Wellman, Barry, and Scot Wortley. 1989. "Brothers' Keepers: Situating Kinship Relations in Broader Networks of Social Support." *Sociological Perspectives* 32:273–306.

Wellman, Barry, and Scot Wortley. 1990. "Different Strokes from Different Folks: Community Ties and Social Support." *American Journal of Sociology* 96:558–88.

Wellman, Beverly. 1995. "Lay Referral Networks: Using Conventional Medicine and Alternative Therapies for Low Back Pain." *Sociology of Health Care* 12:213–238.

Wellman, Beverly, and Barry Wellman. 1992. "Domestic Affairs and Network Relations." *Journal of Social and Personal Relationships* 9:385–409.

Williams, R. G. A. 1981. "The Art of Migration: The Preservation of Kinship and Friendship by Londoners During a History of Movement." *Sociological Review* 29:621–647.

Willmott, Peter. 1987. *Friendship Networks and Social Support*. London: Policy Studies Institute.

Willmott, Peter. 1989. *Community Initiatives: Patterns and Prospects*. London: Policy Studies Institute.

Woolfolk, Robert, and Paul Lehrer, eds. 1995. *Principles and Practices of Stress Management*. 2d ed. New York: Guilford.

3

Neighbor Networks of Black and White Americans

Barrett A. Lee and Karen E. Campbell

Do African-Americans neighbor differently than white Americans? In posing this research question, we address two issues of importance to social scientists. The first concerns the accuracy of a thesis popularized by Fischer (1982; Fischer et al. 1977) and Wellman (1979; Wellman and Leighton 1979), that urbanites' networks of supportive relationships fall largely outside the boundaries of their immediate neighborhoods (see also Webber 1963). According to Fischer and Wellman, advances in transportation and communications have "liberated community," making spatial proximity less relevant than in the past. We contend, however, that most people still establish and maintain ties with their neighbors and that such ties form significant parts of their total personal networks. The "folks next door" not only provide routine assistance but, as informal agents of control, are often influential in socializing children, promoting local safety, and stimulating home improvement activity (Galster and Hesser 1982; Sampson and Groves 1989; Taub, Taylor, and Dunham 1984). In short, there is good reason to believe that proximity continues to shape the social networks of urban residents.

The second issue raised by our research is about the nature of black social life in the contemporary United States. Proponents of the "new disorganization" perspective claim that public policies, demographic and economic shifts, and family breakdown have undermined cohesion among African-Americans in a variety of domains, including inner-city "underclass" neighborhoods (Moynihan 1986; Murray 1984; Wilson 1987). Participating in the social networks of these neighborhoods may lead to negative behavioral outcomes (such as teen pregnancy, poor school performance, criminal activity) and, ultimately, to reduced life chances (Jencks and Mayer 1990). Yet other analysts see local networks as valuable mechanisms through which members of minority groups can obtain resources for coping with and overcoming difficulties. This positive view is consistent with the role played by enclaves in the American urban experience of nonblack ethnic minorities (Massey 1985; Portes and Manning 1986). It also receives backing from several studies of neighboring.

By comparing the local social relationships of black and white Americans, we seek to broaden the debate over the positive and disorganization perspectives while offering a modest corrective to the aspatial community thesis of Fischer and Wellman. We proceed in several steps. First, we introduce compression, avoidance, and composition theories, each of which offers a plausible but distinct explanation for racial differences in neighboring. Second, we recast the three theories in network analytic terms and test them using data from a Nashville, Tennessee, survey. Finally, we go beyond neighborhood limits to examine the place that local ties occupy in the overall networks of Nashvillians.

Compression, Avoidance, and Composition Theories

Compression theory predicts that black city-dwellers should be more involved with neighbors than are whites, and in a greater variety of ways. This prediction arises from the many constraints historically encountered by African-Americans in their attempts to participate in the wider society (Warren 1975, 1981). Discrimination in housing, employment, education, and other institutions has "compressed" black networks territorially as well as racially. Low incomes have further fueled the compression process as limited access to transportation makes long-distance relationships hard to sustain. Residential segregation is the rule even among higher-status blacks with the financial means to move away from impoverished, all-black areas (Denton and Massey 1988). According to compression theory, these factors strengthen the importance of the neighborhood as an interactional arena for blacks, who have fewer options outside its borders than do whites. Thus, necessity rather than choice explains blacks' greater reliance on neighbors for fellowship, information, and support.[1]

Avoidance theory, by contrast, predicts that African-American neighborhoods should be more socially disorganized. It contends that the population mix of these areas discourages interaction with neighbors. As used here, "avoidance" refers only to the local context and does not mean sparse or weak total networks, since ties to people who live farther away may compensate for an absence of neighborhood ties. One version of avoidance theory blames the lack of black contact with neighbors on the demographic homogeneity that is found in public housing projects and other exclusively low-income settings. Mutual distrust and fear of crime presumably lead residents to keep to themselves or, at most, to establish tentative and cautious ties (Merry 1981; Rainwater 1970; Suttles 1968; Wilson 1987).

A second version of avoidance theory emphasizes the internal heterogeneity of African-American neighborhoods (Hannerz 1969; Massey, Condran, and Denton 1987). When neighbors differ in socioeconomic status and lifestyle, they have fewer things in common and are less able to know what to expect from each other. Interestingly, Warren admits the possibility of black residential heterogeneity in his definition of compression—"the compacting of many status groups in a restricted physical environment" (1975, p. 26)—although he does not foresee any negative impact on neighboring. Avoidance theory, however, suggests otherwise. Both its homogeneity and heterogeneity variants indicate that, compared to whites, blacks should be at a disadvantage in neighbor relations because of the perceived unpredictability of nearby residents.

Of course, blacks and whites may differ in a variety of nonracial ways that also can affect neighboring. Gans (1962) has argued, for example, that social class rather than ethnic identity has the decisive effect on informal relations, but that the effect is obscured by the correlation between class and ethnicity (see also Yancey, Ericksen, and Juliani 1976) Similarly, if members of one racial group are more residentially stable or more likely to own their homes than members of another group, then perhaps these local investments, and not race per se, account for variation in neighboring behavior. Such reasoning is central to a third, *composition theory*, which predicts that apparent racial differences in neighboring should disappear after other attributes of black and white urbanites have been controlled. Support for composition theory would challenge compression and avoidance theories, implying that factors besides race influence social participation and the extent to which neighborhoods are organized.

From Neighboring to Networks

The theories under examination fail to spell out anything more precise than an overall white or black advantage. This is hardly surprising in light of the conceptual and empirical treatment of neighboring by sociologists. With few exceptions, the phenomenon has been crudely studied with a handful of survey questions that measure levels of acquaintanceship and contact but little else. Network analysis provides useful tools to overcome these deficiencies. It allows us to conceive of neighboring structurally, as behavior that flows through the ties between a focal individual (or "ego") and particular residents ("alters") of his or her neighborhood.

Once we make this fundamental shift toward a more structural con-
ceptualization, the ties themselves become of primary concern. Taken as
a complete set or, in our terminology, as a neighbor network, they vary
along at least seven dimensions germane to racial variation:

1. *Network size* is simply the number of neighbors with whom a
   person reports some degree of involvement.
2. *Spatial proximity* acknowledges that two neighbor networks of
   equal size may have different consequences for their respective
   egos, depending on the nearness of alters.
3. *Contact frequency*, the first of three aspects of tie strength to be
   considered, reflects how often ties to neighbors are activated.[2]
4. The *intimacy* of these ties, as perceived by ego, also taps the
   strength dimension.
5. So does the *duration* of ties, or how long a person has known his
   or her neighbors.
6. *Content* refers to what is obtained via neighbor ties. Such ties
   may provide conversation, a night out on the town, or other
   inherently fulfilling social benefits, or they may be used for
   instrumental purposes, such as obtaining information or
   assistance.
7. *Multiplexity* is defined as the extent to which ties vary in the
   number of contents. Some neighbors offer many resources,
   others only a few specific ones.

Because the theories of interest to us do not portray neighboring explicitly in terms of network analytic concepts, hypotheses about racial
differences on these seven dimensions must be inferred rather than rigorously deduced. Compression theory, which assigns neighborhood a central position in black social life, predicts that blacks' neighbor networks
should be larger and more spatially concentrated than whites' are, and
that the ties comprising blacks' networks should be more intimate and
longer lasting. Blacks are also hypothesized to use their ties more often,
for both social and instrumental purposes. Hence, they should have access to a wider variety of resources from their neighbors than do whites.

The hypotheses yielded by avoidance theory are opposed on every dimension to those from compression theory. If African-Americans are suspicious, and sometimes even afraid, of neighbors whom they perceive as
unpredictable, their networks should suffer in comparison to whites'. In
particular, avoidance theory suggests that blacks' neighbor networks
should be relatively sparse and spread out, consisting of distant, transitory, specialized ties that are infrequently activated. Finally, no racial dif-

ferences are predicted by compositional theory on any of the dimensions, especially after other relevant variables have been controlled.

Previous Research

Previous research provides little help in evaluating compression, avoidance, and composition theories. Ethnographies of African-American communities, for example, do not make systematic comparisons with white communities, and they emphasize family and peer group relations to the neglect of neighboring. These design features could reflect the operation of spatial constraints, which presumably increase the chances that blacks living near one another are kin or friends (Warren 1975). Such intimates are thought to be of greater value than persons who are "just neighbors." Indeed, some ethnographers (Stack 1974; Uehara 1990; Valentine 1978) support Warren's compression argument by asserting that the ties between black network members are conduits of exchange essential for survival in deprived circumstances.

However, students of "street-corner" groups (Anderson 1976; Liebow 1967) underscore the fluid, shifting character of these ties, which may be short on material aid but which still promote solidarity through identity management and status negotiation. Other researchers, including Merry (1981) and Rainwater (1970), take a more extreme position. In line with avoidance theory, they have documented the truncated social relations born of suspicion and fear among the poorest ghetto inhabitants.

The black ethnography literature does not apply network analysis in a formal sense; it uses network imagery without its measures. To date, surveys have been the most popular way to actually measure networks. The only national survey in the U.S. that includes fairly precise network indicators, the 1985 General Social Survey, shows that African-Americans have smaller "core discussion" networks than whites. Unfortunately, respondents were not asked to designate the geographic location of their discussion partners (Marsden 1987). At the subnational level, Fischer (1982) and Wellman (1979, 1988) describe the neighborhood portions of personal networks, but their Northern California and Toronto studies do not report about black neighborhoods.[3]

Ironically, when network investigators do survey blacks, they frequently leave out whites, thereby perpetuating the difficulties associated with sample homogeneity. Feagin's (1970) study of Boston ghetto housewives is illustrative. He found the housewives' friendship networks to be spatially "encapsulated," with nearby ties utilized often. Another blacks-only analysis (Oliver 1988) examines characteristics of personal networks across three Los Angeles neighborhoods of varying socioeconomic status.

Although the networks of respondents from all three neighborhoods are large and dense, they differ in localization: Those of residents in the lowest-income area (Watts) contain the highest percentage of neighboring ties. Moreover, the multistrandedness of the ties comprising these networks suggests that, for some blacks, neighbor relations rest on kinship and friendship foundations (for further discussion of neighbor-kin overlap, see Logan and Spitze 1994). Thus, Oliver's results appear true to the spirit, if not to the exact predictions, of parts of both compression and composition theories.

Only two network surveys examine the ties that black and white Americans have with their neighbors. In the first, interviews with 104 women in four Kansas City neighborhoods reveal no significant racial differences in the number of neighbors known or in other network attributes, consistent with composition theory (Greenbaum and Greenbaum 1985). However, the racial mix of an area does influence the spatial distribution of neighbor ties: The more heterogeneous the population, the more proximate networks tend to be. The second survey measured network localization for over 1,900 New York City dwellers (Kadushin and Jones 1992). Each respondent could name up to four people with whom he or she "discusses important matters." The researchers define the network as local if 50% or more of its members live in the respondent's neighborhood and if they all know one another. As predicted by the avoidance perspective, fewer black than white New Yorkers have local networks.

Conventional neighboring studies are as ambiguous as those conducted by network analysts, offering mixed support for the three theories (for a review, see Lee, Campbell, and Miller 1991). Against the backdrop of these studies, the mission of our inquiry becomes clear. Using a single sample, we need to compare directly black and white neighbor networks on multiple dimensions.

The Nashville Scene

Our data come from a 1988 survey of Nashville, Tennessee, residents. Though best known as the capital of country music, Nashville is now the twenty-sixth largest city in the U.S., with a metropolitan population of roughly one million. Like other "New South" urban centers, it boasts a diversified, service-oriented economy in which government, education, finance, publishing, health care, entertainment, and tourism all generate a significant number of jobs. Nashville also is reasonably typical of cities elsewhere in the nation, consistently falling in the middle of rankings on a variety of demographic and housing characteristics.[4]

Since the city's founding in 1780, African-Americans have grown in presence. Their numbers increased gradually at first, then surged during and after the Civil War as former slaves and sharecroppers responded to Nashville's lure of opportunity (Doyle 1985a). Many of the newcomers congregated in notorious slums like Black Bottom and Hell's Half Acre. By the late 1880s, a prosperous black bourgeoisie had emerged, living in a corridor that extended west from the central business district to Fisk University. Although the residential separation of blacks from whites would not become marked until after World War I,[5] legal segregation in schools, churches, hospitals, restaurants, and public transportation was the norm from the mid–nineteenth through the mid–twentieth century. The eventual dismantling of this apartheid system vaulted Nashville to the forefront of the Civil Rights movement: It was the first Southern city to desegregate public facilities with a minimum of violence (Doyle 1985b). Much of the credit for that relatively peaceful transition—and for subsequent accomplishments in race relations—belongs to a cadre of local black leaders long known for their political savvy (Rabinowitz 1978).

Despite such successes, Nashville's black population remains socially and economically disadvantaged. Data from the 1990 U.S. census yield a familiar profile. Compared to their white counterparts, local black residents are less likely to be married, to have graduated from high school, and to own their homes. They also are over twice as likely to be unemployed and three times as likely to live in poverty, receiving an annual household income only 59% that of whites. The high level of black-white residential segregation in Nashville (index of dissimilarity = 70) closely approximates the averages calculated for large samples of metropolitan areas (Farley and Frey 1994; Massey and Denton 1987). In light of these patterns, it seems safe to conclude that the nature of black and white Nashvillians' neighbor networks cannot be attributed to an unusual racial context.

South Nashville, the setting for our survey, is wedged between the central business district on the north and interstate freeways on the east and west. It contains several colleges and universities, many of the city's major commercial areas (including Music Row), and approximately two-fifths of the total county population of just over a half-million people. The South Nashville sector juxtaposes affluent, suburban communities of newer, better-quality housing with more traditional inner-city neighborhoods. Census tracts vary widely in racial composition (from 0.3% to 99% black), owner-occupancy (from 9% to 95%), and most other attributes. On a meandering drive through the sector, one would encounter the mansions of an exclusive "silk-stocking" enclave (complete with steeplechase course and polo field), older neighborhoods settled at or before the turn of the century (some solidly working class and some gentrified), and a notorious drug-dealing locale that the mayor symbolically "cleaned up" with a bulldozer a few years ago. Thus, the South Nashville sector covers the range of types of neighborhoods found throughout the city.

The Survey

Our research focused on 81 partial face blocks or "micro-neighborhoods" in South Nashville. Each site is made up of 10 adjacent housing units, five on either side of the street. The sites were selected systematically from a pool of 4,515 partial face blocks stratified by racial composition, tenure mix, and income level (see Lee, Campbell, and Miller 1991 for further details). All people at least thirteen years old living in the 81 micro-neighborhoods were invited to participate in the survey. While such participation could take several forms, the most common was to fill out a questionnaire and complete an hour-long interview. Some people who did not do the full interview did a short "doorstep" version that included key items from the main survey instruments. At the household level, the response rate was 62%: 514 of the 823 households in the 81 sites had one or more members who completed a questionnaire or interview. At the individual level, 994 (or 89%) of the 1,128 eligible people in the participating households took part in the study.

We gathered data on neighbor networks in a series of steps (see Campbell and Lee 1991). During the full interview, respondents were asked (1) which of the residents in the nearest nine or ten houses they knew by name, (2) which of those named residents they had talked with for a minimum of ten minutes in the preceding six months, and (3) which they had visited at home during the same period. After repeating these network-generator questions for the broader neighborhood, we obtained detailed information only about the set of alters identified as "active" ties (the neighbors known by name with whom respondents had recently talked or visited). The follow-up items covered alters' social and demographic attributes, characteristics of the ego-alter relationship, and types of exchanges that had taken place.[6] Both short- and full-interview participants marked the location of their neighbors' homes on a map of the face block and surrounding area.

For this analysis, 18 measures of 7 specific network dimensions have been developed by aggregating information about neighbor ties for each respondent (Table 3.1).[7] Few strong statistical associations exist between measures representing distinct dimensions (only three between-dimension correlations exceed 0.3). There is, however, considerable overlap within dimensions: For proximity, frequency, duration, and multiplexity, the mean intracategory r is greater than 0.6. Nevertheless, we believe that even the most redundant measures get at somewhat different aspects of their respective network dimensions and, thus, have retained all 18 for the initial portion of the analysis.

Results

Basic Differences

How similar are the neighbor networks of black and white Americans? Though not dramatic in magnitude, statistically significant differences are apparent for both measures of network proximity and one measure of size (Table 3.1). Consistent with compression theory, we find that blacks live nearer to their neighbors than do whites. Yet, in line with avoidance theory, blacks know fewer of their neighbors by name. A cleaner pattern emerges for strength of neighboring (panels 3 through 5). Blacks have more intimate and longer-standing ties to their neighbors, and they activate them more often (approximately 80 more times per year). This pattern generally supports compression theory, with a notable exception: Even though the high degree of spatial concentration supposedly experienced by blacks should entail a greater number of kin in their local networks, neighbors are no more likely to be kin among blacks than among whites.

Compression theory also suggests that blacks should benefit more from the content of their neighbor ties. In terms of *socializing*, black Nashvillians have gone to dinner or done something outside the neighborhood with an average of 13% of their neighbors during the last six months. They have turned to similarly modest proportions of neighbors for each of four types of *routine help*: borrowing something small such as a cup of sugar or a tool (16%); receiving assistance in a minor emergency, such as when a telephone is out of order (12%); getting a hand with home repairs or daily chores (13%); and obtaining needed information, such as where to vote (16%). They also have sought *special help* in a selective fashion, drawing on an average of 15% of their active ties to discuss a personal matter, 9% for child-care duties, and 7% for help with a neighborhood problem. The major departure from selectivity is the higher percentage of neighbors (34%) whom black respondents have asked to watch their homes while they were away.[8]

As our summary measures of the socializing, routine help, and special help items indicate, the content and multiplexity of neighbor relations vary little by race (bottom panels of Table 3.1). The absence of significant racial differences lends credibility to the composition perspective.[9] Yet it is somewhat surprising in view of the contrasts just noted. Given the greater strength of black ties, we might expect them to be used for multiple purposes, as predicted by compression theory. In fact, blacks do turn

TABLE 3.1 Mean Differences Between Black and White Neighbor Networks

Network Trait/Measure	Mean on Network Measure for			Significance of Racial Difference[a]	Racial Group with Largest Mean	N of Respondents[b]
	Total	Black Sample	White Sample			
Size						
N of neighbors known by name	14.8	13.2	15.3	.05	W	781
N of neighbors talked/visited with[c]	7.5	7.3	7.6	NS	W	758
% of neighbors talked/visited with[c]	51.4	54.2	50.5	NS	B	758
Proximity						
Mean proximity of neighbors[d]	.7	.6	.7	.01	B	752
% of neighbors on face block	87.5	93.8	85.6	.001	B	752
Frequency[e]						
Mean N of contacts with neighbors[f]	114.6	174.6	96.7	.001	B	596
% of neighbors contacted 2+ times per month	75.3	89.0	71.2	.001	B	596
Intimacy[e]						
Mean closeness to neighbors[g]	1.2	1.5	1.2	.001	B	593
% of neighbors judged close/very close	30.8	40.6	27.8	.001	B	593
% of neighbors who are kin	1.3	1.3	1.3	NS	–	593
Duration[e]						
Mean N of years neighbors known	11.7	15.5	10.6	.001	B	595
% of neighbors known 10+ years	44.6	60.9	39.7	.001	B	595
Content[e]						
% of neighbors socialized with[h]	14.3	13.1	14.6	NS	W	596
% of neighbors giving routine help[i]	36.0	33.3	36.8	NS	W	596
% of neighbors giving special help[j]	41.3	44.2	40.4	NS	B	596

(continues)

TABLE 3.1 *(continued)*

Network Trait/Measure	Mean on Network Measure For			Significance of Racial Difference[a]	Racial Group with Largest Mean	N of Respondents[b]
	Total	Black Sample	White Sample			
Multiplexity[e]						
Mean N of contents per neighbor[k]	1.3	1.4	1.3	NS	B	596
% of neighbors providing 2+ contents[k]	34.1	35.8	33.5	NS	B	596
N of contents from all neighbors[k]	3.4	3.4	3.4	NS	–	596

NS = Not significant

[a]Based on t-test using separate variance estimation.

[b]For Ns above 700, sample composition is 24% black; for Ns below 600, 23% black.

[c]Limited to respondents who knew 1+ neighbors by name; refers to contacts during past 6 months.

[d]0 = neighbor beyond full face block, 1 = on full face block, 2 = on study partial face block, 3 = on respondent's partial face block.

[e]Limited to respondents who talked/visited with 1+ neighbors during past 6 months.

[f]Refers to contacts during past year.

[g]0 = neighbor an acquaintance, 1 = friend, 2 = close friend, 3 = very close friend, 4 = kin.

[h]Refers to social activity outside neighborhood during past 6 months.

[i]Includes lending something small, helping with minor emergency, giving hand with repairs/chores, and providing information; refers to past 6 months.

[j]Includes watching home when respondent away, discussing personal matters, helping with neighborhood problem, and caring for children; refers to past 6 months.

[k]0–9 contents possible; see notes h–j for specific types.

to a higher percentage of their neighbors for special help, and they get more types of help from their neighbors. However, the differences are slight, and levels of white socializing and routine assistance actually exceed those of blacks.

Larger racial differences are evident in the makeup of Nashvillians' neighbor networks. For African-American respondents, 9 out of 10 ties are to black neighbors while less than 2% of white ties are to black neighbors (see also Blackwell and Hart 1982,). The people with whom blacks maintain local relations tend to be older and less educated than those in whites' networks. Moreover, higher percentages of blacks' neighbors are unmarried and either unemployed or not in the labor force.

Such attributes of their neighbors have mixed implications for the benefits that blacks derive from their networks. On the positive side, blacks' neighbors may be physically present much of the time and more available to engage in home-watching, child-care, and other locality-based activities. But the lower socioeconomic status of these neighbors means that they probably can provide only limited access to resources outside the neighborhood (Chapter 4 in this volume).

Multivariate Analysis

The differences reported thus far are a weak test of the avoidance and compression perspectives because they fail to consider nonracial sources of variation in black and white neighbor networks. We use multiple regression to examine four sets of potential causal factors.

Individual Characteristics. Composition theory suggests that if blacks and whites differ in characteristics such as length of residence or the presence of children, then these differences could be responsible for the apparent effects of race on neighboring. To control for this possibility, we have selected ten individual-level antecedents of neighboring identified by previous studies (for citations, see Campbell and Lee 1990, 1992). Such studies propose that participation in neighbor networks depends on locality investments (tapped by housing tenure, length of residence, and birthplace), nurturing duties (gender, presence of children), status resources (education, income), need for support (age), and involvement in competing social relations (marital status, employment status).

Population Mix. Because African-Americans are more apt to live among people they regard as dangerous or unpredictable, avoidance theory holds that the mix of the local population should affect neighboring. Hence, our regressions incorporate dummy variables reflecting the racial, income, and tenure characteristics of respondents' neighborhoods.

We use these variables to evaluate the homogeneity and heterogeneity versions of avoidance theory. Population mix also is operationalized in a more subjective way. Respondents were asked how much their neighbors were like them with respect to race and a variety of other characteristics.[10] We constructed a scale from these questions that taps the perceived dissimilarity or heterogeneity of neighbors.

Spatial Accessibility. Do differences between black and white neighborhoods in physical design and usage affect the accessibility of neighbors? The influence of accessibility on social networks has been asserted but little studied (for exceptions, see Athanasiou and Yoshioka 1973; Caplow and Forman 1955; Whyte 1956). To correct this, our analysis includes an environmental conduciveness scale indicating how many of 18 physical characteristics that may encourage neighborly interaction (front sidewalk, shared driveway, cul-de-sac, etc.) are present for the respondent's house, lot, or face block.[11] We also recorded the number of the five nearest neighbors' front doors visible from the respondent's own front door, and we created an outdoor activities scale measuring the number of times during the last week of good weather that the respondent sat on his or her porch or ate a meal outside.

Neighborhood Perception. Hunter's research on Chicago's "symbolic communities" found that for African-Americans (relative to whites), "the local area is defined as a much smaller social and spatial organization— the street, the block, or the housing project . . . " (1974, p. 104). At issue is whether our methodological procedures (which emphasize the face block) conform more closely to black than white perceptions of the salient domain for neighbor relations, inadvertently distorting the results. Given the larger number of neighbors known by white Nashvillians (see Table 3.1), the likelihood of such a distortion seems doubtful. Nevertheless, an interview question about perceived neighborhood size is included in our analysis.

Neighboring. To assess the influence of individual characteristics, population mix, spatial accessibility, and neighborhood perception on neighboring, we have chosen seven measures from Table 3.1 as dependent variables. Considerations of economy and breadth limit us to a single measure per dimension that corresponds well to the underlying concept (size, intimacy, etc.) and that has a good statistical distribution. The unstandardized regression coefficients in the top panel of Table 3.2 show that race significantly affects several dimensions of networks, always in the direction forecast by compression theory. Blacks have more spatially proximate ties when numerous other factors are controlled. Blacks' ties

TABLE 3.2 Equations from Neighbor Network Regressions[a]

Predictor	% of Neighbors Known by Name (1)	% of Neighbors on Face Block (2)	Mean N of Contacts with Neighbors (3)	Mean Closeness to Neighbors (4)	Mean N of Years Neighbors Known (5)	% of Neighbors Giving Special Help (6)	% of Neighbors Providing 2+ Contents (7)
Race (1 = black)	.300 (1.756)	8.469* (3.431)	72.299*** (15.151)	.308* (.129)	5.617*** (1.116)	-3.569 (5.944)	-1.948 (5.394)
Gender (1 = female)	3.615*** (.920)	-3.379 (1.805)	-5.939 (7.809)	-.011 (.066)	-.570 (.572)	-.609 (3.063)	-.468 (2.780)
Age (years)	-.040 (.045)	.026 (.087)	.951* (.388)	-.003 (.003)	.062* (.028)	-.356* (.152)	-.327* (.138)
Marital status (1 = married)[b]	2.554* (1.164)	-.358 (2.280)	-8.147 (10.117)	-.013 (.086)	.447 (.743)	.421 (3.969)	-.740 (3.602)
Children present (1 = yes)[c]	2.666* (1.033)	-3.655 (2.040)	6.930 (8.789)	-.028 (.075)	-.928 (.645)	-2.872 (3.448)	-4.633 (3.129)
Education (school years completed)	.374* (.190)	-.216 (.371)	-7.247*** (1.635)	-.052*** (.014)	-.657*** (.120)	-.588 (.641)	.211 (.582)
Household income (dollars)[e]	4.928* L5 (2.181) L5	-4.345 L5 (4.259) L5	-3.453 L4 (1.853) L4	-6.252 L7 (1.570) L6	1.887 L5 (1.359) L5	5.233 L5 (7.269) L5	-3.688 L5 (6.597) L5
Employment status (1 = employed)[e]	.316 (1.042)	-4.069* (2.055)	-4.409 (8.875)	-.029 (.075)	.917 (.652)	-3.568 (3.481)	-2.384 (3.160)
Housing tenure (1 = own)	1.431 (1.302)	3.858 (2.567)	-3.481 (11.204)	-.186 (.095)	-1.086 (.823)	6.499 (4.395)	4.328 (3.989)
Length of residence in neighborhood (years)	.344*** (.055)	-.111 (.108)	-1.147* (.485)	.015*** (.004)	.408*** (.036)	-.134 (.190)	-.409* (.173)

(continues)

TABLE 3.2 (continued)

Predictor	% of Neighbors Known by Name (1)	% of Neighbors on Face Block (2)	Mean N of Contacts with Neighbors (3)	Mean Closeness to Neighbors (4)	Mean N of Years Neighbors Known (5)	% of Neighbors Giving Special Help (6)	% of Neighbors Providing 2+ Contents (7)
Birthplace (1 = Nashville)	.107 (.970)	-2.222 (1.910)	9.727 (8.205)	.018 (.070)	1.465* (.603)	-7.044* (3.220)	-2.991 (2.922)
Mixed racial stratum (1 = yes)f	2.554 (1.339)	3.876 (2.613)	-.211 (11.363)	.019 (.096)	-2.739** (.833)	1.648 (4.458)	2.355 (4.046)
Black racial stratum (1 = yes)f	1.401 (2.221)	2.265 (4.376)	-25.031 (19.772)	-.119 (.168)	-1.523 (1.454)	7.973 (7.757)	11.805 (7.040)
Mixed tenure stratum (1 = yes)f	1.907 (1.281)	9.280*** (2.537)	-27.576* (10.996)	-.129 (.093)	.950 (.808)	-.524 (4.314)	-2.337 (3.915)
Owner tenure stratum (1 = yes)f	.381 (1.553)	12.637*** (3.070)	-23.808 (13.308)	-.121 (.113)	.624 (.977)	-.860 (5.221)	.917 (4.738)
Middle income stratum (1 = yes)f	2.046 (1.314)	-2.658 (2.621)	15.090 (11.345)	-.052 (.097)	-.123 (.832)	-9.790* (4.451)	-2.374 (4.039)
High income stratum (1 = yes)f	3.497* (1.693)	-1.722 (3.383)	1.645 (14.460)	-.137 (.122)	-2.634* (1.060)	-13.238* (5.672)	-1.571 (5.148)
Perceived neighbor dissimilarityg	-.594*** (.152)	.064 (.302)	-1.801 (1.304)	-.047*** (.011)	-.135 (.096)	-.254 (.512)	-.470 (.464)
Environmental conducivenessh	.070 (.221)	.398 (.432)	2.503 (1.852)	-.015 (.016)	-.038 (.136)	-.424 (.726)	-.467 (.659)
N of visible front doorsi	-.604 (.351)	.376 (.689)	.917 (2.984)	-.046 (.025)	-.406 (.219)	.934 (1.170)	.762 (1.062)
N of outdoor activitiesj	.201 (.126)	.332 (.247)	1.018 (1.079)	-7.547 L4 (.009)	.014 (.079)	.026 (.423)	.121 (.384)

(continues)

TABLE 3.2   (continued)

Predictor	% of Neighbors Known by Name (1)	% of Neighbors on Face Block (2)	Mean N of Contacts with Neighbors (3)	Mean Closeness to Neighbors (4)	Mean N of Years Neighbors Known (5)	% of Neighbors Giving Special Help (6)	% of Neighbors Providing 2+ Contents (7)
Neighborhood size (blocks)^k	.177	-1.142	-1.965	-.026	.410	.130	.723
	(.355)	(.692)	(3.059)	(.026)	(.224)	(1.200)	(1.089)
Intercept	.540	80.534	190.688	2.911	13.077	79.442	61.739
R^2	.266***	.121***	.275***	.170***	.559***	.062	.075*
N of respondents	515	500	475	473	474	475	475

[a]Unstandardized coefficient on first line, standard error on second line (in parentheses) for each predictor. L after coefficient or standard error indicates number of places to left that decimal should be moved.

[b]Currently married and living with spouse.

[c]Children < 18 years living in parental household.

[d]From all sources, for year prior to survey.

[e]Employed full-time or part-time.

[f]Dummy variables entered for race, tenure, and income strata of respondent's block group, with white, rental, and low-income strata serving as reference categories; see Lee et al. (1991) for further details.

[g]Dissimilarity measured by additive index with range 0–16; see text and note 10 for further details.

[h]Conduciveness measured by additive index with range 0–18; see text and note 11 for further details.

[i]N of 5 nearest neighbors' front doors visible from respondent's front door.

[j]N of times respondent sat on porch or ate meal outside during last week of good weather.

[k]As perceived by respondent; expressed in logarithmic form.

* / ** / *** Value of t or F significant at .05, .01, or .001 level.

also are stronger in terms of contact frequency, perceived closeness (intimacy), and duration. One change from Table 3.1 is that the association between race and number of neighbors known by name—which favors whites when based on the mean difference alone—disappears with the addition of controls. This change fits the reasoning behind the composition perspective, as does the continued absence of racial differences in the content and multiplexity of neighbor ties.

Of course, race is not the sole determinant of Nashvillians' neighborly relations. Length of residence achieves significance in five of the seven equations in Table 3.2, and education and age in four each. The signs for these predictors shift from one dependent variable to the next, sometimes in intriguing ways. For example, longer residence in an area increases both the number of neighbors known by name and the closeness of ties to them, yet it decreases the frequency with which such ties are used. Similarly, ties to neighbors increase in duration but narrow in content with age. The principal effect of education is to lessen tie strength (frequency, closeness, duration), although well-educated people do know a larger number of neighbors.

Only two predictors that are not individual characteristics have more than a single significant effect. Net of other controls (including household income), residents of high-income neighborhoods are acquainted with more of their neighbors than are their counterparts in low- and middle-income areas. However, the former have known their neighbors for a shorter time and are less likely to count on them for special help. Finally, when neighbors are perceived as dissimilar, people tend to know fewer of them by name and to feel less close to them.

Despite the effects of these nonracial factors on neighbor networks, race remains the most important variable. In the four equations in Table 3.2 in which race is significant, it has the largest standardized regression coefficient for the frequency-of-contact dimension, the second largest for duration, the third largest for proximity, and the fourth largest for closeness. This consistent showing confirms that black-white differences cannot easily be explained away by controlling for other variables. Simply put, the influence of race is robust.

The influence of race also appears to be additive. In an extension of the regression analysis, we searched for evidence of interactions between race and other predictors, with little success. Lacking theoretical leads about the nature of such interactions, we used a "blanket" approach, subdividing the sample racially and then re-estimating the regression equations from Table 3.2 separately for black and white subsamples. The subdivision procedure yields a broadly similar pattern of findings for the two groups. In fact, not a single site or respondent attribute significantly influences a network dimension in one direction for one racial group and in the opposite direction for the other in any equation.

On intuitive grounds, the most likely interaction effect to anticipate involves race as an individual and a neighborhood characteristic. Blacks
and whites who live in racially mixed areas should have different kinds
of neighbor networks than those in homogeneous areas. Yet Table 3.3
shows that this is not the case. Comparing subsamples of respondents
from black, white, and mixed neighborhoods, the networks of African-
Americans residing in either black or mixed areas closely resemble each
other on most measures, as do the networks of whites residing in either
white or mixed areas.[12] And when black and white occupants of the
mixed neighborhoods are compared, a familiar pattern of significant
black advantages in tie proximity and strength reappears. Moreover,
these advantages are based on within-race relationships. Despite the potential for interracial contact in mixed areas, over 80% of the ties of black
residents are to black neighbors, while over 95% of the ties of whites in
mixed areas are to white neighbors.

Neighbors in Context

How do neighbors fit into the larger social networks of black and white
Nashvillians? The compression argument, in particular, predicts that the
same forces responsible for heavier neighboring among blacks should result in fewer relationships that extend beyond the neighborhood. Fortunately, our study provides data on ties to people outside as well as inside
neighborhood boundaries. To construct total (i.e., spatially uncon-
strained) *support networks*, we asked respondents to whom they would
turn for a ride (to the post office, store, or work), help in finding a job, a
large loan, care of the family if the respondent was ill, and guidance in
making an important decision. The number of helpers reported ranges
from 0 to 20. The mean of 5.4 is comparable to the size of "core" or intimate networks in previous studies (Campbell and Lee 1991). About one-
fifth of helpers in these networks live in the respondents' neighborhoods
(Table 3.4). However, the percentage is much higher for transportation
assistance (32%) than for other needs.[13]

The support data reveal three noteworthy differences. First, blacks'
support networks contain one less person on average than do whites', a
discrepancy similar to that observed by Marsden (1987) in the General
Social Survey. Second, as compression theory predicts, blacks' networks
are more localized at both the neighborhood and city levels. Roughly
nine-tenths of African-Americans' helpers are Nashville residents, as
compared to three-fourths of whites' (top two rows of Table 3.4). Third,
this difference is consistent in direction and impressive in magnitude for
every kind of support except transportation. Blacks usually have twice as
high a proportion of neighborhood helpers as whites, and a slightly (in

TABLE 3.3   Mean Differences Between Black and White Neighbor Networks in Racially Homogeneous and Mixed Sites

Network Measure	Mean on Network Measure for				Significance of Difference Between [a]		
	Blacks in Black Sites (1)	Blacks in Mixed Sites (2)	Whites in Mixed Sites (3)	Whites in White Sites (4)	(1) & (2)	(2) & (3)	(3) & (4)
N of neighbors known by name	13.0	13.7	15.9	15.3	NS	NS	NS
% of neighbors on face block	92.1	95.7	87.0	84.9	NS	.001	NS
Mean N of contacts with neighbors	149.8	204.8	106.0	93.4	.01	.001	NS
Mean closeness to neighbors	1.5	1.5	1.1	1.2	NS	.001	NS
Mean N of years neighbor known	16.5	15.6	8.4	11.3	NS	.001	.001
% of neighbors giving special help	46.1	41.2	43.5	39.3	NS	NS	NS
% of neighbors providing 2+ contents	39.7	30.1	35.8	32.7	NS	NS	NS
Mean N of respondents	79.6	65.7	115.7	375.7	–	–	–

NS = Not significant

[a]Based on t-test using separate variance estimation.

TABLE 3.4 Mean Differences Between Black and White Support Networks in Degree of Localization

Type of Support/ Localization Measure	Mean on Network Measure for			Significance of Racial Difference[a]	N of Respondents[b]
	Total Sample	Black Sample	White Sample		
Total[c]					
% of helpers in neighborhood	20.5	24.3	19.2	.05	671
% of helpers elsewhere in Nashville	59.0	64.0	57.3	.05	671
Transportation[d]					
% of helpers in neighborhood	32.3	28.5	33.6	NS	663
% of helpers elsewhere in Nashville	62.4	68.7	60.3	.05	663
Job search[d]					
% of helpers in neighborhood	12.7	20.9	9.9	.01	496
% of helpers elsewhere in Nashville	72.8	73.9	72.5	NS	496
Financial assistance[d]					
% of helpers in neighborhood	8.8	13.6	7.3	.05	590
% of helpers elsewhere in Nashville	52.2	60.6	49.6	.05	590
Care during illness[d]					
% of helpers in neighborhood	13.2	18.6	11.4	.05	614
% of helpers elsewhere in Nashville	57.7	63.4	55.8	NS	614
Important decision[d]					
% of helpers in neighborhood	14.0	22.8	11.0	.001	615
% of helpers elsewhere in Nashville	63.5	64.7	63.1	NS	615

NS = Not significant

[a]Based on t-test using separate variance estimation.

[b]Sample is 24–25% black in each panel.

[c]Limited to respondents who named 1+ helpers providing any type of support.

[d]Limited to respondents who named 1+ helpers providing specific type of support.

TABLE 3.5 Summary of Empirical Support for Compression, Avoidance, and Composition Theories

Network Trait	Racial Group with Network Advantage [a] Based on Findings	Theory Best Supported by Findings
Size	neither	composition
Proximity	black	compression
Frequency	black	compression
Intimacy	black	compression
Duration	black	compression
Content	neither	composition
Multiplexity	neither	composition
Localization[b]	black	compression

[a]Reflected in higher scores on measures of trait.
[b]Refers to support network rather than neighbor network.

the job-search and decisionmaking cases) to moderately (financial assistance, care during illness) greater percentage of helpers who live elsewhere in Nashville

Conclusions

Our results show that when blacks' and whites' relations with their neighbors differ, they do so in a manner that best conforms to compression theory (Table 3.5). Compression-inspired hypotheses hold most strongly for the dimensions of proximity, frequency, intimacy, and duration, both at the zero-order level and after individual and site characteristics have been controlled. Within urban neighborhoods, community for African-Americans appears to be a more intense, spatially concentrated phenomenon than it is for whites. Even using a less place-anchored approach to the community concept, the Nashville data suggest a greater localization of black social-support ties—again in line with the compression perspective—although neighbors remain a minority of all those who give social support to blacks. On a few dimensions, the similarities between the races are as predicted by composition theory. For example, blacks and whites maintain active ties with an average of seven to eight neighbors, and they use those ties for roughly the same purposes. The determinants of most network dimensions are similar for the two groups as well.

Apart from their theoretical significance, our findings are reassuring in two ways. First, they converge with the results from an earlier analysis that employed traditional (non-network) survey measures of neighboring to make racial comparisons (Lee, Campbell, and Miller 1991). And second, they parallel those for other social statuses. Elsewhere we have shown that groups marked by high integration or prestige—female, married, and affluent respondents in particular—have larger neighbor networks, as do whites in this analysis (Campbell and Lee 1990, 1992). By contrast, men, the unmarried, and lower-income persons maintain smaller neighbor networks in which ties are more intimate and more often activated, like those reported here for African-Americans. The descriptive lesson to be learned is that the shape of such networks depends on position in the status hierarchy. Near the top, a "broad but shallow" image applies, near the bottom a "narrow but deep" one. However, these characterizations may be less accurate for networks that extend beyond the neighborhood (Fischer 1982).

To be sure, our findings seem out of step with currently fashionable "new disorganization" thinking that structural and institutional changes have weakened black integration and solidarity, most notably for the inner-city underclass. Do the Nashville data challenge this view? They cannot do so directly since our selection criteria excluded occupants of large housing projects and other extreme sites from the sample. Nevertheless, our investigation sounds a warning about the limited scope of the disorganization argument. The vast majority of all blacks with incomes above and below the poverty line live outside of underclass settings in Nashville[14] and throughout the U.S. (Jargowsky and Bane 1990). And among those who reside in other types of neighborhoods (which are well covered by our study), local ties are far from trivial.

In fact, such ties may occasionally prove too strong rather than too weak, especially if they are to lower-status neighbors with modest access to external resources. The possibility has been raised by Granovetter (1973, 1982), who suggests that parochial networks in ethnic neighborhoods can hinder attempts to deal with the extra-local environment (see also Chapter 4, Gans 1962). Ironically, too many futile forays into that environment could explain why some African-Americans turn inward in the first place, developing nearby relations as a response to blocked opportunities. What has not been ascertained is whether these relations "pay off." With regard to collective action, scattered evidence hints that the kinds of intense ties we have found for black residents frequently work against efforts to mobilize politically in the face of problems that threaten neighborhood stability (Crenson 1983; Gans 1962; but see Milburn and Bowman 1991). At the individual level, even less is known about the influence of specific dimensions of blacks' (or whites') local networks on psychological well-being, personal safety, job-search success, and other expressive and instrumental outcomes.

Until these outcomes can be explored, we are left with a two-tiered conclusion. Following composition theory, black-white similarities in nonracial attributes form the foundation of American neighboring. Overlaid on this foundation, though, the societal forces that have slowed blacks' progress in many domains have also encouraged their more extensive neighboring. Thus, race—being black or white—affects neighbor networks much as compression theory says it should. We expect future research to confirm that such racial differences in neighboring have a substantial impact on the quality of urbanites' daily lives.

Notes

We are indebted to Joe Feagin, Claude Fischer, R. S. Oropesa, Thy Phu, Gerald Suttles, Barry Wellman, and Patricia Wittberg, who made helpful substantive and editorial comments on earlier versions of this chapter, and to James Kanan, who provided able assistance with the analysis. Primary support for our research from the National Science Foundation (Grant No. SES-8709981) is gratefully acknowledged. Supplemental support was provided by the Population Research Institute at The Pennsylvania State University (to Lee) and by the Vanderbilt University Research Council (to Campbell).

1. Even when need diminishes, normative pressures toward neighboring may remain strong. From an ethnic community perspective, blacks' minority status and general position in society should make them more likely than whites to have shared experiences that facilitate cohesiveness among group members (Antunes and Gaitz 1975; Olsen 1970). This "we-feeling" fosters the expectation that neighbors will respond if called upon, assuming that they are of the same race. Such an assumption is grounded in the persistently high levels of residential segregation in American metropolitan areas (Farley and Frey 1994), and it holds quite well for the members of our survey sample.

2. It seems reasonable to anticipate some overlap among the different aspects of tie strength, but the correlations should fall well short of perfect. Wellman and Wortley's (1990) analysis partially corroborates this, showing that, for a small sample of Toronto residents, the frequency of face-to-face contact—the typical way that neighbors interact—and tie intimacy are statistically independent of each other (see also Marsden and Campbell 1984).

3. The northern California study excluded localities that were 40% or more black, and the Toronto random sample did not contain any black respondents.

4. Based on 1988 County-City Databook information for the 60 U.S. cities of 250,000 or more in 1970 or 1980, Nashville ranks 25th in growth rate, 28th in proportion black, 23rd in owner-occupancy, 25th in multiunit dwellings, 33rd in educational level, and 30th and 38th in the representation of single-parent households and the elderly, respectively. These rankings are not presented to support the claim that Nashville is perfectly representative of all big cities—because no single place can be—but to point out its lack of glaring peculiarity.

5. As late as 1900, the index of dissimilarity for the two groups (calculated across wards) stood at a comparatively low 34 (Walter 1975). This means that 34% of all black Nashvillians would have had to move to different neighborhoods (wards) to be evenly distributed with whites throughout the city.

6. No limit was placed on how many neighbors respondents could name; the range runs from 0 through 80, with a mean of 15.

7. The far right column of Table 3.1 indicates that N varies across the network measures. Some cases are lost between the first and second rows (because the 23 respondents who knew none of their neighbors by name failed to move beyond the first generator question), and a greater number are lost between the second and third panels (because many respondents had not talked or visited recently with any neighbor, and such interaction served as the criterion for collecting follow-up data on a tie). More cases are lost during the multivariate phase of the investigation, when respondents' social and demographic characteristics are controlled. These characteristics were measured via the questionnaire, but some interviewees failed to complete that instrument. As a result, N ranges from a high of 781 to a low of 473 in Tables 3.1 through 3.4. Fortunately, the attrition process does not differ by race. Blacks comprise slightly less than one-quarter of the respondents at each step in our analysis.

8. We classify these four types of assistance as "special" on conceptual grounds: They all presume a nontrivial degree of trust, intimacy, or commitment in the neighbor relationship. Even the most seemingly mundane of the four, having neighbors watch one's home, is aid that is not treated lightly since it may involve leaving a house key with those neighbors or counting on them to feed the dog.

9. The bivariate character of the t-tests might not appear relevant to the composition perspective, which holds that any zero-order racial differences in neighbor networks should diminish when control variables are introduced. However, our site-selection criteria—favoring relatively stable neighborhoods free of nonresidential land uses (Lee, Campbell, and Miller 1991)—have operated to make black and white respondents more alike on nonracial traits than they would be if chosen from the full range of possible sites. In short, implicit statistical controls are already in place at the level of mean comparisons.

10. The characteristics besides race were age, marital status, income, education, political views, religious values, and general lifestyle. Each item was coded 0–2 (0 = "very much like me," 1 = "somewhat like me," 2 = "not at all like me"), with scores summed across all eight items to create a dissimilarity scale.

11. In addition to these three examples, the scale measures the *presence* of a street mailbox, a driveway fronting on the street, a porch large enough for sitting, chairs or swings on the porch or in the yard, a modest (< 20 yards) setback from the street, close side neighbors (< 20 yards), a lot level with the street, a stop sign at either end of the face block, and a street that is straight and level from one end of the face block to the other. It also measures the *absence* of side fencing, dense front or side vegetation, marked street lanes, and a street extension beyond both ends of the face block.

12. Because very few black respondents live in white areas (< 2% of the population of such areas) and very few white respondents live in black areas (< 5% of the population), these race × racial context subsamples have not been included in the t-tests in Table 3.3.

13. The N also varies by type of support (right column of Table 3.4). For each type, only those respondents able to name any helpers have been included in the t-tests.

14. Based on information obtained from the 1980 census and through personal communications with Metropolitan Development and Housing Agency officials, we estimate that roughly 10% of all black residents of Davidson County live in projects and other government-subsidized housing units likely to be occupied by the extremely poor. The rest inhabit the kinds of neighborhoods included in our low- and medium-income strata.

References

Anderson, Elijah. 1976. *A Place on the Corner.* Chicago: University of Chicago Press.

Antunes, George, and Charles M. Gaitz. 1975. "Ethnicity and Participation: A Study of Mexican-Americans, Blacks, and Whites." *American Journal of Sociology* 80:1192–1211.

Athanasiou, Robert, and Gary A. Yoshioka. 1973. "The Spatial Character of Friendship Formation." *Environment and Behavior* 5:43–66.

Blackwell, James E., and Philip Hart. 1982. *Cities, Suburbs, and Blacks: A Study of Concerns, Distrust, and Alienation.* Bayside, NY: General Hall.

Campbell, Karen E., and Barrett A. Lee. 1990. "Gender Differences in Urban Neighboring." *Sociological Quarterly* 31:495–512.

Campbell, Karen E., and Barrett A. Lee. 1991. "Name Generators in Surveys of Personal Networks." *Social Networks* 13:203–21.

Campbell, Karen E., and Barrett A. Lee. 1992. "Sources of Personal Neighbor Networks: Social Integration, Need, or Time?" *Social Forces* 70:1077–1100.

Caplow, Theodore, and Robert Forman. 1955. "Neighborhood Interaction in a Homogeneous Community." *American Sociological Review* 20:357–366.

Crenson, Matthew A. 1983. *Neighborhood Politics.* Cambridge, MA: Harvard University Press.

Denton, Nancy A., and Douglas S. Massey. 1988. "Residential Segregation of Blacks, Hispanics, and Asians by Socioeconomic Status and Generation." *Social Science Quarterly* 69:797–817.

Doyle, Don H. 1985a. *Nashville in the New South, 1880–1930.* Knoxville, TN: University of Tennessee Press.

Doyle, Don H. 1985b. *Nashville Since the 1920s.* Knoxville, TN: University of Tennessee Press.

Farley, Reynolds, and William H. Frey. 1994. "Changes in the Segregation of Whites From Blacks During the 1980s: Small Steps Toward a More Integrated Society." *American Sociological Review* 59:23–45.

Feagin, Joe R. 1970. "A Note on the Friendship Ties of Negro Urbanites." *Social Forces* 49:303–308.

Fischer, Claude S. 1982. *To Dwell Among Friends: Personal Networks in Town and City.* Chicago: University of Chicago Press.

Fischer, Claude S., Robert Max Jackson, C. Ann Stueve, Kathleen Gerson, and Lynne McCallister Jones. 1977. *Networks and Places: Social Relations in the Urban Setting.* New York: Free Press.

Galster, George C., and Garry W. Hesser. 1982. "The Social Neighborhood: An Unspecified Factor in Homeowner Maintenance?" *Urban Affairs Quarterly* 18:235–255.

Gans, Herbert J. 1962. *The Urban Villagers: Group and Class in the Life of Italian-Americans.* New York: Free Press.

Granovetter, Mark S. 1973. "The Strength of Weak Ties." *American Journal of Sociology* 78:1360–1380.

Granovetter, Mark S.. 1982. "The Strength of Weak Ties: A Network Theory Revisited." Pp. 105–130 in *Social Structure and Network Analysis.* Edited by Peter V. Marsden and Nan Lin. Beverly Hills, CA: Sage.

Greenbaum, Susan D., and Paul E. Greenbaum. 1985. "The Ecology of Social Networks in Four Urban Neighborhoods." *Social Networks* 7:47–76.

Hannerz, Ulf. 1969. *Soulside: Inquiries into Ghetto Culture and Community.* New York: Columbia University Press.

Hunter, Albert. 1974. *Symbolic Communities: The Persistence and Change of Chicago's Local Communities.* Chicago: University of Chicago Press.

Jargowsky, Paul A., and Mary Jo Bane. 1990. "Ghetto Poverty: Basic Questions." Pp. 16–66 in *Inner-City Poverty in the United States.* Edited by Lawrence E. Lynn, Jr., and Michael G. H. McGeary. Washington, DC: National Academy Press.

Jencks, Christopher, and Susan E. Mayer. 1990. "The Social Consequences of Growing Up in a Poor Neighborhood." Pp. 111–186 in *Inner-City Poverty in the United States.* Edited by L. E. Lynn, Jr., and M. G. H. McGeary. Washington, DC: National Academy Press.

Kadushin, Charles, and Delmos J. Jones. 1992. "Social Networks and Urban Neighborhoods in New York City." *City and Society* 6:58–75.

Lee, Barrett A., Karen E. Campbell, and Oscar Miller. 1991. "Racial Differences in Urban Neighboring." *Sociological Forum* 6:525–50.

Liebow, Eliot. 1967. *Tally's Corner: A Study of Negro Streetcorner Men.* Boston: Little, Brown.

Logan, John R., and Glenna D. Spitze. 1994. "Family Neighbors." *American Journal of Sociology* 100:453–476.

Marsden, Peter V. 1987. "Core Discussion Networks of Americans." *American Sociological Review* 52:122–131.

Marsden, Peter V., and Karen E. Campbell. 1984. "Measuring Tie Strength." *Social Forces* 63:482–501.

Massey, Douglas S. 1985. "Ethnic Residential Segregation: A Theoretical Synthesis and Empirical Review." *Sociology and Social Research* 65:315–50.

Massey, Douglas S., Gretchen A. Condran, and Nancy A. Denton. 1987. "The Effect of Residential Segregation on Black Social and Economic Well-being." *Social Forces* 66:29–56.

Massey, Douglas S., and Nancy A. Denton. 1987. "Trends in the Residential Segregation of Blacks, Hispanics, and Asians: 1970–1980." *American Sociological Review* 52:802–825.

Merry, Sally Engle. 1981. *Urban Danger: Life in a Neighborhood of Strangers.* Philadelphia: Temple University Press.

Milburn, Norweeta G., and Phillip J. Bowman. 1991. "Neighborhood Life." Pp. 31–45 in *Life in Black America.* Edited by James S. Jackson. Newbury Park, CA: Sage.

Moynihan, Daniel P. 1986. *Family and Nation.* San Diego: Harcourt Brace Jovanovich.

Murray, Charles. 1984. *Losing Ground: American Social Policy, 1950–1980.* New York: Basic Books.

Oliver, Melvin L. 1988. "The Urban Black Community as Network: Toward a Social Network Perspective." *Sociological Quarterly* 29:623–645.

Olsen, Marvin E. 1970. "Social and Political Participation of Blacks." *American Sociological Review* 35:682–697.

Portes, Alejandro, and Robert D. Manning. 1986. "The Immigrant Enclave: Theory and Empirical Examples." Pp. 47–68 in *Competitive Ethnic Relations.* Edited by Susan Olzak and Joanne Nagel. Orlando, FL: Academic.

Rabinowitz, Howard N. 1978. *Race Relations in the Urban South, 1865–1890.* New York: Oxford University Press.

Rainwater, Lee. 1970. *Behind Ghetto Walls: Black Families in a Federal Slum.* Chicago: Aldine.

Sampson, Robert J., and W. Byron Groves. 1989. "Community Structure and Crime: Testing Social Disorganization Theory." *American Journal of Sociology* 94:774–802.

Stack, Carol B. 1974. *All Our Kin: Strategies for Survival in a Black Community.* New York: Harper and Row.

Suttles, Gerald D. 1968. *The Social Order of the Slum: Ethnicity and Territory in the Inner City.* Chicago: University of Chicago Press.

Taub, Richard P., D. Garth Taylor, and Jan D. Dunham. 1984. *Paths of Neighborhood Change: Race and Crime in Urban America.* Chicago: University of Chicago Press.

Uehara, Edwina. 1990. "Dual Exchange Theory, Social Networks, and Informal Social Support." *American Journal of Sociology* 96:521–557.

Valentine, Bettylou. 1978. *Hustling and Other Hard Work: Life Styles in the Ghetto.* New York: Free Press.

Walter, Benjamin. 1975. "Ethnicity and Residential Succession: Nashville, 1850 to 1920." Pp. 3–31 in *Growing Metropolis: Aspects of Development in Nashville.* Edited by James F. Blumstein and Benjamin Walter. Nashville, TN: Vanderbilt University Press.

Warren, Donald I. 1975. *Black Neighborhoods: An Assessment of Community Power.* Ann Arbor, MI: University of Michigan Press.

Warren, Donald I.. 1981. *Helping Networks: How People Cope with Problems in the Urban Community.* Notre Dame, IN: University of Notre Dame Press.

Webber, Melvin M. 1963. "Order in Diversity: Community Without Propinquity." Pp. 23–54 in *Cities and Space: The Future Use of Urban Land.* Edited by L. Wingo, Jr. Baltimore: Johns Hopkins University Press.

Wellman, Barry. 1979. "The Community Question: The Intimate Networks of East Yorkers." *American Journal of Sociology* 84:1201–1231.

Wellman, Barry. 1988. "The Community Question Re-evaluated." Pp. 81–107 in *Power, Community, and the City*. Edited by Michael Peter Smith. New Brunswick, NJ: Transaction.

Wellman, Barry, and Barry Leighton. 1979. "Networks, Neighborhoods, and Communities." *Urban Affairs Quarterly* 14:363–390.

Wellman, Barry, and Scot Wortley. 1990. "Different Strokes from Different Folks: Community Ties and Social Support." *American Journal of Sociology* 96:558–588.

Whyte, William H. 1956. *The Organization Man*. New York: Simon and Schuster.

Wilson, William J. 1987. *The Truly Disadvantaged: The Inner City, The Underclass, and Public Policy*. Chicago: University of Chicago Press.

Yancey, William L., Eugene P. Ericksen, and Richard N. Juliani. 1976. "Emergent Ethnicity: A Review and Reformulation." *American Sociological Review* 41:391–402.

4

Social Networks Among the Urban Poor: Inequality and Integration in a Latin American City

Vicente Espinoza

A Broad Context for Personal Networks

The Subordination of Social Well-being to Economic Well-being

A persistent social crisis has characterized many Latin American countries since the eighties, from Argentina and Chile in the south to Mexico before and after its free-trade agreement with North America. Most of the crisis has coincided with the implementation of deep economic changes, known as structural adjustment, aimed at stabilizing national economies (Morales and McMahon 1993). The market allocation of resources has been the ubiquitous response of economists and conservative policymakers to overcome inefficient public spending, debt crises, hyperinflation, recession, unemployment, and other economic disequilibria affecting the population's well-being. Promoted by such institutions as the International Monetary Fund (IMF), the American government and Thatcherism, these economic policies have attempted "to subordinate the substance of society itself to the laws of the market" (Polanyi 1957a, p. 72).

The "adjustment" in Latin America has many parallels with Europe's "great transformation" in the nineteenth century. Polanyi (1957a) has shown how the European dream of a self-regulating market became the nightmare of societies unable to achieve social integration if left to the forces of the market. In Latin America, the opening of protected economies to international trade had devastating effects on national industries. Moreover, concomitant cutbacks in public spending reduced welfare provision, and the deregulation of labor relationships weakened unions, leaving workers defenseless. These changes increased unemployment, poverty, and the search for any opportunity to survive in difficult times.

What has been the impact of these economic changes on social integration in Latin America? Ordinary people have had a hard time managing to live under these new conditions. To cope, they have converted their social relationships to economic resources: information about the availability of food, personal services, job openings, and small amounts of money circulates in the narrow streets of impoverished neighborhoods. The pressure to get the minimum resources needed to survive has been so strong that, at times, it has seemed as if all sociability has vanished. The ghost of social disintegration has become a concern for politicians, entrepreneurs, intellectuals, and ordinary people moving through the streets of now-threatening cities.

In this chapter I examine social integration by studying the social networks embedded in the daily life of poor people in Santiago, Chile. I first present the social and political context in which these networks operate. Next, I examine the characteristics of the social networks of the poor and place them within a system of informal social exchanges. Finally, I consider the opportunities that kinship, friendship, and political networks offer for social integration.

The Chilean case is especially suitable for studying the impact of economic restructuring on social integration. Since 1986, Chile's economy has shown signs of stability and sustained growth, along with controlled inflation and reduced unemployment (ECLAC 1993). Although macroeconomic equilibrium and financial reliability have been presented as the satisfactory results of proper structural adjustment, the population's well-being has lagged behind this success and a large percentage of the population is poor (CEPAL 1994; Díaz 1993; ECLAC 1993). This combination of macroeconomic success and popular hardship has been stable and long-term enough that it cannot be attributed to the temporary undesirable consequences of rapid economic change. Hence the caring capacity of Chileans, that is, their survival strategies, has an increased relevance under current economic conditions.

Economic Changes and Social Integration

Poverty has been the immediate result of free-market policies, with the poor receiving few, if any, of the benefits of macroeconomic equilibria. During the 1980s, poverty increased even in countries with large economies and populations, such as Argentina, Brazil, and Venezuela. By the 1990s, 34% of Latin American urban households were poor (ECLAC

1992). In Chile, for example, the number of poor rose from 12% in 1970 (before the economic transformation) to 37% in 1986, and 34% in 1990. When about one-third of the urban population is poor, it is difficult to sustain the idea that mass poverty is temporary.

Even though poverty may diminish slightly, as in Chile or Uruguay in the early 1990s, a sharp inequality remains. The gap between those who are doing well and those who are left out is still so wide that social rewards are meager in comparison with personal efforts (ECLAC 1992). Moreover, the reduction in poverty is a result of economic growth which, in the absence of social or public compensating mechanisms, makes living conditions highly dependent on economic cycles.

To be sure, poverty and inequality are old phenomena in Latin America. But in the past, the middle classes were the bridge between the poor and the affluent. Bureaucrats, politicians, teachers, social workers, professionals, priests, small entrepreneurs, and union leaders linked densely knit communities to societal resources. Typically, patron-client relationships or brokerage systems linked social arenas. They helped people to obtain, for example, retirement payments, support for bank loans, work contracts, and enrollment for children in private schools (Valenzuela 1977; Lomnitz 1971, 1986; Touraine 1976; Cornelius 1975).

The old middle classes were crushed during the period of structural adjustment, and other groups have attained intermediate status positions. The new middle classes, in contrast to the old, only render specialized services to the affluent. Because they do not mediate between rich and poor, they do not play the integrating role that the old middle class did two or three decades ago. The poor are more confined to the alleys of their neighborhoods while the affluent parade their expensive cars on newly built highways. A large gap quarantines the poor from modern society.

The public sector's social policies have not helped smooth the negative impact of economic changes on the population. Rather, they have only given small, temporary help to those sectors most affected by the transformation (Vergara 1990). However, the point would be missed by focusing on the efficiency of social policies to fight inequality. The hidden agenda behind social policies points to the dismantling of the welfare state rather than to mere reductions in its spending (Irarrázaval 1992, Cohen and Franco 1992; ECLAC 1991). Free market orthodoxy has led to many Chilean social services, including health and social security, closing or operating as private enterprises.

A dramatic deregulation of the system of labor relationships has accompanied the process of structural adjustment. Workers not only had to accept unemployment and reduced wages, they also had to learn that "a flexible labor market" is an euphemism for defenseless workers. Unions lost their influence on public policymaking, and the now permissive legal framework favors employers so much that union bargaining has little effect on workplace conditions. After long years of unemployment and political repression, many workers have not returned to their old workplaces and routines. Workers today strive hard to survive, organizing their lives in neighborhood alleys rather than in factories or unions. Thus it is essential to study community life to ascertain how the economic transformation has disrupted social life.

Poverty and decades of military dictatorships have undermined the social fabric of Latin American societies. An authoritarian political context has been historically associated with structural adjustment, and most Latin American countries experienced military dictatorship in the 1970s and well into the 1980s. Although authoritarian regimes in the end gave way to restricted democracies, these have a weak social base (O'Donnell and Schmitter 1986). As long as the state is no longer working to integrate the poor and protect workers, the marginalized populace has to turn away from the state and make their social relationships instrumental to their survival efforts or upward social mobility. Thus the marginal population's response to current state practices results in a splintering of the polity into a myriad of sociability mechanisms. This new social fabric corresponds to microsocial processes of survival intertwined with the overall social organization (Sorj 1991; Roberts 1991; Mingione 1991). Lacking links to social rewards, some people also develop perverse survival strategies to bridge the gap of inequality: street commerce, begging, black-marketeering, drug-trafficking, and theft are components of a more threatening reality (Sorj 1991).

Inequality poses many questions regarding social integration. Some scholars argue that if nobody bridges the inequality gap, the competition of small circles for scarce resources may well bring about the destruction of the existing social fabric without any sound replacement (Sorj 1991; Tironi 1990). Others stress the positive virtues of poverty by emphasizing the poor's cooperation and empowerment in their efforts to survive in the city (Razeto 1990; Friedmann and Salguero 1988). Will the patterns of sociability developed among the poor to cope with structural adjustment be able to support their social integration under a new development model, or will they keep the poor away from the benefits of economic growth?

Social Networks and the Survival Strategies of the Poor

Many Latin American scholars have studied *family survival strategies*, the range of actions adopted by family groups to sustain their daily life.[1]

Scholarship on this area of "social reproduction" has expanded from a focus on the poor to encompass a wide range of groups and practices. Thus far, analysis has usually focused on the functionality of survival strategies for family life, especially on how they compensate for the economic insecurity of daily household life. Case studies have portrayed an array of informal ways of gaining access to economic resources in order to counteract job instability, compensate for insufficient earnings, or find housing. Other family practices, such as the constitution of the family, fertility decisions, consumption patterns, interhousehold cooperation, and migration have also been included in the framework of survival strategies. In spite of their marginal character, these survival strategies are more than desperate attempts to survive. Besides showing how households cope with circumstantial constraints, they demonstrate the active and productive role of the populace.

Many issues remain unsolved. No one has identified the principles that articulate survival practices as a strategy; households move seemingly at random between what is available. Indeed, coping with pressing poverty does not give room for true strategy. "Survival depends on selling one's own and one's family labor cheaply and under whatever conditions are offered" (Roberts 1991, p. 139). Households that scarcely satisfy their basic needs have little chance to exploit their internal resources and depend increasingly on external resources. Without any margin for flexibility, poor households cannot make strategic choices or deal with adverse conditions. They have no real choices in making decisions about their consumption patterns. The behavior of such poor households is far from the rational economic ideal. The rationale of these exchanges is to be found in principles other than optimizing the economic utility of the organization of household resources (Schmink 1984).

I shall demonstrate in this chapter that the economy of survival consists more of managing social ties to gain access to resources than the strategic organization of goods and services. Survival strategies are embedded in social relationships. As such, they are the backbone of community life. Obtaining necessary resources involves dealing with a multitude of relatives, friends, neighbors, coworkers, shopkeepers, organizations, institutions, and the like. Social ties are a household's resource, and obtaining goods and services requires adequate relationships. Resources may exist, but people lacking appropriate contacts cannot get or distribute them.

Thus the core of livelihood is a set of social relations rather than the goods and services obtained or the ways used to acquire them. As long as social relations are a condition for obtaining or circulating resources, the structure of social contacts provides the rationale for the combination of resources. Hence my perspective treats survival practices as social net-

works, analyzing the relationships established in gaining access to resources. From this perspective, a survival strategy is more the management of social ties than an instrumental access to goods and services to
satisfy needs. Consequently, studying the kinds of resources that social
contacts help to channel will enable us to understand how economic survival practices either facilitate or hinder social integration.

Getting the minimum resources necessary to preserve and reproduce
life is the principle that organizes the economic life of poor communities
most of the time. However, scholarship about survival strategies has not
yet linked survival mechanisms to social integration. A starting point for
this is to consider resource flows embedded in community structure. Analysts must choose the appropriate unit of analysis for the study of communities. Intermediate units of analysis in community studies bridge the
gap between the individual and large social processes. Grassroots organizations, domestic units, nonprofit associations, among others, have been
regarded as a mediator or "filter" of individual decisions about labor
force participation, migration, or consumption patterns. They are also
considered a factor explaining different responses to the same structural
conditions (Schmink 1984). Yet such mediating units often remain a black
box: their characteristics are unknown, and decisions about the appropriate units are largely made before analysis begins.

Although households have been widely used as the unit of analysis in
studies of survival strategies, the definition of a household is often arbitrary. Household membership does not equal seeing the family as a kinship nucleus, an organization of consumption, or a system of production.
A definition of household may result in a researcher a priori imposing a
concept of household. Such a definition can create artificial units that do
not comply with historically specific meaning in the community itself
(Collins 1986). For example, most studies of survival strategies conclude
that participants in these strategies outnumber household members
(Wong 1984; Torrado 1981; Oliveira and Salles 1989; Friedman 1984; Wilson 1988; McKee 1987). Such conclusions point to the risk of reifying the
household as a unit of analysis and ignoring forms of access to resources
that involve nonresident family members, other households, or formal
organizations (Schmink 1984). In truth, none of the households exists as
an independent consumption unit. Moreover, transfers between households are crucial to the householding practices of labor force reproduction (Wong 1984; see also Cécora's German data 1993).

Hence it is useful to have a research approach that avoids a priori definitions of the social units that mediate macro and micro processes. From
a structural viewpoint, intermediation may be defined as a set of mutually linked individuals, in other words, a social network. In my study, the

network of survival is a result of the contacts developed in the mobiliza-tion of resources for family consumption. Significant units in the process of survival are obtained as an analytical reconstruction rather than on an a priori basis. Social network analysis overcomes the risk of reifying a unit of mediation because, by focusing on ties, it identifies significant units based on linkages present between individuals.

In such a relational approach, the intersection of a person's set of rela-tionships with the sets of others defines "structurally equivalent" posi-tions, roles, and empirical aggregates in the social structure (Lorrain and White 1971). To define categories, individual functions are qualified by the person's relationships. For example, a woman spending most of her time at home minding household resources may be referred to as a "housewife." However, housewives are similar or different depending on their relations to neighbors, distant kin, their husbands' employers, and so on. A researcher can discern how similar or different two persons are by comparing their sets of relationships. A cluster of structurally similar persons indicates the presence of a significant category. Even though this use of structural equivalence makes relationships an attribute of individu-als, it is less arbitrary than sorting them in terms of researcher-defined units of analysis. Take, for example, this definition of a household: "a reci-procal form of social organization aimed at survival embedded in a kin-ship network" (Mingione 1991, p. 132). A higher density of reciprocal kin-ship ties has to be found for Mingione to speak of a household proper, or else the "social organization aimed at survival" would be a different unit.

The social network approach avoids jumping from one level of analy-sis to the other but moves back and forth by using individual relation-ships as an analytic bridge. The image of community thus attained is con-sistent with other levels of analysis and can still be deconstructed and reconstructed as different sets of relationships. It is still the privilege of the researcher to define the image of the community and use relational data to test multiple hypotheses about community structure.

Social relationships for the reproduction of household members are the starting point—one end of the thread—in the unraveling of the social structure. This involves treating survival strategies as the management of social ties to obtain resources rather than as the optimal allocation of re-sources. The structural equivalence of individuals can also help identify significant units of social reproduction in areas of higher density of rela-tionships. The shifting place of survival practices in social relations may then be established without making one or another unit true by defini-tion. Social network analysis renders the organization of the process of survival theoretically meaningful by placing the economy of the poor within the context of social integration.

Data and Methods

The data for this chapter come from a survey carried out during 1989 in Las Villas, two neighborhoods in Santiago, Chile.[2] The neighborhoods originated in the early 1970s from land seizures, and they now have a similar size and degree of building development. They are in the same locality and have experienced the same social policies. In 1989 Las Villas comprised 2,101 sites and 10,000 people, a large proportion of them poor. It and similar Santiago settlements contain a total of 80,000 households (Espinoza 1992). Women and men from 207 households were interviewed separately, yielding a total of 300 personal networks, encompassing 1,827 members.

My approach follows that devised for the Northern California Communities Study (Fischer 1982). The names of network members were elicited by questions about the contacts people use ordinarily to obtain and distribute survival resources; each respondent had 85 opportunities to identify a network member. Specific questions were constructed after consulting the research literature, fieldwork, and semistructured interviews. Five dimensions of resources were considered: child-care, food, housing, money, and employment. Multiple indicators bear on each variable to provide more reliable information. Some questions allowed the respondent to give the name of two contacts, and some types of resources were treated in more detail. In addition, some 17 questions were asked about particular bureaucratic or market ties. In this way, a total of 102 types of ties were considered.[3]

Social Networks and the Principles of
Access to Resources

The household's basic function in these neighborhoods is to rear children and to care for the elderly. Families have to afford the high cost of maintaining these economically inactive members, a situation encouraging other household members to seek paid employment. Yet resources from paid employment are not enough to cover the basic needs of 69% of households in the sample, a situation similar to other poor Santiago neighborhoods (MIDEPLAN 1992; Schkolnik and Teitelboim 1988). Moreover, while wages from paid work can satisfy the economic needs of some households, the instability of work creates economic insecurity.

Households develop systems of social support, besides regular wages, to cope with the difficulties of daily economic life (Lomnitz 1977; Roberts 1978). Social ties channel goods and services that help families to endure their economic insecurity. These networks of economic support are a typical feature of social organization among the urban poor; a complex prac-

TABLE 4.1   Modes of Access to Resources (percentages of valid cases)

	Mode of Access			
	Social	*Market*	*Bureaucratic*	*No. of Cases*
Child-care	84.9	0.0	[a]	126
School activities	60.7	2.5	N.A.	122
Food and clothing[b]	99.9	54.8	27.6	210
Watching house	92.4	0.0	0.0	210
House upgrades[b]	43.9	34.2	5.3	114
Site uses	36.2	14.8	1.0	210
Job search	71.9	13.8	4.8	210
Job installation	33.3	0.5	3.3	210
Cash donation	13.8	0.0	70.5	210
Credit	72.7	3.3	2.0	150
Emergency cash	40.5	6.2	29.0	210

[a]Time in public day-care was not considered.
[b]Social access includes self-provisioning.
N.A. not applicable

tice of exchanges at the core of community life (Raczynski and Serrano 1985; Lomnitz 1977). Regardless of the kinds of resources channeled, support can come through four modes of articulating households with the larger social structure: *market exchanges, bureaucratic distribution, self-provisioning,* and *interpersonal exchanges* (Polanyi 1957b; Warde 1990; Wellman and Wortley 1990). Each of these four modes has its own rules for integration into the household economy.

This section focuses on the integration of these modes of social articulation into the economy of poor households. My analysis begins with information about the distribution of ties by modes of access for selected resources. Each cell of Table 4.1 displays the proportion of households obtaining a resource for each mode of access.[4]

Social ties give access to all resources. This is the mechanism most households use to gain access to resources, while market and bureaucratic ties are few in number and limited in the scope of resources to which they lead. However, ties vary in the extent to which they provide access to different kinds of resources. The widespread use of ties in many daily family activities reveals their importance for the reproduction of these households. For example, there is such widespread use of ties to get food and clothing that people take it for granted. Extensive ties also develop around child-care, job-searches, and informal credit flows, involving at least 72% of the sample (Table 4.1).

Ties are involved to a lesser extent in obtaining resources such as housing, jobs, or cash. The explanation is twofold. On the one hand, some of these are rather exceptional activities, such as upgrading housing or obtaining jobs. Indeed, ties for constructing housing are neither present for the whole sample nor are they routinely required. On the other hand, the low use of ties can indicate the relative scarcity of some resources in these communities. Many neighbors have only time, information, or small amounts of food to offer others. Hence the informal flow of resources decreases when it comes to items such as skilled work, material resources, or cash.

Access to Resources Through Market Exchanges

Market exchanges operate on a narrow scope, mainly to satisfy households' immediate needs of food and clothing. Other uses of markets to obtain resources are rare, such as hiring workers for housing construction.[5] Low status certainly prevents extended use of the market. For example, none of the children in Las Villas goes to a private school, and nobody pays for baby-sitting. To some extent, market exchanges indicate priorities in the budget allocation of the household's cash resources.

Using credit is bound up with market purchases. One-half of the families get food, clothing, or appliances by negotiating small credits from shopkeepers or door-to-door vendors, who are typical characters of neighborhood life. Door-to-door vendors carry blankets, irons, clothing, or kitchenware in their cargo-tricycles. Like shopkeepers, they sell to patrons on the basis of small but never-ending monthly payments. This is the only way in which many families can obtain small household appliances. Access to this form of credit reflects a difficult short-term situation rather than a higher household status. Indeed, people try to avoid buying on credit because of the suppliers' high prices.

Extra-market mechanisms help manage these credit relationships because both buyers and sellers are aware of many details about their market contacts. There is no clear-cut division between impersonal "pure market" exchanges and personalized relationships. Personal negotiation, rather than retail selling, is the mechanism of delivery. This may well account for the higher participation of poor households in the market. Familiarity with each other helps buyers to negotiate and sellers to control payment.

Engaging in small trade to get some money is another type of market participation. For example, 16% of households rent part of their sites, cabins in their yards, or rooms in their houses. Other people are self-employed, with most of their commercial activity being casual, small-scale trade. Renting or small trade is an economic strategy pursued mainly by women, especially if they are without resources or in short-term financial straits. Unlike established shopkeepers, these women take advantage of their location and domestic appliances to sell such items as flavored ice cubes, loose cigarettes, or homemade pastries. Women also use their skills to sell knitted garments or other crafts, or they may sell surplus goods from factories or the countryside (Raczynski and Serrano 1985). These casual economic practices are both an extension of women's household responsibilities and the means by which they are integrated into the labor force (Benería and Roldán 1987). Not only must women stretch the household budget through nonmarket exchanges, they are also supposed to generate cash.

Taken as a whole, market exchanges have a restricted and weak presence in these neighborhoods. The context of poverty precludes the extensive use of the market and the subsequent commodification of social life. For example, only 8% of the households in Las Villas have credit from large stores. If purchasing power is the measure of social integration through market mechanisms, then people in Las Villas are disintegrated. Moreover, many market relations are subordinated to social relations. In the absence of market-based social integration, the question arises as to whether such integration occurs on another basis. Indeed, the presence of particularistic relationships in these market relationships points to exchanges of resources among network members.

Bureaucracies and Livelihoods

The bureaucratic distribution of resources reaches poor families in two crucial areas of economic life: food and cash. They mainly come through municipal programs attempting to extend the benefits of the social security system to groups having no formal coverage (Vergara 1990). The distribution of resources by bureaucracies intends to maximize target efficiency, but it is not distortion-free. In managing social policies, local bureaucrats identify the needy, select beneficiaries and allocate benefits (Gallardo 1990; Fadda and Oviedo 1994; Rodríguez, Espinoza, and Herzer 1995). Their discretionary power over the delivery of services creates opportunities for group pressure or patron-client practices. Although corruption has not been a dominant trait of the Chilean municipal system, in 1995 some 104 municipalities of 320 in the country were under investigation because of accusations of irregular practices.

Bureaucracies are not important as a mode of social integration among the poor; private or public bureaucracies have minor presence in many aspects of people's daily life. No large-scale subsidies or welfare programs have been implemented on a regular basis in the last decades. The poor have learned that Chile no longer is a welfare state, and they do not expect many benefits from the public sector. For example, only 29% of the respondents believe that some bureaucratic organization will help them in an emergency. Moreover, by stressing target efficiency of its programs, the public sector has abandoned grand interventions (Raczynski 1994; CEPAL 1995).

The Place of Social Ties (and Self-Provisioning) in Survival Strategies

The exchange and distribution of goods and services by means of social contacts are noticeable aspects of social life in these neighborhoods. Social access is more than a mechanism which arises if resources are absent or deficient; it is a key organizing principle of life. Exchanges are regulated by patterns of sociability rather than by price or policy. They sustain links between households by means of nonmarket exchanges, thereby transforming neighborhoods into communities.[6] Are these social relationships a principle of social integration in the absence of market or bureaucratic integration?

To be sure, the households do much self-provisioning. Sixty-five percent of the sample make their own clothes or produce some food for household consumption, and 56% did some household construction or renovation in the year before the survey. Self-provisioning is not an alternative to the use of social contacts outside the household to gain access to economic resources. Households active in these practices are not usually isolated, and they tend to have a significantly higher level of supportive social relationships than other respondents. Making clothes boosts intense social contacts, and knitting is a social practice. As in many other neighborhoods, Las Villas women form knitting groups so that they can talk during their work. Producing for the family is not an autarchic enterprise, and self-help does not preclude intense social exchanges in other fields.[7]

A variety of contacts channel supportive resources to and from the households. How many people are involved in these exchanges? Table 4.2 shows the number of network members by types of resources involved in informal exchanges. The respondents have a total of 1,827 network members, a mean of 8.8 members in the average household's network. Table 4.2 also provides additional information on the number of items exchanged by each network member in every category of resources (out of a total of 18 items). It shows that social contacts play a crucial role in Las Villas's daily economic life. Every household uses social support to gain access to economic resources. That the largest number of contacts occur in labor market exchanges reveals the importance of paid work. Money exchanges come next, showing that cash resources are also the

TABLE 4.2   Number and Percentage of Network Members, Mean Size of House-hold Networks, and Number of Items Exchanged with Contacts in Each Category of Resources

	Network Members	Total (%)	Mean Size	Items by Contact
Job help	684	37.4	3.3	2.1
Monetary	485	26.6	2.3	2.1
Sustenance	445	24.4	2.2	2.2
Child-rearing	301	16.5	2.4	2.6
Homemaking	295	16.2	1.4	2.6
Building	159	8.7	1.4	1.9
All resources	1,827	100.0	8.8	1.8

NOTE: Respondents were not included as network members. Figures correspond strictly to ties.

frequent subject of informal exchanges. A large number of social contacts provide core sustenance (food, clothing, etc.) to the household, while daily household chores such as child-rearing or homemaking use a similar number of ties. Major housing upgrades involve a smaller number of social contacts, but only 54% of the households have done such upgrades.

Las Villas' networks of about 9 persons are smaller in size than the 16 found in urban Northern California (Fischer 1982) and the 17 found in Toronto (Wellman and Wortley 1989; see also Campbell and Lee 1991). However, I looked only at economic support. The members of the Las Villas networks tend to specialize in the kinds of resources they exchange. Except for those involved in child-rearing or homemaking, network members are likely to obtain or provide about two items out of 57 types of support. (Wellman and Wortley 1989, 1990 report similar specialization in Toronto.) Specialized contacts for economic exchanges suggest low multiplexity: These network members do not have many types of relationship with each other. The specialization found in Las Villas seems to reinforce the idea of community disintegration in a context of poverty. By contrast, in highly intertwined communities, network members exchange different types of resources in different contexts of relationships (Wellman, Carrington, and Hall 1988).

Neither the market nor bureaucracies are sound principles of integration in these communities. Do social ties serve this purpose? Social ties can result from so many different conditions that one may be led to assume that ties and patterns of ties are just idiosyncratic. At first glance, specialized ties offer little opportunity for integration. However, the organization of survival cannot be separated from the network through which resources flow. Survival strategies, analyzed as a network, reveal a social structure emerging from the pattern established in the exchanges between members of a social system (Wellman 1988a; Berkowitz 1982). At a microsocial level these networks form the backbone shaping daily life in the community. At a macrosocial level the network structure of these communities offers channels for social integration. Rather than the sometimes suffocating solidarity of densely interconnected communities, the ramifying web of specialized interdependence in Las Villas can knit the community together.

Networks of Informal Exchanges

The specialized participation of network members in exchanges of resources for economic survival does not mean community disintegration because the rationale of access to resources lies in the social ties among network members. My analysis of survival strategies considers first the people involved in exchanges rather than the resources involved or the mechanisms used for their distribution. Contacts among network members are likely to be broader than mere exchanges of resources, and these contacts may also be quite independent of mechanisms or economic decisionmaking.

The influence of social relationships on the exchange of survival resources has seldom received attention in Latin American research (Lomnitz 1977; Didier 1986). Instead most studies have focused directly on the gathering and organization of resources as survival strategies (Roberts 1991; DeBarbieri 1989; Raczynski and Serrano 1985; Schmink 1984; Frías 1977). By contrast, there have been many North American studies of social support networks (reviewed in Wellman 1988b, 1992; Campbell and Lee 1991). Although the sources of uncertainty are quite different in comfortable North American middle-class neighborhoods and desolate Latin American barrios, social contacts in both societies provide and circulate resources.

Who are the members of these networks? Table 4.3 displays the network composition in Las Villas by member's role.[8] Social (nonkin) ties, mainly friendships, and close kinship ties (to spouse, child, parent, sister, or brother) are the two most important roles among network members, comprising 74% of all network ties. This is consistent with previous research on survival strategies stressing the importance of social contacts in economic life and the conversion of social relationships to economic resources (Schmink 1984; Didier 1986; Lomnitz 1977; Roberts 1978). The distribution of people in roles challenges the idea that extended familial exchanges or kinship are the basis of supportive networks. Even if in-laws and distant kin are counted, ties with kin are 38% of the total household and community ties.

TABLE 4.3   Role of Community and Household Ties

Role	Community	Household	Total %
Close kin	13.6	88.6	21.9
Spouse	0.2	23.9	2.8
Child	4.4	48.8	9.3
Parent	2.0	10.4	2.9
Sister/brother	6.8	5.0	6.6
Grandchild	0.3	0.5	0.3
In-laws	9.1	6.5	8.8
Sister/brother	5.4	–	4.8
Child in-law	1.6	3.5	1.8
Parent in-law	1.2	1.5	1.2
Other in-law	0.9	1.5	1.0
Other kin	7.5	3.0	7.0
Uncle/aunt	1.2		–1.0
Cousin	1.5	0.5	1.4
Nephew	2.1	2.5	2.1
Other relatives	0.7	–	0.6
Ritual kinship	2.0	–	1.8
Social ties	58.2	1.0	51.9
Neighbor	33.2	–	29.6
Friend	14.5	1.0	13.0
Acquaintance[a]	4.3		–3.9
Coworker	6.0	–	5.3
Economic ties	11.5	1.0	10.5
Employer	6.8	–	6.1
Customer[b]	4.7	1.0	4.5
Unspecified	0.7	–	0.7
Total	89.0	11.0	100.0
No. of cases	1,626	201	1,827

[a]Includes members of the same organization (0.6 percent).
[b]Includes tenants and hired workers (1.4 percent).

The relevance of friendship ties, as opposed to kinship, leads one to consider the position of the household in the community. Most networks include nonkin from outside the household, with only 11% of economically supportive ties within households. By contrast, networks within households are nuclear families: household network members are 98% kin (including 89% close kin—mainly spouses and children). In short, while households are fairly standard units dominated by close kin, kinship is not central to the overall circulation of social support.

If networks of economic support among the poor largely contain nonkin, one may well ask what kind of sociability operates in them. The

TABLE 4.4   Living Place and Role of Network Members

| | *Immediate* | | *Other* | *Social* | *Economic* | | |
	Kin	*In-laws*	*Kin*	*Ties*	*Ties*	*Total*	*(N)*
Same site	52.2	20.4	15.3	0.8	3.4	15.2	(268)
Close (3 blocks)	17.4	40.1	33.1	70.4	14.9	47.9	(846)
Walking distance	6.1	8.9	9.7	8.6	14.9	8.8	(155)
Have to go by bus	21.0	28.0	36.3	18.7	63.2	25.7	(453)
Outside of Santiago	3.3	2.5	5.6	1.5	3.4	2.5	(44)
N = 100%	391	157	124	920	174	1766	

Chi-square = 861.05 with 16 df, p < .0001
Cramer's V = .35
Number of missing observations = 61

classic debate on this issue is between adherents of what Wellman (1979) calls the "lost," "saved," and "liberated" models of community. Despite arguments in favor of a community freed from physical boundaries, geography still sets limits on the expansion of a community (Wellman 1979, 1988a, 1996; Wellman and Wortley 1990; Harvey 1985). This is particularly true in Las Villas, where people sometimes cannot even afford to take local transport. The boundaries of the Las Villas communities are clear. Most of the ties belong to the neighborhood: 15% of them live on the same site as the respondent; another 48% live less than three blocks away; and 9% more live a somewhat longer walk away. Thus, a total of 72% live within walking distance (Table 4.4). Some 26% of ties live farther away in Santiago, while only 3% live elsewhere. The internal distribution of residence across role categories reinforces the importance of the neighborhood. Only economic ties are not local, probably because scarce economic resources lie outside neighborhood boundaries.

To a large extent, the distribution of social and geographic distance follows the scale hypothesized by Lomnitz (1977) to classify the intensity of exchanges: The closer the kinship relation, the shorter the physical distance and the higher the confidence between partners. Although kin are not a majority of the Las Villas networks, kinship is a vital component in these social networks, since many kin who live nearby actively provide sociability and economic support. Moreover, the neighborhood offers opportunities to establish new strong kinship ties through marriage, and newly married couples tend to remain living there.

Despite the importance of kinship ties, most kin and nonkin contacts merge in a context of physical closeness. Although economic contacts often stretch beyond the neighborhood, such contacts are only a small number of all ties (Table 4.4). The spatial propinquity of network members highlights the opportunities in the neighborhood to form ties. In Las

Villas, kin and nonkin network members live within a territory that has its center at the household site and extends to contiguous alleys.

Thus the groups of the alley constitute a basic unit of sociability, but they do not correspond to an extended family or a complex household as a unit of social structure. Social and physical distance are related, but this is not necessarily associated with kinship. In fact, as many close kin as friends or acquaintances live within three blocks of the average respondent's house.

Reciprocity and Tie Strength

Social and economic dimensions of daily life overlap in Las Villas's networks. Do reciprocal, specialized exchanges of economic resources among neighbors operate on a sporadic, purely instrumental, basis, or do they reflect a continuously strong relationship? Scholars have found that the poor often convert social relations to economic resources, with confidence between partners (*confianza*) being the crucial condition of such exchanges (Schmink 1984; Liebow 1967; Peattie 1970; Lomnitz 1977; Roberts 1973, 1978). Confidence between partners has a close connection with underlying social relations, especially with the strength of ties. Relations established among people are at the base of informal economic exchanges because trust develops principally in well-established relationships. Neither trust nor confidence flourish spontaneously; they take time to grow and mature.

Latin American research has found reciprocity to be the dominant form of exchange among the poor (Roberts 1991; Lomnitz 1977). Scholars have associated strong ties with the necessary trust to engage in informal exchanges and, following Sahlins (1972), with a situation of "generalized reciprocity," that is, in a context of intense sociability that fosters the trust necessary to engage in a wide range of reciprocal exchanges (Wegener 1991; Grieco 1987; Peattie 1970; Lomnitz 1977; Roberts 1973; Sik 1988). In this depiction, social exchanges are a momentary expression of a continued social relationship. This implies that reciprocity or unreciprocated exchanges will occur principally in strong relationships, while more immediate reciprocation will also occur in weaker relationships.

On the other hand, social network research has shown that purely instrumental ties tend to be asymmetrical and weak (Granovetter 1982; Lin 1982). This suggests that scarce resources are likely to be obtained by means of weak ties, thus leading to dyadic relationships based more on mutual interest than on sociability. By contrast, strong ties between symmetrical partners usually accompany exchanges of readily available resources. Analytically, immediate reciprocation could be associated with

TABLE 4.5   Proportion of Immediate Reciprocal Exchanges and Analysis of
Variance by Levels of Strength of Relationship

	Prop.	Std. Dev.	Cases
Entire population	.26	.44	1,791
Strong relations	.32	.47	947
Middle relations	.22	.41	351
Weak relations	.16	.37	493

Analysis of variance:

Source	Sum of squares	D.F.	Mean square	F	Sig.
Between groups	8.55	2	4.27	22.96	.000
Within groups	332.82	1788	.19		

Total cases = 1827   Missing cases = 36 (2.0%)
Eta = .16   Eta squared = .03

weak ties and balanced reciprocity, whereas one-sided, unreciprocated, exchanges should dominate among strong ties, at least in the short or medium term.

Table 4.5 tests the hypothesis that the relationship between immediate reciprocation and strength of ties should be inverse or nonexistent. It shows the proportion of people participating in immediate reciprocation in ties of different strength. An immediate reciprocal exchange is one where the network member is in the position of being both provider and receiver of a specific kind of resource.

Immediate reciprocation is not a widespread characteristic of exchanges in these communities (Table 4.5). Balanced exchanges reach only one-quarter of dyadic relationships. Yet, contrary to the hypothesis, reciprocity increases with the strength of relationships. Balanced exchanges are no evidence of weak relations and are also significant aspects of strong ties.

Although these data show generalized reciprocity, they also reveal its limits. On the one hand, unreciprocated ties, a key characteristic of generalized reciprocity, are more extensive than immediate reciprocation. Many ties only provide or receive help but do not reciprocate immediately. This situation fits the scenario of generalized reciprocity: one-sided exchanges that develop between respondents and network members living nearby, and having similar status and strong, long-established relationships. On the other hand, there are dyadic exchanges that develop amid strong social relations; to some extent, immediate reciprocation is associated with strong ties. This evidence fits the scenario of an organized solidarity, a strategy of community development promoted by nongovernmental organizations (NGOs), more adequately than that of generalized reciprocity (Friedmann and Salguero 1988; Rojas 1988; Razeto et al. 1983).

Strong ties leading to reciprocal exchanges are only part of the phenomenon of social exchange among the poor. The strength of the tie does not vary directly with the social distance of the relationship: strong relations with neighbors or coworkers are as likely as weak relations with kin. An instrumental approach to a strong relation is not as anomalous as it seems. Research in another milieu resembling Las Villas shows low-status people "exploiting" strong ties for instrumental purposes such as job-searching (Wegener 1991).

In which contexts are strong ties more likely to be instrumental? The direction of exchanges should vary according to the interaction between tie strength and the social distance between partners. Table 4.6 shows the strength of ties in the context of the role of network members and the direction of exchanges. A clear contrast appears between unreciprocated (panels A and B) and reciprocated exchanges (panel C). The only noticeable difference between panels A and B is the higher proportion and volume of strong economic ties providing help to the respondent. Hence unreciprocated ties may be analyzed as one phenomenon because panels A and B show similar patterns.

In one-sided exchanges, the percentage of strong ties diminishes with socially distant relations. High levels of friendship and intimacy are almost a rule among close kin, but they are scarce among economic relations. A mother and her daughter probably discuss personal matters, but this is unlikely to happen between customers and shopkeepers. Consistent with generalized reciprocity, a large proportion of unreciprocated exchanges occur in the context of strong ties. Yet less-strong ties account for a large proportion of the unreciprocated exchanges in social contexts.

Panel C shows the relationship between strength of ties and role when both partners reciprocate immediately. Paradoxically, the percentage and volume of strong ties is higher in reciprocated (panel C) than in unreciprocated exchanges (panels A and B.) Strong ties reach the largest percentage of network members (66%). They are indeed important among kin (91%), but they also show significant levels among social (50%) or economic ties (54%). It seems that strong relationships are a condition for, or a result of, continued economic exchanges between nonkin. Whichever the direction of the effect, strong ties are likely to be associated with mutual exchanges between nonkin.

Weak ties making unreciprocated exchanges or strong ties fostering mutual exchanges are not typical features of generalized reciprocity. On the one hand, although strong ties form a large part of unreciprocated exchanges, a high percentage of weak ties are especially active in helping the respondents. Receiving resources from weak ties and not returning

TABLE 4.6   Strength of Relation by Role of Network Members and Position in Exchanges

	Role of Network Members					
	Close Kin	Other Kin	Social Tie	Economic Tie	Total	(N)
	A: Respondent Giving (ego → tie)					
Strength of tie						
Strong	81.3	64.2	37.2	5.9	46.4	(270)
Medium	12.0	17.9	22.3	23.5	20.3	(118)
Weak	6.7	17.9	40.5	70.6	33.3	(194)
Total	100.0	100.0	100.0	100.0	100.0	
No. of cases	75	95	395	17	582	
	B: Respondent Only Receiving (ego ← tie)					
Strength of tie						
Strong	87.1	58.7	43.0	18.0	51.6	(359)
Medium	11.1	25.0	24.2	24.2	21.1	(147)
Weak	1.8	16.3	32.8	57.8	27.3	(190)
Total	100.0	100.0	100.0	100.0	100.0	
No. of cases	171	104	293	128	696	
	C: Mutual Exchanges (ego ↔ tie)					
Strength of tie						
Strong	90.7	67.5	50.2	54.2	65.8	(302)
Medium	7.1	25.0	20.0	16.7	16.8	(77)
Weak	2.1	7.5	29.8	29.2	17.4	(80)
Total	99.9	100.0	100.0	100.1	100.0	
No. of cases	140	80	215	24	459	

Chi-square	Value	DF	P <
Panel A	79.06	6	.0001
Panel B	178.22	6	.0001
Panel C	77.93	6	.0001

them hardly fits solidary practices or deferred reciprocity. On the other hand, strong ties are the highest in percentage and volume among reciprocated exchanges especially in the context of social and economic relations. Immediate reciprocity seems to comply with a principle other than "balanced reciprocity," because strong ties are not likely to command instrumental economic relationships.

Generalized reciprocity by no means exhausts informal social exchanges: strong and weak ties appear consistently in contexts that contradict the theoretical framework. Therefore, reciprocity cannot be equated

FIGURE 4.1   Typology of exchanges based on the characteristics of social ties

	Kinship	Friendship
Strong Ties	Family life Household ties	Mutual aid Organized solidarity
Weak Ties	Extended kin Latent ties	Instrumental ties Economic exchanges

with the strength of social relations because they are different analytical dimensions of informal social exchanges. Hence, an elaboration is required to integrate reciprocity and strength into a common framework by placing unreciprocated exchanges in the context of weak ties, or dyadic exchanges in the context of strong ties. Figure 4.1 presents a schematic classification of exchanges based on tie strength and type of social relationship.

This fourfold scheme presents the strength of ties in the rows of Figure 4.1 and the characteristics of social relationships in its columns. Social relations comprise two categories: kinship and friendship. Although these terms stem from my research in Las Villas, they indicate general types of relationships. Indeed, the classification has immediate resonance with contrasts such as family and comradeship, primary and secondary ties, private and public realms, or home and neighborhood. In more general terms, this could be stated as a difference between communal life and private interest.

In interpreting the columns of Figure 4.1, "kinship" denotes strong norms regulating social life, and "friendship" points to social relations established on the basis of affinity or negotiation of individual interests. Weak ties offer an opportunity for integration, either on kinship or friendship lines, because they are instrumental to reach distant people and scarce resources.

Each of the four cells characterizes one recurrent type of exchange of survival resources that also defines an institution. Strong ties in the context of kinship (the upper left quadrant of Figure 4.1) principally refer to the exchanges that characterize family household dynamics. Weak kinship ties (the lower left quadrant) mostly correspond to nonresidential extended families that are in contact for special events such as ceremonies, emergencies, or occasional get-togethers. Strong friendship ties (the upper right quadrant) mostly correspond to organized solidarity or the celebration of life in community, including friends systematically helping each other. By contrast with the others, the lower right quadrant defines more narrowly instrumental exchanges with the negotiation of interests in an established system of equivalences.

Kinship, Friendship, and Social Integration

The typology of exchanges in Figure 4.1 provides a general context for recognizing differences in social access to resources. Its interpretation may also be extended to the topic of social integration because of the properties of the strength of ties. Because weak ties reach dissimilar people in distant places, they favor the distribution of resources and social mobility. By contrast, strong ties help perpetuate poverty because they merely circulate resources among the poor (Granovetter 1982, 1995).

The following two subsections examine the opportunities for integration within the systems of relations established by kinship and friendship. Typical exchanges through strong and weak ties serve as a guideline for this examination. The first subsection focuses on kinship to examine exchanges occurring both within coresidential families and in extended family relationships. Finding active weak ties among dissimilar kin would indicate that kinship works as a principle of integration in these communities. The second subsection contrasts the characteristics of integration in mutual aid as opposed to social mobility. Strong ties create dynamic small circles of families that need not have kinship ties with each another. Weak ties appear mainly as labor market contacts, thus creating opportunities for economic improvement.

Nuclear Families and Distant Kin

Kinship ties usually cover a broad range, from socially and physically close household members to socially and physically distant kin and in-laws; the system of relationships resembles an extended family. However, household composition almost always shows standard patterns, predominantly nuclear families, evidencing the stability of nuclear family households even in the context of poverty. Las Villas households are not an adaptive mechanism of people facing adverse economic conditions; households were not organized to maximize income generation, shelter the needy, or act as a productive unit. On the contrary, the household's membership follow kinship patterns, and the life cycle explains most of the changes in its composition (Espinoza 1992). Household composition is not a result of economic decisionmaking but depends heavily on kinship relationships. Therefore, households cannot be reduced to their economic functions.

Not economics, but a strong normative system regulates household life: a sense of mutual obligation overrides individual interests, and the authority of the head of the nuclear family (usually a man) tightens the group. Child-rearing is the main task of parents, especially mothers, and it expresses the socializing functions of households in these communities. Helping out with the children is the most typical exchange among family members. These child-rearing exchanges are strongly associated with the private realm. The largest volume occur at home, and many are bilateral. Child-rearing exchanges are usually self-contained in a small circle of intimates, typically close kin or people living in the same place and organized as a household. A typical caregiver would be a mother living with her married daughter or son. Some of the exchanges in the house also develop as mutual child-care, as when brothers or sisters take turns looking after a young child. Thus child-rearing is an exchange occurring in the domain of family relationships; it is characterized by kinship relations, strong ties, similar economic status, and marked age differences.

The private world of the family does not preclude ties with dissimilar persons. Almost every household mobilizes people from outside to look after their children, especially in school-related activities. Providing child-rearing help is also a widespread practice that establishes and maintains relationships between people of similar ages but different statuses. Strong ties involving child-care develop with some alley neighbors. These are mostly women engaging in mutual exchanges with persons of better or similar status either to establish a relationship or to reciprocate past help.

Relatives with different economic statuses tend to have weak ties at most. Moving to middle-class neighborhoods often increases social as well as physical distance between relatives. This hinders frequent contact. More prosperous kin have usually moved socially upward in better times, are elderly people freed from the pressure of child-rearing, or are married to successful small entrepreneurs. These people are still not far from the position of the poor and in many cases they risk falling back into poverty. Since they do not forget that they were once poor themselves, they retain some connection with their friends and relatives (Espinoza 1993). These relationships become latent social ties to people one can count on, especially in emergencies. As is the case elsewhere, these contacts require special management: rituals help keep them alive despite distance or time (Caplow 1982; Grieco 1987; Cheal 1988).

Latent contacts have an instrumental component since extraordinary events such as migration or emergencies may activate these extended kinship ties. These contacts also provide resources for everyday household sustenance. Money is the typical resource obtained through this kind of relationship, although other kinds of support to family sustenance are also available, such as emergency sheltering. This circulation of resources keeps poor households alive.

Although most adults earn money from paid work, their households are usually short of money. Cash from kin and friends provide crucial small change to pay for carfare, cigarettes, school equipment, or to get through the week. Larger amounts cover emergencies such as funerals, lack of housing, or starting a business. Cash gifts through informal networks reach 73% of the households, although only 14% receive them regularly. Almost half (47%) of the monetary exchanges are transfers to the household from network members (28% mutual exchanges of cash and 25% respondent's donations account for the remainder.) Kin provide the highest volume of cash support. They either receive services in return or simply consider the money as a gift.

Getting scarce resources from weak ties with persons of higher economic status is a rational strategy. Respondents efficiently get such money if they are able to reach socially or physically distant network members, and the best way to reach higher status people is through weak ties. The economy of survival through this practice does not involve maintaining emotionally close ties. Those asking for money are predominantly housewives. They must resort to whoever may have the funds, which is rarely their similar-status friends or close kin.

Cash exchanges belong primarily to the world of weak, asymmetrical ties because the difference in status is a condition for engaging in monetary exchanges. Since more resources flow from weak ties, tie strength coincides with status asymmetry. Indeed, latent ties are neither commercial relationships nor simple begging. After all, these weak ties are contacts between relatives or distant friends. People asking for money may relate to their potential source of money with some familiarity but they must keep their distance and formality. In popular culture, this etiquette is referred to as "learning to deal with a rich uncle."

Women often narrate episodes in their life histories of getting some money in this way. They refer to this as going "poker-faced" to visit rarely seen relatives or recently discovered charitable organizations (e.g., Marshall 1984). Women need not be someone's friend to ask for help. They do not find this an easy task, although their impenetrable faces hide the shame of almost begging for money. By contrast, men reject these practices out of pride. They do not want to admit to unemployment or to receiving meals from soup kitchens (Frías 1977; Gallardo 1985). That this is a practice principally maintained by housewives is also reflected in the gender composition of these networks. Women report having contacts with both women and men, while men seldom report seeking resources from women.

In summary, support from kin helps keep nuclear households going. These ties are useful for raising children, getting cash for pressing needs, and overcoming organizational deficiencies. Family relations constitute solidary exchanges among people of dissimilar, albeit close socioeconomic status. These exchanges do not require immediate reciprocation and are typical of generalized reciprocity. Kinship ties may have different resources available at different times. They exchange readily available resources and postpone reciprocating until better times. For example, self-help practices within families involve work applied to the improvement of the group rather than of particular individuals. Deferred reciprocity usually appears in parent-child relationships, involving mutual protection at different stages in the life cycle.

Reciprocal exchanges between kinship ties in extended families do not offer a solid basis for the integration for the poor. People in Las Villas usually belong to a small family system that prevents their social integration through kinship ties. These nuclear families have episodic relations with those distant kin who can provide crucial support. Strong ties among household members dominate kinship exchanges with the result that relations are established among socially similar kin. It is only the rarely contacted weak ties with extended kin that link people of different social statuses. This kinship system is unlike that of Mexico, where kinship relations may fill every rung of the social ladder (Lomnitz 1978, 1986). Extended families are not the backbone of integration in these Chilean communities.

Social Integration in the Realm of Nonkinship Ties

Although limited in number, immediate reciprocity consistently occurs in strong ties with nonkin, that is, friends. These exchanges combine the seemingly incompatible components of strength and interest. They are also forms of organized solidarity and mutual aid because they involve elements of negotiation and formal organization (Friedmann and Salguero 1988; Esteva 1983; Razeto et al. 1983). Such exchanges are the social foundation of what has been termed "the economy of solidarity," a system of co-operative exchanges helping to satisfy individual needs on the basis of strong mutual relationships (Razeto 1990; Mingione 1991).

Goods and Services. Strongly tied friends usually exchange resources such as food or appliances. These are practices in which almost all households engage, with the greatest number of exchanges occurring between network members with very strong relationships. Most homemaking exchanges operate on the basis of immediate return, although these are not explicitly barter or commercial transactions. As many respondents say, "This is not a matter of personal interest; I do not give to obtain a benefit for myself." Yet their explanations conceal the fact that practically every good or service given is continuously returned.

Friendship and intimacy are conditions for developing frequent demands and returns. Asking for favors is something that, as other studies also report, "bothers the person they are asking from" (Correa and Labán 1984). Indeed, some respondents say they never put themselves in a position of having to ask close friends for food or money because they cannot tell the boundary between asking for help and begging. Yet friendship or high personal involvement is a condition that relaxes the rules and bestows dignity upon the demand. (In fact, the small volume of exchanges with middle-to-weak ties shows that network members are unlikely to ask favors from people they do not know well.) The strength of ties, the "trust" stressed by anthropologists, removes concerns about the counterpart taking improper advantage of the relationship (Lomnitz 1977; Roberts 1973, 1978). Therefore, people do not interpret friendship as instrumental to the provision of support, but as a condition of the relationship.

Proper exchanges fuel friendship relationships, but it is also clear that some principle of equivalence must operate to establish an adequate restitution (Lem 1988). Typically, food is exchanged for food: a cup of rice for some oil, sugar for noodles, and so forth. Sharing appliances creates more complex relationships. For example, a daughter using her parents' refrigerator to keep fresh vegetables will allow them to take a lettuce or a few tomatoes from her supplies. In one case, I found three households using one washing machine, moving it from house to house. During the day, somebody carts the machine to another house and then brings it back. At first, I thought this arrangement was a result of difficulties in finding an equitable mechanism to share energy costs. I soon learned that it is the outcome of a dispute between a husband and wife over the rights of an ex-husband's lover to use the machine in her own home.

Alley Circles. The neighborhood is an important context for aid between network members. These exchanges, especially mutual aid, occur in alleys close to the household. Homemaking exchanges occur mostly among women who share appliances or food in durable mutual exchanges: getting a cup of sugar from a neighbor, lending a blender to the girl across the street, or having laundry done in a sister's washing machine, and so forth. These daily activities put the women of an alley in a system of mutual support, while they do what is necessary for the daily functioning of their homes.

Immediate reciprocation in the context of strong ties resembles the "solidary economy" of grassroots economic organizations, for these organizations also hope to develop economic practices and community sociability (Razeto 1990; Rojas 1988). However, homemaking exchanges do not seem to result from the strategies of those development agencies or grass-roots organizations that are trying to cultivate a barrio economy (Friedmann and Salguero 1988; Campero 1987; Razeto et al. 1983). The developers of solidary economy organizations refer to a wider territorial context, such as "the neighborhood"[9] or the "barrio economy." For the purposes of informal exchanges these references are rather abstract. Mutual exchanges occur in the narrow spaces of the alleys between women with strong personal links and involve immediate reciprocation. They are not ties that reach through the wider neighborhood. When contacts are established through the more formal organizations of the solidary economy, they are quickly subordinated to the dynamics of alley circles.

The daily life of poor people has to balance contrasting aspects: strong communitarian bonds and instrumental relations aimed at survival (Campero 1987). On the one hand, there is strength and symmetry in their relationships, many of which are with friends of similar status. On the other hand, social exchanges create a dense web of transactions based on immediate reciprocation. However, exchanges in other fields make extended instrumental use of asymmetrical weak ties.

Getting Paid Work. Questions of employment, especially finding jobs, is an important area of neighborhood activity that involves ties with nonkin. Labor market ties comprise more than one-third of the whole set of ties used by respondents in their survival strategies. Indeed, occupational exchanges are central for households with high levels of participation in paid employment. Moreover, the informal nature of most of the respondents' occupations make these job-related networks a true neighborhood institution. Social contacts have provided job information for as many as 72% of the workers in the sample. Among self-employed workers, social ties also provide crucial resources: tools, raw materials, money, and work space.

Because opportunities for paid work are rarely available directly from close kin, network members find their job opportunities outside the family. The family or the household is not directly involved in paid employment; labor market ties concentrate in the social context and not in households or kinship circles. Although neighbors are a large part of labor market ties, the chances of getting job-related help are increased when people search beyond their immediate surroundings.

Status differences are the most significant aspect of labor market contacts. Low status people receive opportunities for work through ties with higher status persons that often stretch beyond the geographic boundaries of the community. Differences of economic status open connections to other sources of information or links to other networks of labor market contacts. These informal labor markets often involve patron-client relationships (Lomnitz 1978; Middleton 1991).

Labor market exchanges also occur in the neighborhood, among people of similar economic status. The participants need not be paid workers themselves. Contacts in the immediate environment know about available opportunities within the neighborhood or outside of it. They circulate such information, often making it part of a continuous mutual exchange, and they help paid workers to take advantage of it. Patronage is not likely to develop in these exchanges because of the small status differences within the neighborhood. Strong ties among similar people follow the rationale of mutual aid: They help allocate unevenly distributed resources. However, neighborhood labor markets offer poor job opportunities, a typical example being a position as a female domestic worker (for a similar Toronto situation, see Calzavara 1982). Ideally, the distribution of job opportunities in the neighborhood should be part of a solidary economy, a cooperative economic system based on strong mutual relationships (Mingione 1991). In practice, as long as work opportunities are found outside the neighborhood, mutual exchanges of job-related help do not alter the fate of the poor but only help them to cope with poverty.

People use weak or strong ties indiscriminately in searching for jobs. Middle-strength ties are especially important. These ties are clearly not strong, yet some confidence exists in the relationship. This contradictory status appears, for instance, in relationships between employees and employers in small-scale firms. Workers in the informal sector of the economy usually refer to their employers by name, have a daily relationship, and feel close to them despite status differences. Yet these employers will never be considered friends. By contrast, formal labor relations tend to make the employer impersonal; it is "the firm," "the company," or "the enterprise."

Labor market relations extend the system of exchanges beyond the restricted boundaries of kinship and neighborhood. Those exchanges occurring between geographically distant partners with strong status differences are highly instrumental because they involve negotiation and only develop when both partners want to take advantage of the relationship. Economic considerations override social relations in these ties because they have been established to obtain job help. Employment is a scarce resource lying outside the neighborhood. Going outside means entering the world of dissimilarity, usually by establishing relations with higher status people. It is also a world of formal relationships. These are not friends or intimates, but people who provide jobs.

Although asymmetrical labor market ties are purely instrumental providers of resources, they do not always create favorable conditions for negotiation. Some respondents develop asymmetric ties that are strong;

these are usually patron-client ties such as those between a contractor and construction workers (see also Lomnitz 1978). Weak asymmetrical ties, also present in the sample, offer jobs but no opportunities for social mobility because they are too unstable to foster long-term career development. Paid workers in Las Villas are caught in the trade-off between strong ties offering no opportunity for upward social mobility and weak, nonlocal ties offering only unstable jobs.

Conclusions

Years of an authoritarian regime destroyed much of the social fabric of Chile, as has been the case in other Latin American countries. Many voluntary organizations atrophied when put outside the law for allegedly subversive activities. Unions lost their functions, and the patterns of sociability drastically changed. After long years of unemployment and political repression, many workers have not returned to their old workplaces and routines. Instead of the factory and the union, they organize their lives in the alleys of their neighborhoods and have to strive hard to survive. Their lives have more of the characteristics of the poor than of the former working class.

The neighborhoods of the poor are worlds of strong ties whose basic units of integration are nuclear families strongly related to each other. The members of a network of economic support usually correspond to three or four households in the same alley. These informal groups sometimes appear as a formal organization of a few members. In a neighborhood similar to Las Villas, 32% of the organizations had ten or fewer members (Guerra 1991). The alley is the place where most informal exchanges take place; it is the spatial domain of the basic units of the social structure.

Households relate to each other on the basis of social context relationships and not kinship. Rather than a structure based on complexly organized households, Las Villas has a structure of links between independent, nuclear-family households. Multiple exchanges between these households give rise to extensive local, but not coresidential, networks. Strength is the most salient characteristic of the neighborhood ties involved in the economy of survival. Resources circulate among people who are long-time friends and neighbors, and who often are kinfolk. They live close by, visit each other, and meet often. They are the strong, territorially bounded ties that are characteristic of what Wellman has called the "saved community" (Wellman 1979; Wellman and Leighton 1979).

Paradoxically, strong ties do not result in the community integration desired by proponents of the solidary economy because such ties tend to reduce relationships to a small set of intimates (Granovetter 1973). Indeed, the small size of the networks in Las Villas confirms this. Strong ties produce a community structure formed by neighboring small circles that fit together like the pieces of a jigsaw puzzle to produce a larger unity. But the strong cohesiveness of small cliques does not necessarily mean that there is overall social integration (Granovetter 1973). Facing external pressure, communities of strong ties are likely to fall apart. Since the communities are not interconnected, it is difficult even for adjacent cliques to share information or mobilize resources.

By contrast, weak ties are able to connect groups of strong ties (Granovetter 1973). Community integration requires weak ties cross-linking groups to weave an integrating web. Communities integrated by weak ties offer better resistance to external pressure since resources and information circulate faster and further. However, weak ties have no systematic integration in the system of exchanges of the survival economy. They are a scarce resource among the poor.

The weak ties of the people of Las Villas typically are specialized labor market contacts. Optimally, labor market contacts can offer opportunities for upward social mobility and thus foster social integration. Better economic conditions may support social mobility by changing the allocation of the household budget to issues that bear fruit in the long term. Long-term mobility may involve purchasing a house, keeping children in school, or improving job qualifications. Better economic conditions, at least, may help to expand a family's time horizon.

Although present, far-reaching weak labor market ties are a scarce resource in Las Villas. Patronage in the labor market is the immediate horizon for getting jobs subcontracting or in construction teams. Labor markets dominated by strong ties offer few opportunities for social mobility among the poor. The most common patron-client relations provide jobs but tolerate few changes in hierarchy. The reorganization of patron-client relationships is risky for everyone because it creates deep conflicts that often mark the end of an association and lead to a general deterioration of living conditions (Lomnitz 1978; Middleton 1991). These labor market characteristics of Las Villas are common in many Latin American neighborhoods. For the poor, searching for jobs is a mechanism of survival rather than an opportunity for social mobility.

Social Networks and Citizenship

Are these communities doomed to disintegration or will they overcome present seclusion and inequality? We should discard any idea of radical disorganization in these communities: Strong ties among neighbors produce high internal cohesion. Small circles of neighbors help society to survive through economic and political crises. Intense exchanges of resources among alley neighbors allow the poor to resist the impact of free-market policies. However, strong ties do not offer many opportunities for social mobility or for participation in decisionmaking.

Chile's economy has shown sustained growth, the population has attended an average of nine years of school, and public social policies have improved their technical efficiency. Yet communities of the poor still lack the main condition for achieving an integrated society: social mediation to bridge the gap of inequality. The opportunities for people to break the mechanisms that reproduce their poverty rely on elements that are not present in their daily exchanges. In Las Villas, peoples' strategies are confined to the private realm. Sennett (1977) noticed the perversion of fraternity in private worlds: Collective personality cannot emerge from narrow circles. Private circles do not allow people to experience the variegated life of society. Moreover, perverse survival strategies can fill the gap of inequality with the results of crime and violence.

The reduced participation of public bureaucracies in the life of these communities brings citizenship into focus as an issue. If democracy restores the public realm, will ties from the political system offer the urban poor any chance of integration? There is a risk that strong ties will develop in the subordinated relationship of the poor to the political system. Indeed, the typical form of patronage involves a subject group with strong ties to the leader (Valenzuela 1977). Patronage by local leaders linked to the state apparatus is likely to develop in an otherwise disconnected poor community that retains only its strong ties. Patron-client relationships may develop for electoral purposes and for links with the public bureaucracy. Patron-client relationships usually best serve the reproduction of political or bureaucratic elites; they benefit patrons more than they improve the fate of clients. Thus strong ties to the political system would also become a part of the poverty reproducing mechanisms.

Yet public policies could also contribute to the social integration of the poor. Public sector lines of action sometimes address this issue when nobody else seems to show any concern for the fate of the "have-nots" (Anderson 1991; Coleman 1993). Thus far, those Latin American public policies aimed at bridging the inequality gap have repeatedly stressed investment in human capital, especially through education (ECLAC 1991). These policies could be more effective if they were to consider not only the resources of individuals but the social context of their lives. Since alley circles will continue to exist and operate, social policies should treat them as resources rather than as hindrances.

Current social investment intends to target the poor by means of a myriad of small-scale development projects (Rayo and Córdoba 1994). This line of action has been very efficient in channeling resources to poor people, but not so effective in helping them to overcome poverty (CEPAL

1995). If small-scale projects tend to reinforce strong ties among highly cohesive groups they preserve the poor in their current situation and could even provoke community fragmentation (Espinoza 1995). Hypothetically, public policies that develop weak ties could be more effective in the social integration of the poor.

The poor people of Las Villas are not atomized individuals whose achievement will depend on their individual excellence. Yet public policies conceive the poor as objects of policies and do not take into account the organizational resources expressed in their social networks. The social organization of the poor is far from an utopian economy of solidarity, but if any policy aims at improving their living conditions, it must find a way to connect with family initiatives, neighborhood organizations, and small local enterprises. The young, the women, the elderly, the children—everybody in the neighborhood—belong to small circles of families that distribute resources, provide a sense of sociable belonging and inculcate norms.

Does citizenship have any meaning for the poor? Regardless of the answer, to function as a citizen vested with rights and duties makes it necessary to break out of the cage of strong ties. The poor of Latin American barrios spend most of their time managing strong ties in the family and neighborhood, and weaker ties with bureaucratic patrons. A social organization based on strong ties makes inequality appear to be immutable. If neighbors were to find the way to strategic interaction, or public policies were to provide the space, such networks could be the necessary counterbalance to bureaucratic patronage. Participation through such networks in public decisionmaking could open up the boundaries of the community to citizenship and might strengthen citizenship itself.

Notes

I thank Thy Phu, Jimmy S. Smith, and Barry Wellman for their editorial assistance. Parts of this research were supported by Canada's International Development Research Centre, the Ford Foundation, and SUR Professionales Consultores in Chile. Fondo Nacional Desarrollo de Ciencia y Technología (FONDECYT) Project 1940084 provided extra support for additional data analysis. This chapter is dedicated to Marcela Hermoso.

1. For example, Lomnitz 1971, Duque and Pastrana 1973; Torrado 1981; Schmink 1984; Raczynski and Serrano 1985; Valdés 1985; Benería and Roldán 1987; Anderson 1991; Roberts 1991.

2. Fictitious names. A weighting factor was applied to each stratum to compensate for the different proportion of sites in the total. Accordingly, although the sample size is 207, totals appear as 210 in the tables.

3. This includes 13 types for which no respondent could mention any network member who were related to them in that way. Note that I did not ask questions

about emotional support, unlike Wellman's second Toronto study (1982; see also Chapter 2).

4. Resources are a composite measure made up from 57 indicators (see Espinoza [1992] for details). Row percentages in Table 4.1 do not add up to 100 because households may have multiple types of access for the same resource. The number of households in the rows are not always equal to those in the sample because some resources are not required by all of them. For instance, not all households have school-age children.

5. My analysis considers personalized transactions such as credit or hiring, and disregards other routine exchanges such as daily shopping.

6. Gift-giving is a special type of reciprocal exchange that occurs outside of the market. Although it has points of contact with informal exchanges in an economy of survival, gift-giving does not grow out of need and will not be discussed here. It does, however, contribute to the social integration of the community (see Cheal 1988).

7. For a similar analysis of self-provisioning in England, see Pahl 1984.

8. Roles were coded from answers to an open-ended question. Respondents were considered network members only if they belonged to a network of another household member.

9. I use the word "neighborhood" for the Chilean word *poblacion*. The latter has a more specific meaning than the English word, but it is still broadly vague in the context of my argument.

References

Anderson, Jeanine. 1991. *Reproducción Social/Políticas sociales*. Lima: SUMBI.

Benería, Lourdes, and Martha Roldán. 1987. *The Crossroads Of Class and Gender: Industrial Homework, Subcontracting and Household Dynamics in Mexico City*. Chicago: University of Chicago Press.

Berkowitz, S. D. 1982. *An Introduction to Structural Analysis. The Network Approach to Social Research*. Toronto: Butterworths.

Calzavara, Liviana Mostacci. 1982. "Social Networks and Access to Job Opportunities." Ph.D. thesis, Department of Sociology, University of Toronto.

Campbell, Karen, and Barrett Lee. 1991. "Name Generators: Surveys of Personal Networks." *Social Networks* 13:203–221.

Campero, Guillermo. 1987. *Pobladores: Entre La Sobrevivencia y la Acción Política*. Santiago: ILET.

Caplow, Theodore. 1982. "Christmas Gifts and Kin Networks." *American Sociological Review* 47:383–392.

Cécora, James. 1993. *Economic Behaviour of Family Households in an International Context*. Bonn: Society for Agricultural Policy Research and Rural Sociology.

CEPAL (Comisión Económica para América Latina y el Caribe). 1994. *Panorama Social de América Latina*. 1994 Santiago: Naciones Unidas.

CEPAL (Comisión Económica para América Latina y el Caribe). 1995. *Focalización y Pobreza Cuadernos de la Cepal 71*. Santiago: Naciones Unidas.

Cheal, David. 1988. *The Gift Economy*. London: Routledge.

Cohen, Ernesto, and Rolando Franco. 1992. *Evaluación de Proyectos Sociales.* Mexico DF: Siglo XXI Editores.

Coleman, James S. 1993. "The Rational Reconstruction of Society." *American Sociological Review* 58:1–15.

Collins, Jane L. 1986. "The Household and the Relations of Production in Southern Peru." *Comparative Studies in Society and History.* 28(4):651–671.

Cornelius, Wayne A. 1975. *Politics and the Migrant Poor in Mexico City.* Stanford, CA: Stanford University Press.

Correa, Ana María, and María Cristina Labán. 1984. "Estudio de las Características de las Redes Sociales en una Población Marginal de la Comuna de Santiago Como Recurso Potencial Para la Familia y Su Comunidad." Thesis, School of Social Work, Universidad Católica de Chile, Santiago.

DeBarbieri, Teresita. 1989. "Trabajos de la Reproducción." Pp. 235–252 in *Grupos Domésticos Reproducción Cotidiana,* edited by Orlandina de Oliveira, Marielle Pepin Lehauller, and Vania Salles. Mexico, DF: El Colegio de México.

Díaz, Alvaro. 1993. "Restructuring and the New Working Classes in Chile. Trends in Waged Employment, Informality and Poverty 1973–1990." Discussion Paper 49, United Nations Research Institute for Social Development. October.

Didier, Marcelo. 1986. "Redes Sociales y Búsqueda de Ayuda." *Revista Chilena de Psicología* 8(1):3–7.

Duque, Joaquín, and Ernesto Pastrana. 1973. "Las Estrategias de Supervivencia Económica de las Unidades Familiares del Sector Popular Urbano: Una Investigación Exploratoria." Santiago: PROELCE, FLACSO, CELADE.

ECLAC (United Nations Economic Commission for Latin America and the Caribbean). 1991 *Changing Production Patterns: An Integrated Approach* Santiago, Chile: United Nations.

ECLAC. 1992. "Latin American Poverty Profiles for the Early 1990s" LC/L.716 (Conf. 82/6). Document Prepared by the Statistics and Projections Division of ECLAC for the Third Regional Conference on Poverty in Latin America and the Caribbean. Santiago, Chile, November 23–25, 1992.

ECLAC. 1993. *Economic Report on Latin America and the Caribbean.* Santiago, Chile: United Nations.

Espinoza, Vicente. 1992. "Networks of Informal Economy: Work and Community Among Santiago's Urban Poor". Ph.D. Thesis. Department of Sociology, University of Toronto.

Espinoza, Vicente. 1993. "Pobladores y Participación. Entre los Pasajes y las Anchas Alamedas." *Proposiciones* 22:246–251.

Espinoza, Vicente. 1995. "Redes Sociales y Superación de la Pobreza." *Revista de Trabajo Social* 66:31–44. Escuela de Trabajo Social, Pontificia Universidad Católica de Chile.

Esteva, Gustavo. 1983. "Los Tradifas o el Fin de la Marginación" *El Trimestre Económico* 198 (Junio):733–770.

Fadda, Giulietta, and Enrique Oviedo. 1994. "Gestion local de servicios públicos en Chile: Aseo, Vivienda y Educación. Los casos de Talca y Temuco" Pp. 301–332 in *Municipio y Servicios Publicos. Gobiernos Locales en Ciudades Intermedias de America Latina,* edited by Alfredo Rodriguez and Fabio Velásquez. Santiago: Ediciones SUR.

Fischer, Claude. 1982. *To Dwell Among Friends*. Berkeley: University of California Press.

Frías, Patricio. 1977. "Cesantía y Estrategias de Sobrevivencia." *Documento de Trabajo*. Santiago: FLACSO.

Friedman, Kathie. 1984. "Households as Income-Pooling Units." Pp. 37–55 in *Households and the World Economy*, edited by Joan Smith, Immanuel Wallerstein, and Hans-Dieter Evers. Beverly Hills, CA: Sage.

Friedmann, John, and Mauricio Salguero. 1988. "The Barrio Economy and Collective Self-Empowerment in Latin-America: A Framework and Agenda for Research." Pp. 3–37 in *Power, Community and the City*, edited by Michael Peter Smith. New Brunswick, NJ: Transaction.

Gallardo, Bernarda. 1985. "Las Ollas Comunes de La Florida Como Experiencia de Desarrollo de la Organización Popular." *Documento de Trabajo* 248 (Junio). Santiago: FLACSO.

Gallardo, Bernarda. 1990. "Pobreza y Políticas Sociales." *Working Paper*. Santiago: CERC.

Granovetter, Mark. 1973. "The Strength of Weak Ties." *American Journal of Sociology* 78(6):1360–1380.

Granovetter, Mark S. 1982. "The Strength of Weak Ties. A Network Theory Revisited". Pp. 105–130 in *Social Structure and Network Analysis*, edited by Peter Marsden and Nan Lin. Beverly Hills, CA: Sage.

Granovetter, Mark S. 1995. *Getting a Job: A Study of Contacts and Careers*. 2d ed. Chicago: University of Chicago Press.

Grieco, Margaret. 1987. *Keeping it in Family: Social Networks and Employment Chance*. London: Tavistock.

Guerra Rodríguez, Carlos. 1991. "Las Organizaciones Sociales Poblacionales: Un Recurso Para la Aplicación de Políticas Públicas." Ph.D. Thesis, Instituto de Estudios Urbanos de la Pontificia Universidad Católica de Chile, Magister en Asentamientos Humanos y Medio Ambiente.

Harvey, David. 1985. *The Urbanization of Capital: Studies in the History and Theory of Capitalist Urbanization*. Baltimore: Johns Hopkins University Press.

Irarrázaval, Ignacio. 1992. "Comentario." Pp. 73–86 in *La Realidad en Cifras. Estadísticas Sociales*, edited by Sergio Gómez. Santiago: FLACSO/INE/UNRISD.

Lem, Winnie. 1988. "Household Production and Reproduction in Rural Languedoc: Social Relations of Petty Commodity Production in Merviel-les-Beziers." *Journal of Peasant Studies* 15(4):500–530.

Liebow, Elliot. 1967. *Tally's Corner*. Boston: Little, Brown.

Lin, Nan. 1982. "Social Resources and Instrumental Action." Pp. 131–46 in *Social Structure and Network Analysis*, edited by Peter Mardsen and Nan Lin. Beverly Hills, CA: Sage.

Lomnitz, Larissa Adler. 1971. "Reciprocity of Favors in the Urban Middle Class of Chile." Pp. 93–106 in *Studies in Economic Anthropology*, edited by George Dalton. Washington: American Anthropological Association.

Lomnitz, Larissa Adler. 1977. *Networks and Marginality*. New York: Academic Press.

Lomnitz, Larissa Adler. 1978. "Mechanisms of Articulation Between Shantytown Settlers and the Urban System." *Urban Anthropology* 7(2):185–205.

Lomnitz, Larissa Adler. 1986. "La Gran Familia Como Unidad Básica de Solidaridad en México." *Anuario Jurídico* 13:147–163. Primer Congreso Interdisciplinario Sobre la Familia Mexicana, Mexico D.F.: Instituto de Investigaciones Jurídicas, UNAM.

Lorrain, François, and Harrison C. White. 1971. "Structural Equivalence of Individuals in Social Networks." *Journal of Mathematical Sociology* 1:49–80.

Marshall, Teresa, ed. 1984. *Historias de Mujeres de la Ciudad. Historias de Vida en Doce Episodios.* Santiago: SUR.

McKee, Lorna. 1987. "Households During Unemployment: The Resourcefulness of Unemployed." Pp. 96–116 in *Give and Take in Families: Studies in Resource Distribution*, edited by Julia Brannen and Gail Wilson. London: Allen and Unwin.

Middleton, Dwight R. 1991. "Development, Household Clusters, and Work-Wealth in Manta" *City and Society* 5(2):137–154.

MIDEPLAN [Social Planning Ministry]. 1992. *Población, Educación, Vivienda, Salud, Empleo y Pobreza. CASEN 1990.* Santiago: MIDEPLAN, Ministerio de Planificación y Cooperación.

Mingione, Enzo. 1991. *Fragmented Societies: A Sociology of Economic Life Beyond the Market Paradigm.* Oxford: Basil Blackwell.

Morales, Juan Antonio, and Gary McMahon, eds. 1993. *La Política Económica en la Transición a la Democracia: Lecciones de Argentina, Bolivia, Chile, Uruguay.* Santiago: CIEPLAN.

O'Donnel, Guilermo, and Philippe Schmitter. 1986. *Transitions from Authoritarian Rule. Tentative Conclusions About Uncertain Democracies.* Baltimore: Johns Hopkins University Press.

Oliveira, Orlandina, and Vania Salles. 1989. "Grupos Domésticos: Un Enfoque Demográfico." Pp. 11–36 in *Grupos Domésticos y Reproducción Social*, edited by Orlandina Oliveira, Marielle Pepin Lehalleur, and Vania Salles. Mexico DF: El Colegio de Mexico.

Pahl, Ray. 1984. *Divisions of Labour.* Oxford: Blackwell.

Peattie, Lisa Redfield. 1970. *The View from the Barrio.* Ann Arbor, MI: University of Michigan Press.

Polanyi, Karl. 1957a. *The Great Transformation: The Political and Economic Origins of Our Time.* Boston: Beacon Press.

Polanyi, Karl. 1957b. "The Economy as Instituted Process." Pp. 243–270 in *Trade and Market in the Early Empires: Economies in History and Theory*, edited by Karl Polanyi, Conrad Arensberg, and Harry Pearson. Glencoe, IL: Free Press.

Raczynski, Dagmar, and Claudia Serrano. 1985. *Vivir la Pobreza.* Santiago: CIEPLAN-PISPAL.

Raczynski, Dagmar. 1994. "Políticas Sociales y Programas de Combate a la Pobreza en Chile: Balance y Desafío." *Colección Estudios CIEPLAN* 39 (Junio).

Rayo, Gustavo, and Julio Córdoba. 1994. "FOSIS: un Nuevo Concepto de Política Orientada a la Superación de la Pobreza." Working Paper. Santiago: FOSIS.

Razeto, Luis. 1990. *Economía Popular de Solidaridad: Identidad y Proyecto en una Visión Integradora.* Santiago: Area Pastoral Social de la Conferencia Episcopal de Chile.

Razeto, Luis, Arno Klenner, Apolonia Ramírez, and Roberto Urmeneta. 1983. *Las Organizaciones Económicas Populares.* Santiago: Programa de Economía del Trabajo, PET-AHC.

Roberts, Bryan. 1973. *Organizing Strangers*. Austin: University of Texas Press.

Roberts, Bryan. 1978. *Cities of Peasants*. London: Sage.

Roberts, Bryan. 1991. "Household Coping Strategies and Urban Poverty in a Comparative Perspective" Pp. 135–68 in *Urban Life in Transition*, edited by Marc Gottdiener and Chris Pickvance. Newbury Park, CA: Sage.

Rodríguez, Alfredo, Vicente Espinoza, and Hilda Herzer. 1995. "Argentina, Bolivia, Chile, Ecuador, Peru, Uruguay. Urban Research in the 1990s: A Framework for an Agenda." Pp. 223–280 in *Urban Research in the Developing World*. Vol. 3. *Latin America*. Edited by Richard Stren. Toronto: Centre for Urban and Community Studies. University of Toronto.

Rojas, Alejandro. 1988. "Political and Ecological Implications of the Chilean Economy of Solidarity." Paper delivered at the International Conference on the Political Economies of the Margins. Toronto, May 27–29.

Sahlins, Marshall. 1972. *Stone Age Economics*. Chicago: Aldine Atherton.

Schkolnik, Mariana, and Berta Teitelboim. 1988. *Pobreza y Desempleo en Poblaciones. La Otra Cara del Modelo Liberal*. Santiago: PET, Colección Temas Sociales.

Schmink, Marianne. 1984. "Household Economic Strategies. Review and Research Agenda." *Latin American Research Review* 19:87–101.

Sennett, Richard. 1977. *The Fall of Public Man*. New York: Knopf.

Sik, Endre. 1988. "The 'Eternity' of an Institution for Survival" *Innovation* 4/5:589–623.

Sorj, Bernardo. 1991 "Crisis Social y Crisis de las Ciencias Sociales en Brasil." *Revista Mexicana de Sociología* 1/91:107–20.

Tironi, Eugenio. 1990. *Autoritarismo, Modernización y Marginalidad: El Caso de Chile, 1973–1989*. Santiago: Ediciones SUR.

Torrado, Susana. 1981. "Sobre Los Conceptos de 'Estrategias Familiares de Vida' y 'Proceso de Reproducción de la Fuerza de Trabajo': Notas Teórico-Metodológicas." *Demografía y Economía* 15(2):204–233.

Touraine, Alain. 1976. *Las Sociedades Dependientes. Ensayos Sobre América Latina*. Mexico: Siglo XXI Editores.

Valdés, Teresa. 1985. "Mujer Popular: Matrimonio, Hijos y Proyecto: Un Estudio de Casos." *Documento de Trabajo* 255. Santiago: FLACSO.

Valenzuela, Arturo. 1977. *Political Brokers in Chile*. Durham, NC: Duke University Press.

Vergara, Pilar. 1990. *Políticas Hacia la Extrema Pobreza en Chile 1973/88*. Santiago: FLACSO.

Warde, Alan. 1990. "Production, Consumption and Social Change. Reservations Regarding Peter Saunders' Sociology of Consumption." *International Journal of Urban and Regional Research* 14(2):228–248.

Wegener, Bernd. 1991. "Job Mobility and Social Ties: Social Resources, Prior Job, and Status Attainment." *American Sociological Review* 56 (February):60–71.

Wellman, Barry. 1979. "The Community Question." *American Journal of Sociology* 84 (March):1201–1231.

Wellman, Barry. 1982. "Studying Personal Communities." Pp. 61–80 in *Social Networks and Social Structure*, edited by Peter Marsden and Nan Lin. Beverly Hills, CA: Sage.

Wellman, Barry. 1985. "Domestic Work, Paid Work and Net Work." Pp. 159–191 in *Understanding Personal Relationships*, edited by Steve Duck and Daniel Perlman. London: Sage.

Wellman, Barry. 1988a. "Structural Analysis: From Method and Metaphor to Theory and Substance." Pp. 19–61 in *Social Structures: A Network Approach*, edited by Barry Wellman and S. D. Berkowitz. Cambridge: Cambridge University Press.

Wellman, Barry. 1988b. "The Community Question Re-Evaluated." Pp. 81–107 in *Power, Community and the City*, edited by Michael Peter Smith. New Brunswick, NJ: Transaction Books.

Wellman, Barry. 1992. "Which Types of Ties Provide What Kinds of Social Support?" *Advances in Group Processes* 9:207–235.

Wellman, Barry. 1996. "Are Personal Communities Local? A Dumptarian Reconsideration." *Social Networks* 18(3):347–354.

Wellman, Barry, and Barry Leighton. 1979. "Networks, Neighbourhoods and Communities." *Urban Affairs Quarterly* 14 (March):363–390.

Wellman, Barry, and Scot Wortley. 1989. "Brothers' Keepers: Situating Kinship Relationships in Broader Networks of Social Support." *Sociological Perspectives* 32(3):273–306.

Wellman, Barry, and Scot Wortley. 1990. "Different Strokes from Different Folks: Community Ties and Social Support." *American Journal of Sociology* 96(3):558–588.

Wellman, Barry, Peter Carrington, and Allan Hall. 1988. "Networks as Personal Communities." Pp. 130–84 in *Social Structures: A Network Approach*, edited by Barry Wellman and S. D. Berkowitz. Cambridge: Cambridge University Press.

Wilson, Edward William. 1988. "Households and the Problem of Urban Poverty in the Third World." Ph.D. Thesis. University of Pennsylvania.

Wong, Diana. 1984. "The Limits of Using Households as Unit of Analysis." Pp. 56–63 in *Households and the World Economy*, edited by Joan Smith, Immanuel Wallerstein, and Hans-Dieter Evers. Beverly Hills, CA: Sage.

5

The Diversity of Personal Networks in France: Social Stratification and Relational Structures

Alexis Ferrand, Lise Mounier, and Alain Degenne

If one thinks that a society is characterized by a system of values and norms—in a word, its "culture"—then French society cannot be said to exist unless one presents it as a mosaic of cultures similar to that which Robert Park (1925) observed in Chicago. It is not that this diversity is total or that there are grand structural cleavages. It is manageable, but it has not disappeared. Hence any sociological analysis of the French population has to balance global statements with the humility of specific data analyses, with their particular questions and methodological limitations.

Our key question is: How are relations organized in French society? How can we analyze and describe this organization so that readers, by comparing it with other societies, can get a clear view of French particularities? As the contents of ties and the ways in which populations are categorized vary from one country to another, it is meaningless and uninteresting to compare direct statistical measures of relationships. To do this would be to make the same mistake as some international statistical directories do when they present standardized indicators. Instead, a rather abstract picture of reality is needed since only abstract patterns are comparable. As far as relations are concerned, we need to insist more on studying the arrangements and articulations of relational systems than on comparing their composition.

In this chapter we examine how some forms of interpersonal relations are organized in French society. We use data from three national sample surveys to study four types of interpersonal ties and the networks they comprise: friendship *(l'amitié)*, love *(l'amour)*, confidants *(la confidence)*, and mutual aid *(l'échange d'aide)*. Affecting the composition of these networks are processes that are both products and causes of the basic structural cleavages of age, gender, and social status. Thus examining the articulation of these relational systems necessitates forming a social theory and developing a mode of analysis.

First we sketch a few elements of two middle-range theories that have guided our analyses. Although the proposed analyses are common in studies of personal networks, it is worth explaining how we interpret them. Second, we describe how the data were collected and consider how the diversity of interpersonal networks and ties are associated with major sociodemographic characteristics. The next two sections present the heart of our analyses. One section examines how different kinds of interpersonal ties articulate different relational structures. Thus this section analyzes role relationships. The second section examines how different kinds of interpersonal ties articulate social positions, rather than roles.

We caution that the survey data we use constrain our analysis. Because our analysis is based entirely on secondary analysis of data stemming from three surveys constructed for other purposes, we cannot pursue all the inquiries that we would have liked. Moreover, because these surveys were conducted more than a decade ago and were cross-sectional, we lack historical perspective and the ability to study social change. For example, the respondents of different ages are mostly analyzed in terms of their life-courses rather than in terms of generational discrepancies. And in certain cases we must treat the microdynamics of the establishment of relations as a synchronic property of relational systems rather than giving it its proper due as evolving over time.

Two Views of Relational Structures

Articulation Between Kinds of Ties

While there is some validity to considering personal networks as "systems," it is more legitimate to say that personal networks exhibit articulations between relational systems. They are systems of systems. That is, every tie is embedded in a network consisting of the same kinds of ties a person has with others: several friends, workmates, or neighbors who, in turn, may have ties with one another, and be further linked to others. Each kind of tie constitutes a network and a particular system. However, a relation can be multiplex, consisting of at least two different kinds of ties between the same two actors (e.g., a friend is also a workmate[1]). Furthermore, each actor is a member of a widespread network of friendship ties—where the person has other friends—and of a widespread network of ties between workmates—where the person is also linked to other workmates. Hence the relation of two persons as a friend *and* a workmate is an intersection between these two widespread networks of friendship and workmate ties.

In our first approach to studying articulation, let us begin by assuming that *all* friends are also workmates but that all workmates are not friends. Then the friendship network would be a part of the network of workmates. Labor would be the only substructure establishing friendship. In this situation, the structure of the workmate network would impose strong constraints upon possible friendship ties. (However, the specific principles of establishing friendship ties would keep the friendship network from being totally isomorphic with the workmate network.) Because all friends are workmates, those relations based on the social division of labor would constrain the subsystem of friendship ties. Although this is an extreme ideal case, the constraining of one form of relationship by another happens in highly integrated communities, such as villages, urban ghettos, geographically isolated company towns, or organizations (such as IBM or China twenty years ago) that seek to manage both the personal and the work lives of their cadres.

Beyond this extreme case, any relation with two ties is an intersection between tie-specific networks that forms an articulation between those substructures that characterize them. A tie between two persons who are simultaneously friends and workmates articulates the worlds of friendship and coworking. A static reading of these articulations is possible when respondents are asked if certain kinds of ties exist in a relation defined in terms of another kind of tie. But a dynamic reading is also possible when respondents are asked what kind of tie existed *before* the emergence of the tie currently under examination. This can provide information about how a given kind of tie can foster the emergence of another kind: can a neighbor become a friend, a workmate become a confidant, and so forth. (Indeed, the relation may not remain multiplex, as when people cease being workmates but continue to be friends.) The process by which one kind of tie generates another can either be symmetrical—workmates can become friends as much as friends can become workmates[2]—or asymmetrical—there are always more workmates who become friends than friends who become workmates. A systematic asymmetry would indicate, according to Nadel's (1957) formulation, that a tie functions as a recruiter for another.

Another form of articulation in which one kind of tie generates another occurs when a third party who knows two actors on the basis of a given tie leads these two to establish a tie. When the tie that is established is the same kind that the two parties already have, this process allows for the extension and regeneration of a structure, that is, its self-reproduction.

TABLE 5.1   Articulation of Friendship Ties with Other Roles (example)

	Friends	Nonfriends	All (%)
Workmates	15	85	100
Neighbors	05	95	100
Comembers	20	80	100

When the tie that is established is of a different kind, then the structural process initiated by the third party has led to the establishment or renewal of another structure of relations. In this latter situation, the two structures are interdependent.[3]

On a higher level of analysis, the nature and strength of these various articulations constitute a structural property of the patterns and interconnections of systems of different kinds of relationships: friends, workmates, and so on. In such analyses, our focus is not directly on multiplexity or transitivity themselves, but on the ways in which they allow a description of the cross-sectional and dynamic connections between relational systems. Hence, at the level of an actor's personal network, various forms of articulation between these particular relational systems can be analyzed.

Given these general principles, we can now address a methodological issue. Let us assume that friends can also be workmates, neighbors, or members of the same organization ("comembers"). To measure the strength of intersection (articulation) between these relational systems, we need an exhaustive count of all friendship ties and all other related ties. This might produce the results shown in Table 5.1 (an artificially constructed case study).

The surveys we are using in our analysis do not enable us to know the *total* number of friends, workmates, and so on that people actually have in their networks. Because all of them are national, random-sample surveys, they statistically generalize to the same type of actors' actual networks, with the same number of kinship, friendship, and neighborhood ties. Yet we really do not know the parameters of these actual networks. But we do know that for a given population, 3% of the confidant ties are also workmate ties and that 14% of the mutual aid ties are also workmate ties. Because the number of actually available workmates is essentially identical across surveys, comparing these percentages shows that the system of mutual aid is more closely related to the system of workmates than is the system of confidants.

Thus the analysis in this chapter implies that there are actual networks, unknown but homogeneous throughout the surveys. By *comparing kinds of ties* we can obtain an outline of a relational structure as an articulation of specific systems of ties with one another. However, it can only be a partial outline of the structure, since the ties examined deal with limited domains of social life.

Is there a single "French" relational structure? Probably not. Social differences manifest themselves in the diverse ways in which ties articulate with one another. The first substantive section of this chapter will describe the diversity of these modes of articulation, especially according to gender and age.

Positional Articulation Between Kinds of Ties

The second way of approaching articulation between systems of relations is through the classic formulation of Laumann and Pappi (1976, p. 6), defining a social structure as "a persisting pattern of social relationships among social positions. A social relationship is any direct or indirect linkage between incumbents of different social positions." This defines a structure in sociometric terms as the specific arrangement of ties among "positions" in contrast to our previous use of the term "structure" as the articulation of kinds of ties with one another. Let us go back to Laumann and Pappi: "There exists a multiplicity of social structures in any complex social system that arises out of the many possible types of social relationships linking positions to one another." This admits, just as we do, the existence of different relational systems, each having "its own logic of social and functional constraint" (1976, p. 7).

How may these different systems be linked to one another? How do Laumann and Pappi conceive of the articulation of relational systems? "for any given relationship-specific structure, there exists a principle of systematic bias in channeling the formation of . . . relationships between certain kinds of positions and the avoidance of such relationships between others" (1976, p. 7). Unfortunately for our purposes, after discussing the main theories of social differentiation, the authors define positions only within *one* structure, that of the division of labor. This poses a problem for a structural approach to analyzing social life because the sociometric arrangement for each particular relational system allows actors to be assigned positions that are specific at each time. This theoretical inconsistency has been noted by Blau, who asks: "Do we first analyze social relations and distinguish positions on the basis of differences in patterns of relations, or do we start by categorizing people by social position to examine the patterns of relations among them?" (1982, p. 277). Blau shows that the former approach is more apt for emerging microsocial processes while the latter approach is more suitable when social positions "have become crystallized." However, his answer is rather pragmatic and not theoretically grounded.

The general assumption of almost all network analysts is that the actor's position in those processes that make up the relational system of production *more or less strongly* determines positions in other relational structures. Even nonmarxists seem to hold this view implicitly. Such analyses use the actors' positions in the division of labor as a reference in order to examine the probability that a particular kind of tie exists between two actors with different positions within this basic structure (e.g., Laumann 1973). This raises two issues:

1. To what extent is a relational system articulated with the division of labor? To what extent do empirical data show that the relations of this system, instead of being randomly distributed among any positions, are channeled by systematic "biases" to particular positions?

It is possible to compare different relational systems with respect to these issues. The extent to which different systems are analogous with each other can provide partial conclusions about their *autonomy or interdependence* from each other. Although such conclusions would only be partial, they would also be theoretically significant. The extent of the interdependence that exists between the various domains of social life is a structural property of those social systems that help us comprehend their dynamics of change. For instance, an economic crisis might set off a major social explosion. The social milieus' ability to respond to the ways in which they are affected by such an economic crisis would depend partly on the degree of interdependence of all the relational systems that make up these milieus, and not just the strictly economic domain. In a similar analysis, Grafmeyer (1991) notes that the bourgeoisie of Lyon are organized without an emphasis on occupational status. One can be socially bourgeois without being economically bourgeois.

2. The second issue addresses the *meaning*, rather than the degree, of interdependence. Is it possible to believe that one structure is caused by another? (In practice, one always implicitly does this more or less.) For example, are men often married to women who are clerks only because clerical occupations tend to be feminine? Or do women become clerks because they often are wives? Does, or does not, the structure of trade unions affect the economic structure? We raise these questions because they are interesting and important, but unfortunately, the data we have available provide no answer.

The relational and positional approaches to articulating social systems have guided the analyses introduced in the two parts that follow. As they do not describe the same structural properties, they are not integrated. Schematically, they recall two of the origins of network analytic thought: (a) a social anthropological concern with the ways in which institutionalized roles combine; (b) a continuation of the sociometric spirit in the sociological analysis of social stratification.

Definitions and Data

Four Kinds of Ties

Before examining our results, we specify the four kinds of ties that we shall analyze in this chapter: friendship, love, confidants, and mutual aid.

Friendship. A tie between two persons is supposed to be unselfish and egalitarian. Guided at first by the mere pleasure of sociability, it can also exhibit unconditional assistance that is not fettered by concerns of short-term reciprocity. An increase in the number of friends can strain the amount of attention a person can give to any one tie. A friendship tie is often perceived as being incompatible with a close kinship tie, a love tie, or a significant difference in status.

Love. Operationally defined in the surveys as a current tie with one's latest sexual partner, it is based on the exchange of pleasure within social prescriptions and is usually regarded as reciprocal. When two lovers constitute a couple in a household, they are an economic unit of consumption. In such cases (the majority of the ties), love ties can include exchanges of economic resources. When lovers are parents, love ties also entail social reproduction through the education of children.

Confidants. Confidants exchange confidences about emotional and sexual matters. It is a tie based on the exchange of speech, information and advice dealing with a private domain of one's life. Such ties can involve processes of influence and control. When exchanges of confidences concern sexual relations, they bring about an articulation between sexual and nonsexual networks.

Mutual aid. Mutual aid is operationally defined in this chapter as the exchange of services between households rather than between individuals.[4] Mutual-aid ties are part of a network in which resources are exchanged. Their exchanges of aid may not be egalitarian. Note that our definition of mutual aid is limited only to services and does not include the emotional aid that many studies of social support also take into account (Wellman 1992b).

The Surveys

The Survey of Modes of Life. This survey of 6,807 households representative of all of France was carried out between November 1988 and November 1989. It provides a detailed description of the households, their homes, the members of their households, and their close relatives. It records mutual aid between households and close relatives, and it describes the help provided by a wife to her husband in his paid work. Each type of activity distinguishes between services provided by household members and those provided by network members outside of the household. Diaries for weekly expenditures and time use were completed by the housewives and, if necessary, their husbands. A second questionnaire further specified the content of each activity. (An appendix provides descriptive statistics for all the surveys used in this chapter.)

The survey's module lists opportunities for *exchanging goods and services*—services given, services received, and services both given and received. This enables us to describe those households with whom the respondents exchange aid. Several types of services are identified in this module: services related to children (child-care, taking them to school), services about daily life (shopping, housework), and more specialized or incidental services: sewing, making preserves (such as jellies), plant and animal care, odd jobs, and heavy work. For every household with which there has been an exchange, the module enumerates the kind of tie with the household (kinship, neighbor, workmate, friend), the household's composition, the location of the residence, and the household head's occupation.

The Survey of Sexual Behavior.   Between November 1991 and February 1992, the *Agence Nationale de Recherches sur le Sida* (National AIDS Research Agency) surveyed 20,055 randomly chosen persons aged eighteen to sixty-nine living in French households. The questionnaire allowed the estimation of frequency of potentially hazardous behaviors, as well as the number of sexual partners and the use of tests to detect AIDS. In addition, a questionnaire for measuring the frequency of various sexual practices and analyzing the sociological and psychological factors associated with them was administered to two subsamples: 2,271 persons with potentially hazardous sexual behavior and 2,549 persons as a reference sample.

The subsample questionnaire used a social network name generator: "Besides the person you live with, with how many people do you speak about romances, sexual problems or diseases, your life as a couple." This allowed the respondent to identify up to three *confidant* relationships, and provide information about the confidants' sociodemographic characteristics, length of relationship with the respondent, frequency of interaction, role relationship, reported sexual behavior, and changes in this behavior since the emergence of AIDS. We also obtained data about each respondent's *most recent sexual intercourse* with his/her customary household partner. In our analyses for this chapter, we treat confidant and sexual ties separately.

The Survey of Contacts Between Persons. This survey aimed to describe and analyze various forms of sociability: neighborhood, work relations, kinship, fellowship, going out, and so on. Jointly conducted by the
Institut National de la Statistique des Études Économiques (INSEE) and
the Institut National d'Études Démographiques (INED) in 1982–1983, the
survey was carried out from a random sample of 8,000 addresses representative of the French population according to the 1975 census. Surveys
were administered to 5,900 households, representing 16,400 persons,
during eight waves of four to five weeks. The data were obtained
through questionnaires (questionnaire A for an adult of the household,
questionnaire B for a randomly chosen individual) and seven-day diaries
filled in by the respondents.

The *friendship* module of this survey obtained information about the respondents' relationships with their three best friends: sociodemographic
information, duration of the relation, context, geographical proximity,
frequency of meetings or exchanges through the mail or over the telephone, presence of spouse in these exchanges, membership in a group of
friends as opposed to an independent dyadic tie between the respondent
and the network member.

The Size of Networks

As is the case for all other studies of personal networks, our information
is limited to only the small number of strong ties about which the respondents reported. These do not represent the size of actual networks because survey procedures do not enable us to study the thousand or more
other interpersonal ties that most respondents probably had.[5]

There is substantial variation in the number of persons with whom respondents interact. For instance, the number of confidants about emotional or sexual matters ranges from 0 to 10, with a mean of 2.3; the number of households involved in mutual aid exchanges ranges from 0 to
over 100, with a mean of 3.0. This variance can be analyzed in terms of
the respondents' sociodemographic characteristics.

For every kind of tie examined, women's networks are somewhat
smaller than men's. The difference is chiefly noticeable for friendship
ties: a mean of 2.4 for women versus 3.4 for men. The lower relational ex-
pansiveness of women expresses the differences between—and perhaps
the interdependence of—female and male roles. Often, a woman marries
not only a man but his network as well, to the detriment of her own
friendship ties. This French phenomenon is quite different from what
Wellman (1992a) found in Toronto, Canada, where women's relationships dominate in marital households.

The effects of age on different kinds of ties are manifested at different stages of the life course. The number of confidant relations dealing with emotional and sexual matters diminishes slightly and regularly with age. The number of friends is stable until the age of sixty, and then it decreases. Aid exchanges vary according to major changes in a household's life course. For respondents under the age of forty, the beginning of occupational life and the raising of young children generate exchanges between nearly four other households. Then the number of households involved in such exchanges tends to decline: to slightly over three other households for those between the ages of forty and fifty, and to less than three households for those between ages fifty and seventy.

This variation in the size of networks according to the kind of tie that comprise them reveals the heterogeneity of changes that make up the life course. The more the relationships pertain to practical ends, such as mutual aid, the more they vary according to the evolution through the life course of the problems that individuals and households happen to face. The more the relationships deal with an individual's personality, identity and emotional life—such as friendship ties do—the steadier is their number through the life course.

The Articulation of Ties Within Relations

Confidants and Mutual Aid

General Tendencies. The surveys about exchanging confidences and aid asked respondents about what other kinds of ties exist in the same relationship: kin (inside and outside of the respondents' households), neighbor, workmate, friend. The association of these relationships with being confidants or providing mutual aid indicates the articulation of different kinds of relationships.

Aid exchanges were found twice as often in kinship ties (55%) as in friendship ties (23%; see Table 5.2). Conversely, confidants are found more than twice as often in friendship ties (62%) than in kin (24%). These percentages show the *strength* of the articulation of mutual aid and confidences with friendship and kinship. Over half of mutual aid ties are "stuck" to ascriptive kinship ties, as if the exchange of domestic services needs both the intimacy and the solidarity so often characteristic of kinship ties. Moreover, confidences about emotional and sexual matters are so often included in friendship ties that it is possible to imagine that both types of ties satisfy a single relational logic. Two constituents of the actors' relational structure begin to emerge: *kinship + aid*, and *friendship + confidants*.

As for other kinds of ties, neighboring fosters mutual aid but does not warrant exchanging confidences about personal life.[6] Workmates show

TABLE 5.2 Association of Mutual Aid and Confidant Ties with Kind of Tie

	Kin		Friends		Neighbors		Workmates		Total
	M	CV	M	CV	M	CV	M	CV	
Mutual Aid	55%	.95	23%	1.77	15%	1.72	3%	4.87	96% [a]
Confidant	24%	1.77	62%	.78	–	–	14%	2.50	100%

M = Mean   CV = Coefficient of variation
[a] 4% have another kind of tie

the opposite pattern: exchanging confidences but no mutual aid outside of the workplace. We can therefore expand the original equations:

$$\text{Mutual Aid} = \text{Kinship} + \text{Neighboring}$$

$$\text{Confidants} = \text{Friendship} + \text{Workmates.}$$

The picture we obtain is that people get help in domestic situations from kin and neighbors, but they confide in their friends and workmates. Friendship and workmate relations are more voluntary, which means they can be more easily broken if confidences are betrayed. Moreover, friendship and workmate relations are less densely knit so people have less ability to socially control indiscretions revealed through confidences.

Gender and Age. The data just presented aggregate networks pertaining to all population categories: men and women, young and old, etc. But is there *one* "French" relational pattern or several distinct patterns?

With respect to *confidant* relations, there is much social diversity within France. For example, the coefficients of variation ("CV" in Table 5.2) of the distributions for each kind of tie go from 0.78 for friendship to 1.77 for kinship to 2.50 for workmate ties.[7] Although confidant relations are strongly and consistently articulated with friendship, the articulation between confidants and other roles is subject to significant social variation.

Therefore, we need to examine how variations in how kinds of ties articulate with one another may depend on the actors' positions with respect to rift lines in society. We focus here on gender and age—which will be found in further analyses below—for they are very general phenomena that make our comparisons easier. To simplify analyses, we shall only comment on contrasting results; the reader can refer to the tables for a more detailed approach.

The *gender rift* is strong for confidant ties but not for mutual aid. Women confide in kin (29%) more than men do (18%), but women confide less in workmates (10%) than men do (19%; Table 5.3). To put it an-

TABLE 5.3   Age Group Articulation Between Ties and Roles

	Family (%)	Neighbors (%)	Workmates Schoolmates (%)	Friends (%)	Others (%)	All (%)
Mutual aid						
18–24	57	4	2	36	1	100
25–39	53	12	3	29	3	100
40–49	48	18	4	26	4	100
50–59	54	19	3	19	5	100
60–69	62	18	0	15	5	100
Confidant						
18–24	28	–	4	68	–	100
25–39	25	–	17	58	–	100
40–49	21	–	19	61	–	101
50–59	26	–	18	56	–	100
60–69	14	–	13	73	–	100

other way, while men confide in workmates about as much as they confide in kin, women are three times more likely to confide in kin than in workmates.

At every age, mutual aid is chiefly articulated with kinship and confidants with friendship. These are the preferential and dominant articulations. They weaken somewhat in the middle ages, only to become strongest at ages sixty to sixty-nine (the upper end of the ages surveyed).

By contrast, less dominant roles decrease somewhat regularly with age. For aid exchanges, friendship declines from 36% to 15%, while for confidants, kinship declines from 28% to 14%. Aging seems to have a systematic and linear effect, with these secondary modes of articulation becoming increasingly recessive. Aid networks disengage from friendship, and confidant networks disengage from kinship. As we have seen, this disengagement will be compensated in later life by the strong influence of the dominant role.

With regard to mutual aid, the decrease of kinship is compensated by the increase of neighborly relations from the age of twenty-five onward. If kinship is always dominant with respect to mutual aid, then neighborly relations are complementary or concurrent (as is also the case in Toronto: see Wellman and Wortley 1989). With regard to confidant relations, the decrease of friendship ties is compensated for by the increase of workmate ties between the ages of twenty-five and sixty. The age of twenty-five, with marriage and paid work usually begun, sees the onset of the standard equations: *aid = kinship + neighboring*, while *confidants = friends + workmates*. There are variations in the sources of aid and confidences. One does not necessarily need more or less support as one grows older, but the sources of aid and confidence change over time.

Thus the variations shown in Table 5.3 express changes in the principles of articulation between kinds of ties. A synthesis of these changes can be expressed as rules of structural dynamics:

	Confidants	Mutual aid
Dominant relational role:	friend	kin
Weak complementary role:	workmate	neighbor
Recessive role:	kin	friend

As one grows older, the importance of the complementary role continuously increases from being weak at the beginning of adult life to competing with the dominant role in midlife. However, the dominant role becomes stronger again as people attain their sixties. In fact, it is at its strongest in this older age group.

How can we comprehend these rules? As for any variation by age, they can be comprehended as stemming from either the social logic of the life course or from the logic of cultural deviations between generations. Without having decisive arguments available for either position, we favor the assumption of changes connected to the life-course.

Thus the regular decrease of family involvement as emotional and sexual confidants can be interpreted as the gradual autonomous development of individual emotional life, which leads people away from their ascriptive family ties. To view this in another perspective, individuals speak about love and sex in the sphere of achievement: friendship and work life.

Urbanization. Urbanization does not put an end to mutual aid, despite the fears of the "Community Lost" argument (see Wellman's 1988 review). The composition of mutual aid ties varies with population size in complex ways. Although one mutual aid tie out of five is a neighborhood tie in a rural area, there is no effect of the degree of urbanization on the proportion of neighbors in aid exchanges in places ranging in size from towns of 20,000 up to the Paris urban area. By contrast, the more a place is urbanized, the higher the proportion of friends who exchange mutual aid: from 17% in rural areas to 30% in the Paris urban area. Kinship ties comprise 58% to 55% of aid ties in places of all sizes, except for Paris where they comprise only 49% of such ties.

The extent of urbanization does not affect confidant ties to the extent that it affects mutual aid. However, Parisians have a lower proportion than other French people of confidants who are their friends.

It is the logic of the articulation of ties that is important. Mutual aid and confidant relations are differentially influenced by the *accessibility* of network members. Although confiding in a friend can be done over the telephone, it is not yet possible to water a friend's plants remotely. Thus for practical reasons, less material aid from kin is asked for by Parisians, as their kin tend to live farther away than their friends. However, the assumption of a special Parisian "subculture" (Fischer 1982) is also plausible, with friendship ties being especially voluntary and supportive in this milieu.

Education.   The weight of family relations for both aid and confidant relations is greater among people with the least education. Conversely, the more education, the higher the proportion of friends exchanging aid and confidences. These differences likely originate less in subcultural variation among adults (with more educated people being "less traditional") than in relational forms of childhood socialization. The educational system cumulatively defines pupils as individuals who must prove themselves. This orients them toward autonomous friendships rather than toward ascriptive kinship ties.

How Ties Generate Ties

Three Processes of Establishing a Tie.   Personal networks are dynamic realities and the duration of ties in them is variable. Some come to an end while others get established. We examine here *genetic articulations between relational systems,* using as an example the genesis of friendship and stable sexual ties in a relation.

Respondents were asked in the surveys how they encountered the members of their networks. Three processes are possible:

1. There already was a direct ego-alter relationship, and another kind of tie was added to it.
2. Ego and the future alter already shared the same acquaintance, and their ties with this third party fostered the establishment of a direct ego-alter relationship. Not only is this a shift from an indirect link to a direct one, it is also the emergence of a tie that may be different from those that had fostered the contact. Thus it is an effect of the transitivity of interpersonal ties between two different relational systems.
3. Ego and alter already were participating in the same social context, and this shared participation allowed them to become acquainted and establish a particular kind of tie. This is a shift

from a shared and weak membership role to a stronger, direct interpersonal tie.

We can show how a relation can arise out of other relations by examining the types of third-party relations or social contexts that have fostered these ties. We can also shed light on an important structural property: If we assume that the relation which allowed Ego and Alter to establish their new relation is likely to last, then these two relations are "chained" along with their central roles (Nadel 1957). They are interrelated as to their future, for each type of tie exerts some social control on the type of tie even though they each are private and personal relations. Therefore, it is important to differentiate those first encounters that arose out of a relation with a third party—situations in which "chaining" is relevant—from contextual encounters—situations in which there is more uncertainty about the involvement of third parties. However, if we assume that the existence of the same indirect tie with a third party implies the potential existence of that tie between partners,[8] then we can regard as analogous (1) the transformative process of adding a new kind of tie to an existing relation, and (2) the process of a shift from an indirect link to a direct one through the emergence of a specific kind of tie.

Unfortunately, preexisting relations (1) and (2), and (3) encounter contexts were not classified identically in the two surveys being analyzed here. Because of this heterogeneous data, we must consider the different logic of contact separately for each survey.

The Origins of Sexual Ties

A respondent's first contact with a future sexual partner can result from the expansion of an existing relationship, an introduction by a third party (family member, neighbor, workmate, or friend), or from an encounter in a social context (associations, holidays, cafés). Regarding the respondent's most recent sexual partner, 96.9% are the persons with whom respondents usually live (i.e. one's "spouse," "mate," or "partner"). Yet less than 10% of the initial contacts of these sexual ties stem from the family framework—an institutionalized form of sexual life—or the neighborhood—the descendant of the former village marital arena (Table 5.4). Thus kinship, a network largely marked by the incest taboo, does not introduce the individual to sexual relations. Moreover, kinship, the network of institutionalized continuing sexuality, has little influence on establishing new relations of sexuality, whether institutionalized or not. Just as neither kinship nor the neighborhood are much involved in exchanging sexual confidences, they hardly contribute to the establishment of sexual ties.

TABLE 5.4 Three Types of Generating Ties

	Transformation of a Relation			Relations Shared with a Third Party			Comembership of a Relation	
	Neighbor (%)	Workmate + Schoolmate (%)	Kin (%)	Kin + Neighbor (%)	Workmate (%)	Friend (A + B) (%)	Dances/ Night Clubs (%)	Other (%)
Sexual relation	–	–	–	9	23	19+21	28	–
Friendship relations	20	39	11	–	–	11	–	19

TABLE 5.5   Age Difference in the Articulation of Ties and Roles

	Kin (%)	Neighbors (%)	Workmates/ Schoolmates (%)	Friends (%)	Others (%)	All (%)
Latest Sexual Relation						
18–24	0	8	26	27+16	23	100
25–39	0	9	23	18+22	28	100
40–49	0	8	25	23+20	24	100
50–59	0	14	18	20+23	25	100
60–69	0	5	28	10+15	42	100
Friendship Relations						
18–24	11	10	47	17	15	100
25–39	10	16	45	12	17	100
40–49	10	22	36	10	22	100
50–59	14	24	37	9	16	100
60–69	12	27	29	9	23	100
70 and over	13	33	24	9	21	100

We do note that family influence is greater in rural areas (12%) and in the Paris urban area (16%) than in medium-sized communities (less than 10%). Does this imply that the family makes greater efforts to control patrimony: land in rural areas and other types of inheritance among the Parisian bourgeoisie? This is merely a speculation.

If not kin or neighbors, then who? Workmates and schoolmates introduced a future sexual partner to 23% of the respondents, friends made the introductions for 19%, while leisure contexts fostered 21% of the ties. It is not surprising that friendship ties and leisure contexts foster encounters with future sexual partners; there is an analogy of form (elective) and content (ludic) between friendship ties and sexual ties. But the spheres of work and school, supposedly repressing sexuality in their instrumental preoccupations, are also the origins of nearly one-fourth of sexual ties. School is even more prominent for respondents with higher educational levels. For example, 36% of the graduates of higher education were introduced to their sexual partners by schoolmates, as compared to only 16% for nongraduates.

The weight of workplace relations is more significant for those under the age of fifty (23% to 26%) than it is for those aged fifty or more (Table 5.5). For the older age groups, kinship is a somewhat more active mediator. At the other end of the age range, friends are an especially important source of introduction of sexual partners for respondents aged eighteen to twenty-four.

The Origins of Friendship Ties. As previously suggested, the origins of friendship ties were surveyed in terms of whether they are a transformation of an existing role, such as neighbor, or stem from an encounter fostered by a third party.[9] About three-fifths of the friendship ties (59%) develop from the transformation of existing relations (Table 5.4): 39% are former workmates or schoolmates, while 20% are former neighbors. The sphere of occupational relations frequently overlaps its narrow domain by fostering the establishment of voluntary friendship ties. The other process that fosters friendship, contact through a third party, occurs as frequently through the mediation of other friends (11%) as through kinship (11%).[10]

There appears to be a decreasing importance with every twenty-year age-group of the role of workmates and schoolmates in fostering friendship: about 46% under the age of forty, 36% between forty and fifty-nine, and only 29% thereafter (see Table 5.5 above). The role of friends as third parties also decreases, declining from 17% under the age of twenty-five to 9% over the age of fifty. Conversely, the percentage of neighbors who become friends increases from 10% among adolescents to 33% among those over seventy. As for friendships fostered by kin, their proportion is low to the age of fifty (10%), but increases slightly thereafter.

Thus the conditions governing the establishment of friendship ties change substantially between youth and old age. The two salient facts being that friendship networks progressively decouple from occupational networks and they become increasingly incapable of self-generation through friends introducing their friends to each other. It is probable that these changes are associated with journeys through the life course rather than that behavior has changed between generations. Best friends change through the life course (Wellman et al. 1997). With aging, the recruitment of friends becomes less articulated with the occupational sphere and more closely articulated with neighborhood and diverse memberships in other social milieus.

These general tendencies are modulated by educational levels and urbanization. Respondents with high educational levels are more likely to select best friends among workmates and schoolmates, while respondents with low educational levels are more likely to select best friends among neighbors. In addition, best friends are more apt to be workmates in large cities, especially in Paris, than in smaller places.

Conclusions and Implications

In this section we have examined the multiplexity of interpersonal relations, the fact that they contain various kinds of ties. We have examined how different relational contents are compatible and how this multiplexity accompanies certain formal characteristics, such as the frequency of encounters or feelings of closeness. We shifted the level of interpretation beyond the dyad by regarding the surveys about personal networks as yielding significant information for comprehending relational systems. We have assumed that each kind of tie can form a relational system with its own logic, and we have wondered how these different systems are articulated with each other.

Two systems of voluntary relations, stable sexual ties and friendship, appear to be *incapable of self-generation*. Unlike preindustrial times, new marriages (i.e., sexual ties) do not now depend upon existing ones: Kinship relations do not generate them. These data show that new friendship ties rarely depend on existing ones. Hence both sexual and friendship ties have the major structural property of being reproduced exogenously.

One-fourth of the sexual ties and one-third of the friendship ties are linked to occupational sociability. These proportions are important, since friendship and sexual ties pertain to the realm of elective, egalitarian, and enjoyable interaction, while work is in the domain of hierarchical, rationally oriented action. Indeed, the dependence of sociable friendship on the sphere of labor allows us to understand the extra-occupational losses that people experience when they lose their job.

If we put aside considering the process of establishing ties and examine the current articulations of relational systems, it is obvious that the mutual aid network is strongly linked to kinship and the confidants network to friendship. The strength of these articulations at the level of statistical observation prompts us to formulate two quite different types of assumptions.

On the one hand, one can wonder about the possibility of *structural homologies*. For example, we can consider that, in principle, a kinship network contains a potentially high density of ties and therefore exerts strong social control. If those aid ties that are not linked to kin are linked instead to friends and neighbors who are in densely knit cliques, then we can say that exchanges of aid are linked to any densely knit system and not just to kinship.

On the other hand, one can wonder about the *normative principles* that account for the compatibility of ties. For example, kinship fosters very long-term reciprocities within whose framework more routine—and rarely egalitarian—exchanges of aid take place. And both friendship and exchanges of confidences suppose tolerance toward the other and the other's behavior. So two kinds of interpretation can be proposed. Ties can be compatible either because they need the same normative orientation or because they need the same structural constraints, or because they need both.

Occupational Stratification and
Relational Milieus

In this section we consider socio-occupational categories as defining positions within a particular structure: that of stratification linked to production. Fundamentally, such social stratification categories classify people in terms of the social resources they have that provide certain living conditions. But to what extent does the structure of such stratification govern and foster other aspects of social life? We approach this question by examining how the four kinds of ties studied here are associated with the structure of stratification.

Homophilia

The Sociological Meaning of Homophilia.   Homophilia, the inclination of individuals to establish ties with people like themselves, is the most common way by which the composition of an individual's network is likely to diverge from a random distribution. In this section we examine the extent to which different kinds of ties are homophilous by belonging to the same socio-occupational category. We also consider what other types of preferential selections are liable to emerge.

One way to interpret homophilia is in terms of individuals' relational strategies: Who chooses whom? This is the domain of social psychology, which has paid especial attention to preferential selections of marriage partners. Those spouses exhibiting the same social characteristics have a "homogamous marriage."

Let us change this perspective slightly. If a statistically defined category (or "class") of persons occupying the same economic position establishes ties with persons occupying any other position, then that class does not relationally form an actual social group for they are people who establish ties with anybody. By contrast, if people occupying the same class are mostly inclined to see each other and to have few contacts with people from other classes, then their class tends to form an actual group. Thus homophilia measures the social consistency and bounding of a group as defined by its occupational position.

All societies should be regarded as being differentiated, and all societies exist because there are exchanges between the various categories that comprise them. We can think of highly cohesive, constituted, and clearly identified subgroups that must exchange with others because they generate various resources within the framework of the social division of tasks. The Indian caste system is a well-known example. The fact that a class exhibits certain attributes (possesses certain social resources) and exchanges them with other classes is part of the overall structure of those exchanges, which are vital for each class and for the society as a whole. Hence homophilia, the preponderance of internal ties within a class and the lack of contact with other classes, would indicate the class's marginality and exclusion from the "market" of social transactions.

Thus relations between and within classes must reach a certain balance: Internal relations must exist for the cohesion of the class and external relations for overall social cohesion.[11] To address this matter, we examine ties here that pertain exclusively to the domestic and private sphere of everyday life. Consequently, we are not able to propose an outline of "the structure" of French society, but can only examine specific substructures of this society. Yet we cannot directly find in our analysis the fundamental exchanges of these substructures to ascertain whether they are linked to labor and economic activities, or to the institutionalization of power relations. Hence these exchanges cannot be regarded as being linked directly to the social division of tasks. Rather, the relations examined here are in the domain of sociability where they indirectly foster the production and reproduction of social identities. Moreover, the complex multidimensional realities created by these ties are better called "milieus" than more precisely bounded "groups."

In short, by examining homophilia from the standpoint of socio-occupational categories—structural positions—we are trying to answer two indissoluble questions: Which positions seem to generate a relational milieu, and in so doing isolate themselves and create identifiable elements of social structure? Which elements are linked, more or less strongly, to each other?

The Respondents' Social Positions and Measures of Homophilia. Since the surveys we are reanalyzing did not use the same socio-occupational categories, we must use rather broad classes to maintain comparability. The different makeup of categories in the different surveys account for the apparent differences in the class composition of the national samples. (However, all the surveys show that women's positions differ from men's.) For certain kinds of ties, this represents a structural constraint of the actors' distributions, which will be taken into account. Table 5.6 shows the proportion having ties with members of the same occupational category. Unfortunately, differences between the surveys means that the data are reported in different ways for each kind of tie:

1. For mutual aid, relations between the household head and network member.
2. For confidant and sexual ties, the data are shown separately for male and female respondents.
3. For friendship ties, the data are only for male respondents.

Knowing the occupational distribution of French society, we can also compare the observed proportions (taken from Table 5.6) with those that would be randomly expected (Table 5.7). The probabilities of interindividual ties among and within social categories depends on the relative size of the categories (Blau and Schwartz 1984). Therefore the demographically possible proportion of homophilous ties should vary according to the way the population is classified, irrespective of any specific social logic.

The observed data (Table 5.7) record *preferences* of only those respondents reporting at least one social tie. This does not take into account the relational and structural importance of the respondents who completely *lack ties*. Consequently, our data compel us to analyze social systems through preferential prescriptions—distributions of choices—but does not provide much information about proscriptions, impediments, or interdicts. It is unfortunate that the lack of ties is most often treated as a social-psychological, individual phenomenon when it is also a social fact

To take into account the relative sizes of categories and the lack of ties between some categories, it is necessary to give up the measurement of homophilia that is based exclusively on existing ties. One first needs to calculate the *expected frequency* obtained when the probability of a relation among persons belonging to two given classes is proportional to their size. Hence we have constructed a matrix (not shown here) of the ties that would exist if anyone would choose anyone else without regard to their categories. Of course, this matrix contains homophilous cells whose total indicates the overall proportion of expected homophilous selections. The second row of Table 5.7 ("% expected") indicates this expected proportion of homophilous ties.

When we examine the deviation between the frequency of existing ties observed and the expected frequency,[12] the differences are clear. For example, where 35% of friendship ties are "expected" to be homophilous, 55% are observed to be. This suggests a social world in which strong rules lead people to select friends similar to themselves.

The difference between the proportions of observed and expected homophilous friendship ties is 20% (55% − 35%). Thus *socially induced homophilia* is a ratio of 20/100 and not of 55/100, as one might believe by looking only at the observed data. This leads to a softer view of preferential selection rules and of their influence on structuring the relational space of a society. We shall compare the four kinds of ties and examine a few identifiable structural tendencies.

The Role of Socially Oriented Selections in Relational Systems. The first property of these relational systems to be considered is their *degree of existence*: What is the proportion of those existing ties that do not corre-

TABLE 5.6 Nature of Categorization and Homophily for the Four Surveys

Relation	Aid	Confidant		Sexual		Friendship
		M	F	M	F	
1 Farmers, artisans, sales workers, executives	17.2	7.4	3.2	10.2	6.3	15.4
2 Managerial workers and higher professional, intermediate occupations	29.5	24.1	18.6	33.5	21.8	20.5
3 Clerks, blue-collar workers	51.2	40.8	51.4	46.5	56.2	51.9
4 Never had paid work (schoolchildren, students, housewives)	2.1	–	–	9.8	15.7	12.2
5 Never had paid work (under 60, unemployed)	–	9.2	15.3	–	–	–
6 Retired over 60	18.5	11.5	–	–	–	–

Categories of	Household Heads	Individuals	Individuals	Individuals
Present or	Cited	–	Cited	Cited
Former occupation	Cited	–	–	–
Present occupation	–	Cited		

TABLE 5.7   Observed and Expected Percentage of Homophilous Ties

		Confidant		Sexual	
Relation	Aid	All	M⇒F	M⇒F	Friendship
% Observed	50	50	45	52	55
% Expected	38	30	29	36	35

spond to expected intercategorical ties (i.e., the total deviation). These deviations have a value close to 40 for mutual aid, friendship, and the most recent sexual tie, while the deviation is above 50 for confidants (Table 5.8).[13] Therefore, the observed data for the four kinds of ties shows that they are partially established in terms of prescriptions, impediments, and social interdicts. But only partially. If out of 100 ties, we observe 40 "anomalies," we would have to change the categories of the respondent and the network member of 20 relations (40/2) in order to get an equiprobable distribution of ties between all categories. It also means that 80 relations out of 100 have been established as an outcome of the random chance that two individuals would be linked with each other.[14]

A first conclusion can be drawn: *The social rules of mating deviate only selectively and partially from the relational flux between socio-occupational categories.* The great majority of ties are established without members of a category systematically choosing themselves or only one other category. Most relations arise according to the constraints imposed by the demographic distribution of the population into various categories. Our analysis has revealed the effects both of these demographic constraints and of socially oriented selections.

The World of Men and the World of Women. Heterosexual relations, by definition, link two persons of opposite sexes. Because men and women are differently distributed among socio-occupational categories, there are two distinct social stratifications rather than one. Therefore heterosexual social ties tend to go from one stratification system to another and to link different levels of stratification. For example, the occupational

TABLE 5.8   Total Deviation Between Matrices of Observed Ties and Expected Ties

		Confidant		Sexual	
Relation	Aid	All	M⇒F	M⇒F	Friendship
Total deviation	41	51	59	41	41
Degrees of freedom	9	16	16	9	9

category of "clerk" is mostly feminine, whereas other categories are mostly masculine. Hence most men are more likely to be connected to a female clerk than to women of their own occupational category. This means that at the societal level, there are stronger linkages between the male category and the female clerk category than there are between male and female categories at the same stratification level. *Thus differences in gender are associated with two stratifications, and each heterosexual interpersonal tie is a link between these two worlds.*

Heterosexual ties are one of the factors that foster the maintenance and reproduction of status differences between men and women. Because men and women usually establish stable sexual relations and households form consumption units, men's higher incomes are shared with and financially compensate for women's lower incomes. This "allows" women to be in occupational positions that on average are lower than men's and strongly affects power relations within households.

It is possible to neutralize statistically the gap between women's and men's social stratifications. We first calculate the expected probabilities of ties, taking into account men's and women's respective distributions among social positions by using the proportions of women and men in the various categories as marginal totals. Just as in the analysis of stratification in the previous section, this procedure will neutralize the fact that *demographically* men have great chances of encountering female clerks. This neutralization enables us to identify those preferential selections that are *socially* related.

Similarly, we can compare the distributions of male-female stable sexual partnerships with the distributions of male-female confidants. We find that deviations from "expected" gender links between occupational categories are stronger for confidant relations than for stable sexual partners. This suggests that *if the logic of social selection exists in the domain of sexual life, it influences exchanges of confidences more than sexual intimacies.*

Overall, stable sexual ties are not more oriented towards stratification systems than other types of interpersonal relations. Indeed, they seem rather commonplace. By comparing the selection of a stable sexual partner with other types of selections, and by measuring all possible deviations from "expected" links between male and female occupational categories, we obtain a reference point for comparisons that is usually lacking in analyses of mate selection.

Socioeconomic Orientations of Interpersonal Selections

Having established the overall nature of how socioeconomic categories are linked, we can now examine these linkages in more detail. There can be two social logics:

TABLE 5.9   Percent of Homophilous Preferences By Kind of Tie

Relation	Aid	Confidant M⇒F	Sexual M⇒F	Friendship
Percent of Homophilous cells in total deviation	30	43	44	48

1. Members of each socioeconomic category prefer to choose persons who belong to their own category, that is, the same milieu. This is a tendency that fosters homophilous selection.
2. Members of a particular category systematically establish ties with one or more categories, perhaps because they have more prestige, more economic and informational resources (Lin 1987), or more emotional and human resources (Wellman 1992a).

To analyze these issues, we shall examine all the deviations between the selections expected and those observed. Our goals are to ascertain whether there is a preference for homophilous selection, and whether strong preferences arise between certain categories.

Homophilous Selections.   The tendency for homophilous selection varies according to the kind of ties: it represents 30% to 48% of the choices that deviate from a random distribution (Table 5.9). This relative part is very significant and nearly reaches the maximum possible of 50%.[15] Hence, *the tendency for homophilous selection is dominant among the social selection processes.*

Friendship (48%) is the kind of tie with the strongest homophilous orientation; that is, people are most likely to have friends within their own socioeconomic category. Hence there is a tendency towards bounding relational spheres because all categories are neither equally nor randomly connected.

By contrast, *aid relations* between households are much less homophilous than friendship: 30% of the total deviation in aid relations are in homophilous cells. Although the level of social selectivity is similar to friendship (the total deviation, homophilous and nonhomophilous is similar), the nature of social selectivity is different. Unlike friendship, aid exchanges are usually between households of different socioeconomic categories rather than between households of the same socioeconomic category. We assume that different socioeconomic categories tend to have different kinds and amounts of resources available (see also Lin 1987). Therefore, exchanges of aid are likely to be asymmetrical in quality (a socially meaningful exchange of unmeasurable phenomena such as love, information, or emotional support) and quantity (a transfer in one direction of goods, services or money). Moreover, this difference between friendship and aid suggests that the relational substructures produced by interpersonal ties—the links between socioeconomic categories—have not arisen out of analogous selection processes.

Diversity and Convergence of Relational Substructures. In addition to the deviation from expected distributions of homophilous ties, ties between two different socioeconomic categories can also deviate from expected probabilities. The existence of systematic heterophilic selections or rejections is the second major characteristic of relational structures. Although homophilous relationships are a major structuring logic, they cannot by themselves provide a picture of the relational substructures studied here. We address the following question: What are the homophilous or intercategorical relations that deviate the most from a distribution proportionate to the size of categories?

Let us compare the structures of *friendship* and stable sexual ties. For both friendship and sexual ties, homophilous relationships are the largest deviations from random expectations (Table 5.10). Such choices within one's own socio-occupational category are the basis of the structures. For both friendship and sexual ties, those in Category 1 (farmers, artisans, sales workers, executives) and Category 2 (managerial workers and higher professionals, intermediate occupations) tend to choose partners from Categories 1 and 2, thereby bounding their relational spaces. This stresses the overall structure strongly.[16] Those in Category 3 (clerks, blue-collar workers) also form sexual ties and friendships with persons from their own category.

In the overall structures, the status of Category 3 (clerks and blue-collar workers) appear chiefly as *relational deficits*. They have deficits with Category 4 (never-been-salaried students, homemakers, etc.) of –16 for friendship ties and –23 for sexual ties, and of –16 for friendship with Category 1 (farmers, artisans, sales workers, and executives). Note that with the exception of homophilia, all of the friendship and sexual "links" (deviations) between categories are negative.[17]

Taking all of the deviations together reveals that the basic structure is the homophilous tendency for friendships and sexual ties to be established between members of the same socio-occupational category. In addition, the structures are characterized by:

1. A lack of ties between Category 3 (clerks, blue-collar) and Category 4 (students, homemakers, never been salaried);
2. A lack of ties between Category 3 and Category 1 (sales workers, executives).

TABLE 5.10 Proportion of Each Cell in Total Deviation of Matrix

Relation	Friendship				Sexual				Aid			
	1	2	3	4	1	2	3	4	1	2	3	4
INDEX:												
1 Farmers, artisans, sales workers, executives	+9	–	–16	–	+7	–	–	–	–	–10	–14	-
2 Managerial workers and higher professional; intermediate occupations	–	+22	–	–	–	+18	–	–	–	–	–	–
3 Clerks, blue-collar workers	–	–	–	–16	–	–	+17	–23	–	–25	+19	+8
4 Never had paid work (schoolchildren, students, housewives)	–	–	–	+13	–	–	–	–	+2	+7	–	–
Total												
proportion of homophilous cells	48%				44%				30%			

The lack of ties that we have observed is not the inevitable complementary effect of the overrepresentation of homophilous selections. The lack of ties between Categories 3 and 4 (Table 5.10) may be due to the anomalous nature of Category 4, which includes persons who have never done paid work, young persons who have not yet entered the labor force, homemakers, handicapped persons, students, and so on. A large number consists of women who have never done paid work, such as homemakers. The relatively low-status men of Category 3 probably do not have sufficient income and wealth to be stable sexual partners (husbands) of women who have never done paid work. The world of the wage-earning working class (Category 3) is relationally locked in on itself. Paid work versus not doing paid work appears to be a strong dimension of the social structure in this category which has the strongest economic constraints.

The lack of ties between Categories 1 and 3 (see Table 5.10) is sociologically more interesting, since it exhibits the classic rift in France between the worlds of independent workers and the wage-earning working class. The social differences between these two categories are well known and have been documented by many economic, social, and cultural indicators. The lack of ties shows that these categories are also separated by a *significant sociorelational distance*. Thus, in addition to the already known differences between these strata, we have identified the existence of a social barrier that greatly hinders the establishment of friendship and sexual ties and is a strong characteristic of these relational structures.

Besides studying the affinity ties of friendship and sex, we can examine in a similar way the relational substructure: *exchanges of aid*.[18] Because we study exchange relations between households and not individuals, we base our socioeconomic categorization on the occupational status of the household member whom the respondents designated as household heads, generally a man.

We noted earlier that aid exchanges have a weaker tendency for homophilia than do friendship or sexual ties: Only 30% of the deviations from randomly expected stem from a homophilous preference. However, the more detailed information in Table 5.10 shows that aid exchanges are very selective, with only the households of Category 3 showing a strong homophilous tendency. Two intercategorical linkages are slightly overrepresented:

1. Category 4 (never worked) and Category 2 (managers and higher professionals): +7%;
2. Category 4 and Category 3 (clerks, blue-collar): +8%.

These positive social "preferences" seem to be characterized by need, with Category 4 households whose head has never worked getting support from Category 2 and 3 wage-earners, although not from the self-employed members of Category 1. Yet the real logic of the table is elsewhere. The substructure of exchanges is most strongly characterized by the *reciprocal rejection of the working population categories,* both self-employed and wage earning:

1. Category 1 self-employed workers and Category 2 managers and professionals: −10% of the deviations;
2. Category 1 self-employed workers and Category 3 clerks and blue-collar workers: 14% of the deviations;
3. Category 2 managers and professionals and Category 3 clerks and blue-collar workers: 25% of the deviations.

Thus the logic of exchanges calls for a different language than the logic of friendships and sexual partners. It does not exhibit the voluntary "preferences" that friendships and sexual relationships do. For a few households (2%), aid exchanges appear as a form of solidarity between working people and never-worked people. Most of these may be mainly parental support of young adults who have not yet entered the labor force. But for a much larger part of France, the exchanges seem to be based on the interdiction or impossibility of service exchanges between distant social positions. The constraints of the principle of reciprocity act less to favor relations with certain categories than they do to forbid relations with socially different categories.

Conclusions

The ties examined in this chapter—love, confidants, friendship, aid exchanges—are important components of the vast domain of elective or voluntary relationships. Although people have socially consistent preferences in their relationships, these networks are less socially structured than they initially appear. By inserting the constraint of the demographic distribution of the population into the analysis, we have diminished the apparently strong rule of social selections.

Besides, this is a diversified domain. Contrasting configurations and heterogeneous logics arise for different kinds of ties. Although the global events of social selection are about the same for these various relationships, their patterns are different. For example, homophilous selection is the strongest in the friendship realm. By contrast, aid relations are less homophilous but are more apt to connect the not-employed category with the paid workers of Categories 2 and 3. Thus, even if the unemployed are helped by the employed, they are not apt to be friends or sex partners. Each kind of tie exhibits a different logic of linking categories.

A picture of the "total" relational reality of French society would be based on the superposition of these and other matrices. Although this is not methodologically possible it is sociologically relevant, since the ties between people often cumulate in practice: For example, friends often exchange services and confidences (see also Wellman and Wortley 1990). The actors, linked by the totality of their different relations, constitute a third dimension of network linkages, in addition to the relational and positional linkages that this chapter has discussed.

The data suggest that French society has the dual property of (1) strongly and rigidly reproducing differences between categories, but (2) synchronically linking them by means of multiple relational substructures with overlapping effects. If this is so, then the strong consensus that underlies the popular view of a "French" social order may only be the effects—at the level of cognitive representations and cultural values—of an inability to think of oneself (and one's strata) as being cut off from the rest of society.

Appendix: Descriptive Statistics for Mutual Aid Relations, Confidant Relations, Latest Sexual Relations, and Friendship Relations

	Cited Relations (Mean)	Document Relations (Mean)	Kin (%)	Neighbor (%)	Colleague Schoolmate (%)	Friend (A+B) (%)	Other (%)	All (%)
All								
Aid relations	3.0	3.0	55	15	3	23	4	100
Confidant relations	2.3	2.3	24	–	14	62	–	100
Last sexual relation	–	–	–	9	23	19+21	28	100
Friendship relations	2.8	1.4	11	20	39	11	19	100
Sex								
Aid relations								
Males	3.1	3.1	56	15	8	23	4	100
Females	2.8	2.8	52	15	2	26	5	100
Confidant relations								
Males	2.4	2.4	18	–	19	63	–	100
Females	2.2	2.2	29	–	10	61	–	100
Last sexual relation								
Males	–	–	–	11	22	17+23	27	100
Females	–	–	–	8	24	21+18	29	100
Friendship relations								
Males	3.4	1.4	9	20	40	13	18	100
Females	2.4	1.3	13	20	38	11	18	100

(continues)

Appendix (continued) Descriptive Statistics for Relations

	Cited Relations (Mean)	Document Relations (Mean)	Kin (%)	Neighbor (%)	Colleague Schoolmate (%)	Friend (A+B) (%)	Other (%)	All (%)
Age								
Aid Relations								
18–24	3.9	3.9	57	4	2	36	1	100
25–39	3.8	3.8	53	12	3	29	3	100
40–49	3.2	3.2	48	18	4	26	4	100
50–59	2.6	2.6	54	19	3	19	5	100
60–69	2.5	2.5	62	18	0	15	5	100
70 and over	2.1	2.1	63	20	0	11	6	100
Confidant relations								
18–24	2.4	2.4	28	–	4	68	–	100
25–39	2.3	2.3	25	–	17	58	–	100
40–49	2.3	2.3	21	–	19	61	–	100
50–59	2.2	2.2	26	–	18	56	–	100
60–69	2.2	2.2	14	–	13	73	–	100
Last sexual relation								
18–24	–	–	–	8	26	27+16	23	100
25–39	–	–	–	9	23	18+22	28	100
40–49	–	–	–	8	25	23+20	25	100
50–59	–	–	–	14	18	20+23	25	100
60–69	–	–	–	5	28	10+15	42	100

(continues)

Appendix (*continued*)   Descriptive Statistics for Relations

	Cited Relations (Mean)	Document Relations (Mean)	Kin (%)	Neighbor (%)	Colleague Schoolmate (%)	Friend (A+B) (%)	Other (%)	All (%)
Friendship relations								
18–24	2.9	1.6	11	10	47	17	15	100
25–39	2.9	1.4	10	16	45	12	17	100
40–49	2.9	1.4	10	22	36	10	22	100
50–59	3.0	1.3	14	24	37	9	16	100
60–69	2.5	1.2	12	27	29	9	23	100
70 and over	2.7	1.0	13	33	24	9	21	100
Socio-occupational Categories								
Aid Relations								
1	2.3	2.3	63	16	1	15	5	100
2	3.5	3.5	48	14	3	30	5	100
3	3.7	3.7	51	14	3	28	4	100
4	3.0	3.0	53	15	3	25	4	100
5	2.8	2.8	59	17	2	19	3	100
6	3.5	3.5	49	–	0	42	4	100
Confidant relations								
1	2.3	2.3	14	–	16	70	–	100
2	2.5	2.5	17	–	18	65	–	100
3	2.3	2.3	21	–	17	62	–	100
4	2.2	2.2	33	–	13	54	–	100
5	2.3	2.3	23	–	20	57	–	100
6	2.5	2.5	21	–	2	77	–	100

(*continues*)

Appendix *(continued)* Descriptive Statistics for Relations

	Cited Relations (Mean)	Document Relations (Mean)	Kin (%)	Neighbor (%)	Colleague Schoolmate (%)	Friend (A+B) (%)	Other (%)	All (%)
Last sexual relation								
1	–	–	–	13	19	21+20	27	100
2 –	–	–	–	7	33	22+7	31	100
3	–	–	–	9	24	22+21	24	100
4	–	–	–	9	26	17+21	27	100
5	–	–	–	10	16	17+27	30	100
6	–	–	–	4	20	31+19	26	100
Friendship relations								
1	3.1	1.2	13	26	26	11	23	100
2	4.3	1.7	10	12	49	11	18	100
3	3.5	1.6	9	15	48	11	17	100
4	2.5	1.3	12	19	39	12	18	100
5	2.6	1.0	12	22	36	12	18	100
6	2.3	1.3	10	23	42	9	16	100
Degree of Urbanization (Number of Inhabitants)								
Aid relations								
<5,000	2.8	2.8	58	20	1	17	4	100
5,000–20,000	2.9	2.9	58	16	2	20	4	100
20,000–100,000	2.9	2.9	57	15	2	22	4	100
100,000–1 Million	3.1	3.1	55	15	2	24	4	100
Paris	3.2	3.2	49	15	3	30	3	100

(continues)

Appendix (*continued*) Descriptive Statistics for Relations

	Cited Relations (Mean)	Document Relations (Mean)	Kin (%)	Neighbor (%)	Colleague Schoolmate (%)	Friend (A+B) (%)	Other (%)	All (%)
Confidant relations								
<5,000	2.2	2.2	24	–	14	62	–	100
5,000–20,000	2.3	2.3	25	–	13	62	–	100
20,000–100,000	2.1	2.3	26	–	15	59	–	100
100,000–1 Million	2.3	2.3	23	–	12	65	–	100
Paris	2.4	2.4	24	–	17	59	–	100
Last sexual relation								
<5,000	–	–	–	12	20	17+23	28	100
5,000–20,000	–	–	–	3	20	18+27	32	100
20,000–100,000	–	–	–	7	25	11+18	39	100
100,000–1 Million	–	–	–	8	27	23+22	20	100
Paris	–	–	–	16	24	27+ 9	24	100
Friendship relations								
<5,000	2.9	1.3	13	24	34	9	20	100
5,000–20,000	2.8	1.3	11	22	38	10	19	100
20,000–100,000	3.2	1.5	10	10	40	12	18	100
100,000–1 Million	2.6	1.3	11	17	41	14	17	100
Paris	2.9	1.4	10	15	45	13	17	100

Notes

Translated from French by Philipe Sicard and edited by Barry Wellman.

1. We use the term "workmate" to denote those coworkers to whom network members feel socially close.

2. Chapter 6 in this volume shows the many ways in which Hungarian friends help each other to find work in the same organization.

3. It is thus necessary to distinguish conceptually between a relational structure's (1) ability for *endogenous reproduction* through transitivity, and (2) the structure's ability for *exogenous reproduction* through establishing structures of different kinds of ties.

4. In practice, Wellman and Wellman (1992) and Chapter 4 in this volume show that the great majority of exchanges among individuals really operate as exchanges between households.

5. Even for those ties that we do have information about, we can only learn something about the nature of the relationship between the respondents and the members of their networks. We do not have information about ties between the members of the respondents' networks.

6. Indeed, in the pilot study for the sexual behavior survey, there was such a low frequency of neighbors exchanging confidences about their sexual behavior that the full survey did not ask about neighbors (Ferrand and Mounier 1991). Whatever the French feel about the biblical commandment not to "covet thy neighbour's wife," they certainly do not talk to their neighbors about it.

7. The coefficient of variation gives an indication of the dispersion of a distribution.

8. This assumption has been implemented by Ronald Burt's *Structure* computer program, which can take into account the strength of such indirect ties.

9. Unfortunately, this survey did not inquire about the third way of establishing a tie: through participation in the same social context (see Feld 1981).

10. This survey did not ask explicitly if neighbors, workmates, or schoolmates are third parties that foster contact between future friends. Such relationships are presumably subsumed here under "other friends," i.e., nonkin.

11. An idea developed by Merton (1957), perhaps inspired by Durkheim (1893). See also Merton (1965).

12. The matrix of expected proportions is calculated as for the chi-square, except for the important fact that marginal rows and columns are not the sums of the cells, but proportions of persons in each category of population that would name zero, one, or several relations. An expected cell value is the proportion of all possible ties that would be found in the cell under the hypothesis of independence, better defined here as the hypothesis of pure demographic constraint.

13. For the overall socio-occupational categories, the *total deviation* is the sum of deviations (in absolute value) between the observed proportion of homophilous ties and the expected proportion under the assumption of independence. For each of the four kinds of ties, we use the percentages computed for the table as a whole. Three of the four tables have the same structure and are strictly comparable (4 x 4). The confidants table uses five categories and thus has a different structure (5 X 5). Because the partition of confidant relations is made among

different and more numerous classes, the degrees of freedom appear in terms of the deviation calculated. An approximation to neutralize the sole effect of table structure can be made using the same formulas as in Cramer's V. This approximation shows that the deviations for confidant relations are of the same order of magnitude as for the other three kinds of ties.

14. A single "abnormal" tie entails a deficit in one cell of the matrix and an excess in another. Hence it produces two deviations. This is the case for the overall matrix. For a given category, the lack of ties with certain categories is not the mechanically complementary effect of overrepresentation of, for example, homophilous selections. Indeed, except for monogamous sexual relations, each person could mention several relations as well as being mentioned by others several times. The more a category increases the average number of relations per actor, the more it is likely to be able to be both homophilous and open to other categories.

15. The homophilous cells almost always show a positive deviation. People tend to overselect alters who are similar to themselves. Each tie governed by a social preference has a positive and negative effect in the matrix: a total of two deviations. Then a specific set of cells must show a net deviation that is either positive or negative.

16. We allow here for the proportion of each intercategorical tie in the total deviation as it appears in Table 5.10. They are not weighted by the volume of the expected number of ties. Then we print boldface cells in which the deviation is strong, even if its contribution to total deviation is weak because of the demographic composition of the population.

17. This is not an inevitable algebraic effect of homophilous tendencies on all of the other cells of the matrices. Note, for example, the positive aid links between categories in Table 5.10.

18. We omit from analysis here the fourth kind of tie, relations between *confidants*, because their socio-occupational categories are not comparable to the three other kinds of ties.

References

Blau, Peter. 1982. "Structural Sociology and Network Analysis." Pp. 273–280 in *Social Structure and Network Analysis,* edited by Peter Marsden and Nan Lin. Beverly Hills, CA: Sage.

Blau, Peter, and Joseph Schwartz. 1984. *Crosscutting Social Circles.* Orlando, FL: Academic Press.

Bozon, Michel and François Heran. 1987. "L'aire de recrutement du conjoint." *Données sociales:*338–347.

Degenne, Alain, and Marie-Odile Lebeaux. 1991. "L'entraide entre les ménages: un facteur d'inégalité sociale?" *Sociétés Contemporaines* 8:21–42.

Durkheim, Émile. 1893. *De la division du travail social.* Paris: Alcan.

Feld, Scott. 1981. "The Focused Organization of Social Ties." *American Journal of Sociology* 86:1015–1035.

Ferrand, Alexis, and Lise Mounier. 1991. "La confidence: des relations au réseau." *Sociétés Contemporaines* 5:7–20.

Ferrand, Alexis, and Lise Mounier. 1991. *Relations sexuelles et relations de confidence.* Rapport pour l'Agence nationale de recherche sur le Sida.

Ferrand, Alexis, and Lise Mounier. 1993. "L'échange de paroles sur la sexualité: une analyse des relations de confidence." *Population* 5:1451–1475.

Fischer, Claude. 1982. *To Dwell Among Friends.* Berkeley: University of California Press.

Grafmeyer, Yves. 1991. *Habiter Lyon.* Lyon: Presses Universitaires.

Heran, François. 1987. "Comment les Français voisinent." *Economie et Statistiques, Report No. 195.*

Heran, François. 1988. "La sociabilité, une pratique culturelle." *Economie et Statistiques,* Report No. 216.

Heran, François. 1987. "Trouver à qui parler: le sexe et l'âge de nos interlocuteurs." *Données sociales* 1990. INSEE, Reports Nos. 364–368.

Laumann, Edward. 1973. *Bonds of Pluralism.* New York: Wiley.

Laumann, Edward, and Franz Urban Pappi. 1976. *Networks of Collective Action: A Perspective on Community Influence Systems.* New York: Academic Press.

Lazega, Emmanuel. 1992. "Les relations de travail des Français vues par l'enquête 'Contacts entre les personnes.'" Report. Paris: PIRTTEM.

Lin, Nan. 1987. "Social Resources and Social Mobility: A Structural Theory of Status Attainment." Presented to the International Sunbelt Social Network Conference. Clearwater Beach, FL. February.

Merton, Robert K. 1957. "Patterns of Influence: Local and Cosmopolitan Influentials." Pp. 387–420 in *Social Theory and Social Structure.* Glencoe, IL: Free Press.

Merton, Robert K. 1965. *Social Theory and Social Structure.* New York: Free Press.

Nadel, S. F. 1957. *The Theory of Social Structure.* London: Cohen and West.

Park, Robert. 1925. "The Urban Community as a Spatial Pattern and a Moral Order." Pp. 55–68 in *Robert E. Park on Social Control and Collective Behavior, edited by* Ralph Turner. Chicago: University of Chicago Press.

Rogers, Everett M., and D. K. Bhowmik. 1986. "Homophily–Heterophily: Relational Concepts for Communication Researchers." *Public Opinion Quarterly* 34:523–538.

Sociétés Contemporaines. 1991. Special Issue on "Production domestique," 8.

Sociétés Contemporaines. 1991. Special Issue on "Réseau sociaux," 5.

Spira, Alfred, and Nathalie Bajos, groupe ACSF. 1993. *Les comportements sexuels en France. La* Documentation Française, Paris.

Wellman, Barry. 1988. "The Community Question Re-evaluated." Pp. 81–107 in *Power, Community and the City,* edited by Michael Peter Smith. New Brunswick, NJ: Transaction Books.

Wellman, Barry. 1992a. "Men in Networks: Private Community, Domestic Friendship." Pp. 74–114 in *Men's Friendships,* edited by Peter Nardi. Newbury Park, CA: Sage.

Wellman, Barry. 1992b. "Which Types of Ties and Networks Give What Kinds of Social Support?" *Advances in Group Processes* 9:207–35.

Wellman, Barry, and S. D. Berkowitz, eds. 1988. *Social Structures: A Network Approach.* Cambridge: Cambridge University Press.

Wellman, Barry, Renita Yuk-lin Wong, David Tindall, and Nancy Nazer. 1997. "A
    Decade of Network Change: Turnover, Persistence and Stability in Personal
    Communities." *Social Networks:* 19(1):27–50.
Wellman, Barry, and Scot Wortley. 1989. "Brothers' Keepers: Situating Kinship Re-
    lations in Broader Networks of Social Support." *Sociological Perspectives*
    32:273–306.
Wellman, Barry, and Scot Wortley. 1990. "Different Strokes from Different Folks:
    Community Ties and Social Support." *American Journal of Sociology* 96:558–588.
Wellman, Beverly, and Barry Wellman. 1992. "Domestic Affairs and Network Re-
    lations." *Journal of Social and Personal Relationships* 9:385–409.

6

Network Capital in Capitalist, Communist, and Postcommunist Countries

Endre Sik and Barry Wellman

Eastern Europe as Network Societies

Our Argument

People and organizations use networks everywhere, but they use them more in communist and postcommunist countries than in capitalist countries. One might think that the elaborate bureaucracies of communist countries make networks less necessary. In fact, the inherent rigidities and shortages of communist bureaucracies, paradoxically, made the use of networks more necessary. Nor has the end of communism lessened the need to use networks, for the permeability, fluidity, and uncertainty of postcommunism have fostered even greater reliance on networks. Thus our argument in this chapter is twofold:

1. People relied on network capital more in Eastern European communist countries than they did in the developed capitalist countries of Western Europe and North America.
2. In the current postcommunist era, people in these countries rely on networks even more than they did under communism.

These hypotheses are general, referring to ideal types rather than concrete societies. Although our examples are Hungarian, we believe that they broadly represent communist and postcommunist societies in Eastern Europe.[1] We do not rigorously test our hypotheses but illustrate their application with case studies of common situations. If our illustrations are robust and our assumptions sensible, then we can draw certain conclusions about how networks vary between societies.

The Ubiquity of Networks

By arguing the extraordinary presence of networks in Eastern Europe, we do not wish to imply that only Eastern Europeans use networks heavily. Indeed, a central argument of this book is that networks are an important form of social capital in every society, including affluent core Western societies. Everywhere they are an essential way by which people, households, and organizations survive and thrive, along with the more visible means of market exchanges and state distributions (see also Wellman 1992). As Wellman argues in the Introduction, the use of social networks is one of the five basic means by which people and institutions acquire necessary resources—along with market exchanges, state distributions, and, to a lesser extent, self-provisioning and coercive appropriations (see also Polanyi 1957; Wellman and Wortley 1990). Such networks operate both independently of, and supplementary to, the processes by which the market and the state provide resources.

There are three ways to back the thesis that networks are everywhere an important form of social capital:

1. Building networks and manipulating them for cooperation, assistance, or investing in relationships are basic characteristics of the human race. Though the extent to which these characteristics are present in any culture can differ, network capital is still a general form of social capital, just as human or physical capital (wealth) are—and this is true in capitalist as well as in communist or postcommunist societies (Kropotkin 1902).
2. Investing in network capital should be a rational choice. In every society there are situations (minor troubles, temporary imbalances) when using networks is the best means to cope. It is less costly, more effective, more easily accessible than any other alternative such as the household, market purchases, or acquiring state redistributions (see also Polanyi 1957; Wellman and Wortley 1990). To the extent that these troubles are present in affluent capitalist societies, network capital is an auxiliary institution there, specializing in providing sociability, emotional support, and assistance for domestic needs and informal health care (Wellman and Wortley 1990). Without denigrating the importance of such social support, it is clear that the networks of comfortable Westerners rarely provide the kinds of assistance for economic or political matters that communist and postcommunist societies do. The exceptions are at the margins: (a) the Western elite's use of networks for dealing with major

political and economic issues; and (b) the use of networks for survival of those Westerners who are facing hardship, such as the residents of ghettos (Liebow 1967) and immigrant workers in sweatshops.

3. Network capital is not only useful for coping; it is also useful for grabbing opportunities. All agents of the economy can use their network capital offensively: to retain power, to increase advantages, to fight opponents, and so on. Therefore, it is not surprising that ambitious people carefully invest in and maintain network capital. Examples are numerous, such as the craft- or guildlike groups in some professional labor markets (Abbott 1988). Moreover, networks in capitalist societies are often superimposed on markets in everyday circumstances. For example, there are personal networks between buyers and sellers in local markets (Plattner 1989; Mintz 1961; Farberman and Weinstein 1970; White 1992) and business executives often make personal deals to avoid the rigidities of contracts (Macaulay 1963; Burt 1992).

The Role of Network Capital

Just as people use their financial capital to purchase things on markets and their human capital to gain better access to markets and state distributions, they also use *network capital*, their connections with people and organizations. In addition to providing direct access to resources, network capital channels financial capital among actors and provides the interpersonal and interorganizational basis by which people use their human capital to gain surer access to state distributions and markets. Just as "no man is an island", both financial capital and human capital fundamentally require the connections made through network capital in order to organize and apply their resources. Such network capital can assume many forms, such as altruistic, long-lasting, and multipurpose relations; short-term instrumental relations; asymmetric patron-client relations; corrupt, exploitative, unequal exchanges.

The scope and role of network capital varies among societies: It is a simultaneous function of its culture, its past and present social organization, and the changing socioeconomic situation (Granovetter 1985, 1992). The *volume* of an economic actor's[2] network capital is equal to the size and number of the networks that it can mobilize in case of need. The *value* of an actor's network capital is a function of the number and availability of network members, and the resources and amount of network capital that these members themselves possess. There are two ways in which network capital can operate in relation to the market and the state: as a substitute or as an addition. When network capital is a substitute, it is used as an institution independent of the dominant institutions, as when people exchange among themselves the goods and services needed for survival (see also Chapter 4 in this volume). More commonly under communism and postcommunism, network capital was an addition, operating within the framework of the state and the market.

Our fundamental comparisons in this chapter are between ideal-type communist, postcommunist, and capitalist societies. We argue that both the volume and the value of network capital in communist societies is greater than in capitalist societies and greater still in postcommunist societies. We further suggest that these ideal-types are valid differentiators, so that variations in the volume and value of network capital among societies is smaller than between them. Because it is not possible to compute network capital precisely for societies, we use simple comparisons: Has there been *more* or *less* network capital in communist, postcommunist, and capitalist societies?

Why Is There More Network Capital Under Communism Than Under Capitalism?

Network Capital as a Substitute for State and Market

Our basic argument in this section is that the volume of network capital was greater in communist countries than in capitalist countries in the past few decades because of (a) their historical differences in social structure and culture, and (b) because the greater socioeconomic pressures and rigidities in communist countries gave network capital more opportunities to operate.

Network capital as a substitute for state and market is an auxiliary, and often temporary, alternative institution competing with these dominant institutions. In every society from ancient to modern times, various forms of network capital have persisted through auxiliary and small institutions such as altruism, barter, and reciprocity (Polanyi 1957; Sik 1988a; Dalton 1982). In this subsection, we describe several ways in which network capital was used as a substitute in communist countries: the reciprocal exchange of labor (REL) among workers to deal with routine problems, emergencies, and the special case of house-building, and managers' reciprocal transactions (MRT) in aid of their organizations. Although REL connects households and MRT connects organizations, both institutions had the same operational rules of balanced reciprocity (Sahlins 1972) and the same troubleshooting roles in the complex political economy of the communist market-state.

Support Among Households. A pervasive feature of communist Hungary was the reciprocal exchange of labor, in which households exchanged their labor on a nonmarket basis (see Sik 1988a for further discussion). Belying Western notions of the pervasiveness of the communist state, the state largely left such villages alone and increasingly abandoned the provision of houses. The reciprocal exchange of labor, always important in Hungary, became an even more important form of network capital, especially in rural towns and villages. Despite modernization and communism, such villages have remained relatively closed because of their physical isolation and fears that external forces will harm them. Such villages live under the double oppression of hostile nature and outside society, functioning to a great extent independently of the distant communist political structure. Their constrained opportunities, lack of external contact, and small size make their interpersonal networks densely knit, tightly bounded, and simultaneously supportive and conflictual.

Troubles are eternal and ubiquitous in such rural communities and coping resources scarce. The inertia characterizing small cultures and the community's dense and overlapping systems of personal networks have provided a suitable environment for the reciprocal exchange of labor to thrive as the principal means of dealing with problems. A survey of one village-like town, Vésztö, with a population of approximately 10,000, revealed that all of the households are interhousehold donors and/or recipients of material support and information (Table 6.1).[3] A majority of townspeople have been involved in almost all kinds of transactions, with the slight exceptions of lending money (49%) or lending assets (48%). The transactions that tend to occur most frequently are health care, gifts, and help with part-time farming. Material exchanges are more widespread than providing information exchanges, such as help in finding jobs or giving advice.

Most routine troubles are problems that need immediate care and are usually small in value and unexpected. Households often help each other deal with routine and urgent crises by exchanging services or lending tools and household items. Commercial repairmen do not bother making minor household repairs or lending tools. The needed goods and services would be too expensive for such townspeople to purchase on the market, even in the unlikely event that they are available. And people rarely obtain help from the chronically limited resources of the state.

The more prevalent the kind of transaction, the more likely it is to have been reciprocated, and the more likely that a majority of those who have provided all kinds of transactions have reciprocally received the same kind of help in exchange. (Wellman, Carrington, and Hall 1988 found similar reciprocity in westernized Toronto.) The major exceptions are that only slightly more than one-quarter of the townspeople have received reciprocal help in (major) trouble, in lending money, and in lending as-

TABLE 6.1   Frequency and Direction of Transactions by Type of Transaction

	% Households Supplying Support	% Households Involved in Symmetric Support (both directions)
Reciprocal care	87	64
Gifts	87	77
Taste of food[a]	86	85
Pig killing	82	64
Repairs	73	41
House building	68	67
Lending tools	67	42
Finding jobs	61	40
Giving advice	56	40
Help with trouble	54	26
Farming	54	47
Lending money	49	27
Lending assets	48	26

[a]A traditional and ceremonial rite of sending a taste of sausage to a network member.
SOURCE: Sik, 1995, p. 35.

sets. This apparent asymmetry may reflect the fact that many townspeople have not had the opportunity to reciprocate in these less common types of support.

The Case of House-building.   Hungarians also rely on reciprocal exchanges of labor to deal with problems that are not emergencies, but can be planned for or anticipated in advance. The role that network capital plays in house-building under communism and postcommunism is a good example. Most households have only been able to afford to pay for building materials and basic construction work. Shortages, inflation, and monopolistic gouging have led land and building costs to rise, increasing an already severe financial burden on households. Obtaining necessary permissions, getting increasingly scarce building material, and organizing construction tasks has taken a lot of time and has put severe burdens on the households' financial resources. Furthermore, the high rate of rural commuters and the better urban market for illegal construction labor has led to the rapid increase of rural wages. In the monopoly situation created by the labor shortage, rural and suburban house-builders who lack skill and knowledge have been at the mercy of the limited number of construction workers and artisans (such as plumbers) available for hire.

To be able to build their own homes, house-builders generally have had to borrow money from other households, reduce consumption, and do much of the work themselves. Men are largely responsible for this work, yet the one or two men in a typical rural household do not provide enough manpower for the many phases of the work to be done. The men's labor is already occupied on weekdays for an average of eight to ten hours. Yet it is also the men's duty to organize house-building, to obtain the necessary permissions, and to obtain materials. This takes a good deal of time during construction and crucially affects cost.

Households feel a good deal of urgency in finishing the work. Land and material have consumed scarce financial resources. House-building disrupts the lives of household members. The whole household drives itself to do the work. Their leisure time (weekends, evenings, and holidays) is consumed by house-building, with other activities subordinated to it. The situation is worsened because the household must live in cramped conditions and may even have to move several times during construction. There is never enough time because income-generating work cannot be suspended for long lest the crops die and cash for construction materials run out. Constantly rising construction costs and the threat of bad weather place further pressures on the household to finish building quickly (Kenedi 1983). It is better to move into the new house before severe winter conditions arrive, yet house-building has to stop at the onset of winter.

Thus time constraints and the labor-intensive nature of construction make it difficult for ordinary households to build homes using household members' own labor or using only labor bought on the market. These households are caught between the Scylla of self-exploitation and the Charybdis of exploitation by the local construction market. To cope, they must use their network capital to obtain labor. These townspeople do not rely on their interpersonal ties for their cheapness, pleasantness, or efficiency, but because they can only construct their homes by drawing on their network capital. Typically, they depend on anyone who has the needed skills or the available time: friends, relatives, and even distant acquaintances. These exchanges are not altruistic. Careful record-keeping and pervasive communication among these densely knit townspeople enable careful accounting of who has done what for whom and for what reason. The accounts give due weight to the skills involved. An electrician's help is worth more than a laborer's and will be so rewarded when the current house-builder helps, in turn, the electrician, or perhaps his brother-in-law. The densely knit and bounded nature of the town ensures that most of the help stays within the town, that debts frequently can be repaid through helping a mutual relation, and that social control can be exercised to encourage network members to repay their obligations.

Under such circumstances the proportion of Hungarian house-building using informal work increased from 25% in 1977 to 52% in 1989

TABLE 6.2   House Construction in Hungary by Type of Builder, 1977–89 (%)

Year	State	Market	Self-help	Total
1977	58	17	25	100
1980	58	15	27	100
1982	55	14	31	100
1985	46	14	40	100
1987	43	14	43	100
1989	32	16	52	100

SOURCE: Farkas and Vajda, 1989, p. 134.

(Table 6.2) and 56% in 1991. Moreover, such informal work (combining domestic work, altruistic help, and reciprocal exchanges of labor) has accounted for even higher percentages of working hours and participants. One study has estimated that such informal work in 1988 accounted for 74% of the house-building hours worked, and that 90% of construction workers built their own houses or were in REL situations helping others to build houses (Farkas and Vajda 1989). The following account gives the flavor of two of these transactions:

> Uncle Mihály, my neighbor, also helped to erect the roof, for I had helped him with the building of his cottage and a stable. He had asked me to go and help because he was afraid of a change for the worse in the weather. He said he paid a man, who had begun building the cottage, 150 *forints* [about US$2 at that time] a day, and he offered me the same amount. I took four or five days off my work, and put my nose to it. I would not have asked him for any money, since he had also done me good turns when, for instance, I needed some tools or help with this or that, but he insisted, because that was the surest way of making me stay on the spot all the time . . .
>
> A former workman of mine, a house painter and decorator, also helped me with making adobe walls. He is a strong young man. We knew he would also need help since he was a newly-wed. In return, I painted the rooms of his house. Everybody should help with what they are most skilled at. So the painting cost less than we would have paid to a stranger, though the most important thing was that there was somebody to do the work, because, in the summer, house painters are in great demand and they are hard to get.

Networks Among Managers and Their Organizations.   It would be a mistake to assume that only households used networks extensively in communist societies or that firms relied only on their relations with state organizations and, in the later stages of communism, on market forays. In reality, communist enterprises could not rely on ineffectual contract law to settle disputes and enforce obligations. Nor could they obtain needed goods and services from the bureaucratic, prodigal, and expensive state organizations. Even if they could find such goods and services, the absence of open markets meant that they could not buy them. Most fundamentally, shortages and bureaucratic regulations caused uncertainties that immobilized market and state redistributions.

This situation forced every actor in the economy to erect and maintain defensive institutions. For instance, managers revived the seemingly outdated, traditional institution of reciprocity because they were aware that they must maintain barter networks to survive. They created and used network capital to provide sources of reliable, fast information, and to ensure the exchange of goods and services that would enable them to survive the permanent shortages and the paralytic over- and underregulation of the redistributive state. Their links were *dual* (Breiger 1974): Just as ties between managers helped organizations to make the necessary sub rosa exchanges, ties between organizations brought managers into the juxtaposition necessary for building personal relationships (see also Czakó and Sik 1988). These ties between managers and organizations, which we call managers' reciprocal transactions, had several consistent principles:

1. The primary aim of transactions is to facilitate the operation of the organization (or the unit that the manager represents within it). Since managers personify their organization's interests in the course of these transactions, MRT has been a personalized form of interorganizational coping network. Troubleshooting transactions solved unexpected problems in purchases, production, or sales that the manager or firm could not solve alone. Such transactions involved supplying information, labor, products, money and services through loans, short-term rentals, long-term leases, gifts, or the sale of products not meant for sale. Network members mutually accepted risk, especially when a product or money is involved. For example, the assisting partner would temporarily provide a resource that his organization might need later.

2. No officially accepted procedures exist: neither bureaucracy, nor formal hierarchy, nor written commitments. In the absence of formal procedures, systems of norms provided security to network members, guaranteed the performance of the agreement, and reduced the risk entailed by the transactions' unofficial status. MRT has been a gentleman's agreement,[4] strengthened by personal trust, common defencelessness, interdependence, illegality, and "alegality" when the law was in limbo.[5] Managers have behaved with a group consciousness that

emphasizes solidarity, loyalty, and ceremony. Since honesty and reliability ensure that members observe the norm of reciprocity, such traits have been highly valued. Breaching the norm has entailed severe punishment. For instance, the "debtor" partner who fails to meet his obligations expels himself from the mutual-aid network.

3. Relationships can be either horizontal—between managers at similar levels in similarly situated enterprises—or vertical "soliciting" of help between managers or units on different levels of the hierarchy. As the organizational power of managers involved in soliciting differs greatly, so too do the results of bargaining. Although the network members were in uneven positions, both eventually won. Firms procured resources cheaply, they jumped the queue for goods that are in permanent shortage, or obtained better-quality goods. They received favors such as looser deadlines, long-term credit, foreign exchange, and alterations in state economic plans. In exchange, the grateful firm supported the higher organization by overfulfilling its quota, being loyal in organizational shake-ups, and deliberately producing the scarce goods desired by the higher organization. Hence patron-client relations have been "probably more widespread and pervasive in communist than in other industrial societies" (Eisenstadt and Roniger 1984, pp. 190).

4. Firm-centered transactions are embedded in personal networks among managers. Both hierarchical or horizontal reciprocal transactions have been based on personal relationships which originated through the managers' common contexts, such as school, place of work, association, membership, origin, and which were concomitant with the managers' official positions. To initiate a manager's reciprocal transaction, network members used both their personal relationships and official positions. This means that MRT has been neither a private affair nor a purely official contact. And while the overlap between organizational networks and personal networks increased the efficiency of both, it also distorted them because the overlap made it impossible to separate the intertwined interorganizational and interpersonal networks.

5. Managers' reciprocal transactions are maintained through implicit and explicit ceremonies. Ceremonial MRTs have preserved and strengthened personal networks. Partners have engaged in preventive investment, meeting and keeping in touch even when there is no need for help. Managers knew that only well-founded and well-kept contacts would be useful for defending their

TABLE 6.3 Percentage of Managers of Agricultural Cooperatives Involved in MRT Transactions in a Given Year

	Got	*Gave*
Agroker[a]	77	33
Production system[b]	70	93
Local school	46	79
Police	43	32
Military	35	26
Village council	29	75
Village party organ	21	31

[a]Oligopolistic state-run commercial firms that handle all kinds of agricultural goods.

[b]Nonprofit associations of agricultural firms. They determine allocation of the means of production (high tech) and the innovation of flow.

SOURCE: Czakó and Sik, 1988, p. 24.

positions. Though the forms of keeping in touch were not strictly prescribed, any kind of interaction might be used that preserved the warmth of the relationship: friendly greetings, courtesies, symbolic favors, smaller gifts, and invitations. Violating the norms observed in ceremonial transactions created the risk of a deteriorating relationship that might lower the likelihood that a manager would receive future benefits.

Managers' reciprocal transactions were widespread and frequent as the case of exchanges among agricultural enterprises illustrates (Table 6.3). In every organization, at least 95% of the managers engaged in loan transactions, and 85% engaged in such other network transactions as renting scarce goods, leasing on good terms, and selling a not-for-sale product. Most engaged in at least one transaction per month. One-third of managers gave—and one-fourth received—help at least weekly.

Although the organizations listed in Table 6.3 are formally of equal rank, the direction of transactions reveals the imbalance of their network relations. Agroker, an oligopolistic state-run enterprise involved in every kind of agricultural good, is an example of this. Not only did Agroker's power to allocate machinery give it a preeminent place among managerial contacts, it also had widespread offices, so it had much discretion about how helpful it could be to a specific neighbor. Agroker received more than twice as many favors as it gave. Agrotek, the state monopoly that imported, exported, and allocated major farm machinery, did even better, receiving six times as many favors as it gave. At the other extreme, the relatively resourceless town council, local school, and local party organization gave more favors than they received.

Summary. MRTs were so prevalent under communism that we have chosen to discuss them as a substitute for, and not merely a superimposed addition to, the operations of the communist state. The prevalence of MRTs stemmed from deficiencies in the system of economic institutions—especially in relationships through which their enterprises acquire needed resources. The managers' transactions prevented emergencies, solved crises in production or economic management, and alleviated some of the shortages typical of communism. All the defects that appeared in the communist economy have had a basic role in producing these transactions: the structural and technical shortcomings of distribution, the overcentralized organization of production and trade, the overbureaucratized and overpoliticized management of firms, and the unachievable system of regulation.

Although troubles, disorders, and scarcities may turn up in capitalist systems, they were a stable feature of the communist economy, a symptom of its normal state. This is because communist enterprises acquired their necessary resources through two institutional systems—state redistributions and the state-controlled market—the operation of which was essentially determined by uncertainties caused by shortages and bureaucratic regulations. Under such circumstances, every actor in the economy was forced to respond to this situation in order to survive. This is why MRT (just as REL), the seemingly outdated institution of reciprocity that is characteristic of traditional economies, was revived and flourished under communism. As the underlying situation did not magically change in the rapid transition from communism to postcommunism, MRT and REL continue today in Hungary. Indeed, we argue later in this chapter that such practices flourish even more under postcommunism.

Network Capital Superimposing State and Market

Networks not only substituted for state and market, they were also superimposed additions to the operations of the communist state and markets. Buyers and sellers, entrepreneurs and bureaucrats, principals and agents used their network capital to reorganize state and market to their advantage. Cooperating or competing, they relied on networks to cope with their lack of market or bureaucratic power and to grab opportunities to cheat market and state powers. The networks had many guises: monopolies and oligopolies, cartels and cliques, "mafia" and clan, ethnic enclaves, patron-client and long-lasting buyer-seller relationships, bribery and corruption. In this subsection, we describe two ways in which network capital has been superimposed on the communist state and market: the monopolization of the academic labor market, and corruption and bribery in the state hierarchy and the market.

The Academic Labor Market.   One might think that academia, as an intellectual elite, would rigorously control the meritocratic selection of its members as a bureaucratically screened open competition largely free from the influence of network connections. Yet all over the world white-collar jobs are often allocated via personal networks (Dornstein 1977), and well-developed informal networks (buddy networks) defend the existing professional labor markets against "outsiders."

In communist Hungary, structural elements of the academic labor market, especially in the social sciences, have further heightened the role of network capital: (a) As the financial problems of the state worsened, the supply of casual academic labor (for part-time and short-term jobs) increasingly exceeded demand. (b) As academia has been a state monopoly, the extent of the demand depended solely on the state budget, while jobs have been concentrated in a few state-dominated universities and research centers. (c) To reduce costs, academic institutions have made many jobs part-time or casual (short-term contractual). (d) Although the typical employee has at least one university degree and an additional full-time job, total income is barely enough to get by (Sik 1986–1987).

Taken together, these labor market characteristics produced a market where the demand was state-dominated, oligopolistic, and shrinking, and where the supply consisted of formally nonorganized, well-educated, low-paid scholars seeking short-term solutions to the economic uncertainty created by the inadequacy of their incomes. This situation has largely continued until the present time. In this shrinking and state-dominated academic labor market, the only way to gain access to a casual job has been to have contact with the few places that have funds or positions available. The greater one's network capital, the more likely one could acquire information before others and, with luck, get a decent contract.

Job-seekers have used the elements of their network capital that are within the labor market, seeking help from patrons, bribes, peers, and workplace cliques. Yet it is not surprising that to obtain these scarce, important transitory prizes, job-seekers (and their agents) have also used networks that are outside the academic labor market, such as ties with friends, spouses, ex-spouses or ex-lovers, and bridge partners. Indeed, most transactions are embedded in such extramarket networks. These other ties often have been members of a densely knit group, a structural form well suited to controlling information and mobilizing collective support. Thus the smallest unit of organization of this labor market is not the individual but an extramarket primary group.

Yet all of the academic and extramarket primary groups have usually been intertwined and form a large network. The transactions of this network have tended to become embedded in a long-run series of reciprocal

exchanges that encompassed both academic and extramarket relationships. Such long-term reciprocity made these networks flexible enough
to survive conflicts among different subcircles and powerful enough to
exclude those outside their charmed circles.

Why has network capital been so crucial in the allocation of jobs in the
academic labor market?

1. Because academic work is both autonomous and nonmanual, it
   cannot be regulated and a worker's ability to do the job cannot
   be anticipated precisely. Because jobs are casual or short-term,
   they are not crucial to the organization. Those with jobs to
   dispense have preferred to minimize the time spent selecting
   candidates and to maximize the reliability of those selected. As a
   result, this academic job market is inherently closed,
   personalized, and particularistic (Dornstein 1977; see
   Granovetter 1974 for similar American situations).
2. There is a tradition of "status" (in the Weberian sense) in the
   labor market. The use of networks has maximized the efficiency
   of the market and minimized its risks as credible people have
   been hired quickly (Dornstein 1977). Because casual jobs are
   tenuous and must be done on short notice, the bargaining
   position of casual employees is weakened by the quick and
   personal nature of the selection process, as well as by the lack of
   a legal framework and the absence of trade unions. Yet the
   sponsorship and referral system has also helped privileged
   insiders to retain their power and has reinforced the continuity
   of the networks. The system has encouraged clannish
   inequalities between patron and client, and between patron and
   patron. Patrons have used the legitimating ideology of labor-
   market efficiency to maintain their long-term interests. The
   success of their networks in obtaining jobs for members has
   reinforced the continuity of networks and legitimated norms of
   loyalty to the mutual-aid cliques within them.
3. As noted above, the majority of the transactions of this casual
   academic labor market have been embedded into the operation
   of densely knit, extramarket networks. The inertia of such
   networks has been great because they have been long-lasting
   and have often been reinforced through cliquish norms.

The bad and worsening market conditions, the monopolistic and state-
dominated nature and the uncertainty of casual jobs, and the inertia of
existing networks thus explain why investing in network capital is ex-

tremely important in the Hungarian academic labor market. Similar conditions have been present in other casual white-collar labor markets.

Corruption in the Markets. Under communism, the fundamental feature of the market was eternal scarcity, while the fundamental feature of the state was its inherent complement, overregulated bureaucratic hierarchy. The state treated the economy as a complete hierarchy commanded by the Politburo through deputies and lower-level agents. The only task of enterprises at the bottom of this hierarchy was to carry out the plan, and the state tried to control them thoroughly in order to achieve this end.

In practice, such control was imperfect. Information was lost and distorted as it traveled in both directions because both higher and lower levels found it costly and time-consuming to process it. Subordinates, responding to a variety of moral, career, and material incentives, were only imperfectly controlled by their superiors. Further confusion ensued when multiple superiors in complex hierarchies issued conflicting orders. New plans and orders could not be carried out without changing many of the orders that were already being implemented. Making changes while maintaining coordination was organizationally impossible (Montias and Rose-Ackerman 1981).

Both scarcity and overregulated bureaucracy offered fertile soil for widespread, continuously reinforced, and therefore, ever increasing, corruption. Galasi and Kertesi (1987, p. 373) use game theory to analyze the inherent logic of the spread of market corruption. Their starting point is the "uncorrupted" situation where both the price and the worth of an espresso is three forints:

> There emerged the institution of the so-called "extra espresso": those customers who wish to have a better (stronger) coffee pay two forints more. This amount goes to the waitress who makes the coffee and who, in turn, prepares a five forints' worth of espresso for the bribers. Since she only has so much coffee in stock which she gets through official channels and she does not steal, the transaction is possible only if she "economizes" on the coffee given to non-bribers. Thus those who pay the official price (3 *forints*) only get one *forint*'s worth of coffee. The waitress fares well since she earns an extra two *forints* for every briber without any extra work or cost. The bribers also fare well since they get 5 forints' worth of coffee for their five *forints*, while if they had paid three *forints* they would have got one *forint*'s worth of coffee. On the other hand, non-bribers fare badly since they get one *forint*'s worth of coffee for three *forints*.

Galasi and Kertesi argue that if two buyers can opt to pay either the official or corrupt price, both will choose the latter in the long run. However, this choice is to their detriment because both pay more and get lower quality.

Under communism, corruption spread and prevailed in the market. The process illustrated by the game theory model has emerged in every situation where there has been no competition, and when the seller can influence the quality of goods and services or shorten the wait for them. Moreover, once the custom of giving tips, bribes, and "thank you money" became part of the structure of a culture, it necessarily spread throughout the society.

Where corruption in capitalist countries has been focused on selling goods (e.g., bribery to obtain contracts), corruption in communist countries focused on obtaining goods. People and organizations routinely engaged in corrupt practices to distort the order of rationing, cheat the official plan, and obtain scarce materials and jobs. Because people had more network capital available than goods and cash, they used their network connections to survive and to grab resources. Because such ties went outside of the formal hierarchy, they were illegal or, at least, alegal. Yet network capital was the only resource available in abundance and hence the only way that people could make the system work for them.

The spread of corruption was hastened by the speed by which information traveled about the rules of the game, such as appropriate behavior, etiquette, and amounts to pay. Moreover, the inertia built into the process of networking increased the chance that latecomers would not be immediately aware of changes even if the original actors decreased or ceased their corruption. Although the actors in the Galasi-Kertesi model behaved as if they were on an isolated island, in real life actors also teach each other how to behave and teach the rest of society as information flows through their networks. Norms emerged to define appropriate behavior, such as the proper amount of bribery. These norms spread rapidly through the networks, socialized other actors, and became embedded as new cultural traits. And it was not just the rules of behavior that spread. At the same time, the acceptance of bribery as a fact of life decreased the cognitive dissonance of committing a sin. A pro-bribery culture emerged and became reinforced.

Why Is There More Network Capital Under Postcommunism Than Communism?

Postcommunism has not only produced a rather incomplete shift from state distributions to market exchanges. Along with the expansion of buying and selling on the market, there has been an increased use of network capital as an addition to (although not a substitute for) market and state activity. This is because postcommunism contains several characteristics that increase the uncertainty of economic actors, including the rapidly changing legal framework, the new political machinery of a multiparty parliamentary system, newly opened borders, and the emergence of new entrepreneurial and unemployed strata. These developments have created new challenges for households, organizations, and state authorities (see also Kennedy and Galtz 1996). Such challenges contain both threats and unique opportunities, which often give quite unexpected and almost unknown cost-benefit structures and durations. Under these circumstances, everyone invents, develops, or copies strategies and tactics *to cope* (to protect against threats) or to *grab* (to make a fortune).

In this section, we present four typical situations in postcommunist Hungarian society in which network capital is of great importance as a means of coping or grabbing. The first example shows the role of network capital as a means for ordinary households to cope with everyday economic problems in a society that has grown more impoverished. The next two examples show the importance of network capital as a means of both coping and grabbing, for new entrepreneurs established after the collapse of communism, and for old entrepreneurs who have persisted after communism and are adapting to the new situation. The rapid proliferation of entrepreneurs makes Hungary rather unique in Eastern Europe: 10% of the active labor force were entrepreneurs in 1993 (most of them were self-employed) and more than 40% of Hungarian employees worked in the private sector. Finally, we elaborate briefly on the unique characteristics of postcommunism: the role of network capital in the speedy shift to privatization.

Coping with Everyday Consumer Crises

The already extensive culture and practice under communism of using intra- and interhousehold networks has increased under postcommunism. Paradoxically, under postcommunism, the market has become less of an alternative for most people because prices have been increasing and incomes have been decreasing. At the same time the state sector has been shrinking since the mid–1980s and is now not able to offer a defensive solution for people in trouble. Under these circumstances the use of networks has increased in a society where such networks already are abundant and well-maintained, the family is deemed to be the "natural" unit of reproduction, and the household is the "normal" unit for the production of well-being. Hence, relying on intra- and interhousehold networks involves few costs for establishing them, or for learning and teaching how to use them.

As most postcommunist problems and crises have been domestic (even if they are the result of larger-scale societal problems of job and in-

TABLE 6.4   Percentage of Household and Network-Capital-Based Transactions
in Postcommunist Countries

	Bulgaria	*Czechoslovakia*	*Hungary*	*Poland*	*Romania*
Household production[a]	94	91	81	75	95
Reciprocity[b]	76	53	60	49	56
Connection[c]	70	33	37	48	48
Bribery[d]	30	13	17	38	60

[a]One or more of the following time uses: growing food, building or repairing
the house, queuing an hour or more a day.
[b]Exchanging help with friends in growing food, building or repairing houses,
shopping, baby-sitting, or transportation.
[c]Using connections to get things done without formal payment.
[d]Using connections to get things done involving money payments.
SOURCE: Rose and Haerpfer, 1992, p. 87.

come shortages), the family/household is the natural unit for exchanges.
The transaction-cost approach offers some explanations as to why households choose domestic work and interhousehold transfers so frequently
to cope with their problems in postcommunist societies (Pollak 1985).[6]
The household's lack of efficiency and low economy of scale are of little
importance in accomplishing domestic work and interhousehold barters.
Moreover, interhousehold networks have advantages over market
economies in providing low-cost access to a large labor pool, diverse human capital, and flexibly organized domestic production. These factors
also decrease the negative effects of the interplay between economics and
emotions that are common in household and interhousehold relations.

Thus it is natural that all kinds of network capital are widely used as a
means to cope in postcommunist societies. Table 6.4 shows that the situation is not peculiar to Hungary. Household production, as the core of every
network-based economic activity, has been the most widely used means of
coping. Reciprocity, essentially the use of interhousehold networks to obtain more domestic service, care, and production, is next in importance, except in Romania where bribery seems to have been more widespread.

Because interhousehold networks are densely knit, tightly bounded,
and solidary, there are low costs in organizing, operating, monitoring,
and evaluating them. These interhousehold networks differ profoundly
from the opportunistic, uncertain behavior of often transitory market and
state agents in the postcommunist era. As a shrinking producer of welfare, the postcommunist state has been unable to offer a solution for the
troubled well-being of the populace (Sik 1988b). With decreasing gross
domestic product and real wages, there are fewer opportunities to earn
additional income in the second economy (Sik 1992) and fewer house-

holds can afford to buy goods in the formal market. Yet the opening of markets has created more awareness of—and demand for—a much wider variety of higher-quality goods and services.

In hard times, loyalty to the household tends to increase as it is the principal thing that families can control. With the hedgehoglike pulling back to the family household of those who had left to seek their fortune, there is a special interest in increasing household assets. The increased size of the household creates more opportunities to organize the domestic division of labor more flexibly and to allocate each chore to the household member who is best at it. Economies of scale also become more possible. Thus, the efficiency of production increases while the chance of conflict decreases.

At the same time, people expand their investment in their intra- and interhousehold network capital. Unlike paid work, which is organized on an individual basis, the household-based economy encourages exchanges between households, with individuals acting as agents of their respective households. Thus interhousehold networks under postcommunism have become an even more efficient way of coping with ordinary problems and extraordinary crises. There are few financial costs in establishing, searching for, and learning how to use networks. Indeed, household-centered production results in fewer negative spillovers and more self-monitoring, making family loyalty an even more preferable option. The densely knit networks foster collective work for the common good. Moreover, people have more time and opportunity to help fellow network members than they do to earn the money that would enable them to buy goods and services.

The Networks of Postcommunist Entrepreneurs

In the early stages of postcommunism, privatization has offered a unique and temporary occasion to make a fortune because the rules of the game are uncertain and changing. There are excellent opportunities to seize the moment and increase one's market position and power. The role of corruption has skyrocketed because the state retains key positions in financial and economic policymaking and politics are unstable. Even though the political regime changed with the transition to postcommunism, the institutional structure and the operation of the lower economy that produces low-tech, cheap goods and services has hardly changed.

All of the wheeling and dealing practices of using network capital that developed under communism have remained valuable assets for coping with problems and seizing opportunities. Indeed, network capital has become more important (compared to other alternatives) in the transition from communism to postcommunism, because the East European cultural background favors it, flourishing networks were created under communism, and such networks provide available and relatively reliable means to deal with decreasing state control, increasing opportunities, and daily and long-term uncertainty (see also Czakó and Sik 1988). This is especially true in the case of privatization, since money is a necessary but insufficient condition to make a bargain. Only a handful of people know which are the juiciest parts of the fruit, and even fewer have the desire or power (or access to the real power centers) to put their ideas into practice. This uncertainty of knowledge explains why intensive search is rational, and such searching is best done through networks.

Investment in developing know-how, position, and vertical and horizontal networks (Csanádi 1991; Czakó and Sik 1988), was especially useful for those bureaucrats in the party and state authorities who could manage to do these things. As some cadres developed experience with the informal second economy, they became readier to abandon their power in the first (state) economy and invest in private enterprises. This was especially true for the younger, well-educated state technocrats who spoke foreign languages, were familiar with the protocol of the market, and whose networks extended beyond the Hungarian economy. The preparation of these influential people for active participation in private enterprises facilitated the nonviolent transformation to the postcommunist economy (Nee 1991).

The inertia of corruption and connections provides the cultural and structural bases of intensive networking. The role of social structure seems to be more important than that of culture because both Western multinationals and small sharks seek to acquire network capital. Since they do not have the language, the local knowledge, or the local network capital, they hire brokers (mostly former deputy ministers and middle-rank technocrats) who possess much network capital. These brokers have expert knowledge: They speak foreign languages and have foreign ties, possess second-economy entrepreneurial skills as well as first-economy connections, know who should be bribed and how, and they understand the etiquette of lobbying (Czakó and Sik 1988; Csanádi 1991; Nee 1991 Böröcz 1992, 1993).

Indeed, we can see clearly, as if in a laboratory, how network capital facilitates setting up a business:

1. The rules of the game are both over- and underregulated.
    Although the massive bureaucracy has continued from the communist era, its attention has shifted to controlling the new entrepreneurs. But the bureaucrats lack the staff and expertise because they were trained to administer the communist state and are still preoccupied with ministering to its widespread

remnants. Moreover, because of new responsibilities, overwork, comparative loss of income in inflationary times, and loss of perquisites and status since communism, the bureaucrats are now more corruptible.

2. With laws constantly changing, no one can be certain what is or is not legal. To cope, people must use their network capital to gather information and obtain favors from officials. Yet using such networks further corrupts bureaucracies and distorts markets.

3. Network capital is especially important in the informal economy, where trust is everything (Mars and Altman 1983). Trust is vital for defending against state agents and for attacking other cliques. It is not surprising that the most active networks in the informal economy are organized around nonmarket networks of kin, friends, and neighbors. Ethnic minorities have an advantage here because their shared culture and mutual ties foster trust and strengthen existing networks. For example, Poles and Romanians are active in black-marketing and smuggling, Arabs and Turks in illegal currency dealings, and Gypsies in a variety of activities. Such groups rely on their networks as a low-cost and high-efficiency way to deal with being a marginal, sometimes oppressed, minority (see also Light and Bonacich 1988).

4. People have responded to their lack of wealth and state credit by pooling through their networks. Not only do they create a greater pool of wealth and state access in this way, but their joint networks create more network capital by enabling them to reach out to more diverse social circles (Granovetter 1973, 1982; Wellman and Leighton 1979). The case of the Three Graces illustrates how friends and kin use their ties to create a business.

Starting an Enterprise—The Three Graces. Once upon a time under communism, three editors of a state publishing house became friends. They shared each other's ability to work hard, endure hardship, and survive troubled times. They had followed each other in two subsequent jobs and still maintained good working relations. So, when postcommunism came, they decided to set up their own business. Their assets were their trust in each other, their expertise in the publishing business, and, last but not least, their contacts in Hungary and abroad in all necessary dimensions of publishing: contacts with translators, editors, typists, printing houses, market dealers, and so on.

As the three women did not have any money, they accepted a fourth partner, a Swede who lent the necessary seed money and who was a brother-in-law of one of them. Yet there was still not enough money to lease office space and equipment, let alone to cover the costs of printing and publishing a book. Therefore, one person's living room was converted into an office, and her telephone was used as an office phone. Fax and copying services were either stolen or received as informal aid from friends and relatives working in other offices.

These solutions all involved intense networking. Family members, friends, friends of friends and their friends were constantly used as information channels in learning how to set up a bank account, which bank is reliable, who to contact to jump the huge queue for obtaining the proper business license before a deadline, how to find a resourceful but cheap accountant, how to beat taxes, social insurance, and customs systems, and so on. Strong ties such as family members and best friends were asked to do voluntary work including translating, writing advertisements, going to the post office, selecting potential books, and waiting at home for urgent phone calls. Family and friends were asked to tolerate the disappearance of the Three Graces from their domestic and social lives.

Networks also were useful for obtaining initial contracts. One husband's firm gave an order for the publication of a book, another arranged an advertising contract, a Canadian friend arranged contacts with Toronto publishers, and another friend arranged a contract for a yearlong project involving many books. Of course, contacts with the most important business partners had preceded the formal establishment of the venture. The Three Graces received generous terms of payment from people they already knew in the book business: publishers, printers, houses, translators, and editors. This gave them the margin of time between earning money through selling books and paying their printing bills. Translators and editors also accepted promises of future profits instead of requiring immediate payment. Over time, the business survived and now is even prospering.

Protecting an Existing Enterprise—The Budapest Taxi Drivers. On Thursday, October 25, 1990, the Hungarian government raised gasoline prices by 76%. By late afternoon, thousands of angry taxi drivers were protesting in front of the Parliament building. Within hours, they had blocked all Danube bridges and controlled the main streets in and out of Budapest. On Friday, the Austrian border was closed, and the international airport, offices, factories, and schools were paralyzed. On Saturday, food ran low. Some people became afraid for the future, while others picnicked in the middle of the empty bridges. People frolicked in the noticeably less-polluted air. The tension grew hourly as truck and bus drivers, peasants with tractors, and private cars joined the blockade. On Sunday, the government met with representatives of employees and employers in a televised all-day roundtable discussion that was watched by the whole country. The result was a compromise: The drivers demolished their blockade, while the government reduced the price increase and pardoned the blockaders. An ordinary Monday followed the long weekend of rebellion (see also Sik 1994).

Why were the taxi drivers able to organize a blockade and beat the system? Each driver normally works independently and entrepreneurially, with no hierarchical differences or specialization. Yet a driver is not isolated from his colleagues. The taxi radio network routinely coordinates the dispatch of cabs, and in emergencies, this network rapidly relays information about accidents, robberies, and so on. In ordinary situations the radio is a communication channel for sending messages to others, calling families, setting up dates, searching for rare commodities, reporting traffic jams, and the like.[7]

Thus, the radio network has been the basis of a *social* network with well-developed patterns for cooperating on the job and dealing with other problems. There are densely knit ties among drivers and a collective self-identity that supports cooperation without formal organization. The network is more technically developed than the government's communication systems. It is maintained psychologically by the drivers' sense of solidarity; it is maintained socially by the drivers' organizational skills, personal relations, and frequent use of network capital. The speed, straightforwardness, and lack of ambiguity offered by the radio network and supported by the drivers' subculture facilitated the widespread, simultaneous actions that were crucial for staging the rebellion. However, solidarity means more than a taxi driver turning on his radio. Each driver must believe that other drivers feel the same way and will do what the radio instructs.

The taxi drivers' blockade is a clear example of the development under postcommunism of network capital that originally arose independently of the state as part of the informal second economy of late communism. Transactions under communism in this hidden but visible market have socialized drivers and customers to market processes, such as bargaining and calculating costs and benefits. The drivers especially became socialized to a special type of entrepreneurial behavior: profit-seeking in a shortage economy that lacked a banking, taxation, or credit system, and that was under the perpetual surveillance of the police. Then, in the late 1980s, as a last communist effort to use the informal second economy as a tool to reform the formal first economy, the taxi drivers were transformed and made visible as small entrepreneurs. By the end of communism, they had developed a collective culture, self-organization, joint maintenance activities, and monopolistic practices. Their quasi-corporate network flourished.

Networks such as this that had been established during communism did not disappear in the change to postcommunism. In the short run, the institutional structure and operation of low-tech goods and services have hardly changed. Therefore, the practice of using network capital to cope and grab retains an important role. Meanwhile, postcommunism's uncertainty and severe economic conditions encourage people to stick to already developed troubleshooting mechanisms. The most widespread and important of which is their network capital.

Conclusions

There is more network capital under communism than under capitalism, and there is even more under postcommunism than under communism. To be sure, people in all societies use network capital to grab opportunities and to cope with difficulties, and corruption is hardly a unique feature of communism and postcommunism. Compared to using markets or accessing state resources, networks often are more easily and quickly accessible, less costly, and more effective.

As Wellman argues in the introduction to this book, network capital pervades all societies. Does this ubiquity negate our argument that network capital is more important under communism than under capitalism? We believe that although network capital is a crucial and non-system-specific form of social capital, there are cultural, historical, political, social, and structural factors that justify our argument for its especially important role under communism:

1. There was a strong base of networks in Eastern Europe before the arrival of communist states. Communism came into power in the eastern semiperiphery of Europe, historically the locale of rural, peasant societies. For example, in 1930, approximately 51% of the Hungarian population and 80% of the Bulgarian population worked in agriculture, as compared to 7% in England, 29% in Germany, and 36% in France (Berend and Ránki 1974). To live in a peasant society means to live in a specific type of production and reproduction system: household- and village-based, seasonal and labor-intensive agricultural activity, tightly bounded and densely knit networks, impositions from outside and above, and underdeveloped communication with the outside. The underdeveloped communication and dense, bounded infrastructure meant that household- and kinship-orientedness were key elements. Hence personal networks were relatively strong, homogeneous, and local (Fél and Hofer 1973). Even cities were relatively small, with a population largely composed of first-generation rural migrants who retained strong active ties to their villages. In short, communism came to power in postpeasant, small-community societies in which the population had well-maintained network

capital and where ecological circumstances contributed to the usefulness of relying on this capital.

2. Due to cultural and historical factors, network capital was more widespread under communism than under capitalism. The communist party-state fought against civil organizations and cultural traditions, fostering industrialization, urbanization, and statism. The peasant community and work culture disappeared, voluntary and charitable associations were destroyed, and occupational and settlement systems were transformed. Yet the rural peasant culture partially survived the period of communism and resurfaced when the time was ripe (Szelenyi 1988). Patterns of familism, localism, inheritance, and mutual support continued and strengthened.

3. Despite the communists' attempts to destroy some elements of network capital, structural pressures and opportunities under communism nevertheless were strong and persistent enough to increase the momentum of network capital. Although communism destroyed much tradition and changed Hungary's occupational structure (and to a lesser extent its settlement structure), in less than a generation communism could not change the culture and nature of precommunist network capital. In some ways, the half-century of communism actually strengthened network-oriented culture. Although state-dominated economies had existed in most precommunist Eastern European countries, communism's elaborate central and local administrations and large-scale banking and manufacturing systems favored bureaucratic procedures on the one hand, and corruption and patron-clientelism on the other hand (Berend and Ránki 1974).

4. In rural areas, all alternatives were worse than network reciprocity. Households used their network capital to cope with shortages and to improve their housing. Throughout Hungary, managers relied on network capital to troubleshoot, while academics used network capital to get scarce jobs in a shrinking labor market. In the regulated market and totalitarian hierarchy, corruption became widespread as a means for survival and success.

In short, the greater rural element, more closed economies and communities, greater bureaucratic rigidities, and more clientelistic bureaucracies of Eastern European communist countries have enabled network capital to proliferate more than in their capitalist counterparts. Yet several reasons have combined to make network capital even more important under postcommunism than it was under communism. To understand why, we must consider the social, economic, and political factors that provided the "ideal" environment for networks to flourish:

5. As network capital has high inertia and was quite widespread under communism, it should be at least as prevalent under postcommunism, unless it has been destroyed or become less useful. In communist Hun-

gary, the almost peaceful coexistence of the first (formal) and second (informal) economies encouraged a strong culture of networking to develop. Participants were socialized to place high priority on using networks to avoid or overcome troubles. At the same time, this culture increased the momentum of existing network capital. It also made investment in this asset increasingly profitable. This culture and ever increasing network capital could not disappear in the course of transformation to postcommunism. And why should it disappear if it has been so effective for so long? Without exception, in every postcommunist country, people feel that networking—especially with foreign ties—guarantees success.

6. Because market and bureaucracy frequently malfunction under postcommunism, network capital is an even more useful means to cope and grab. The failure of the distorted and subordinated communist markets, and the greater presence of an over- and underorganized state and bureaucracy have resulted in the greater use of networks. Whether superimposed on or substituted for market and state, networks under these circumstance clearly thrive.

7. The transition from communism to postcommunism involves growing uncertainty that is manifested by increasing incidents of minor troubles, crises, calamities, opportunities that must be seized instantly, changes in the rules of the game, and new games with new players. People who lack other alternatives tend to use network capital when conditions worsen or uncertainties prevail. Consequently, network capital increasingly is important for households and firms as a means to cope and grab. This is not only because of the inertia of former practices, but because people rationally rely on their already existing behavioral patterns, skills, and heavy investment in network capital. Under postcommunism, both the culture of networking developed during the communist period and investments in network capital are assets that are proving effective for coping with economic troubles and exploiting available opportunities.

Notes

We appreciate the editorial assistance of Thy Phu. Support for this chapter has been provided by the Kellogg Institute (Notre Dame University), the Wissenschaftszentrum Berlin für Sozialforshung (Germany), and the Social Sciences and Humanities Research Council of Canada.

1. And perhaps beyond. See Nee and Matthews's (1996) review of China's societal transformation.

2. An economic actor could be a person, household, organization, state, etc.

3. This survey was conducted under Sik's supervision in southeastern Hungary. There was a large area embracing the town covered by isolated farmhouses. Husbands and wives were interviewed in about 10% (222) of the households.

Questions about relationships (e.g., kin or friend) were answered separately by husbands and wives. Questions about dealing with troubles were divided between husbands and wives, depending on whether the trouble was generally considered to be a man's job (e.g., lending tools, building houses) or a woman's household job. Our definition of "trouble" covers (a) minor, unforeseeable problems in everyday life (e.g., something breaks down, the household runs out of a small item, a tool is missing); (b) cases that present some rare but foreseeable difficulty for which a household can plan (e.g., building a house, agricultural work, pig-killing); (c) unexpected major emergencies (e.g., shortages of cash, natural disasters, accidents, illnesses). Troubles, although also occurring in affluent communities, are a part of the "normal" life of small settlements.

4. Very few women were managers.

5. We are grateful to Detelina Radoeva for suggesting this term.

6. Two remarks with respect to the limits of the transaction-cost approach for our analysis. First, the approach emphasizes the lack of economies of scale and of the efficiency of household production. Yet these aspects are of limited importance in evaluating the role of households and interhousehold networks in coping with problems. Second, the approach has focused solely on the individual household and ignored the role of interhousehold networks. Yet such networks can substantially soften the obstacles of household production by providing a greater labor pool, more diverse human capital and material resources, more flexibility in organizing and timing household production, and by decreasing the negative effects of problems within a single household.

7. Our analysis has been especially aided by Mars's (1982) description of social relations among "hawks," "wolves," and "vultures." The cab drivers are socially organized as "vultures."

References

Abbott, Andrew. 1988. *The System of Professions: An Essay on the Division of Expert Labor.* Chicago: University of Chicago Press.

Berend, Ivan T., and György Ránki. 1974. *Economic Development in East-Central Europe in the 19th and 20th Centuries.* New York: Columbia University Press.

Böröcz, József. 1992. "Dual Dependency and the Informalization of External Linkages: The Hungarian Case." *Research in Social Movements, Conflicts and Change* 14:189–209.

Böröcz, József. 1993. "Simulating the Great Transformation: Property Change under Prolonged Informality in Hungary." *Archives Européennes de Sociologie* 34:81–107.

Breiger, Ronald. 1974. "The Duality of Persons and Groups." *Social Forces* 53:181–190.

Burt, Ronald. 1992. *Structural Holes.* Chicago: University of Chicago Press.

Csanádi, Mária. 1991. "Structure, Cohesion and Disintegration of the Hungarian Party-System." Pp. 325–350 in *Democracy and Political Transformation,* edited by György Szoboszlai. Budapest: Hungarian Political Science Association.

Czakó, Ágnes, and Endre Sik. 1988. "Managers' Reciprocal Transactions." *Connections* 11:23–32.

Dalton, George. 1982. "Barter." *Journal of Economic Issues* 16:181–190

Dornstein, Miriam. 1977. "Some Imperfections in the Market Exchanges for Professionals and Executive Services." *American Journal of Economics and Sociology* 36:113–128.

Eisenstadt, Samuel N., and Luis Roniger. 1984. *Patrons, Clients and Friends.* Cambridge: Cambridge University Press.

Farberman, Henry A., and Eugen A. Weinstein. 1970. "Personalisation in Lower Class Consumer Interaction." *Social Problems* 17:449–457.

Farkas, János, and Ágnes Vajda. 1989. "How to Build a House and the Housing Reform in Hungary." Pp. 81–91 in *Hungary under the Reform.* Budapest: Research Review on Social Sciences.

Fél, Edit, and Tamás Hofer. 1973. "Tanyakert-s, Patron-Client Relations and Political Factions in Atany." *American Anthropologist* 75:787–801.

Galasi, Péter, and Gábor Kertesi. 1987. "The Spread of Bribery." *Acta Oeconomica* 38:371–389.

Granovetter, Mark. 1973. "The Strength of Weak Ties." *American Journal of Sociology* 78:1360–1380.

Granovetter, Mark. 1974. *Getting a Job.* Cambridge, MA: Harvard University Press.

Granovetter, Mark. 1982. "The Strength of Weak Ties: A Network Theory Reconsidered." Pp. 105–130 in *Social Structure and Network Analysis,* edited by Peter Marsden and Nan Lin. Beverly Hills, CA: Sage.

Granovetter, Mark. 1985. "Economic Action and Social Structure: The Problem of Embeddedness." *American Journal of Sociology* 91:481–510.

Granovetter, Mark. 1992. "The Sociological and Economic Approaches to Labor Market Analysis: A Social Structural View." Pp. 233–263 in *The Sociology of Economic Life* edited by Marc Granovetter and Richard Swedberg. Boulder: Westview Press.

Kenedi, János. 1983. *Do-it-yourself.* London: Pluto Press.

Kennedy, Michael, and Naomi Galtz. 1996. "From Marxism to Postcommunism: Socialist Desires and East European Rejections." *Annual Review of Sociology* 22:437–458.

Kropotkin, Petr. 1902. *Mutual Aid.* Boston: Extending Horizons.

Liebow, Elliot. 1967. *Tally's Corner.* Boston: Little, Brown.

Light, Ivan, and Edna Bonacich. 1988. *Immigrant Entrepreneurs.* Berkeley: University of California Press.

Macaulay, Stewart. 1963 [1992]. "Non-Contractual Relations in Business: A Preliminary Study." Pp. 265–283 in *The Sociology of Economic Life,* edited by Mark Granovetter and Richard Swedberg. Boulder: Westview Press.

Mars, Gerald. 1982. *Cheats at Work.* London: Allen and Unwin.

Mars, Gerald, and Yochannan Altman. 1983. "The Cultural Bases of Soviet Georgia's Second Economy." *Soviet Studies* 35:546–560.

Mintz, Sidney. 1961. "Pratik: Haitian Personal Economic Relationship." Proceedings of the Annual Spring Meeting of the American Ethnological Society.

Montias, M., and R. Rose-Ackerman. 1981. "Corruption in a Soviet-Type Economy: Theoretical Considerations." Pp. 53–83 in *Economic Welfare and Economics of Soviet Socialism,* edited by R. Rosefielde. Cambridge: Cambridge University Press.

Nee, Victor. 1991. "Sleeping with the Enemy." *Working Papers on Transitions from State Socialism* No. 92.1. Ithaca, NY: Cornell University.

Nee, Victor, and Rebecca Matthews. 1996. "Market Transition and Societal Transformation in Reforming State Socialism." *Annual Review of Sociology* 22:401–435.

Plattner, Stuart. 1989. "Economic Behavior in Markets." Pp. 210–221 in *Economic Anthropology,* edited by Stuart Plattner. Stanford: Stanford University Press.

Pollak, Robert. 1985. "A Transaction Cost Approach to Families and Households." *Journal of Economic Literature* 23:581–608.

Polanyi, Karl. 1957. "The Economy as Instituted Process" Pp. 243–270 in *Trade and Market in the Early Empires,* edited by Karl Polanyi, Conrad Arensberg, and H. Pearson. Glencoe, IL: Free Press.

Rose, Richard, and Christopher Haerpfer. 1992. "New Democracies Between State and Market." University of Strathclyde: Studies in Public Policy, No. 204.

Sahlins, Marshall. 1972. *Stone Age Economics.* London: Tavistock.

Sik Endre, 1986–1987. "A Casual Labor Market." *Angewandte Sozialforschung* 14:63–71.

Sik, Endre. 1988a. "Reciprocal Exchange of Labor in Hungary." Pp. 527–547 in *On Work,* edited by Ray Pahl. London: Basil Blackwell.

Sik, Endre. 1988b. "New Trends in the Hungarian Welfare System: Towards 'Self-Welfarization?'" Pp. 281–296 in *Shifts in the Welfare Mix,* edited by Adalbert Evers and Helmut Wintersberger. Frankfurt: Campus Verlag.

Sik, Endre. 1992. "From the Second to the Informal Economy." *Journal of Public Policy* 12:153–175.

Sik, Endre. 1994. "The Vulture and the Calamity or, Why were Hungarian Cabdrivers Able to Rebel Against increased Gasoline Prices?." Pp. 275–291 in *Transition to Capitalism?,* edited by János Mátyás Kovács. New Brunswick, NJ: Transaction Publishers.

Sik, Endre. 1995. *Measuring the Unregistered Economy in Post-Communist Transformation.* Eurosocial Report. No. 52. Vienna: European Centre.

Sorokin, Pitirim. 1941. *Man and Society in Calamity.* New York: Greenwood Press.

Szelenyi, Ivan. 1988. *Socialist Entrepreneurs: Embourgeoisement in Rural Hungary.* Madison, WI: University of Wisconsin Press.

Wellman, Barry. 1979. "The Community Question." *American Journal of Sociology* 84:1201–1231.

Wellman, Barry, and Barry Leighton. 1979. "Networks, Neighborhoods and Communities." *Urban Affairs Quarterly* 14:363–390.

Wellman, Barry, and Scot Wortley. 1990. "Different Strokes from Different Folks: Community Ties and Social Support." *American Journal of Sociology* 96:558–588.

White, Harrison. 1992. *Identity and Control.* Princeton: Princeton University Press.

7

Getting a Job Through a Web of *Guanxi* in China

Yanjie Bian

As China moves from a state economy to a market economy, how do people obtain jobs? On the surface, it is a shift from a system where the state assigned people to job slots, to a situation in which people scramble on their own to attain positions. In reality, interpersonal and interorganizational relations have helped people find jobs in both the state and the market systems.[1] In this chapter I consider the use of connections in China to obtain jobs, and its implications for the analysis of occupational attainment, occupational mobility, and social stratification.

The process of occupational attainment is of great interest to sociologists studying social stratification and mobility. While status-attainment scholars attribute one's occupational attainment to one's ascribed and achieved statuses (Blau and Duncan 1967), and labor-market researchers relate to one's employer position in a segmented economy (Stolzenberg 1978), network analysts draw our attention to the role of interpersonal ties in job searches. Among others, Granovetter (1981) has argued that capitalist market economies are run on an imperfect system for diffusing information. Consequently, personal networks are used to collect information about jobs and thus become an important mechanism through which people are matched to occupations. In a study of managerial, professional, and technical workers in the Boston area, Granovetter (1974) showed that, although his respondents obtained information about jobs through formal means, such as direct application and employment advertisements, more than half of them learned about job openings from their relatives, friends, and, especially, casual acquaintances. Although there have been inconclusive findings on whether weak interpersonal ties (i.e., acquaintances) are more effective in obtaining job information than strong ties (i.e., relatives and friends), the use of personal networks for job-searches has been considerably studied in North America (Boorman 1975; Lin, Ensel, and Vaughn 1981; Calzavara 1983; Bridges and Villemez 1986; Marsden and Hurlbert 1988), Western Europe (DeGraaf and Flap 1988; Wegener 1991), and East Asia (Xiong, Sun, and Xu 1986; Watanabe 1987, 1994).

This chapter examines how personal networks affect job-searching in Communist China. My research interest is not in the imperfect diffusion of employment information, but this is not because the Chinese system is a perfect one. On the contrary, in a centralized economy like China's, information about jobs is rarely made available to job-seekers because it is internally circulated among government agencies, state employers who are allocated labor quotas, and school and residential authorities who screen job applicants (Bian 1994b). Indeed, control of information about jobs is a precondition for allocating jobs to carry out centrally imposed plans (Walder 1986; Davis 1990; Lin and Bian 1991; Bian 1994a). Under these circumstances, personal networks are not used for obtaining information about jobs, but for getting assistance from those who have the authority to control information and to allocate jobs.

I will show that within the system of control and allocation, job-seekers in a Chinese city use both strong and weak interpersonal ties to obtain help from job-control agents, but that strong ties are especially useful because of mutual trust and reciprocal obligation among relatives and friends. Acquaintance ties lack these characteristics, which are central to personal networks in the Chinese society. Specifically, I will describe how Chinese people have used *guanxi*, or intimate and reciprocal interpersonal connections, to obtain desirable jobs in two periods: before and after radical changes toward marketization at the beginning of the 1990s. I begin with a review of network theory and research on job-search processes.

Strength of Ties and Job-search Research

Interpersonal ties can be strong or weak. Granovetter (1973) suggests four dimensions to measure the strength of a tie: the amount of time spent in interaction, the emotional intensity, the intimacy, and the reciprocal services that characterize the tie. These dimensions are correlated with each other (Marsden and Campbell 1984) and intermixed with role relations and a kin-nonkin dichotomy (Bott 1957; Lin, Ensel, and Vaughn 1981; Wellman and Wortley 1990). Studies from North America (Wellman and Wortley 1989, 1990; Wellman 1992) have shown that strong ties are more useful than weak ties for emotional support. For example, family ties and close friends can help one with emotional problems caused by undesirable life events (Lin, Dean, and Ensel 1986). Yet Granovetter (1973, 1974, 1982) has argued that weak ties are superior to strong ties for some instrumental actions such as getting a job.

According to Granovetter, weak ties tend to link persons across social groups of close interpersonal relationships. Thus, the weak tie between any individual and his or her acquaintance becomes "not merely a trivial acquaintance tie, but rather a crucial bridge between the two densely knit clumps of close friends" (Granovetter 1982, p. 106). A person can access job information, or other resources that are not usually available, by using the bridges to other social circles that weak ties provide. For example, in a study of professional and managerial job-changers in a Boston suburb, Granovetter (1974) found that people learned more job information from those with whom they spent smaller amounts of time than from those with whom they spent more time. This information gave these people a greater opportunity to change jobs with higher status or income.

Granovetter's "strength of weak ties" theory has inspired students of labor markets. However, their research has shown that the impact of weak ties on job-search outcomes does not conform to a simple, linear formulation. Lin and his associates have shown in a study in upper New York state that the tie strength between job-seekers and their contacts is only indirectly related to status attainment, and is mediated by social resources (e.g., friends' power, status, or wealth) that are embedded in personal networks (Lin, Ensel, and Vaughn 1981; Lin, 1982; Lin and Dumin 1986).

There have been inconclusive findings on the relationship between tie strength and social resources. The likelihood that weak ties bridge social resources was not replicated in studies of Chicago (Bridges and Villemez 1986) and Detroit (Marsden and Hurlbert 1988). In a recent study of German workers, Wegener (1991) found that individuals with low-status jobs benefit from their close friends more than their acquaintances for job-mobility purposes. He argues that *real* social networks are heterogeneous, containing both strong ties and weak ties. In a heterogeneous network, persons of low status can choose among strong ties for accessing social resources within the network, but persons near the upper end of their network's status continuum must rely on weak ties to contact someone of a status outside the status range of their own network.

Watanabe (1987, 1994) shows that the strength of weak tie theory is not applicable to Japan. In a 1985 sample of 2,593 male workers in the Tokyo area, Watanabe found that network ties were useful in channeling workers into small firms but not into large ones. Large firms relied on examinations and other formal means to screen job applicants, which left little room for personal networks to play a role in recruitment. Such formal procedures were not required or were considerably less effective in small firms. Consequently job-seekers used their social ties to obtain jobs in small firms. Strong ties enabled workers to learn about jobs in these small firms and to receive high pay and an immediate identification with the company, resulting in a high rate of job satisfaction. The mutual trust created on the basis of kinship, regional networks, and long-term tenure at work seemed to be the reason that job information was transmitted through a chain of strong ties rather than through weak ties.

If the studies from the United States and Germany indicate that class structure is a condition under which job information and social resources tend to be mobilized by social ties of differing strengths, then the Japanese study points to the need to analyze institutional contexts in which these ties are used in job-searches. In a recent study of China (Bian 1997), I have argued that such an institutional analysis is a key to understanding why strong ties are especially useful in job-searching processes in China, a state socialist country to which I now turn.

Job Control in China's Cities

From shortly after the 1949 Communist revolution through the late 1980s, the Chinese government implemented a rigid job assignment program (Bian 1994a) based on Maoist ideology that the "socialist" labor force is not a commodity but a national resource that requires centralized planning (He et al. 1990; Tang 1990). This program aimed to control the size, growth, and distribution of urban jobs. Food rationing, household registration, and centrally imposed labor quotas were the administrative means used to implement the program (Whyte and Parish 1984; Walder 1986). Searching for jobs in the state and collective sectors was officially prohibited—not a trivial matter, as more than 95% of urban jobs were located in these sectors (State Statistical Bureau of China 1989, p. 101). Educated youths could not pursue jobs, but waited for state assignments after graduation from school. Once assigned, they faced administrative restrictions on switching between places of employment (Davis 1990). Under these circumstances, the first job became the most important component of the development of an individual's career (Lin and Bian 1991; Bian 1994a).

Job assignments were implemented in all cities. In each city, jobs and job information were controlled by three authorized agents: government labor officials, heads of hiring organizations (employers), and school and residential leaders. Government labor officials planned and allocated labor quotas for employers; they had information on all the jobs to be assigned in the year and the greatest authority in determining assignments of who would work where. Although employers were allowed to submit proposals to a designated local government office about the number and kinds of new workers they wished to hire, the final decision rested with the government. When assignments were being made, employers sent hiring announcements to designated schools or residential districts. Since youths waited for jobs either at their schools (right after graduation) or at their residences (during the years when school graduates could not possibly all be assigned jobs), school and residential leaders, as well as employers, screened the applicants and made recommendations to the government labor office.

Formally, youths waiting for assignment were kept away from information about jobs until they received notification of their assignments from the local government labor office. Informally, they all tried to learn about jobs and mobilized their networks and those of their parents to secure good assignments. They would not have done this if the process were strictly subject to government regulations or if they were confident about its fairness. Indeed, some did not have any useful ties of their own and could not possibly locate any through their networks. However, personal networks helped many to learn about jobs and to influence control agents during various stages of the job-assignment process.

Interpersonal Ties in the Process of Job Assignments

Even in centralized China, with its powerful control agents and powerless job-seekers, the web of social relationships is important. People's family ties, kinship networks, work colleagues, neighbors, and friendship circles, to name a few, are *communities* into which they grow and on which they depend (see Bian [1994b] for China, and Wellman [1979, 1988; also Introduction] for a more general discussion). These networks are much closer to individuals than the formal structure of the Communist party-state. Social relationships around an individual provide an immediate expressive and instrumental support that the formal structure of the party-state does not. People rationally cultivate and utilize their social connections to satisfy their personal interests. In a culture that emphasizes the exchange of favors among intimate ties (Fried 1953; Hwang 1987; Yang 1989, 1994), these same people are obligated to assist others who are closely connected to them.

Tactics used by control agents to manipulate the job-assignment process varied according to their level of specific power. School and residential leaders could recommend their favored persons to "good" organizations, even though the recommended persons may not have the formally announced qualifications. Heads of the hiring organizations would do a "favor" for these school and residential leaders by accepting the recommendations, because they, in turn, would suggest other names whom they favored to be included on the recommendation list. Finally, government labor officials could request that school or residential leaders recommend someone whom the officials favor and have an organization hire that person. Compliance from school and residential leaders and heads of hiring organizations was expected, not merely because they were subordinates to government officials, but because they would then be permitted to recommend or recruit some of their favored candidates (Bian 1997).

The effectiveness of the party-state's formal structure ensured that control agents and job-seekers worked with each other on the basis of mutual, established trust. It was against party rules for job-seekers to use personal networks to influence control agents and for the agents to do favors for their social ties. In the eyes of the party officials, as well as those of the general public, such actions should and would be punished. The risk of exposure for either player was not terribly high, given that a large number of officials and job-seekers were suspected of this type of action (Bian 1994b), yet the action was nonetheless unauthorized, and the risk had to be minimized by mutual trust.

Mutual trust is a characteristic of some strong ties but not of weak ties. Weak ties do not have this characteristic because persons in a weak relationship know little about one another or feel little intimacy with one another (Granovetter 1974; Lin, Ensel, and Vaughn 1981; Marsden and Campbell 1984; Wegener 1991). Strong ties, however, differ. Mutual trust and reciprocal assistance are what strong ties, such as family ties and close friends, represent (Wellman and Wortley 1989, 1990). A family tie or friendship between two individuals deteriorates or vanishes when commitment to either component is no longer shared by the parties involved (Fisher 1982).

China's job-control policies in the mid-1950s through the late 1980s created an institutional context in which mutual trust was required when job-seekers wanted to obtain assistance from control agents. Because strong ties have the merit of mutual trust, strong ties are expected to be heavily used in job-search processes in China. The fact that many job-seekers are not in contact with control agents but still can indirectly obtain help from them raises the question about the web of what Chinese people refer to as *guanxi,* or intimate and reciprocal interpersonal connections.

Guanxi, Favors, and Patronage

Although the Chinese term *guanxi* literally means "relationship" or "connection," it actually refers to the interpersonal connection in a dyad in which the involved parties have high intimacy to each other and a mutual understanding of reciprocal services between them (Bian 1997). So *guanxi* implies a strong dyadic link and the obligation to exchange favors between the parties involved. The extent to which people can benefit from their *guanxi* depends on the specific institutional context in which the networks are structured. For example, job-seekers' successes in influencing control agents to secure good assignments depend on their position in a web of *guanxi* woven around these agents.

In the context of job assignments, control agents had a high degree of local centrality in their communities. There they were surrounded by their strong ties and by weak ties whose other strong and weak ties were located farther away. Government labor officials not only had local centrality but also system centrality, since they also were surrounded by the control agents of the two other groups. When a job-seeker was a strong tie with a control agent, the opportunity to learn about jobs and obtain help from the latter was great. The stronger the tie, the greater the mutual trust. On the other hand, being in the same intimate circle, the control agent would be obligated to do a favor for the job-seeker, who has the same obligation to pay back the control agent and would have plenty of opportunities to do so.

When a job-seeker had a weak tie with a control agent, the opportunity for assistance from the latter was not as great because mutual trust and reciprocal obligations were not present. But the opportunity for assistance greatly increased when a strong-tie intermediary linked the job-seeker to the control agent; the intermediary acted as a bridge and offered mutual trust to both job-seekers and control agents. In this situation, the control agent trusts and has the obligation to assist the intermediary, who will pass the benefit on to the job-seeker.

When job-seekers used intermediaries to contact control agents, the exchange of favors became complicated. When one intermediary was used, there were three exchanges: (1) between job-seeker and intermediary, (2) between intermediary and helper, and (3) between job-seeker and helper. Exchanges of favors for (1) and (2) were not completed immediately, since these were exchanges between strong ties. However, friendship was immediately reinforced, creating an even stronger basis for further exchange of favors.

Exchanges of favors for (3) differed. Immediate transactions were expected by both parties: helpers offered a job to job-seekers, and in return, job-seekers gave a gift of substantial value to the helpers. Job-seekers often consulted their intermediaries about selecting an appropriate gift at a proper price. These intermediaries gave advice on this gift because they did not want to lose face (Hwang 1987; Bian 1993).

There were situations in which more than one intermediary was involved. However, the more intermediaries there were, the higher the costs for job-seekers. Thus, a cost limitation would have to be set by the job-seekers relative to their expectations about jobs to be received. Moreover, three groups of job-control agents (government labor officials, heads of hiring organizations, and school and residential leaders) were also likely to be introduced into these indirect relations. These agents formed a patronage network themselves, with government officials being the patrons and heads of hiring organizations and school/residential leaders being clients.[2]

The web of *guanxi* in the job-assignment context was a patronage network (Eisenstadt and Roniger 1980; Flap 1990). When job-seekers had direct contact with control agents, they formed a simple structure in which patrons (control agents) were linked directly to disconnected clients (job-seekers). The resulting structure is an "open triangle," in which patrons exchange resources with their clients, who do not exchange with each other (Singelmann 1975). In the case of job assignments in China, control agents as patrons controlled valued resources (jobs) that job-seekers as their clients wanted. In this "lopsided" relationship (Pitt-Rivers 1954), job-seekers depended on control agents. Control agents were willing to help because their clients were both loyal and beneficial to them, and because of the mutual trust established between the patrons and the clients. But control agents depended equally on their clients for continued loyalty and rewards. Although these returns might not be relevant to the position of control agents at work, they were important for these agents' maintenance of position and power in their intimate circles (family, kinship, friendship, neighborhood, etc.). After all, their clients were likely to be members of one of these circles.

When job-seekers (clients) were indirectly connected to control agents (patrons) via a common third party (intermediary), a pyramidal structure (Scott 1972) formed in which the intermediaries joined the ultimate patrons and the ultimate clients. The intermediaries were patrons to job-seekers but clients to control agents. These go-betweens operated with the resources of other persons. They helped transfer jobs from control agents' hands to job-seekers' hands. At the same time, they sent gifts backward from the job-seekers to the control agents. Their own resource in this situation was the mutual trust that they had with both their patrons (control agents) and their clients (job-seekers). Because the go-betweens did not merely give but also took, they strengthened their friendships with both patrons and clients. Since both control agents and job-seekers benefited from the go-betweens, both owed a good deal to them.

Guanxi and Getting a Job in China:
The 1988 Tianjin Survey

The data for this study come from a 1988 survey of adult residents in Tianjin, the People's Republic of China. Tianjin is in the north of China, eighty miles east of Beijing, with its downtown area twenty-five miles inland from the east coast of the Pacific Ocean. It is the land and sea gateway to China's capital, Beijing, as all the people in eastern China (about 70% of the country's population) must go through Tianjin to reach Beijing. Tianjin is also the birthplace of the modern manufacturing industries of North China, a harbor city that transports one-tenth of China's imports and exports, and a center of higher learning and scientific and technological research.

I will now show how Chinese persons used *guanxi* to get their first jobs in a period from the 1950s to the 1980s. The 1988 survey was based on a multistage random sampling procedure and offers a data-set of 945 persons who had worked in the civilian labor force at the time of the survey.[3]

The socialist transformation of the mid-1950s created a state-controlled economy in both rural and urban areas, which fostered a low standard of living through the 1970s. Although political campaigns have been a constant reality, the Cultural Revolution of 1966 to 1976 moved postrevolutionary China into a period of political and economic crisis. Since the death of Mao Zedong in 1976, leaders starting with Deng Xiao-ping have led a government campaign known as "market reforms" aimed at decentralizing the economy by introducing market mechanisms (Lin 1989; Nee 1989).

These transformations have had strong impacts on job-searches and the use of *guanxi*. Some of our Tianjin respondents entered the labor force before the socialist transformation in the mid-1950s (N = 140). Among them, 53% found their first urban jobs through their personal networks. As economic and political control tightened between 1953 and 1965, this number declined to 37% (N = 262) and slid further to 30% during the Cultural Revolution (N = 268). In light of the market reforms begun in the late 1970s, the number of respondents who found their first urban jobs through personal networks grew to 57% (N = 278).

Characteristics of Social Ties in First-job Searches

Table 7.1 displays the information about social ties used by some respondents during their search for first jobs. Respondents were asked if there was "someone" (commonly understood to be *guanxi* in China) who provided help during their search for their first jobs. This someone is termed here as a "helper." If there was a helper (45.1%), the respondents were further asked if there was "someone else" who made the connection between the respondent and the helper. This someone else is termed here an "intermediary." Thus, three dyadic relations are identified:

1. R-H refers to the tie between respondent and helper;
2. R-I refers to the tie between respondent and intermediary;
3. I-H refers to the tie between intermediary and helper.

TABLE 7.1 Social Ties Used in Getting a First Job

Strength of Tie	All R-H Ties	Direct R-H Ties	Indirect R-H Ties	R-I Ties	I-H Ties
N using social ties*	428	234	194	194	194
Role relations (%)					
Relatives	43.2	58.5	24.7	25.8	57.2
Friends	17.8	16.7	19.1	54.6	41.2
Acquaintances	39.0	24.8	56.2	19.6	1.6
Intimacy (%)					
Very well (high intimacy)	44.2	69.7	13.4	73.2	73.7
Well (medium)	27.6	23.1	33.0	24.2	24.2
Not well (low)	28.3	7.3	53.6	2.6	2.1
Mean for intimacy (x 10)**	21.6	26.2	16.0	27.1	27.2
Characteristics of ultimate helper					
% in supervisory positions	67.1	53.8	83.0		
% in the state sector	72.9	64.5	83.0		
Mean score of work-unit rank (x 10)	32.7	29.2	36.9		
Mean score of occupational status	85.6	82.4	89.3		

*Social-tie users are 45.1 percent of the total respondents (948).

**Value assignments are 3 = very well, 2 = well, 1 = not well. This intimacy measure is used in regression analysis presented in Tables 7.2 and 7.3.

Notations: R = respondent; H = (ultimate) helper; I = intermediary.

The strength of these dyadic ties is measured by role types (relatives, friends, and acquaintances) and intimacy (knowing each other "very well," "well," or "not well"). Direct R-H ties tend to be strong rather than weak: 43% are relatives, 18% are friends, and 39% are acquaintances. Among them, 44% know each other "very well" (high intimacy), 28% know each other "well," and 28% know each other "not well" (low intimacy). More than 45% of the social-tie users confirm that their helpers are found through at least one intermediary. By comparison, weak ties are much more heavily used in job-searches in Western countries (Granovetter 1974; Lin, Ensel, and Vaughn 1981; Bridges and Villemez 1986; DeGraaf and Flap 1988; Marsden and Hurlbert 1988; Wegener 1991). Also, Granovetter (1974) reported that 67% of the respondents in his Boston study used intermediaries to learn about their jobs.

Overall, direct-tie users tend to have strong ties with their helpers (data in the second column of Table 7.1). This contrasts sharply with indirect-tie users, whose relationships with their helpers on the average are weak. In this group, more than half the ties are acquaintances who tend to be in a low-intimacy relationship. But both respondents and their helpers tend to have high levels of intimacy with intermediaries. Unlike the West, the direct ties between these Chinese job-seekers and intermediaries, and between intermediaries and helpers, are predominately strong.[4]

Access to Social Resources Through Social Ties

How has the nature of the three dyadic ties affected one's access to a helper independent of one's own characteristics and the characteristics of one's father? Four dependent variables measure Lin's (1982) concept of social resources, in this case the status characteristics of helpers: supervisory position, work sector, workplace rank, and occupational prestige.[5] The primary variable is whether a helper holds a supervisory position. Such a position allows an individual to engage, directly or indirectly, in the decisionmaking process of job assignments. Therefore such an individual is in a position to help a job-seeker. Indeed, 54% of direct-tie users use helpers with supervisory positions (Table 7.1). The percentage increases to 83% for indirect-tie users. Clearly, it pays to go through an indirect route to search for an able helper. The helper's work sector (state versus nonstate) and the employer's workplace rank[6] are used to measure the structural positions that helpers hold in the state economy. Finally, the helpers' status is also measured by their occupational prestige.

Table 7.2 presents regressions predicting a person's access to social resources. Model I assumes that job-seekers are in direct contact with their ultimate helpers. It shows that the less the intimacy between the job-seek-

TABLE 7.2   Logistic and OLS Regressions Predicting Access to Social Resources

| | Variables: Ultimate Helper's Status | | | | | | | |
| | Supervisory Position | | Work in the State Sector | | Rank of the Work Unit | | Occupational Status scale | |
Independent Variables	(I)	(II)	(I)	(II)	(I)	(II)	(I)	(II)
Strength of tie measures								
Intimacy for R-H	-1.17**	-.52**	-1.06**	-.62**	-.56**	-.41**	-5.54**	3.40**
Intimacy for R-I	—	1.03**	—	.73**	—	.24*	—	4.34*
Intimacy for I-H	—	1.00**	—	.64**	—	.16	—	6.92*
Characteristics of respondents								
Education	.03	.02	.07**	.05	.16**	.01	3.88**	2.06
Party membership	.07	.20	.09	.04	.18	.05	3.41	3.85
Sex (male = 1)	.31*	.89*	.15	.08	.10	-.003	-.20	.93
Age (x 10)	.06	.01	.02	.05	.18**	.23**	.14*	-.53
Father's status								
Work in the state sector	.03	.03	.09	.09	.11	-.46	1.34	.81
Rank of work unit	.08	.16	.04	.05	.18**	.28**	.83	2.25
Occupational status (x 10)	.18**	.06	.02	.01	.02	.01	.19**	.07
Intercept	11.18**	5.12**	10.25**	4.79**	5.97**	2.11**	8.65**	61.95**
Chi-square	674.42	256.27	680.34	263.83				
R²					.25	.30	.23	.20
N of cases	428	194	428	194	428	194	428	194

NOTES:

Logistic regression coefficients are obtained for the dichotomous dependent variables (supervisory position and work in the state sector) and metric OLS regression coefficients are obtained for the continuous dependent variables (rank of work unit and occupational status scale).

Significant levels are denoted: * p < .05, ** p < .01.

Notations: R = respondent; H = (ultimate) helper; I = intermediary.

ers and their ultimate helpers, the more likely it is that they have access to helpers with supervisory positions who work for high-ranking employers in the state sector or whose occupational prestige is high. Model II goes further to assume that, although people may have weak links with ultimate helpers, their direct connections with intermediaries—and the connections between these intermediaries and the ultimate helpers—tend to be strong. When these direct connections are strong, they tend to provide access to useful helpers who are cadres, who work for high-ranking employers in the state sector, or whose jobs are prestigious. Thus, weak as well as strong ties promote access to social resources. A direct weak tie brings useful social resources to oneself, but when an ultimate helper is indirectly available, strong ties tend to be the bridges.

Social Resources and First-job Status

The state sector has been in high demand among job-seekers (Lin and Bian 1991; Bian 1994b) because the measure of the administrative rank of the workplace to which a person was assigned is also an important dimension of job assignments. Entering a high-rank organization has meant a greater opportunity to gain access to organization-related resources such as housing and collective welfare programs (Walder 1992), home location and community resources (Logan and Bian 1993), membership in the Communist party, and promotions to bureaucratic positions (Bian 1994a). Administrative rank is a scale indicating the hierarchical level of a work unit.[7] Finally, occupational status is measured by a standard socioeconomic index (Lin and Xie 1988).[8]

As Table 7.3 shows, attained status can be predicted from the job-seeker's and the father's characteristics,[9] as well as by the characteristics of one's helper in the job-assignment process. The helper's supervisory position and work-unit rank showed more consistent and stronger effects on attained status than the helper's sector and occupation. This is understandable, because individuals holding a supervisory position or working in a high-ranking organization retained political and organizational power that could be used to serve their interests and those of their *guanxi*. No significant effects of the strength of ties are expected on attained status (Lin 1982). Unlike Wegener (1991), I do not find interactive effects of the strength of tie to the ultimate helper and the job-seeker's position (education, party membership, and the father's work-unit rank) on attained status. Although social resources tended to be available from helpers with whom job-seekers probably have weak ties, they also tend to be indirectly linked to the ultimate helpers: common intimate friends or relatives bridge the gap between job-seeker and ultimate helper.

TABLE 7.3   Logistic and OLS Regressions Predicting First-job Status

	Dependent Variables: First-job Status					
Predictors	Work in the State Sector		Rank of the Work Unit		Occupational Status Scale	
Social resources (helper's)						
Supervisory position	.32**	.31**	.23*	.63**	1.66*	2.83*
Work in the state sector	.47**	.45**	.21	.28	2.84*	3.61*
Work-unit rank	.12*	.14*	.17**	.17*	1.03*	1.31*
Occupational status	.02	.03	.04	.02	.15**	.10*
Characteristics of respondents						
Education	.26**	.27**	.19**	.21**	5.87**	5.87**
Party membership	.45**	.23	.15*	.13	.53	2.10
Sex (male = 1)	.03	.05	.08	.16	−2.92*	−3.67*
Age (x 10)	.05	.03	.11**	.06	3.29**	3.59**
Father's status						
Work in the state sector	.11*	.15*	.07	.12	.48	.83
Rank of work unit	.02	.01	.37**	.44**	1.17	1.44
Occupational status (x 10)	.02	.01	.05	.01	−.05	−.01
Strength of tie measures						
Intimacy for R-H	−.08	−.05	.05	.04	1.43	.43
Intimacy for R-I	–	.02	–	.02	–	−3.18
Intimacy for H-I	–	−.09	–	.04	–	−1.40
Intercept	4.09**	4.21**	−1.38	.01	4.95**	43.99**
Chi-square	406.73	181.62				
R²			.25	.26	.35	.35
N of cases	428	194	428	194	428	194

NOTES:

Logistic regression coefficients are obtained for the dichotomous dependent variable (work in the state sector) and metric OLS regression coefficients are obtained for the continuous dependent variables (rank of the work unit and occupational status scale).

Significant levels are denoted: * $p < .05$, ** $p < .01$.

Notations: R = respondent; H = (ultimate) helper; I = intermediary.

Guanxi in the Emerging Labor Markets

The 1988 data provide a picture of guanxi and the job-searching process in China before radical changes in the early 1990s toward marketization. Despite a military crackdown on pro-democratic movements in 1989, China's economic reforms have not slowed. With the central government giving up its control on the prices of industrial and consumer goods and their allocation, the economy has become decentralized. For example, prices on all but eleven categories of industrial products have been deregulated since 1993 (Hong, Liu, and Chen 1994). The state sector, which absorbed more than 70% of the urban labor force in 1990 (State Statistical Bureau of China 1991, p. 97), has been greatly affected. When I visited Tianjin officials in March and April of 1993, they estimated that only one-third of the city's state enterprises were profitable, another third struggled to survive, and still another third had gone bankrupt. A large number of state workers have become jobless. To survive, they (and others who quit their state jobs) work in the booming "market" sector consisting of international and domestic joint ventures, foreign firms, private companies, family businesses, and subcontracted workers. To secure the housing and medical benefits provided by state employers, some state workers have formally maintained their employment status in the state sector, but to make more money they actually work in the market sector (Barnatnan et al. 1994; Jia 1994).

These changes are accompanied by the abolition of job-assignment programs. In 1993, waiting for job assignments became optional. All those in need of jobs now try to find a job by themselves, to avoid the manual work and low wages that comes with a state assignment. Thus, a state assignment is the last option to be considered by urban residents. Most manual and low-paying jobs in the state and market sectors are being taken by surplus rural laborers who have flooded to the cities.

The desirable jobs are those in both the state and market sectors that pay well or provide large nonsalary incomes. Many market jobs have high wages, especially those in international joint ventures and foreign firms. Some state jobs pay only a moderate salary but offer numerous large bonuses due to the profits generated by these state firms, such as those in railway and chemical-engineering industries in Tianjin. Some government jobs, which are prone to abuse of power and corruption, allow occupants to obtain "hidden" incomes. Both state enterprises and government offices provide subsidized housing and an array of collective benefits that are not offered by international joint ventures and foreign firms. Indeed, since 1993, some internationally connected firms in the market sector have started to offer subsidized housing to some of their employees to avoid the loss of valuable human resources (Francis 1996).

Direct application and personal networks have become the predominant ways for job-seekers to learn about desirable jobs. Because both the diffusion of job information by employers and the search for jobs by individuals have become normative, mutual trust is no longer an issue as far as job information is concerned. Consequently, both strong ties and weak ties are useful in acquiring job information, although the weak ties usually provided a wider range of information for the fifteen graduate students I interviewed.

These fifteen students were graduating with master's degrees in sociology from Peking University in Beijing and Nankai University in Tianjin. All of them used their personal networks to learn about jobs but they also used newspapers and casual acquaintances. They sent their applications directly to employers they had learned about from newspapers, relatives, friends, and acquaintances. Although all of them started their job-searches by using someone from their somewhat intimate circles, most of them learned *useful* information from someone who was not a member of these circles. Nine of them, at the time of the interviews, were in the middle of getting a job; all nine of them wanted to work in South China where high-paying jobs were believed to be found. Four people had each received at least two offers, but were still trying to find a better one elsewhere.

Although mutual trust seems irrelevant to acquiring information about available jobs, it is important for securing offers of jobs. This is especially true for managerial and technical jobs whose occupants' long-term tenure and loyalty to employers are expected. Four of the fifteen graduate students had received job offers and were becoming managers; all of them had been recommended by a third party who was trusted by their prospective employers. In two of these four cases, the third party was a relative.

Guanxi and exchanges of favors are usually behind job offers. Desirable jobs tend to be located in profitable firms, so people try to get jobs in these firms. Competition and the desire to keep labor costs low make it difficult to obtain jobs in profitable firms. But these firms, like all other firms, are connected to and dependent upon other parts of the society: business licenses are issued by the government, water and electricity are supplied by state utilities bureaus, raw materials and tools are purchased from suppliers, products are distributed by dealers, and financial and taxation matters are subject to inspections by government officials. Long-term business connections represent personalized *guanxi* between the heads of profitable firms and the government officials and business partners. Thus, routine activities arranged to promote transactions may be used as if they are the favors offered by one party to exchange those from the other party. Job offers by profitable firms are common favors. Mr. Cao, the director of a profitable state-owned motorcycle repair company in Tianjin, told me the following story:

> Most workers [in my company of about 100 employees] came to work [at the company] because they have *guanxi* [with me, other managers of the company, or the heads of businesses or government offices with which the

company has "business" connections]. I wanted to partition our company into five shops in order to attract foreign investments and reduce sales taxes [by meeting the requirements of a state policy to promote new, international joint ventures]. When I requested licenses for these shops from the Bureau of Industries and Commerce [of the district in which the company is located in early 1993], the bureau chief wanted me to hire two persons he had promised to help find jobs in profitable firms. I had to satisfy his request, otherwise who knows when the licenses would be issued. Afterwards, the Utilities Bureau [of the district] wanted me to do the same for them when we requested the bureau replace the electric wire system in these shops. Then, oil suppliers, the water station, the health bureau, the district hospital [whose services are used by the workers of the company], schools [in the district], etc., etc., all came to ask about jobs. You could not possibly decline these requests because they are all my old *guanxi* with whom I do business on a daily basis. They say to me, "Oh, old Cao, please help me, just once, your company has made a lot of money, you can hire a couple of people, it won't hurt you, and this is the first and the last time I ask you to help, please!" In fact, I sometimes ask them to help me out, for the matters concerning my company as well as my family, myself, and *guanxi* of mine. So, I feel obligated to help them, also.

Conclusions

In this chapter I have explored why the job-search process in China differs from that of Western countries in North America and Europe. In the West, weak ties more strongly facilitate the diffusion of job information than do strong ties (Granovetter 1974; Boorman 1975), although they may not lead to better jobs (Calzavara 1983). In China before radical changes toward marketization in the early 1990s, both jobs and job information were controlled to satisfy the needs of central planning and state job assignments. Thus, individuals who wished to learn about jobs and to obtain help from job-control agents to secure good jobs were best facilitated by their strong ties with the control agents. Strong ties have the merit of mutual trust, which is a necessary component of interpersonal connections in the job-search process in China.

A 1988 Tianjin survey supports this argument. Forty-five percent of those who had worked in the civilian labor force at the time of the survey found their first jobs through their personal networks. This was the most important step in their career development, since switching between employers was highly restricted. These respondents used strong ties (in terms of both role types and intimacy) more heavily than weak ties. When job-seekers were not in contact with control agents or had weak relationships with the latter, they tended to locate a common third party who had a strong tie with both the job-seekers and the ultimate helpers.

The reason was simple: mutual trust provided by strong-tie intermediaries reduce the risk of exposure of "misconduct," as defined by the government, and it warranted the exchange of favors between job-seekers and helpers. The intermediary was a bridge between job-seekers and control agents.

This situation occurred in a special institutional context, and it is by no means a universal phenomenon. But to say that the bridging of strong ties is uniquely Chinese is equally untrue. Strong ties tend to act as bridges when an exchange of resources or favors between social actors (individuals or organizations) is unauthorized or when mechanisms for their operation are unavailable in the formal social structure. Thus, mutual trust is required to link these actors in order to reduce the uncertainties and potential risks that are likely to occur otherwise. Bridges are also useful when these actors are not in contact; their common strong ties that offer mutual trust will bridge the gap (see also Bian 1997). In the United States, Whyte's (1955) *Street Corner Society*, Banfield's (1961) study of a wheeler-dealer type of transaction central to the operation of political machines, and Coleman's (1988) analysis of New York City Jewish jewelers' businesses show how mutual trust and patron-client networks work in various situations (see also Malinowski 1922; Ziegler 1990; Hamilton 1991).

Rapid changes in China in the early 1990s have significantly altered the institutional contexts of government job control. Job assignments have been abolished, and the diffusion of job information by employers and the search for jobs by individuals has become legal and normative. Consequently, mutual trust has become irrelevant as far as the diffusion of job information is concerned. But, as both employers and job-seekers are living in the web of *guanxi*, exchanges of favors are still normative conduct. According to my limited observations, strong-tie intermediaries are often used to strengthen mutual trust and to "generate" a job offer. Thus, understanding the importance of mutual trust and the bridging nature of strong ties continues to be necessary for understanding Chinese job-search behavior under the current situation of radical change.

Notes

Funding for this study comes from a NSF grant (SES-9209214), a grant-in-aid and a 1993 summer research fellowship from the University of Minnesota Graduate School, and a travel grant from the China Center of the University of Minnesota. I thank Mark Granovetter and Harrison White for stimulating conversations that led to the preparation of the manuscript, Barry Wellman for his helpful editing, and the University of Minnesota and the Hong Kong University of Science and Technology for being supportive homes.

1. See also Chapters 4, 6, and 9 in this volume.

2. Tarkowski (1981) observed that the Polish economy was operated through the patronage networks of central government officials, local officials, and factory managers. Although these agents were formally linked through work ties in the bureaucratic structure of the state, patron-client relationships developed through these work ties and were the actual mechanisms through which resources and incentives were distributed from the central government to the state-owned institutions. Walder (1986) analyzed similar patron-client networks between factor managers, shop-floor supervisors, and political activists that were seen as a basis of authority structures in the Chinese workplace. (See also Chapter 6.)

3. Details of the sampling procedure can be found in Bian (1994a, Appendix A).

4. Because information about the strength of tie between the intermediary and the helper was solicited from the respondents, errors might exist due to inaccurate recollections, particularly if the respondents did not know exactly what relationships were between them. But the respondents I interviewed all believed that they "knew" exactly what kinds of relationships were between their ultimate helpers and intermediaries and how strongly their relationships were because the intermediaries "told" them so. In fact, a job-seeker usually asked the intermediary for this information to make sure that the ultimate helper would be willing to help because of his or her strong tie to the intermediary. Similarly, the intermediary would also want to tell the respondent this information to guarantee that the ultimate helper would definitely help.

5. Although status characteristics of intermediaries are also important, for simplicity the respondents were only asked to specify the status characteristics of their ultimate helpers.

6. An official rank assigned to employers to denote whether they are managed by central ministries, municipal bureaus, or lower-level government offices.

7. The value assignments are (1) section or lower, (2) department, (3) division, (4) bureau, and (5) higher.

8. The Lin-Xie (1988) socioeconomic index is a Chinese version of an American index (Duncan 1961). In this study, it is based on 16 occupational categories of the respondents. The 19 occupational categories and the corresponding Lin-Xie SEI scores are presented here in a low-to-high order: unclassified occupations (60.31), unskilled worker in industry (65.00), unskilled worker in commerce or service sector (69.06), skilled worker in industry (70.29), skilled worker in commerce or service sectors (70.94), staff, clerical worker below section level (87.12), primary school teacher (89.16), middle-ranking cadre (90.59), low-ranking technical professional (92.21), high-ranking cadre (100.43), private-sector workers (101.79), middle-ranking technical professional (104.36), middle and high school teacher (108.59), college or university assistant instructor or instructor (114.45), high-ranking technical professional (117.09), and college or university associate professor or professor (126.78). Data for education and income required by the calculation of the index also come from the respondents.

9. These results have been confirmed by status-attainment studies in China (Parish 1984; Blau and Ruan 1990; Lin and Bian 1991; Bian 1994a).

References

Banfield, Edward C. 1961. *Political Influence*. New York: Free Press of Glencoe.

Barnatnan, Joyce, Peter Engardio, Lynne Curry, and Bruce Einhorn. 1994. "China: The Emerging Economic Powerhouse of the 21st Century." *Business Week* (May 17, Special Report):54–65.

Bian, Yanjie. 1993. "Vertical Interpersonal Connections and Resource Allocation: Cadre Networks in the Chinese Economy." Presented at the annual meeting of the American Sociological Association, Miami Beach, August.

Bian, Yanjie. 1994a. *Work and Inequality in Urban China*. Albany, NY: State University of New York Press.

Bian, Yanjie. 1994b. "*Guanxi* and the Allocation of Jobs in Urban China." *The China Quarterly* 140 (December):971–999.

Bian, Yanjie. 1997. "Bringing Strong Ties Back In: Indirect Ties, Network Bridges, and Job Searches in China." *American Sociological Review* 62 (3):366–385.

Blau, Peter M., and Otis Dudley Duncan. 1967. *The American Occupational Structure*. New York: John Wiley.

Blau, Peter M., and Danching Ruan. 1990. "Inequality of Opportunity in Urban China and America." In *Research in Stratification and Mobility* 9:3–32.

Boorman, Scott A. 1975. "A Combinatorial Optimization Model for Transmission of Job Information though Contact Networks." *Bell Journal of Economics* 6:216–249.

Bott, Elizabeth. 1957. *Family and Social Network: Roles, Norms, and External Relationships in Ordinary Urban Families*. London: Tavistock.

Bridges, William P., and Wayne J. Villemez. 1986. "Informal Hiring and Income in the Labor Market." *American Sociological Review* 51:574–582.

Calzavara, Liviana. 1983. "Social Networks and Access to Jobs: A Study of Five Ethnic Groups in Toronto." Toronto: Centre for Urban and Community Studies, University of Toronto. Research Paper No. 145.

Coleman, James S. 1988. "Social Capital in the Creation of Human Capital." *American Journal of Sociology* 94 (Supplement):S95-S120.

Davis, Deborah. 1990. "Urban Job Mobility." Pp. 85–108 in *Chinese Society on the Eve of Tiananmen*, edited by Deborah Davis and Ezra F. Vogel. Cambridge, MA: Harvard University Press.

DeGraaf, Nan Dirk, and Hendrik Derk Flap. 1988. "With a Little Help from My Friends: Social Resources as an Explanation of Occupational Status and Income in West Germany, the Netherlands, and the United States." *Social Forces* 67:452–472.

Duncan, Otis Dudley. 1961. "A Socioeconomic Index for All Occupations." Pp. 109–38 in *Occupations and Social Status* edited by Albert J. Reiss, Jr. New York: Free Press of Glencoe.

Eisenstadt, S. N., and Louis Roniger. 1980. "Patron-Client Relations as a Model of Structuring Social Exchange." *Comparative Studies in History and Society* 22:42–77.

Fischer, Claude S. 1982. *To Dwell Among Friends*. Chicago: University of Chicago Press.

Flap, Henrik Derk. 1990. "Patronage: An Institution in Its Own Right." Pp. 225–243 in *Social Institutions: Their Emergence, Maintenance, and Effects*, edited by Michael Hechter, Karl-Dieter Opp, and Reinhard Wippler. New York: Aldine de Gruyter.

Francis, Corinna-Barbara. 1996. "Reproduction of *Danwei* Institutional Features in the Case of China's Market Economy." *China Quarterly* 147 (September): 839–859.

Fried, Morton H. 1953 [1969]. *Fabric of Chinese Society: A Study of the Social Life in a Chinese County Seat*. New York: Octagon Books.

Granovetter, Mark. 1973. "The Strength of Weak Ties." *American Journal of Sociology* 78:1360–1380.

Granovetter, Mark. 1974 *Getting a Job: A Study of Contacts and Careers*. Cambridge, MA: Harvard University Press.

Granovetter, Mark. 1981. "'Matching' Persons and Jobs: Theoretical Perspectives." Pp. 11–48 in *Sociological Perspectives on Labor Markets*, edited by Ivar Berg. New York: Academic Press.

Granovetter, Mark. 1982. "The Strength of Weak Ties: A Network Theory Revisited." Pp. 105–130 in *Social Structure and Network Analysis*, edited by Peter Marsden and Nan Lin. Beverly Hills, CA: Sage.

Granovetter, Mark. 1985. "Economic Action and Social Structure: The Problem of Embeddedness." *American Journal of Sociology* 91:481–510.

Hamilton, Gary G., ed. 1991. *Business Networks and Economic Development in East and Southeast Asia*. Hong Kong: University of Hong Kong.

He, Guang, Qiang Qiu, and Lan Fu, eds. 1990. *The Labor Force Management in Contemporary China* (*Xiandai Zhongguo Laodongli Guanli*). Beijing: Chinese Social Sciences Press.

Hong, Tang, Jian Liu, and Xiao Chen. 1994. "Central Planning to Remain Despite Reform." *China News Digest* (May 11):22.

Hwang, Kwang-kuo. 1987. "Face and Favor: The Chinese Power Game." *American Journal of Sociology* 92 (January):944–974.

Jia, Qingguo. 1994. "Reform Ideology, Political Commitment and Resource Transfer: An Alternative Model for the Explanation of China's Economic Reform." *Journal of Contemporary China* 5:3–24.

Lin, Cyril Zhiren. 1989. "Open-ended Economic Reform in China." Pp. 95–136 in *Remaking the Economic Institutions of Socialism*, edited by Victor Nee and David Stark. Stanford, CA: Stanford University Press.

Lin, Nan. 1982. "Social Resources and Instrumental Action." Pp. 131–147 in *Social Structure and Network Analysis*, edited by Peter Marsden and Nan Lin. Beverly Hills, CA: Sage.

Lin, Nan, Walter M. Ensel, and John C. Vaughn. 1981. "Social Resources and Strength of Ties: Structural Factors in Occupational Status Attainment." *American Sociological Review* 46:393–405.

Lin, Nan, and Mary Dumin. 1986. "Access to Social Resources." *Social Networks* 8:365–385.

Lin, Nan, Alfred Dean, and Walter M. Ensel, eds. 1986. *Social Support, Life Events, and Depression*. New York: Academic Press.

Lin, Nan, and Wen Xie. 1988. "Occupational Prestige in Urban China." *American Journal of Sociology* 93:793–832.

Lin, Nan, and Yanjie Bian. 1991. "Getting Ahead in Urban China." *American Journal of Sociology* 97:657–688.

Logan, John R., and Yanjie Bian. 1993. "Access to Community Resources in a Chinese City." *Social Forces* 72:555–576.

Malinowski, Bronislaw. 1922 [1953]. *Argonauts of the Western Pacific*. London: Routledge and Kegan Paul.

Marsden, Peter V., and Karen E. Campbell. 1984. "Measuring Tie Strength." *Social Forces* 63:482–501.

Marsden, Peter V., and Jeanne S. Hurlbert. 1988. "Social Resources and Mobility Outcomes: A Replication and Extension." *Social Forces* 66:1038–1059.

Nee, Victor. 1989. "A Theory of Market Transition: From Redistribution to Markets in State Socialism." *American Sociological Review* 54:663–681.

Parish, William L, Jr. 1984. "Destratification in China." Pp. 84–120 in *Class and Social Stratification in Post-Revolution China*, edited by James Watson. New York: Cambridge University Press.

Pitt-Rivers, J. A. 1954. *The People of the Sierra*. London: Weidenfeld and Nicolson.

Scott, James C. 1972. "Patron-Client Politics and Political Change in Southeast Asia." *American Political Review* 66:103–127.

Simmel, Georg. 1950. *The Sociology of Georg Simmel*. Translated, edited, and with an Introduction by Kurt H. Wolff. New York: Free Press.

Singelmann, Peter. 1975. "The Closing Triangle: Critical Notes on a Model for Peasant Mobilization in Latin America." *Comparative Studies in Society and History* 17:389–409.

State Statistical Bureau of China. 1989. *Statistical Yearbook of China: 1989* (*Zhongguo Tongji Nianjian: 1989*). Beijing: Statistical Press of China.

State Statistical Bureau of China. 1991. *Statistical Yearbook of China: 1991* (*Zhongguo Tongji Nianjian: 1991*). Beijing: Statistical Press of China.

Stolzenberg, Ross M. 1978. "Bringing the Boss Back in: Employer Size, Employee Schooling, and Socioeconomic Achievement." *American Sociological Review* 43:813–828.

Tang, Yunqi, ed. 1990. *A General Inquiry into China's Labor Management* (*Zhongguo Laodong Guanli Gailan*). Beijing: Chinese Cities Press.

Tarkowski, Jacek. 1981. "Poland: Patrons and Clients in a Planned Economy." Pp. 173–88 in *Political Clientelism, Patronage and Development*, edited by S. N. Eisenstadt and Rene Lemarchand. Beverly Hills, CA: Sage.

Walder, Andrew G. 1986. *Communist Neo-Traditionalism: Work and Authority in Chinese Industry*. Berkeley: University of California Press.

Walder, Andrew G. 1992. "Property Rights and Stratification in Socialist Redistributive Economies." *American Sociological Review* 57:524–539.

Watanabe, Shin. 1987. "Job-Searching: A Comparative Study of Male Employment Relations in the United States and Japan." Doctoral dissertation, University of California at Los Angeles.

Watanabe, Shin. 1994. "Job-Matching Processes Among Japanese Male Workers: Job-Finding Methods, Social Networks, and Mobility Outcomes." Working Paper, Department of Sociology, Sophia University, Japan.

Wegener, Bern. 1991. "Job Mobility and Social Ties: Social Resources, Prior Job, and Status Attainment." *American Sociological Review* 56:60–71.

Wellman, Barry. 1979. "The Community Question." *American Journal of Sociology* 84 (March):1201–1231.

Wellman, Barry. 1988. "The Community Question Re-evaluated." Pp. 81–107 in *Power, Community and the City*, edited by Michael Peter Smith. New Brunswick, NJ: Transaction Press.

Wellman, Barry. 1992. "Which Types of Ties and Networks Provide What Kinds of Support?" *Advances in Group Processes* 9:207–235.

Wellman, Barry, and Scot Wortley. 1989. "Brothers' Keepers: Situating Kinship Relations in Broader Networks of Social Support." *Sociological Perspectives* 32(3):273–306.

Wellman, Barry, and Scot Wortley. 1990. "Different Strokes from Different Folks: Community Ties and Social Support." *American Journal of Sociology* (November):558–588.

Whyte, Martin King, and William L. Parish, Jr. 1984. *Urban Life in Contemporary China*. Chicago: University of Chicago Press.

Whyte, William Foote. 1955. *Street Corner Society*. 2d ed. Chicago: University of Chicago Press.

Xiong, Ruimei, Qingshan Sun, and Zhisong Xu. 1986. "Strength of Ties and Job Change Behaviors of Employees in Manufacturing Industries." *Sociological Journal of the National University of Taiwan* 18 (November):1–24.

Yang, Maifair Mei-hui. 1989. "The Gift Economy and State Power in China." *Comparative Studies in Society and History* 31:25–54.

Yang, Maifair Mei-hui. 1994. *Gifts, Favors, and Banquets: The Art of Interpersonal Relations in China*. Ithaca, NY: Cornell University Press.

Ziegler, Rolf. 1990. "The Kula: Social Order, Barter, and Ceremonial Exchange." Pp. 141–68 in *Social Institutions: Their Emergence, Maintenance, and Effects*, edited by Michael Hechter, Karl-Dieter Opp, and Reinhard Wippler. New York: Aldine de Gruyter.

8

Personal Community Networks in Contemporary Japan

Shinsuke Otani

Beyond the Group

Except for kinship, the study of personal community networks is new in Japan. Although many Western studies have documented the existence, scope, and importance of personal community networks (e.g., Laumann 1973; Wellman 1979, 1988, 1990; Fischer 1982; Wilmott 1987), there have been few analyses of non-Western societies (but see Blau, Ruan, and Ardelt 1991).

Most Japanese studies have analyzed specific affiliations separately (kinship, friendship, neighborhood, and workmate ties), without assessing the whole set of ties in community networks (Otani 1993b). Even in the field of family sociology, where the most information about personal ties (kinship) has been accumulated in Japan, few studies have looked broadly at egocentric networks (e.g., Nojiri 1974; Seki 1980) as opposed to household-centered networks. Hence, there has been little analysis of the fit between kinship ties and other relationships, such as neighboring and friendship.

Instead, sociologists have focused on kinship ties (see Megro's 1992 review). Analysts have noted that there have been two types of kinship relationships in Japan: *Dozoku* relationships are inter *ie* (household) networks based on *ie* patrilineal ties, whereas *shinrui* relationships are composed of both affinal and consanguineal relatives (Morita 1985). Until recently, most Japanese family sociologists have focused on household-to-household networks based on the *ie* and *dozoku* systems (traditional family kinship structures) rather than on person-to-person networks. Although many researchers have recently recognized that *dozoku* relationships are declining and *shinrui* relationships are becoming more important, there have been few empirical studies of egocentric *shinrui* networks. And while many Japanese studies have looked at household-to-household networks in neighborhoods, few studies have examined egocentric networks that stretch beyond the neighborhood to include ties with kin and friends (Matsumoto and Nozawa 1994; Otani 1995).

The many analyses asserting the unique nature of Japanese interpersonal relationships *(Nihonjinron)* have often used stereotypical images such as the "group model" (Mouer and Sugimoto 1986; Befu 1980). For example, Nakane (1970) has used phrases such as "personal relationships in a vertical society," to contrast the importance of "vertical" or hierarchical ties and group solidarity in the Japanese context, with "horizontal" or egalitarian ties and individualism in the Western setting. Similarly Fukutake (1989) has stressed that the concepts of *ie* and *mura* (household and village as community) are most important in understanding Japanese "familistic social relations." He has noted that the *mura* along with *ie* was the mold from which modern Japanese society was formed. At the time of the Meiji Restoration (1886), some 90% of the population lived in villages and more than 80% were engaged in agriculture. Almost all Japanese lived and died in the *mura* in which they were born. Rice agriculture, incorporating irrigation systems, required collective labor by the villagers. Community solidarity was interwoven with a stratification system based on land ownership. This unitary and hierarchical nature of *mura* shaped Japanese social character into conformist behavior, with an orientation toward extended families (see Fukutake 1980).

Such analyses grasp the traditional form that personal networks take in Japanese society, but they do not fully explain the features of these networks in contemporary urban-industrial Japan. We must view two aspects of personal networks to understand contemporary Japanese society: not only the remaining traditional forms of personal networks that have provided the basic structure for Japanese culture, but also the changes that have occurred in these personal networks. Japanese scholars have placed too much stress on traditional forms and have paid too little attention to recent changes in them. Analyzing Japanese personal community networks from these two viewpoints can contribute to rethinking Japanese social relations and to better understanding the differences and similarities between Japanese and Western societies.

Comparing Japanese and North American Networks

The Surveys

Between 1987 and 1989, I conducted three surveys to gather information about Japanese community networks.[1] The data discussed in this paper derive mainly from a 1989 random-sample mail survey of 1086 adults (aged twenty and over) in five cities located in the Chugoku and Shikoku regions of southwestern Japan (Chugoku-Shikoku Survey): Hiroshima (1985 population = 1,044,118), Okayama (572,479), Matsuyama (426,658), Uwajima (71,381) and Saijyo (56,516). Hiroshima, Okayama, and Matsuyama are typical prefectural capitals, while Uwajima and Saijyo are smaller cities with rural characteristics.

To measure networks, I asked respondents two questions:

1. "How many intimate kin, coworkers, neighbors, and friends do you have (people you get together with frequently)?"
2. "What is the relation of the person outside your home to whom you feel closest? 1. kin; 2. neighbor; 3. coworker; 4. friend (other than 1, 2, 3)?"

For comparisons, I use data from the 1977 Northern California Community Study, the 1968 and 1978 East York Social Network Studies, and the 1985, 1986, and 1987 U.S. General Social Surveys (GSS). Fischer (1982) interviewed 1,050 adults living in fifty Northern California communities. Wellman (1979) conducted a 1968 random-sample survey of 845 adults aged eighteen and over residing in the Toronto borough of East York (1971 population = 104,645), and in the 1978 survey, he reinterviewed a small subsample (33) of the original respondents (Wellman 1982; Wellman, Carrington, and Hall 1988). The GSS is an annual cross-sectional survey of American adults (Davis and Smith 1992). The 1985 and 1987 GSS asked questions about social networks and the 1986 GSS included a special module of social support and network items (Burt 1984, 1986, 1987; Marsden 1987). Although the basic procedures of each survey were different, they make possible a rough comparison between Japan and North America. This comparison is especially meaningful in the case of intimate networks in Chugoku-Shikoku versus Toronto (Table 8.2) because of the similar wording used in both surveys.

How Does the Composition of Networks Differ?

Two things are apparent when comparing the composition of personal networks in Chugoku-Shikoku, Northern California, and the U.S. General Social Survey (Table 8.1). First, Japanese respondents name fewer kin than do Americans. The mean number of kin named in the Northern California study is 7.7, compared to only 4.4 in Japan. Different survey methods may explain part of this difference: the Chugoku-Shikoku Survey focused on more urbanized respondents than the Northern California Survey, and the category of kin in Northern California included spouses.

TABLE 8.1   Mean Number of Network Members by Role Type

	Japan[a] (Chugoku-Shikoku)	U.S.[b] (N. California)	U.S.[c] (GSS 1986)
Network size	14.1	18.5	7.4
Kin	4.4	7.7 (close = 4.3) extended = 3.4)	–
Coworkers	2.7	1.8	0.9
Neighbors	2.7	1.9	1.5
Friends	4.1	7.1	5.0
All nonkin[d]	9.5	10.8	7.4

[a]The Japanese study used a mail survey to ask respondents to estimate the number of associates they had. The wording was: "How many intimate kin, co-workers, neighbors, or friends do you have? (i.e., people with whom you get together frequently)."

[b]The Northern California study asked respondents to name key people using ten questions asking about various kinds of social support.

[c]The 1986 GSS question was: "Thinking now of close friends not your husband or wife or partner or family members but people you feel close to." "How many close friends would you say you have?" "How many of these close friends are people you work with now?" "How many of these close friends are your neighbors now?" There is no way in this survey to distinguish kin from friends, and they are recorded in this table as friends.

[d]"All nonkin" include coworkers, neighbors, and friends (as a residual category).

Second, the Japanese name more neighbors and coworkers than do Americans, with a mean of 1.9 in Northern California, 1.5 in the U.S. nationally, and 2.7 in Japan. The mean number of coworkers listed is 1.8 in Northern California, 0.9 in America, and 2.7 in Japan. Greater Japanese involvement with neighbors and co-workers also is apparent in the role composition of intimate networks (Table 8.2). About 65% of the Torontonians name kin as their closest intimate as compared to only 45% of the Japanese. Only 4% of the Torontonians name a neighbor and 4% name a coworker, as compared to 11% and 12% of the Japanese.

Kinship Ties

Although some sociologists have found that the Japanese have less frequent contact with relatives than do Westerners, there has been much debate about these findings. After comparing Japanese data to the Detroit area study (Blood et al. 1956), Koyama (1970, p. 337) concluded that kinship relations in Japan continue to have many traditional and formal elements, although contacts among relatives are less frequent. Morioka

TABLE 8.2   Percentage Composition of Networks

	Japan (Chugoku-Shikoku)	Canada[a] (Toronto) Ranked Closest	U.S.[b] (1985, 1987 GSS) 1st Person named
All kin	45	65	47
Child	8	13	10
Parent	7	19	18
Sibling	22	21	10
Other Relative	6	12	9
Coworker	11	4	13
Neighbor	12	4	9
Friend	33	28	31
Total	100%	100%	100%
No. of Cases	1058	811	2044

[a]The 1968 Toronto question (asked in person) was: "Who are your six closest intimates (the persons outside your home that you feel closest to)?" The 1989 Chugoku-Shikoku question (by mail) was: "What is the relation of the person outside your home to whom you feel closest? 1: Kin, 2: Neighbor, 3: Coworker, 4: Friend (other than 1, 2, 3)?"

[b]The U.S. data are average percentages of 1985 GSS and 1987 GSS using the same wording: "Looking back over the last six months, who are the people with whom you discussed matters important to you?" First person is spouse (parent, sibling, child, other family member, coworker, group member, neighbor, friend, adviser, or other?)

(1964) has argued that a cultural pattern has not yet been established for contact between parents and nonresident children. He contends that a traditional cultural pattern based on the *ie-dozoku* system still survives. That is, according to tradition, day-to-day contact between parents and children is usually limited to courtesy calls or emergencies. The exception is frequent contact with an adult child who lives in the same home, usually the eldest son.

However, Ohashi and Shimizu (1973) argue that the higher rate of parent/child coresidence in Japan compared to the West is a major reason for low contact with kin outside the household. They point out that the ratio of three-generation families in Japan is remarkably high (Chugoku-Shikoku = 17%). For example, the percentage of people aged sixty or older residing with a married child is 31% for men and 42% for women, compared to only 1% and 2% in the U.S. (Morita 1985, p. 239). Moreover, my own data show that the Japanese name fewer parents and children as closest associates outside their home than do Canadians (Table 8.2). These facts support Ohashi's theory that cohabitation patterns affect kinship ties among the Japanese.

Neighborhood Ties

Profound differences between Japanese and American neighborhoods help explain why the Japanese have a larger percentage of their relationships with neighbors. Japanese neighborhoods *(mura)*, traditionally have frequent local activities and have contained many densely knit relationships. There is a sense of obligation among immediate neighbors and many reciprocal relationships (Dore 1958; Vogel 1963; Bestor 1989). Although such relationships are becoming less important in contemporary Japan, the Japanese still neighbor more than Americans.

Chonaikai (urban wards or neighborhood associations), which exist nationwide and are based on semicompulsory household memberships, also play an important role in promoting neighborhood cohesiveness and support networks (e.g., Curtis 1971). *Chonaikai* are responsible for a variety of local activities, such as printing announcements of neighborhood associations, organizing trips for local clubs, and organizing local sports (Ben-Ari 1991). In the Chugoku-Shikoku survey, 92% of the respondents belong to *chonaikai*, and 72% participate in *chonaikai* activities or meetings. These features of Japanese neighborhoods probably account for why the Japanese name more neighbors as close associates than do North Americans.

Coworker Ties

The portrayal of the firm as a corporate family has been central to managerial ideology in Japan since the nineteenth century (Dore 1973; Nakane 1970; Cole 1979). Central themes in accounts of Japanese work life and organization are the high degree of work-group cohesion, the close and personal relations between workmates and supervisors, and the overall solidarity and familial character of the firm (Lincoln and Kalleberg 1990). Many company employees in Japan often spend their after-work hours with coworkers and people from other firms who they know through work (Atsumi 1979, 1980). Although this is also true in the West, the frequency and extent of the practice is far greater in Japan. Lincoln and Kalleberg (1990) point out that the Japanese report an average of two close friends in the company as compared to less than one for Americans. Atsumi argues that these social relationships *(tsukiai)* are based on a Japanese cultural pattern that is imbued with a sense of obligation or social necessity among white-collar employees. The social milieus of Japanese paid workers strongly affect the nature of personal community networks. Japanese men who are heavily engaged in paid work spend a considerable amount of time with workmates, while "kitchen widows" (the wives of such workers) are at home interacting with neighbors and kin. Moreover, the traditional patterns persist of parent/child cohabitation, and social relationships, arising from a sense of obligation. Indeed, these differences in cultural context and social setting between Japan and North America affect the nature and development of personal community networks.

Personal Background and
Personal Community Networks

In what ways are Japanese networks similar to those of North Americans? In his Northern California study, Fischer (1982) notes that women tend to be more involved with relatives than men, and that the more education and income people have, the more friends and neighbors they have as close associates. Although Japanese data are quite similar, there is one exception. According to the Northern California data, better educated people are especially likely to name neighbors as close associates (Fischer 1982).By contrast the Japanese data show the opposite: better educated people choose a lower percentage of neighbors as intimates. I believe that this is because the Northern California survey excluded predominantly black communities and non-English speakers and sampled from more socially homogenous neighborhoods (Deng and Bonacich 1991). Hence, educated Northern Californians may be more likely to name neighbors as intimates because their neighbors tend to be more similar to them in socioeconomic status, whereas the Japanese reside in neighborhoods that are more socioeconomically heterogeneous.

To understand this difference between the Japanese and Northern Californians, we should take into account two differences in urban settings that can affect the characteristics of personal networks. The first is residential mobility: Americans move more frequently and farther away from home. Indeed, many are committed more to careers or lifestyles than to places (Long 1988). The Japanese have been less mobile than Americans because they traditionally have a strong attachment to their hometown. The percentage of the American respondents who were living in a different state at the age of sixteen is 33% (average rate of the 1985, 1986, and 1987 GSS), while only 17% of the Japanese respondents report having lived in a different prefecture at the age of sixteen (Chugoku-Shikoku Survey). The mean number of years spent living in their current city is 20.4 for the Americans, and 31.8 for the Japanese. The Americans have lived a mean of 10.5 years in their current dwelling, while the Japanese have lived almost twice as long in theirs, 20.0 years. These differences are remarkable because American states are larger than Japanese prefectures, and the Chugoku-Shikoku respondents are more urban than the national GSS sample.

TABLE 8.3   Composition of Networks According to Respondents' Personal
Characteristics

	Kin		Coworker		Neighbor		Friend	
	Japan	U.S.	Japan	U.S.	Japan	U.S.	Japan	U.S.
Sex								
Male	40	40	14	18	9	8	37	34
Female	49	51	8	10	14	9	30	30
Age								
20–39	31	47	14	16	7	7	48	32
40–59	47	42	12	17	12	9	29	32
Over 60	58	52	4	5	16	12	22	31
Education (years of school)								
< 11 Years	48	53	11	8	18	12	24	28
12–15 Years	50	46	9	14	11	7	31	32
> 15 Years	32	39	14	20	7	7	47	35
Income								
< $20,000	45	49	8	6	16	9	31	35
$20,000–$40,000	43	50	13	15	10	6	35	29
> $40,000	44	43	13	24	9	9	35	24
Total	45	47	11	13	12	9	33	31

NOTES: Japanese data are from the 1989 Chugoku-Shikoku survey. U.S. data are
an average percentage of 1985 and 1987 GSS. Income calculated at US$1.00 =
¥150.

Nevertheless, many of the same tendencies appear in both the U.S. GSS
and the Japanese data (Table 8.3). For example, older respondents choose
as intimates a higher percentage of neighbors and a lower percentage of
coworkers; more educated respondents choose more friends; higher-in-
come respondents choose more coworkers. These similarities between
such different countries suggest that there may be commonalities in the
personal communities of developed countries.

Gender differences are of special interest because Japanese attitudes
differ profoundly from those held by most Americans. In America
(1985–87 GSS), 24% agree that "women should take care of running their
homes and leave running the country up to men," while in Japan
(Chugoku-Shikoku), 76% agree that "men should work and women
should stay home." Indeed, few Japanese working women are heavily
engaged in both domestic and paid work. In the Chugoku-Shikoku survey, 17% of the women have never done paid work outside their homes, 35%
have done such work but quit when they married or had a child, 20%
quit (usually on marriage) but have returned to doing paid work, while
only 16% currently are doing paid work and 12% have had other patterns
(such as quitting when married, returning to paid work later, and then

quitting again). These data tell us that the work situation of women in Japan differs profoundly from that in America (see Kamo 1993). Yet women in both countries tend to be somewhat more involved than men with kin and neighbors and less involved with coworkers and friends (Table 8.3).

Urban Features of Personal Networks

Many sociologists have discussed the transformations occurring in personal networks throughout contemporary Western societies. Fischer (1982) suggests that urbanism has reduced involvement with the traditional complex of kin, neighborhood, and church and has slightly increased involvement in the more modern and voluntary contexts of work, secular associations, and footloose friendship. He describes urban personal networks as being "more selective." Wellman (1979) expands the definition of community to take into account far-flung, sparsely knit ties that stretch beyond the boundaries of neighborhood or kinship solidarities. He points out that contemporary urbanites juggle limited memberships in multiple, specialized, interest-based communities rather than immersing themselves fully in solitary, local, or kinship groups. Mayer (1963) describes narrowly-defined, single-stranded networks as characteristic of an urban style distinct from a rural style of broadly defined, multistranded networks (see also Boissevain 1974; Wellman 1979). Wireman (1984, p. 3) develops the concept of warm and friendly "intimate secondary relationships" for modern or urban types of personal networks that occur in formal settings and have limited goals: They involve "the individual rather than the family; commitment that is limited in time and scope and with a relatively low cost of withdrawal."

Can these same transformations in personal networks be seen in a Japanese society that has been undergoing rapid urbanization? I examine this question by comparing friendship networks in large central cities (Hiroshima, Okayama, and Matsuyama) with those in small rural cities (Uwajima and Saijyo).

Similar tendencies (i.e., the more urban the respondents' communities, the fewer kin and the more friends they name) can be seen when the Japanese data are compared with the Northern California data while controlling for level of urbanism (Table 8.4). In Japan, as in Northern California, urbanism reduces respondents' involvement with the traditional complex of kin and neighbors and increases their voluntary involvement with friends. This suggests that the effects of urbanism on promoting nontraditional ties is a Japanese as well as a Western phenomenon.

Networks in Japan, as in Toronto, are not local residential groups. Rather, the data suggest that Japanese urbanites also possess far-flung,

TABLE 8.4   Average Number of Associates in Each Role, by Urbanism

(Population Size)	Kin	Nbors	Frnds	Cwks	NetSz	NonKin
Chugoku-Shikoku, Japan						
Large central cities	4.0	2.5	4.5	2.9	14.0	10.0
Hiroshima (1,038,198)	3.8	2.4	4.7	2.4	13.5	9.6
Okayama (566,672)	3.8	2.4	4.1	3.4	13.9	10.0
Matsuyama (426,658)	4.2	2.6	4.7	2.9	14.5	10.3
Small rural cities	5.0	2.9	3.7	2.4	14.2	9.2
Uwajima (71,381)	4.4	2.9	3.9	2.1	13.4	8.9
Saijyo (56,516)	5.6	3.0	3.5	2.8	15.0	9.3
Northern California						
Regional core	4.3	1.6	8.6	2.1	15.9	12.3
Metropolitan	6.4	2.0	7.4	2.3	17.6	11.7
Town	7.4	1.9	6.6	1.6	17.3	10.2
Semirural	7.2	2.2	5.3	1.2	15.5	8.7

NOTE: Size of Japanese cities from national census of October 1, 1985.

KEY: Kin   = Kin
       Nbors   = Neighbors
       Frnds   = Friends
       Cwks   = Coworkers
       NetSz   = Network Size
       NonKin   = Nonkin

sparsely knit ties characteristic of the "community liberated" model (Wellman 1979). Only 12% of network members in Japan, as compared to 22% in Toronto, live within walking distance (Table 8.5; Wellman, Carrington, and Hall 1988). That over 50% of the respondents report single-stranded networks and intimate secondary relationships, even in small cities, indicates that the features of personal networks described by Western sociologists also exist in contemporary Japan.

Networks in large cities are even more liberated. There is a high proportion of friendship ties (as compared to kinship and neighboring), relationships are more specialized, and they are more limited in the scope and duration of their commitments (Table 8.6).

Heterogeneity of Networks

Many American sociologists have focused on homophily and homogeneity in personal relations, a tendency for friendships to form between those who are alike in some respect (Lazarsfeld and Merton 1954; Verbrugge 1977; Laumann 1973). Yet cities tend to be relatively heteroge-

TABLE 8.5   Percentage of Network Members by Residential Distance

Japan[a]	Chugoku-Shikoku Total	Large Central Cities	Small Rural Cities
Same neighborhood (Chonaikai)	12	10	16
Same city	57	58	55
Same prefecture	21	18	25
Outside prefecture	10	15	5
Total (p < 0.01)	100	101	101

Toronto, Canada[b]	Intimate Ties	Significant Ties
Same neighborhood (0–1 mile)	18	22
Metro Toronto (1.1–30 miles)	50	45
South central Ontario (31–100 miles)	17	13
Further away (> 100 miles)	15	21
Total (p < 0.01)	100%	101%

[a]Large central cities: Hiroshima, Okayama, Matsuyama; small rural cities: Uwajima, Saijyo.

[b]Toronto data (1978) from Wellman, Carrington, and Hall (1988, p. 149). Significant ties are non-intimate relationships that are actively thought about and maintained. Intimate ties are those active ties that are socially close.

TABLE 8.6   Percentage of Japanese Respondents Reporting Urban Forms of Relationships

Single or Multistranded Networks[a]	Single-Stranded	Multistranded	Total
Large central cities	57	44	101
Small rural cities	50	50	100
Total (p < 0.05)	54	46	100

Friendship Preference[b]	Intimate Secondary	Primary	Total
Large central cities	61	39	101
Small rural cities	57	43	100
Total	60	40	100

[a]"Which statement better expresses your daily behavior?
   A: When I go out, I do not go out with the same friends. [Single-Stranded];
   B: When I go out, I do go out with the same friends [Multi-Stranded]"

[b]"Which statement better expresses your desire?
   A: I like to have friendships, but I want commitments limited in time and scope with a relatively low cost of withdrawal. [Intimate Secondary];
   B: I prefer friendships that are deep and long lasting. [Primary]"

TABLE 8.7   Percentage of Heterogeneous Network Members by U.S. City Size

City Size (,000)	<10	10–99	100–499	>500	Total
Gender	25	27	26	26	26
Education[a]	47	41	44	34	42
Age[b]	31	27	30	25	29
Race[c]	4	6	13	22	8
Religion[d]	26	37	28	41	33
Party ID[e]	39	38	41	31	37

NOTE: Includes only respondents who name nonkin as the first person with whom they discussed matters important to them in the 1985 GSS and 1987 GSS.

[a]*Education:* <12 years; 12–15 years; 16+ years

[b]*Age:* <40; 40–59; 60+

[c]*Race:* white; black; other

[d]*Religion:* Protestant; Catholic; Other/none

[e]*Party Identification:* Democrat; Republican; Independent/other.

neous milieus (e.g., Wirth 1938; Fischer 1975, 1982, 1984). Indeed, Fischer (1975) argues that the heterogeneity of cities increases their homogeneity because people are able to select similar associates out of the large urban population pool.

To see if urbanism increases the homogeneity of Japanese networks, I analyzed the connection between urbanism (city size) and homogeneity of networks in GSS (1985 and 1987) data. The GSS survey asked about personal characteristics (sex, education, age, race, religion, and party identification) of the first person with whom respondents said they discussed important matters. I classified as having "heterogeneous" relationships those respondents whose characteristics were not the same in category as those of the first person with whom they consulted.[2] Contrary to Fischer's argument, urbanism does not increase the homogeneity of networks, especially with regard to race and religion (Table 8.7). In fact, the opposite tendency appears. This finding supports Deng and Bonacich's (1991) conclusion that the blackness of black networks is not strengthened by urbanism, and Blau's (1977) contention that the greater heterogeneity of large cities promotes more intergroup relations. It also suggests that Fischer's (1975) subcultural theory may have overemphasized the homogeneity of networks in cities.

I use my Japanese data to demonstrate the possibility and importance of heterogeneous networks in cities. I rely on only one measure of heterogeneity: whether respondents and their network members come from the same hometowns or prefectures. One reason for this is negative, as I do not have other information about the heterogeneity of networks. The other, a positive reason, is to test my hypothesis that the heterogeneity of

TABLE 8.8   Percentage of Mixed Ties of Japanese Nonkin Network Members by City Size

Total	N	Same Hometown[a]	Same Prefecture	Different Prefecture	
All Non-Kin[b] (p < 0.005)					
Large Central Cities	332	27%	39%	34%	100%
Small Rural Cities	251	47%	36%	18%	101%
Friends Only[c] (p < 0.005)					
Large Central Cities	197	30%	35%	35%	100%
Small Rural Cities	151	52%	35%	14%	101%

[a]"Where is this person's (closest associate's) hometown?"
  1) Same city, town, or village = "Same Hometown"
  2) Not same city/town/village, but same prefecture = "Same Prefecture"
  3) Different prefecture = "Different Prefecture"
[b]Includes only respondents of subsample who named nonkin as their most intimate associate (neighbor, coworker, friend).
[c]Includes only respondents of subsample who named "friend" as their most intimate network member.

hometowns in personal networks is important for those Japanese who have a strong localistic attachment to place. The presence of heterogeneous interactions with intimates, which I call "mixed ties," displays the possibility of encouraging unconventionality and breaking through traditional (localistic) Japanese culture.[3] Those living in large cities are more likely to name as their closest intimate a nonkin (and especially a friend) whose hometown differs from theirs (Table 8.8). Moreover, the proportion of spouses who came from the respondents' hometowns is also lower in the large cities. These findings suggest that urbanization increases the possibility of interaction and marriage between people whose hometowns are different. Although closer examination of various other factors—such as socioeconomic status, age, and lifestyle—are necessary to conclude that urbanism increases the heterogeneity of Japanese networks, we can at least say that intimate nonkin ties in large cities are more mixed than those in small cities. More significantly, "mixed ties" affect consciousness, irrespective of urbanism. The more widely mixed the respondents' ties, the more unconventional and cosmopolitan are the opinions that they express (Table 8.9).[4]

Such findings indicate that "mixed ties"—social relationships between people from cultural contexts—are as important in Japanese society as they are in the West (see Simmel 1890, 1908; Park 1928; Granovetter 1973; DeVos 1976; Burt 1992). They create opportunities for the intersection of social spheres, which can help to break through traditional values and to develop cosmopolitanism. Although I have focused in this chapter on

TABLE 8.9   Percentage of Mixed Ties Among Unconventional and
Cosmopolitan Japanese

	N	Women work[b]	Nonconform[c]	Cosmopolitan[d]
Hometown	198	49	57	71
Same prefecture	212	51	62	71
Different prefecture	152	64	65	84
Total	1086	50	59	71
		(p < 0.05)		(p < 0.05)

[a]Includes only respondents who named nonkin as their most intimate associate (neighbor, coworker, friend).

[b]*"Please tell me whether you agree or disagree with the following statement: Men should work, and women should stay home."* (percentage of respondents who answered "disagree")

[c]*"I think it isn't necessary to conform myself to the way of the world."* (percentage of respondents who answered "agree")

[d]*"Of the following statements, which statement better expresses your opinion?*
   A: Officials of Matsuyama (or other survey city) should be people who were born and raised in Matsuyama, because they best know the manners and customs of Matsuyama.
   B: Officials of Matsuyama (or other survey city) need not be people who were born and raised in Matsuyama. Their ability is most important." (percentage of respondents who answered "statement B").

only one type of mixed tie, the heterogeneity of hometowns, I suggest that many kinds of mixed ties are important in social life, such as relationships with people of different lifestyles, value orientations, gender, age, and socioeconomic status. For example, in other research, I have found that the more heterogeneous the membership of Yokohama voluntary associations (e.g., hobby groups, sports clubs, welfare groups, social interest groups), the more viable and creative are their activities (Otani 1986). Furthermore, heterogeneous groups discussed public and community matters more while private matters (such as family problems) dominated discussions in homogeneous groups

Conclusions and Implications

1. Differences of social setting between Japan and North America continue to affect personal community networks. The Japanese name fewer kin as intimates than do North Americans because the pattern of parent/child cohabitation based on traditional kinship structures (*ie-dozoku* systems) continues in contemporary Japan. Relationships among neighbors and coworkers in Japan are stronger than in North America because

traditional personal relationships arising from a sense of obligation persist in Japanese neighborhoods and workplaces.

2. Despite differences in cultural context, the characteristics of personal networks described by Western sociologists also exist in contemporary Japan. There are similarities in the relationship of personal characteristics to network characteristics. Although kinship and friendship ties predominate in both countries, Japanese women tend to be more involved than men with kin and neighbors and less involved with coworkers and friends. Older people have a higher percentage of neighbors as intimates, respondents who are more educated have more friends as intimates, and respondents with high incomes have a larger number of intimate ties with coworkers.

3. Urbanism, even in Japan, reduces people's involvement with associates drawn from the traditional complex of kin and neighbors and increases their involvement with people drawn from the more voluntary contexts of footloose friendship. Thus, Japanese urbanites possess the far-flung, sparsely knit ties that are characteristic of the "community liberated" model (Wellman and Leighton 1979). Although this is especially true in big cities, more than half of the Japanese surveyed, even in small cities, favor new forms of footloose friendship.

These findings suggest two important trends in Japanese personal community networks. One is the continuation of the traditional forms of personal networks that have provided the basic structure for Japanese culture. The other is the growing individualism in Japanese urbanized society. Until now, research on Japanese networks has emphasized the first trend and failed to grasp the latter. Of course, it is important to take into account the fact that social settings based on traditional Japanese culture affect the nature of Japanese personal community networks, but it is wrong to overemphasize the cultural uniqueness of Japanese society.

Notes

I am indebted to Claude S. Fischer and Barry Wellman for comments on earlier drafts of this paper, to Barry Wellman, Beverly Wellman, and Thy Phu for copyediting, to Matsuyama University, and to the Survey Research Center, University of California, Berkeley, where I was a visiting scholar, 1990–1991.

1. In 1987, 269 people were interviewed in person in Matsuyama, a central city in the Ehime prefecture (Matsuyama Survey). In 1988, a survey of 890 people was conducted by mail in four prefectural capitals (Matsuyama, Takamatsu, Kochi, and Tokushima) in the Shikoku region (Shikoku Survey). Response rates of the Chugoku-Shikoku Survey ranged from 34% (Hiroshima) to 53% (Saijyo). For more details, see Otani (1992, 1993a).

2. For example, I classified a man as "heterogeneous" if he chose a woman as the first person with whom he discussed matters important to him.

3. As an index of "mixed ties," "same hometown" describes Chugoku-Shikoku respondents whose hometowns are the same as their closest intimate, while "same prefecture" indicates that their hometowns differ but their home prefectures are the same.

4. The proportion of unconventional respondents was not associated with the size of the city. The percentage of respondents who held unconventional opinions about women working in Hiroshima was 48%, in Okayama 55%, in Matsuyama 44%, in Uwajima 54%, and in Saijyo 48%. The rate of unconventional opinion expressed about cosmopolitanism was 54% in Hiroshima, 64% in Okayama, 64% in Matsuyama, 57% in Uwajima, and 55% in Saijyo. The proportion of cosmopolitan respondents was strongly associated with the size of the city. This conclusion remains the same when the size of the city is controlled.

References

Atsumi, Reiko. 1979. "Tsukiai: Obligatory Personal Relationships of Japanese White-Collar Company Employees." *Human Organization* 38(1):63–70.

Atsumi, Reiko. 1980. "Patterns of Personal Relationships: A Key to Understanding Japanese Thought and Behavior." *Social Analysis* 5/6:63–78.

Befu, Harumi. 1980. "The Group Model of Japanese Society and an Alternative." *Rice University Studies* 66(1):169–187.

Ben-Ari, Eyal. 1991. *Changing Japanese Suburbia: A Study of Two Present-Day Localities.* London: Kegan Paul.

Bestor, Theodore C. 1989. *Neighborhood Tokyo.* Stanford: Stanford University Press.

Blau, Peter M. 1977. *Inequality and Heterogeneity.* New York: Free Press.

Blau, Peter M., Danching Ruan, and Monica Ardelt. 1991. "Interpersonal Choice and Networks in China." *Social Forces* 69(4):1037–1062.

Blood, Robert, and Morris Axelrod. 1956. *A Social Profile of Detroit:1955.* A Report of the Detroit Area Study of the University of Michigan.

Boissevain, Jeremy. 1974. *Friends of Friends: Networks, Manipulators and Coalitions.* Oxford: Basil Blackwell.

Burt, Ronald S. 1984. "Network Items and the General Social Survey." *Social Networks* 6:293–339.

Burt, Ronald S. 1986. "A Note on Sociometric Order in the General Social Survey Network Data." *Social Networks* 8:149–174.

Burt, Ronald S. 1987. "A Note on the General Social Survey's Ersatz Network Density Item." *Social Networks* 9:75–85.

Burt, Ronald S. 1992. *Structural Holes: The Social Structure of Competition.* Cambridge: Harvard University Press.

Cole, Robert E. 1979. *Work, Mobility, and Participation: A Comparative Study of American and Japanese Industry.* Berkeley: University of California Press.

Curtis, Gerald L. 1971. *Election Campaigning Japanese Style.* New York: Columbia University Press.

Davis, James A., and Tom W. Smith. 1992. *The NORC General Social Survey: A User's Guide.* Newbury Park, CA: Sage.

Deng, Zhong, and Phillip Bonacich. 1991. "Some Effects of Urbanism on Black Social Networks." *Social Networks* 13:35–50.

DeVos, George A. 1976. *Responses to Change: Society, Culture, and Personality.* New York: Van Nostrand.

Dore, Ronald P. 1958. *City Life in Japan: A Study of A Tokyo Ward.* Berkeley: University of California Press.

Dore, Ronald P. 1973. *British Factory–Japanese Factory: The Origins of Diversity in Industrial Relations.* Berkeley: University of California Press.

Fischer, Claude S. 1975. "Toward a Subcultural Theory of Urbanism." *American Journal of Sociology* 80(6):1319–1341.

Fischer, Claude S. 1982. *To Dwell Among Friends: Personal Networks in Town and City.* Chicago: University of Chicago Press.

Fischer, Claude S. 1984. *The Urban Experience.* 2d ed. New York: Harcourt Brace Jovanovich.

Fischer, Claude S., Robert Max Jackson, C. Ann Steuve, Kathleen Gerson, Lynne McCallister Jones, and Mark Baldassare. 1977. *Networks and Places: Social Relation tion in the Urban Setting.* New York: Free Press.

Ford, W. Scott. 1973. "Interracial Public Housing in a Border City: Another Look at the Contact Hypothesis." *American Journal of Sociology* 78(6):1426–1477.

Fukutake, Tadashi. 1980. *Rural Society in Japan.* Tokyo: University of Tokyo Press.

Fukutake, Tadashi. 1989. *The Japanese Social Structure: Its Evolution in the Modern Century.* 2d ed. Translated by Ronald P. Dore. Tokyo: University of Tokyo Press.

Granovetter, Mark S. 1973. "The Strength of Weak Ties." *American Journal of Sociology* 78:1360–1380.

Kamo, Yoshinori. 1993. "Determinants of Marital Satisfaction: A Comparison of the United States and Japan." *Journal of Social and Personal Relationships.* 10:551–568.

Koyama, Takashi. 1970. "Rural-Urban Comparison of Kinship Relations in Japan." Pp. 318–337 in *Families in East and West: Socialization Process and Kinship Ties,* edited by R. Hill and R. Koning. Paris: Mouton.

Laumann, Edward O. 1966. *Prestige and Association in Urban Community: An Analysis of an Urban Stratification System.* New York: Bobbs-Merrill.

Laumann, Edward O. 1973. *Bond of Pluralism: The Form and Substance of Urban Social Networks.* New York: Wiley.

Lazarsfeld, Paul F., and Robert K. Merton. 1954. "Friendship as Social Process: A Substantive and Methodological Analysis." Pp.18–66 in *Freedom and Control in Modern Society,* edited by Morroe Berger, Theodore Abel, and Charles Page. New York: Van Nostrand.

Lincoln, James R., and Arne L. Kalleberg. 1990. *Culture, Control, and Commitment: A Study of Work Organization and Work Attitudes in the United States and Japan.* Cambridge: Cambridge University Press.

Long, Larry. 1988. *Migration and Residential Mobility in the United States.* New York: Russell Sage Foundation.

Marsden, Peter V. 1987. "Core Discussion Networks of Americans." *American Sociological Review* 52 (February):122–131.

Matsumoto, Yasushi, and Shinji Nozawa. 1994. *Families and Personal Networks in Urban Settings.* [In Japanese] Tokyo: Nissei kiso Kenkyujyo.

Mayer, Phillip. 1963. *Townsmen or Tribesmen: Conservatism and the Process of Urbanization in a South Africa City.* Cape Town: Oxford University Press.

Megro, Yoriko. 1992. "Between the Welfare and Economic Institutions: Japanese Families in Transition." *International Journal of Japanese Sociology* 1:35–46.

Morioka, Kiyomi. 1964. "Studies of Kin-Family Networks in America: A Rising Trend in Family Sociology." [In Japanese]. *Monthly Bulletin of Family Courts* 16(1):1–57.

Morita, Saburo. 1985. "Changes in Family and Kinship Structure in Japan: A Reconsideration of the Nucleating Family Hypothesis." Pp. 221–249 in *Family and Community Changes in East Asia,* edited by K. Aoi, K. Morioka, and J. Suginohara. Tokyo: Japan Sociological Society.

Mouer, Ross, and Yoshio Sugimoto. 1986. *Images of Japanese Society: A Study in the Structure of Social Reality.* London: Routledge and Kegan Paul.

Nakane, Chie. 1970. *Japanese Society.* Berkeley: University of California Press.

Nojiri, Yoriko. 1974. "Family Social Network in Modern Japan: An Application of Path Analysis." [In Japanese] *Japanese Sociological Review* 98:37–48.

O'Brien, David J., and Mary Joan Roach. 1984. "Recent Developments in Urban Sociology." *Journal of Urban History* 10(2):145–170.

Ohashi, Kaoru, and Shinji Shimizu. 1073. "Some Problems of the International Comparative Study on Kinship Interactions and its Reconsiderations." [In Japanese]. *The Meiji Gakuin Sociology and Social Welfare Review.* 37:1–40.

Otani, Shinsuke. 1986. "Characteristic of Urban Voluntary Associations in Yokohama City." [In Japanese]. Pp. 59–89 in *Urbanization and Voluntary Associations,* edited by Noboru Ochi. Yokohama: Civic Culture Center at Yokohama City University.

Otani, Shinsuke. 1992. "Social Network Study of Five Cities in the Chugoku, Shikoku Regions of Japan: Survey Report and Questionnaire." *Matsuyama University Review* 3(6):149–183.

Otani, Shinsuke. 1993a. "Comparative Studies of Personal Networks between Japan and North America." *Matsuyama University Review.* 5(2):129–150.

Otani, Shinsuke. 1993b. "A Critical Review on Studies of Personal Networks in Japan." [In Japanese]. *Matsuyama University Review.* 5(3):239–254.

Otani, Shinsuke. 1995. *Personal Community Networks in Modern Cities.* [In Japanese]. Kyoto: Mineruba Press.

Park, Robert E. 1928. "Human Migration and the Marginal Man." *American Journal of Sociology* 33(6):881–893.

Seki, Takatoshi. 1980. "A Study on Kinship Relations of Urban Families." [In Japanese]. *Gendai Syakaigaku.* 7(2):3–37.

Simmel, Georg. 1890 [1976]. "The Intersection of Social Spheres." Pp.95–110 in *Georg Simmel: Sociologist and European,* edited by Peter Lawrence. Nairobi: Nelson.

Simmel, Georg. 1908 [1971]. "The Stranger." Pp. 143–149 in *Georg Simmel: On Individuality and Social Forms,* edited by Donald N. Levine. Chicago: University of Chicago Press.

Verbrugge, Lois M. 1977. "The Structure of Adult Friendship Choices." *Social Forces* 56(2):576–597.

Vogel, Ezra F. 1963. *Japan's Middle Class: The Salary Man and His Family in a Tokyo Suburb.* Berkeley: University of California Press.

Wellman, Barry. 1979. "The Community Question: The Intimate Networks of East Yorkers." *American Journal of Sociology* 84(5):1201–1231.

Wellman, Barry. 1982. "Studying Personal Communities.' Pp. 61–80 in *Social Networks and Social Structure,* edited by Peter Marsden and Nan Lin. Beverly Hills, CA: Sage.

Wellman, Barry. 1985. "Domestic Work, Paid Work, and Network." Pp. 159–191 in *Understanding Personal Relationships,* edited by Steve Duck and Daniel Perlman. London: Sage.

Wellman, Barry. 1988. "The Community Question Re-evaluated." Pp. 81–107 in *Power, Community, and the City,* edited by Michael Peter Smith. New Brunswick: Transaction Books.

Wellman, Barry. 1990. "The Place of Kinfolk in Personal Community Networks." *Marriage and Family Review* 15(1/2):195–228.

Wellman, Barry. 1992. "Men in Networks: Private Community, Domestic Friendships." Pp. 74–114 in *Men's Friendships,* edited by Peter Nardi. Newbury Park, CA: Sage.

Wellman, Barry, and Barry Leighton. 1979. "Networks, Neighborhoods and Communities." *Urban Affairs Quarterly* 14 (March):363–390.

Wellman, Barry, Peter J. Carrington, and Alan Hall. 1988. "Networks as Personal Communities." Pp. 130–184 in *Social Structures: A Network Approach,* edited by Barry Wellman and S. D. Berkowitz. Cambridge: Cambridge University Press.

Williams, Robin, Jr. 1964. *Ethnic Relations in American Communities.* Englewood Cliffs, NJ: Prentice-Hall.

Wilmott, Peter. 1987. *Friendship Networks and Social Support.* London: Policy Studies Institute.

Wireman, Peggy. 1984. *Urban Neighborhoods, Networks, and Families: New Forms for Old Values.* Lexington: Lexington Books.

Wirth, Louis. 1938. "Urbanism as a Way of Life.' *American Journal of Sociology* 44(July):3–24.

9

Using Social Networks to Exit Hong Kong

Janet W. Salaff, Eric Fong, and Wong Siu-lun

Background

On July 1, 1997, the red flag of the People's Republic of China was hoisted over Hong Kong as the British colony reverted to China. This looming event gave rise to great anxiety in Hong Kong for more than a decade. It was widely believed in the West that most Hong Kong families fled for political reasons. But, if that were the case, emigrants and nonemigrants would differ mainly by their political views, or by the economic backing to act on these views. Our study finds that this is not the case. Instead, emigrants and nonemigrants differ mainly by their social networks. Emigrants are linked abroad through kin and friends and other people close to them, while the nonemigrants have constructed few of these ties.

The Chinese value networks. As do Westerners (Wellman 1990), the Chinese rely on networks for quick help when they are under pressure, for daily needs, such as child-care and other practical help, and emotional support. Networks also affect decisions about major changes in life events, such as the decision to emigrate. The fund of daily support provided by kin is of great help where people feel uncertain about uprooting. But people use friendship ties as well. Friends can help in different ways from kin. That kin and friendship ties differ in the decision to emigrate is the topic of this chapter.

How Chinese families draw upon social networks when they decide to emigrate is an important area of research. From the study of Chinese social networks we can address several theoretical issues. First, we develop a class-based model of emigrant networks, because the social background of contemporary international migrants is diverse. A class-based model of emigration networks broadens our understanding of the ways that kinship networks shape migration decisions. The migration literature documents that people with kin abroad can migrate more easily, and that network migration is self-sustaining. Unfortunately, most of these studies only explore the migration decisions of poor, uneducated, and rural migrants from developing countries (see Massey et al. 1987).

Yet in recent years the immigrant population to the Western receiving countries has changed, and now kinship networks enter the migration decision in more complicated ways. The new immigrant population is composed of people from varied socioeconomic backgrounds, who are less homogeneous than in the past. They include the longstanding category of labor migrants who have little education and are poor, and who enter the new country to search for menial jobs. Next, a large number of immigrants are professionals from higher educational strata who seek occupations that will develop their careers and sustain their lifestyles. A large number of new immigrants are entrepreneurs who bring capital with them to invest in the new country. Finally, refugees may eventually become citizens.

The types of immigrants are diverse, and social networks shape their migration decisions in a number of ways. Although most research acknowledges this, few studies have tried to differentiate how people from different socioeconomic backgrounds look to others they know when they decide to migrate (Findley 1987). A study of the emigration decisions of Hong Kong Chinese is an excellent place to begin, because Hong Kong emigrants come from varied social backgrounds. Here we compare how working and middle classes structure their social networks. We look at the ways they draw upon these social networks when they decide to move across the seas.

As well, social network analysis mainly focuses on how people *actually* draw upon networks for support. Most studies on immigrants are retrospective, asking how kin networks helped them adjust. By showing how potential emigrants plan an immense change in *anticipation* of help from kin, we can broaden the scope of social network analysis.

Our main contribution is to contrast families that intend to emigrate from those that will not take that step. Among the ways they differ is in the networks that link them abroad. These families, drawn from various social groups, further differ among themselves. We will explore how the definition and use of these ties are distinct among families by social class.

To do so, we divide this chapter into three parts. The first part outlines a model of emigration, drawing on the discussion from literature on network analysis and immigration. In the second part, we test the model on a survey of Hong Kong respondents, who represent the typical new North American immigrants from Asia. These people were still living in Hong Kong when we met them. Some were making plans to emigrate, while others were not. We discuss how these people, from a range of socioeconomic backgrounds, perceive the role of networks in the decision to exit Hong Kong. By combining quantitative and qualitative analyses, we hope to give an in-depth discussion of how kinship networks enter migration decisions of people from a range of socioeconomic backgrounds.

The Impact of Networks on Migration

Social networks provide actual help for new immigrants that lowers the risks and increases the net returns of emigrating. Studying the migration of families from four communities in Western Mexico to the United States, Massey and his associates found that the first immigrants that settle in a new place face high costs (Massey et al. 1987; Massey and Espana 1987). However, these costs are reduced as more immigrants arrive and each builds a set of social networks. These social networks are crucial for newcomers to find a job or get economic support (Portes and Sensenbrenner 1993; Light 1972; Hugo 1981). As more migrants return to their home communities, they further solidify the social process, providing potential leavers with unique access to social and economic ties at their destination. When they first arrive in the United States, lower-class Mexican immigrants find a place to stay, a job, or borrow money from kin (Massey et al. 1987). This is also the case for Philippine and Indonesian rural migrants to Manila and Jakarta (Lopez and Hollnsteiner 1976; Temple 1974).

Social networks are also the major sources of information about the destination, allowing potential migrants to form pictures of a strange land that encourage them to move there. Grunig's (1971) research on Columbian peasants showed that the information flow from relatives and friends is crucial. Those who plan to migrate regard information from relatives and friends as a reliable basis for making a move. Studies of black migration from the American South to the North at the beginning of the century also found that personal letters and occasional visits of migrants back home brought news of excitement about the city and of job prospects, in turn inspiring more to move (Spear 1967).

However, not all networks serve the same functions. Various types of social networks have their own levels of closeness and support. Kinship networks contrast with other types of social networks because they can be very dense. If they are densely knit, kin can give money and share resources, which colleagues and neighbors rarely do (Wellman and Wortley 1990). Yet not all kin networks give concrete support. Bott (1957), who pioneered the study of personal networks, suggested that the family's social background greatly shapes its network structure, more specifically the density of networks. Because of their limited geographical and social mobility, lower-social-class families have strong kin ties. Applying this finding to international migration, the dense kin networks of the working class can help them in material ways and lower the costs of moving. As well, working-class people usually form friendships from similar social backgrounds who have limited social resources. Those who emigrate must themselves adjust to a harsh new environment. They cannot offer their working-class friends much help.

By contrast, because better off families move and change their jobs often, they do not have dense social networks that link neighborhood, work, and kin (Bott 1957). Their kin and friends tend to be more loosely linked. Because of their financial independence, middle-class immigrants do not require much material support when they arrive in a new country, but they do need information about good jobs, good neighborhoods, and schools. Here they can profit from the emotional support and useful information from colleagues, classmates, and other peers, network members generally connected to them by loose ties (Burt 1992; Granovetter 1982). For instance, in his study of emigrating Argentine physicians to the United States, Portes (1976) found that most had received encouragement and information from close medical colleagues abroad, not kin.

In short, we have outlined a framework to explain the social networks and migration decisions of people from a number of backgrounds. Working-class families expect their kin to give them financial support and concrete help, and those with emigrant kin are more likely to emigrate. In contrast, more affluent families do not depend on their emigrant kin to leave. But their friends can be useful for forging pathways to a job.

The Setting

Historical experiences nuance the Chinese use of networks. Before 1949, the Chinese state did not reach down to the lower levels of society. No lords demanded that vassals put fealty to the reign above that to their family. No powerful set of religious institutions competed with the family. Overseas Chinese who emigrated to foreign shores had even less chance to use formal political institutions. In the Chinese diaspora, people traveled widely looking for work. While most intended to return to China, few did so, creating links for further migration. As ethnic outsiders with no state of their own, they looked to kin they could trust for support. In a similar way as those who went to Singapore, San Francisco, or Thailand, as "outsiders" to the colonial state and its institutions, Hong Kong Chinese had to rely on kin and friends in political and economic dealings.

A British colony on the edge of China's Gwangdong province, Hong Kong was from the outset an immigrant city (Skeldon 1991; Kwong

1993). Following the victory of the Chinese Communist Party in 1949, over 1 million new immigrants arrived. Some brought machinery and know-how from Shanghai and other Chinese coastal cities, and formed a local entrepreneurial class that produced textiles, and later, garments. Others became low-cost labor. With these immigrants of diverse social backgrounds eager to begin their new lives and the sociopolitical events of later decades, Hong Kong became a prosperous node in international trade, "the most internationalized city in East Asia" (Kwong 1993, p. 146).

Hong Kong people lacked deep roots to the colonial city-state. As sojourners in their own city, they moved readily to places where they could find work, and Hong Kong became an emigrant city. The social class of postwar emigrants has varied over the years. This was partly due to changing Western immigration policies, but after a core of emigrants set up homes abroad, they sponsored others in their families when they could. The first wave of emigrants were mainly poor. The Western economies drew on unskilled immigrant workers, and Britain had not yet set up barriers to Commonwealth members. Poorly educated New Territories villagers left in large numbers to man British restaurants (Watson 1975). Gradually, the skills of those who went abroad changed. As Hong Kong society developed a strong middle class tied intellectually to Western nations, many sent their children abroad to study. The students often remained, and these links prompted more people to go back and forth.

In line with its need for more skilled workers, North American immigration policy shifted to stress human capital. In Canada after 1967 a point system was introduced that privileged applicants with needed skills and education, and which led the way to a middle-class brain drain. Thus, by the 1980s, as Hong Kong's uncertain prospects sparked ideas about leaving, Western immigration policies favored young, well-educated, English-speaking professionals, technicians, and managers with financial means (Richmond and Verma 1978; Kwong 1991; Wickberg et al. 1982).

People emigrate from Hong Kong for a number of reasons today. Foremost, we might think that political worries push people out of Hong Kong. It is true that many Hong Kong people are concerned about Chinese politics towards Hong Kong. All worry about corruption. The working class expected 1997 to usher in chaos, and the middle class feared the loss of property (Salaff and Wong 1994). Responding to this future political sea change, and wanting the skills and capital of Hong Kong people, some countries opened their immigration doors wider to Hong Kong people. About 60,000 Hong Kong Chinese emigrated in 1992, half to Canada. However, we find that, although political concerns are widespread, attitudes alone cannot determine who plans to exit and where they go.

Education and money also figure in who can exit Hong Kong. Although many Hong Kong people emigrate, they are not exempt from the stringent criteria that other immigrants face. Those of working age usually need a firm economic base to be acceptable. Thus, most Hong Kong emigrants need to be employable abroad and show that their educational, skill, and capital levels provide a sound economic base. Nevertheless, neither political concerns nor human capital determines who leaves and why they leave.

In addition to political concerns and economic ability to leave and be accepted abroad, we find that connections to the receiving countries forge crucial chains in international migration. Emigrants use their networks to leave Hong Kong. For one reason, since potential immigrants have to show that they will make good abroad, having kin sponsor them is one assurance to the authorities that they will do well. Family reunification is given credit in most receiving nations. The core circle of family members (parents and unmarried children) have priority, although members outside the inner circle can sponsor kin. This sets the stage for networks to help future immigrants. Further, networks include both kinship and friendship. There is considerable variation in who chooses these twin types of networks. Our research story focuses on how people from different class backgrounds access their resources to leave Hong Kong and to be received in the new land.

Method

Our study combines quantitative data from a large survey with qualitative data from a small number of in-depth interviews. The survey data of kinship networks and other factors associated with the emigration decisions of people from different social classes come from a large-scale representative survey of 1552 Hong Kong respondents, conducted in Hong Kong, in 1991.[1] The questionnaire gathered demographic and socioeconomic data, and questioned respondents on their family's plans to emigrate. The respondent was selected according to the random selection grid of each person over eighteen years old living in the household. Thus, the interviewer did not always choose the head of the household, and the respondent could be an adult offspring or the father of the household head who had retired and was living with his son's family. Use of these data to understand international migration decisions is legitimate because international migration is a household economic strategy that reflects a joint decision of the family, not solely an individual (Stark 1984). In particular, emigration decisions in Chinese society involve the whole family, even the extended family. Thus, the decision of any family member still represents the joint decision of the family. Further, these data reflect the characteristics of the general population in Hong Kong.[2]

The year after the survey, we interviewed thirty of the respondents about their social networks and emigration decisions. We were able to reinterview most annually from 1992 through 1997 to update our information. The qualitative interviews went further than the survey questionnaire and located the wider kin circles, friends, and colleagues of both husband and wife. In describing their views of the importance of networks in emigrating, and how networks enter into their plans, we discuss how they use contacts, and whether they feel people need networks to emigrate. We place the networks they use in the context of their lives. Here we focus on how social networks, which affect the job-search prospects in the new country, influence the emigration decision. We do not try to assess the entire range of family emigrant needs here, because finding a job usually ranks first and therefore is an important place to begin.

For the tables based on the survey population, we divided the respondents into four major social groups according to occupation. The affluent group includes managers and professionals. There are the petty bourgeois businesspeople. The lower-middle class consists mainly of white-collar workers. Finally, the working class is composed of menial and seasonal workers. We classified married respondents' households by the highest occupation of either spouse.[3]

In choosing the families for our qualitative study, we tried to locate the first ten from each class group that we could contact. We further sought to interview equal numbers of emigrant and nonemigrant households from each group. We have only three major social groups here, since we reclassified the petty bourgeois as either middle class or working class, based on their assets. There were two single men and twenty-eight married couples, and we categorized their households according to the highest paid occupation of either spouse. This was the husband in all cases but one. Sixteen households had applied for visas and fourteen had not.

We should take a moment to clarify our concepts. When asked, Chinese usually take kinship as referring to members of the nuclear family, and extend this to include patrilineal members. Nevertheless, in practice they will turn to the female line as well, to get resources quickly (Baker 1979; Salaff 1998). Hong Kong Chinese are especially likely to define meaningful kin broadly (Lau and Kuan 1988). Although we look principally at the ways Hong Kong families draw on their immediate relations within the nuclear family, we also take note of the help they seek from those related by blood or marriage outside their immediate circle, whether the male or female line. This is easier to do in the qualitative

TABLE 9.1   Average Kinship Ties by Emigration Status Controlling for Class

	Average Number of Kin Living Abroad		
	Emigrants	Nonemigrants	Average
Affluent class	0.61	0.87	0.67
Petty bourgeois	0.69	0.54	0.56
Lower middle class	0.53	0.50	0.50
Working class	0.72	0.36	0.38

cases, where we can ask each family a lot about who they recognize as related. Here, too, only the qualitative cases inquired systematically about friends and colleagues abroad.

We classify an *emigrant household* as one in which any member has actually submitted an immigration application form to a major Western nation. This classification has the advantage of measuring the actual migration actions taken by the household instead of their vague intentions to emigrate.

Networks and Emigration

Many Hong Kong families have kin abroad. Those we surveyed had a mean of 0.52 family members abroad, an average of one for every two households (Table 9.1). The working class has the fewest family members abroad and the affluent middle class the most. Emigrants average nearly twice the number of kin abroad as those who are not emigrants. In three of the four class groups, emigrants have more kinship ties overseas than do nonemigrant households.

But when we look at the variation in kin ties between emigrants and nonemigrants among the class groups, we find another trend. We find the most dramatic difference in the number of kinship ties between emigrant and nonemigrant households in the working class. The petty-bourgeois businessmen, mainly with family businesses, follow. The lower-middle class has a small difference, while the affluent middle class actually reverses the finding. Thus, the difference in kin ties abroad between emigrants and nonemigrants is greatest for the "familistic" social groups—the working class and petty bourgeois in family firms.

Previous studies of North American immigrants have found that immigrants tend to be between twenty and thirty years old (Jasso and Rosenzweig 1990), with low education, and single (Borjas 1990). The second set of factors consists of anticipation of employment and opportunities for a good education for their children abroad, and concern over the high cost of living and low quality of life at home. Finally, we include consideration of the political situation. How important was the widespread political uncertainty over Hong Kong's return to Communist China in 1997 in spurring emigration?

In reporting the household characteristics by emigration status, we relate the social and demographic features and the political and economic concerns of the adult respondent to the emigrant status of their households. The emigrants are more highly educated (Table 9.2). Whereas 84% of the nonemigrants have less than high school, 92% of the emigrants have at least completed high school. Further, the affluent dominate the emigrant, but not the nonemigrant, population. Emigrants are slightly younger than nonemigrants. Emigrants are as likely to be married as nonemigrants. However, their attitudes do differ somewhat: Emigrants are more concerned about politics, jobs, the environment, and education for their children in Hong Kong than nonemigrants. But these differences in attitudes are not statistically significant.

Our next step is to disentangle the full effect of kinship ties on emigration, controlling for: demographic factors (including age, education, and marital status), economic and social expectations, and political concerns. Table 9.3 suggests that there are great class differences in motives for emigration.[4] Yet these do not lie in political views. Although popular argument emphasizes the importance of political factors in the Hong Kong emigration wave, the analyses do not support these assumptions. The coefficient of political concerns is not statistically significant for any of the class groups. The working class may be concerned about the political future, but this concern is not by itself enough to propel them out of Hong Kong. As well, the greater the concern about their children's education and the more education they have themselves, the more likely a working-class family is to emigrate. Yet few of these same factors suggested in the literature much affect the emigration decisions of the affluent and middle classes. In sum, the analyses point out the overriding importance of kinship ties on emigration decisions for the working class, but not the middle classes. Middle-class families may not emigrate because they have kin abroad.

To learn why kinship ties are more important in the emigration plans of working-class than of middle-class families, we studied a smaller number of families over time. We wanted to learn whether there were systematic variations in our sample between emigrant and nonemigrant kin networks that lead abroad. In this smaller sample, we could be more precise about their emigrant kin, and moreover could talk with them about others who influenced them to emigrate. We have learned that emigrants have a wide range of kin abroad. To facilitate comparisons with nonemigrants, we enumerate here only those siblings who emigrated. Because we are interested in the siblings who form social networks with our respondents and who are "at risk" of emigrating from Hong Kong,

TABLE 9.2 Household Characteristics by Emigration Status

	Emigrants	Non-Emigrants	Total
Socioeconomic Variables			
Education			
University Education	9%	· 10%	10%
	(N = 51)	(N = 98)	(N = 149)
Post–high school technical	5%	6%	6%
certificate	(N = 30)	(N = 62)	(N = 92)
High school completion	78%	6%	32%
	(N = 434)	(N = 58)	(N = 492)
Less than high school	8%	67%	45%
	(N = 43)	(N = 660)	(N = 703)
Kindergarten only	0%	7%	0%
	(N = 0)	(N = 7)	(N = 7)
No schooling	4%	10%	7%
	(N = 2)	(N = 102)	(N = 104)
Social classes			
Affluent class	63%	30%	34%
	(N = 105)	(N = 334)	(N = 439)
Petty-bourgeois	10%	13%	12%
	(N = 16)	(N = 140)	(N = 156)
Lower-middle class	9%	11%	11%
	(N = 15)	(N = 125)	(N = 140)
Working class	19%	46%	42%
	(N = 32)	(N = 506)	(N = 538)
Demographic Variables			
Age (years)	36	41	40
Marital status			
Single	27%	23%	24%
	(N = 50)	(N = 315)	(N = 365)
Married	70%	67%	68%
	(N = 128)	(N = 920)	(N = 1048)
Separated	1%	2%	2%
	(N = 1)	(N = 24)	(N = 25)
Widowed	3%	8%	7%
	(N = 5)	(N = 105)	(N = 110)
Political and Economic Concerns			
Political situation	2.2	2.4	2.4
Employment opportunity	2.5	2.8	2.7
Quality of life	2.6	3.0	2.9
Education of children	2.5	3.0	2.9

NOTES: For political situation, the score represents an average of three questions: "Below are some political factors that may influence people's decision to emigrate or not. Please indicate the importance of each factor to you: a) Democratization in Hong Kong; b) political stability in Hong Kong; c) social stability of Hong Kong before and after 1997." For the questions regarding economic opportunity, quality of life, and education of children, respondents were asked how important each of these factors was to them. The scores ranged from 1 to 5: 1 was most important.

TABLE 9.3   Estimates of Logit Model of Selected Factors on Emigration Status

	Affluent Class	Petty Bourgeois	Lower-middle Class	Working Class
Socioeconomic Variables				
Education	0.03**	0.03**	0.03	0.02**
Demographic Variables				
Age	−0.01	−0.01	−0.02	0.00
Marital Status				
Single	−0.22	0.76	1.75	1.05
Married	−0.34	2.00	2.54	0.70
Separated	6.77		−2.71	−4.36
Network Ties				
Number of Family Members and Relatives living abroad	0.09	0.45**	0.36	0.38**
Political and Economic Concerns about Hong Kong				
Political Situation	−0.02	−0.38	0.21	−0.08
Employment Opportunity	−0.19	0.04	−0.02	−0.02
Quality of Life	0.01	−0.24	−0.50	0.11
Education of Children	−0.06	−0.56**	−0.34	−0.43**
Cost of Living	0.49**	0.68**	0.09	0.33**
Intercept	−2.92	−3.98	−3.47	−4.08
Log likelihood	305.21	91.194	171.383	262.932
χ^2	43.48	30.92	220.42	25.95
DF	11	10	11	11
N	506	132	189	602

$p^{**} < 0.05$
$p^{*} < 0.1$

we leave out from our calculations those who had never lived in Hong Kong, such as those in China or the Philippines. Our interviews revealed that siblings who live in China or Southeast Asia are not part of the networks leading to emigration to developed countries. Emigrants have more siblings who emigrated from Hong Kong than nonemigrants have (Table 9.4).

We also asked emigrant applicants whether they had other friends and colleagues who had already gone abroad. We expected that having emigrant friends would also propel our respondents outward. Those with friends and colleagues who had already emigrated could count on them for help or tips about life overseas. Those with friends who were applying could form a reference group of like-minded people, who would assure each other that it was all right to exit. We found that friends are important to future emigrants: thirteen of the sixteen applicants have friends, neigh-

TABLE 9.4   Emigrant Siblings of Emigrants and Nonemigrants

	Percentage of Emigrant Siblings of Total Number of Siblings
Emigrant respondents	
working class	36
lower middle class	37
middle class	51
Average (N = 194)	42
Nonemigrant respondents	
working class	12
lower middle class	8
middle class	26
Average (N = 125)	13

NOTES: These data are from the subsample of 30 respondents.

The total number of siblings refers to those that lived in Hong Kong before emigrating (see text).

bors, or coworkers who had emigrated and with whom they keep in touch. In contrast, nonemigrants had not kept in touch with acquaintances abroad. Indeed, few could think of any close friends who had emigrated. These findings, taken together with our survey material on a larger group of Hong Kong families, reveal the importance of looking further into the relations abroad of emigrant and nonemigrant families.

Working-class Ties

In Table 9.1 we saw that the emigrant kin of emigrant working-class households that were surveyed almost double those of nonemigrant working-class households. Emigrant working-class households have a mean of 0.7 relatives living abroad, while nonemigrants have a mean of 0.4 relatives. Indeed, having a greater number of relatives living abroad increases the likelihood that the working class will emigrate (Table 9.3, results of logistic regression).

The in-depth interviews confirm these findings from our survey. Working-class families emigrate with an eye to those kin who have already left. Their ties to kin had run deep even while they lived in Hong Kong. Kin assistance is widespread and many-stranded among these working-class Chinese. In the work world, kin help these families get a job or get trained. They work together or start a firm with kin. Although finding a job was the most common form of mutual help in the work world, kin help in other ways, as when a father gives his son capital to start a business. The small businesses of the working class greatly depend on kin as economic pillars. Moreover, in nearly all the families there is exchange of child-care: Relatives care for youngsters so that women and men can work.

There are also important material exchanges that do not have to do with work. Kin may have bought a house jointly or lived together. Non-material help, like advice, was often common, as was visiting and dining out together. Kin may help with daily chores.

Emigrants. Given the many ties of assistance among the working class in Hong Kong, we can understand why emigrants follow kin abroad. We met ten working-class families, of whom four applied to emigrate. Three sought to exit through kin support.

One route for people without wealth is emigration through joint family action. To even think of emigrating, their close kin have to offer them jobs. Such people are completely dependent on kin to be able to leave; they use the family links that have already been established as bridge-heads. Thus, a working-class family's emigration decision may flow from the family business in Hong Kong. We interviewed a traditional work-ing-class applicant, who depended entirely on the family business for a job, a home, and a visa out of Hong Kong. His father and three elder brothers ran a small frozen meat enterprise that supplied Chinese dim sum restaurants. The father is the formal head of the family, and the sons were like paid staff. Although each has a claim to the family property, none has any free capital to use on his own. The whole family made a concerted effort to establish themselves in Canada, aiming to avoid the chaos they expected 1997 to usher in and to leave their crime-ridden Hong Kong neighborhood. Their firm's fortunes were declining, and they were ready to wind it down. The family coordinated their man-power and funds, working closely as a unit. After emigrating, the family reestablished two businesses in a new Chinese settlement in suburban Toronto. With only middling education, they speak rudimentary English and mainly can find good work in the ethnic economy (Zhou 1992). One by one, the members of the family emigrated, until it came to our respon-dent, the fourth son. He submitted an immigration plan to the Canadian government based on his participation in the new family business. His plans depend entirely on densely knit relationships and agreements among brethren. Should one of the sons have a falling out or the family economic plans fall through, family entrepreneurs have no independent resources to succeed. Indeed, this has happened in this case, and our re-spondent's attempt to join his family firm has hit a snag. As a result, he remains in Hong Kong and has no other emigration outlet.

Having kin abroad not only helps people to find a job, it also provides practical help to emigrate. Siblings and in-laws may buy homes together in the new country, or they may put together an investment package to qualify for a visa. For instance, we spoke with a part-time restaurant helper, married to a truck driver, and the mother of two teenage daughters and an autistic son. Her elder brother sponsored her for an American visa and offered her a job. As family reunification was the legal basis for their application, she can only consider emigration because she expects to find work in her brother's Boston restaurant. This is similar to the earlier experience of others in her family:

> By working in Brother's restaurant kitchen, Father earned more than US$1,000 dollars a month. He said that he could earn as much in one month as he could working in China for several years! But now they are old. He does not work now. At first, my sister-in-law planned that Mother would live with her, because she needed someone to babysit her children, so she could work in the restaurant. But after a while, my mother did not want to continue. Living together is very difficult. So she and my father moved into a senior citizen's home. My brother doesn't need to support them. There is good welfare for the old people. Altogether, we are six brothers and sisters. I'm the youngest. All have applied, and some feel that they are almost successful. My third sibling is most enthusiastic about emigrating. She's a housewife and her husband works in a Chinese restaurant here. They have money. My elder brother said he would help her buy a house to prepare for her coming. He'll rent it out until she arrives.

Few working-class families have ever lived outside of Hong Kong, China, or Macau. They have little firsthand experience of other places, and they depend on those they know in foreign lands to give them information about life abroad. In most cases, these are kin. Those working-class folk applied to immigrate to one country only, largely because they could count on kin support in only one place. The disadvantage is that they have little option should they be turned down.

Those with fewer kinship links have fewer emigration alternatives, and thus are less likely to succeed. For example, one respondent works with his sister as a guard for the corrections department. Unmarried, without dependents, his sister has been accepted under the British right of abode scheme for members of the civil service in sensitive jobs. Upon her urging, our respondent also applied, but was rejected. Without other kin abroad, he has no alternative plan of action, and he just gave up the emigration effort.

Working-class families with kin abroad try to mobilize them in order to emigrate; three of the four emigrants sought to follow kin. The fourth, a shop clerk married to a bank messenger, did apply to emigrate to Singapore without any kin there. They filled out an application in the aftermath of the Tiananmen Square incident of June 4, 1989, when the Singapore government trumpeted its welcome to Hong Kong Chinese immigrants. They enjoy travel and pride themselves in having visited many areas of China. They were open to the chance to visit a new place, and thought they would check Singapore out. However, they had no response, most likely because they lacked the technical skills that the Singapore authorities have sought. It seemed to them that their application had been rejected. As they are without kin in Singapore, they know no one who can offer them a job there. They have been sanguine about this and have not banked on this chance to leave. As the wife told us, "Well, it was a whim, an opportunity presented itself to apply. We don't really expect to go there." In this case, having kin in Singapore would have been their main entry card. Without kin they do not realistically stand a chance to be accepted as new immigrants.

In these ways, migrant kin determine the exit of Hong Kong–based working-class families. Kin that already have a foothold abroad may have opened small businesses serving the ethnic community. If they can offer a job, their close kin can get the security they need to voyage to a strange port, and they can also have enough points for a visa. This is one of the few ways that working-class families can succeed in emigrating. For without jobs in the working-class community, they had little chance to survive in a distant world that was then in recession, and whose language they speak poorly.

Nonemigrants. The nonemigrant working-class families in our sample have fewer contacts abroad and are afraid to venture to where they have no links with people upon whom they can depend. For instance, ten years ago, a construction worker came from South China to Hong Kong illegally, following his elder brother, who had also arrived illegally. He sought refuge with his maternal uncle, a construction worker, who introduced him to the business. His elder brother before him also had been in construction and then branched off into the interior design business. The two brothers bought an apartment together, and they have sometimes worked together in construction. Proud of his close ties with Hong Kong kin, he argues:

> How can I emigrate? I don't know anyone. How could I find work? I have an uncle in the States, whom I've never seen. If I passed him in the street, I wouldn't recognize him. There's no feeling between us. He couldn't help me at all. Among my close relatives, nobody intends to emigrate, so we never talk about it. Among my workmates, it's the same story.

Ties with kin are partly an issue of definition. While he has a relative that lives in the U.S., he has no socially recognized link with him. He cannot mobilize those ties, and to him this is the same as "not knowing any-one" overseas.

The nonemigrant working class have not lived outside the region and have no personal ties abroad. With limited experiences abroad, without links outside of the Hong Kong region, they are unable to exit. Not only do they accept living in Hong Kong, many are satisfied with life there. Most important, they lack the meaningful kin ties that could influence them to want to exit or could help them leave the colony. The road stops in Hong Kong.

Although nonemigrant working-class families average fewer kin abroad than the emigrants, many have siblings abroad. When we asked those with siblings abroad why they have decided not to follow them, their answers were mainly that they did not have enough money and their siblings could not offer them work. For instance, a supermarket clerk, married to a butcher, told us about her sister and brother-in-law who had immigration papers for Singapore, sent abroad by the husband's company. Our respondent could not turn to them for support in any emigration effort of their own.

> They emigrated there just to have a visa. To have a protection from 1997. Ab-solutely, living in Hong Kong is better than Singapore. So, they wanted to earn as much as possible before 1997. My sister's husband is a surveyor. The way he went to Singapore is good. He was transferred by his employer, so that he had a job. Everything is under a plan. Then after ten months, his em-ployer transferred him back to Hong Kong. The whole family returned two days ago. Still, I think they want to emigrate eventually, and they bought a flat there. After they returned to Hong Kong, they rented it out. But I haven't thought about leaving myself. To emigrate you need a good financial situa-tion. At least, you need a large sum of money, to buy a house and give the children education. Then, you will not worry about having an income at least for the first few years. If you don't have that, emigration to another country will be very risky. Although we have relatives overseas, we'd have nothing else to rely on.

Although we expected that these working-class folk could count on friends and neighbors who had already emigrated to help them, we found that their friends do not influence them to leave. While they might find comfort in learning about the plans of these people to leave, they cannot lean too heavily on these contacts. Their friends, who have jobs like theirs, cannot give them a job that is good enough to warrant emi-grating, or a job that will get them a visa. Further, these working-class friends have their own kin to support.

The young clerk in a dry cleaning store, married to a bank messenger, had applied to emigrate to Singapore. She also keeps in touch with friends in North America, and has found a novel way to contact a former neighbor in Toronto and a former coworker in San Francisco. Last Christmas, she used the store fax to send greetings to these friends. "It's unusual and it only costs 10 Hong Kong dollars!" But she felt:

> We can't depend on our friends to emigrate. Actually, I don't like San Francisco very much. So I think I'd travel there, but not settle down. You know, it is difficult to find a job over there and we have few relatives and friends who could take care of us. If I had a lot of money, I might live there, as I would not need to bother about making a living. However I do not have much money. So I think my friend who has emigrated would not influence me.

A short-order cook, who retired as a shipboard chef, recalled how a friend once encouraged him to emigrate:

> In 1964, my friend in Australia offered me a job to work in his restaurant, but I declined. It's not worth it to earn a living in such a distant place. It's not easy to return to Hong Kong [to visit] because the airplane ticket is very expensive. Everywhere is more or less the same. You need to work to earn a living. Since I didn't do so in the past when I got that chance, which cost me nothing, I won't now. Now, emigration is quite expensive!

Even if the cook were to take up this offer today, the restaurant job that he turned down more than three decades earlier could not now get him a visa, since immigration policies have changed. It is rare that friends of working-class folk can offer them jobs abroad. It is mainly a family firm run by middle-class kin that can do so.

In sum, where dense ties provide links to jobs, which is a necessity to working-class emigrants, they might consider exiting. However, most have such dense ties only to working-class kin who cannot help them.

The Lower-middle and Affluent Middle Classes

While the middle class have more kin abroad than any other group, emigrants actually have fewer kin than nonemigrants. Similarly, while the lower-middle and affluent social classes with kin abroad are more likely to want to emigrate than those without kin, the relationship is not statistically significant when other variables are controlled (Table 9.3). This points to the contradiction that we study in this chapter: Although the affluent have more kin abroad than the working class, they do not depend on these kin to emigrate as much as do the working class.

The qualitative data suggest why emigrant kin can provide an opportunity for, yet do not determine, the exit of their Hong Kong–based middle-class families. It is true that the middle class also finds kin ties useful in Hong Kong and abroad. They use such ties to get emotional support, child-care from grandparents, and help in finding places to live. Yet they do not relocate abroad mainly to get such support from kin. In fact, it is hard for young parents in North America to get their kin to help with household chores and child-care (Man 1994). Nor are young middle-class parents always keen on having the grandparents teach their children. As for the middle-class elders, they cannot always get the daily on-going help from family that they used to get in Hong Kong (Ikels 1983).

What mainly sets the middle classes apart from the rest is that emigrant kin are not able to give them work abroad, for a number of reasons. Few have worked in family enterprises in Hong Kong. Rather, most have worked in complex bureaucracies where they have not had kin as coworkers. Their occupations are specialized, and many have degrees, diplomas, or certificates. It is hard for them to find such professional and semiprofessional jobs through kin. Finally, many in the higher reaches have enough money to set themselves up in jobs. Thus, while many have kin abroad, whom they want to live near, their kinship networks are not enough to propel these middle-class families outward.

Lower-middle-class Families

Our study contains ten lower-middle-class couples; all work in bureaucracies in the public and private sectors. Four families have applied to emigrate. The way they apply is distinctive. Most take advantage of their civil service status to apply as special emigrants to Singapore or England. Here they do not follow kinship ties, although some have kin abroad. A civil servant, policewoman, and a teacher pursued their political options and tried to get papers for the UK and Singapore. Kinship connections did not help them.

These three families have not used kin ties. They do have relatives abroad (Tables 9.1 and 9.4), but only one of the four applied through these channels. The reason that few use kin ties to emigrate is because their family economies are separate from kin. The lower middle class cannot depend on kin to emigrate, because the kinds of jobs they hold are not secured through kin. In Hong Kong, they rarely work with kin. And so while lower-middle-class emigrants have kin abroad, they are less likely to draw on these kin to emigrate. Rather, they depend on qualifications achieved through advanced study and legitimated by diplomas.

These middle-class employees are afraid that if they emigrate, they cannot get similar jobs abroad. Some work for Hong Kong government bodies, and they cannot qualify for the kind of work elsewhere. Those with customers know that their work depends on local contacts. None have the necessary licenses or certification to start again in their lines of work. Those who are semiprofessionals would have to compete in the North American market, and they worry that North American ethnic politics would create hardships for them as employees. For instance, a nurse has heard that foreign hospitals gave immigrant nurses the hard and dirty jobs. The situation is similar for those of somewhat higher class status. None could qualify easily for the same level of job abroad, and those who are middle-aged are too advanced in their careers to try a new line of work.

Hong Kong semiprofessionals and other lower-middle-class families earn too little for most investment categories of Canadian immigrants, which grants residence to families investing C$250,000 (around US$160,000). (Other countries have similar programs.) They lack the higher education, specialized training, and funds to qualify as "independent" immigrants to Canada and Australia, the countries to which most Hong Kong people emigrate, and where friends and relatives live. Since they have little capital, they cannot set themselves up in business abroad.

They have enjoyed a spurt in their incomes in recent years, which they fear they cannot match abroad. Partly this is because both spouses work. In most lower-middle-class couples we interviewed, both husband and wife work to maintain a solid household economy. In eight of the couples, wives earn wages, as civil servant, police clerk, teacher, factory worker, nurse, and cleaning lady. While only two are high-earners, wives are proud of their input to the household income, and worry that they cannot get such jobs abroad.

Lacking property, these lower-middle-class couples did not fear that their assets would be confiscated when the Communists took over in 1997. Comparing their current improved economic position against past poverty, most are hopeful about their future in Hong Kong. Although they have few grand economic hopes for themselves, they are not eager to reject the solid living standard they enjoy in Hong Kong for an uncertain life abroad. These nurses, technicians, civil servants, assistant engineers and school teachers earn good salaries and look forward to promotions in Hong Kong through fixed steps on career ladders. They have no extra savings, and they fear that if they exit, they could not get their retirement pensions. Thus, without the promise of equivalent jobs abroad, they are loath to leave.

Only one of these lower-middle-class couples used its kinship ties in an application to immigrate. A middle-aged telecommunications technician and his wife, a nurse, have kin in Canada and Australia. The wife first applied to immigrate to join her sisters in Canada, but was rejected. Australia turned the couple down as well. They then tried to emigrate to

New Zealand, thinking it would be easier from there to get into Australia. With two of his brothers, the technician organized an investment package for the occasion. But the jerry-built firm did not pass official scrutiny, and they were compelled to abandon their immigration goal. That the family did not have enough resources to convince the authorities of three countries supports our point that if their kin hold similar positions, they cannot materially help lower-middle-class couples to emigrate.

Unable to get jobs in their line of work from kin, the lower-middle class use other channels. A civil servant status helps the most, because Singapore and England remain options for those who have quasi-political civil servant jobs. We interviewed a woman who is a clerk in the police force, whose husband had been a Hong Kong constable, and is working in a Manchester, England, karate studio. As a young man, her husband had studied karate in his uncle's martial arts studio. He then studied with the instructor of the world-famous martial arts expert Bruce Lee, became proficient, and began to teach in a community center. He later joined the police force. While at a training course, he met a British constable, who had come to Hong Kong hoping to meet Bruce Lee's coach and train with him. Our respondent made the necessary introductions. In early 1989, the British constable invited our Hong Kong respondent to Manchester to teach in his studio and arranged for him to have working papers.

This emigrating couple may be seen as a deviant case to the lower-middle class we met, for they obtained help from a combination of friends, kin, and the bureaucracy. The husband had been close to his kin in Hong Kong. He trained in the martial arts with his uncle; he had initially bought his Hong Kong flat together with his younger sister. His sister also traveled to Manchester to complete a course of study; her brother and his karate students made the arrangements. Our respondent received concrete help in finding work abroad from a coworker. But in the end, because friendship was not enough to qualify him and his family for a passport, he and his wife took the crucial emigration step through the wife's civil service connection. In the wake of the June 4, 1989, Tiananmen Square incident the constable became afraid of remaining in Hong Kong after it reverted to China. Still a member of the correctional services, his wife qualified for the right of abode in England for herself, with eligibility extended to her husband. She and their son have emigrated to Manchester to join her husband.

Those who have no kin abroad are reluctant to leave. But even with kin abroad, those holding modest salaried posts may not join them. They worry that they cannot easily fit into an enterprise that their foreign kin might run. If the work relationship falters, they will be left without an independent base of their own and no economic recourse. Should the jobs that kin offered them not work out, they could find no other suitable work.

Indeed, these lower-middle-class workers pride themselves on being independent. The main form of help kin give each other in Hong Kong is to lend money or give it outright, such as in buying a house or paying for a sibling's schooling. People pool their resources to support their older parents. However, they do not consider giving or receiving money as a gift, such as a wedding gift, as creating dependency on kin.

A land inspector, who is married to a part-time sewing-machine operator, decided not to emigrate, even though his niece's family asked him to join her in moving to Australia. His relatives offered him a job in a firm they hoped to open. He refused, because he felt that his work as a civil servant was stable, and he did not want to depend on other people and receive any advantage from them.

> I told my niece I wouldn't go. Her husband is a professor of pharmacy in USA. But they live in Taiwan. He is doing some research and patented a new medicine. He always goes to different places to deliver lectures. They are very rich. They want to open a pharmacy in Australia, and asked me to go there to do some clerical job. But I don't want to rely on my relatives. I am independent. I don't want to depend on them and receive their help. On the other hand, I will lose my pension if I resign. After consideration, I decided not to emigrate.

Affluent Middle-class Families

Although Table 9.1 shows that affluent emigrants have more kin living abroad than the nonemigrants, the logistic regression in Table 9.3 shows that the effect of kin living abroad on emigrant decisions is minimal and statistically insignificant. The affluent class includes businessmen and well-trained professionals. Although one of the ten we interviewed works alongside kin in a flourishing family firm, the others have little occupational contact with kin. Regardless of whether they work closely with kin or not, they seek emigration in similar ways that are mainly independent of kin.

Although the eight affluent middle-class families who have visas to exit Hong Kong are technically "emigrants," only four have used them to emigrate, and two of those have returned to work in Hong Kong. The main response was hesitation to emigrate unless the 1997 change of regime precipitates a crisis. Their visas are for "insurance purposes." Indeed, several have applied for papers to immigrate to more than one country, revealing their limited commitment to exit Hong Kong.

Only one, an unmarried member of a family with sisters living in Alberta, Canada, was granted a visa in the family reunification category. The rest applied to immigrate under the business or "other independent" categories, or as the right of abode granted to civil servants and civic leaders who were felt to be at risk after 1997 because of their role in the colonial administration. While several of these affluent respondents have visas to places where they have kin, they are not economically dependent on these kin, for they can immigrate as businessmen or independently, without their kin's sponsorship. The affluent, with their own channels for immigration, can choose not to depend on emigrant kin for jobs or money. Instead, they are more likely to seek help from networks of schoolmates and former colleagues.

Although their well-placed kin living abroad can offer positions to those they sponsor, these affluent respondents do not depend on these jobs. To be sure, some use offers of convenient "paper" jobs to satisfy the requirements of the immigration authorities, but they do not actually expect to take up the jobs so offered. For instance, a manager of the computer section of an investment bank has a wide range of choices and expects to be offered a visa to the United States. He has been granted residence in Singapore, although he does not plan to exit unless civil strife erupts in Hong Kong. Having his brother offer him a job is also part of his plan. He is close with this brother, whose young son lives with him and his parents.

> I applied for the right of residence in Singapore in 1989 and just recently renewed it. It will expire in 1999. I've got the right, but I have done nothing yet besides gaining the principal approval. I need to immigrate with the letter of employment. My brother will also go with his wife and child. Elder Brother became a waiter in a Chinese restaurant when he was 12 and finished only primary school. Later he became a manager. Then ten years ago, he opened his own restaurant with investments from other partners. There are branches in China, Australia and Singapore. They are expanding the business rapidly. Any one of his companies can offer me a job at short notice. As I understand from those policies, there is no regulation about what kind of job you need to get. It doesn't have to match your technical abilities. You just need to have a job offer, that's about it, and you can get to go.

Well-established applicants do not want to take help if it shows friends and relatives they are "needy," because many feel quite comfortable in Hong Kong. Thus, while many have kin abroad, the affluent do not feel beholden to them. They tell us that their decision to emigrate does not turn on having kin abroad. Businessmen with family firms in Hong Kong have their own fund of resources and do not count on kin abroad for daily support. They would be embarrassed to be seen in this way, for depending on kin to emigrate is the same as having poor business acumen. Middle-class emigrants who ask for help from their kin abroad often feel placed in the position of a supplicant. Many are too proud to be seen asking for help when they do not need to. They dislike what they refer to as "depending on" kin, or having kin "depend on" them.

In another instance, the brother and sister of an estate manager have emigrated, as have his wife's sisters. His sister, who had worked in China, convinced the entire family that life in Hong Kong under the Communists would be hard. Even in this case, the process of emigration does not greatly depend on kin. He says that although the family shares opinions, apart from this, "the issue of emigration is just like religion, we talk little about it. We all have our own families, we should handle our problems ourselves independently." Our respondent's family received some moral support and a bit of practical help from kin in their quest to emigrate. His wife and son visited her sister to see if they could acclimatize to Toronto. Her brother-in-law drove them around to look at neighborhoods and houses to buy. But they did not get economic help from kin in the emigration process. Nor would they, in turn, assist her sister and brother-in-law, who are returning to Hong Kong. Our respondent family will get some help in adjusting abroad, such as finding a place to live, if they decide to emigrate. But that level of help is not much, and so, like others in their class, they say that their decision to emigrate does not depend on kin.

Just as many middle-class emigrants are reluctant to seek help from kin, not all kin want to be involved in helping them to immigrate. Kin may not even recognize the bond if the tie is weak and if there have not been any exchanges between them. On their part, kin on distant shores seem to fear they cannot legitimately get supplicants off their rolls once mutual aid begins, and are reluctant to extend help. Many affluent Hong Kong Chinese are concerned that if they recognize that kin have claims on them, they will be supporting these kin for a long time. Hence, while many do assist kin, others may not, or may do so in ways that are unacceptable to the recipients. If their kin help them to immigrate, families worry they will owe their kin too much.

Former work colleagues who had emigrated were more important than kin in attracting a site engineer and his wife, a software saleswoman, to Canada. "Compared with Australia, I have got more friends and some uncles in Canada," said the wife. When we further asked how closely they keep in contact with their uncles, she was silent for a few seconds, and the engineer mentioned they do not keep in touch. His wife explained, "My husband does not welcome people's help" because he does not wish to depend on help from kin. Furthermore, when they reluctantly contacted his Canadian relatives in order to increase their immigration points, the relatives refused to recognize this appeal for help. "We have cousins in Vancouver and Toronto, but our relatives are not useful. They didn't even answer my fax. They are afraid if they get involved, they can never get rid of us. Friends are more reliable." In the end, this engineer got a visa as an independent immigrant, and his relatives did not help at all.

The kinship contacts of these affluent couples are spatially and socially spread out. Most have emigrant kin in many different countries. They are not all tied tightly to their kin contacts. But they also have other resources. Friends, colleagues, and classmates are crucial.

All the middle-class families that would emigrate have kept in contact with friends abroad, and they have the most extensive circles of friends who will emigrate. They keep in touch with colleagues who have been eligible to leave Hong Kong, and they also maintain contacts with classmates who have left. These loosely textured "weak links" are most characteristic of the better educated and well-off who maintain contact with their classmates years after they finish school. The Hong Kong middle class have struggled to complete school by passing entry and school-leaving tests. They are from a school system that selects students rigorously at a young age, but does not put them in a position of competing against classmates to remain in school. Many in our sample have gone through postsecondary education in part-time evening schools. Their schoolmates have been through a lot with them, as they cooperated, not competed, when studying. Because of this shared travail, they feel they can trust and depend on their schoolmates. For instance, the engineers in our sample received their training part time in the Building Trades courses given in Hong Kong Polytechnic. For six years, they went to school several nights a week after work. That grueling stint cemented ties that still bind a decade later.

Affluent emigrants feel that these emigrant friends are important, and sometimes more than emigrant kin. Depending on classmates for help is common for our middle-class respondents. Friends are already established and can give the newcomer a first job. The job can be permanent, or if it does not work out, it helps tide them over while the new immigrant settles in and learns the ropes. Further, those classmates in the same trade can give the newcomer information that leads to a job (Granovetter 1974; see also Chapter 7). The affluent do not feel that this is a form of dependence, for they have their own funds and many contacts to help them.

A managing director of a factory has obtained visas from several countries. Although his sister lives in Canada, he has excluded that country as an immigration possibility. "We haven't even bothered to visit Toronto. It's too far for our children to travel there, and we don't like the weather," his wife said. "If we haven't even bothered to visit her, how could we want to live there?" Instead, they chose Singapore as their destination, because it is a place where the managing director knows many classmates and people he has met through business. Singapore is also closer than Toronto to their China-based business. The family has already bought a house there as part of their immigration package. Another of the managing director's brothers will immigrate to Singapore as a teacher, but our respondent claims he is not drawn by this relation. He chose to apply for Singapore papers because of the flexible immigration conditions, and because his classmates there can help him work out his business arrangements.

The site engineer, who received his diploma in Hong Kong Polytechnic, is employed by a large Hong Kong construction firm. On the side, he has opened a small interior design firm, with classmates as shareholders. Yet another polytechnic classmate immigrated to Vancouver: "I bought my Vancouver (Canada) house there with his help. I never even went there; he helped me care for it. Then when I was ready to sell it, he helped me too. My classmate told me not to immigrate because the economy for construction is so bad. But if I do immigrate, I'll probably work with him at the start." The middle class see friends' offers of jobs as one possible strategy that they can leave or take up if conditions work out.

When middle-class men describe working with former classmates, it is clear they are thinking of egalitarian relationships. They do not feel that by agreeing to work together they are depending on friends. Because it is understood that each side is ready to put up capital, such relationships with friends do not make them feel like they are getting handouts. Classmates know each other's skills and talents. For this reason, many future middle-class emigrants say that friends more than kin can help them immigrate.

Implications

There are many social-class differences in the Hong Kong Chinese use of networks, and these begin before they leave home. We have stressed job connections between kin. We have argued that finding work abroad is important for all but the young and elderly who plan to emigrate. In planning to go abroad, the Hong Kong people we interviewed think ahead from a position of strength. Most feel that they have accomplished much in Hong Kong, and it would be hard to duplicate their success abroad. So they cast ahead in their minds to how they can establish themselves well elsewhere. Some will depend on kin to help them with jobs when they emigrate. But not all. Depending on kin for support seems rooted in class and other structural features.

The working class usually draw on personal ties to find jobs, and many work with kin in Hong Kong. Working-class immigration applicants perceive that a job offer is crucial for them to survive at their destination. When they emigrate, they will not have the money to live on without working. Thus they must get a job right away in the new country. Lacking cultural capital (language and contacts), working-class immigrants are also likely to look for jobs that can be supplied by the ethnic and kin enclave (Zhou 1992). Having kin from similar backgrounds should be a boon and not a problem in learning about those jobs they can get. The shape of their kin networks further helps them out. They can call upon densely knit kinship networks for help adjusting to the new environment. Strong ties, most characteristic of working-class kinship networks, ensure that kin actually come through with jobs and give material help as well. In contrast, their friends cannot promise such help abroad. The friendships that the working class had were usually forged in the jobs they held, but they usually have not been proprietors of establishments with enough resources to extend to old friends. Indeed, their friends may be struggling themselves in the new climate.

By contrast, few lower-middle class, semiprofessionals, or affluent established professionals with certificates, diplomas, or degrees find work through kin while living in Hong Kong. Many are employed in specialized bureaucracies and their kin may not be well placed to give them the kind of work for which they have spent many years training. Yet the lower-middle class and affluent families differ in some key ways. Lower-middle-class families have little savings. By contrast, the affluent do not need immediate financial support when they arrive in a new country, for they bring money with them. What the lower-middle class and the affluent both need most is to find positions in their lines of work. Close kin may not be able to give them such job information. Indeed, getting a job from a person with whom they are densely tied is likely to give them poor information (Granovetter 1982; Burt 1992; Calzavara 1983). Such information is spread best over sparsely knit networks of classmates.

The affluent tell us of the value of having networks of weak ties abroad if they seek to immigrate to a new land. For this reason, they keep track of their classmates and exchange information with them, whether or not they intend to emigrate. If they do decide to leave Hong Kong, they are likely to look up classmates and former colleagues.

In sum, we find that kinship networks affect the migration decisions of families from lower socioeconomic backgrounds because they need material help. People expect to receive basic financial support and have other direct, immediate needs met by those densely tied to them in many-stranded relationships. These are likely to be kin. By contrast, those from higher socioeconomic levels may choose to immigrate to a foreign city because they have family there. Yet it is not economic help that their kin extend. Kin abroad can offer them a harbor, by giving them information about housing and schools. But kin may not be the only ones able to do this (see Wellman 1990), and the affluent emigrants are less directly affected by kinship networks when they plan to leave Hong Kong. They are as likely to be affected by friendship networks that may help them look for jobs in the new country.

Our findings suggest that future analyses of international migration decisions should explore the kinds of situations people are leaving from and the kinds of capital people bring with them. There are some without high income and education, and their only resources are in kinship ties. As they are unlikely to have exchanged resources with friends and neighbors, they cannot draw upon these resources when they leave Hong Kong. Given the current prosperous climate for most of the working class in Hong Kong, those who lack kinship ties abroad will not plan to emigrate. In contrast, those with money, education, and other cultural capital like the English language also have a past of exchanging favors and resources, such as helping out friends or even investing in their friends' enterprises. These are more likely to spread their contacts widely when they seek to emigrate.

Thus it is useful to distinguish between migrants with low and those with high income and education. We need to look for the structural basis of network contacts. Most models of international migration note that the poor follow their close kin to a new country. They live with these kin, find a job in the ethnic enclave, and may not have to learn another tongue. In short, they find refuge in what has been called an institutionally complete ethnic community. These factors apply to the working-class emigrants of past years (such as Mexico, as found by Massey et al. 1987) more than to the affluent and middle classes that have been leaving Pacific Rim countries for political or professional reasons, who have far more choices. Even if we do attend to the new migrants, future studies should venture away from a modified push-pull economic analysis or the study of attitudes. We must consciously compare structural components of networks in the study of international migration.

Notes

We thank the following bodies for financial support: Hong Kong Universities Grants Association; The Canada-Hong Kong Project, Joint Centre on Asian Pacific Studies, University of Toronto/ York University; Initiatives Fund, Institute for International Programmes, University of Toronto; Office of Research Services, University of Toronto; and Centre of Urban and Community Studies, University of Toronto. Barry Wellman and Ivan Light, Department of Sociology, UCLA, gave intellectual support for our exploration into how networks connect international migrants.

1. A total of 3098 addresses were randomly sampled with the help of the Census and Statistics Department in Hong Kong. Trained interviewers visited each address. They randomly interviewed only one household even if there was more than one household at the address. A total of 1595 interviews were successfully completed. However, 43 interviews contained inconsistent information. These interviews were dropped to increase reliability, leaving 1552 interviews for the final analysis.

2. A comparison of the demographic characteristics of the respondents and the general demographic characteristics in the 1991 Hong Kong Population Census finds that distributions of sex, age, marital status, education, and occupation are highly similar. However our survey sampled fewer of the very wealthy than are found in the census. It is easier for the affluent to avoid a university interviewer than a Census Department interviewer who has more resources and the mandate of the law.

3. In this analysis, we used occupation as a proxy of social class. Although we depend on only one indicator, this measure avoids introducing less reliable proxies, such as education and income in the classification. Many of Hong Kong's successful businessmen are not highly educated. Promotions to senior positions in many large and small corporations are based on experience, kinship and personal connections, and performance, as much as educational levels. In addition, many respondents are reluctant to report their actual income. As a result, neither education nor income is a reliable indicator of the social class of the household.

However, using occupation to categorize social class also creates problems. First, the questionnaire included managers as a response category, yet we do not know the size of firm—is it a family firm or a large *hong*? The category "business managers" represents a wide range of income distributions with the majority (72%) in the low income groups (earning under HK$20,000 per month). Most are proprietors of market stalls or small family businesses. Next, we cannot identify whether the manager is a business owner or employee. To avoid confusion in the interpretation of results related to small-business managers, we separate this group in our analysis of the survey data into the petty bourgeoisie category. This problem of classification does not arise in the qualitative case study, however, where we had more information about each family.

4. We employed logistic regression in Table 9.3 because the dependent variable is a dichotomous variable, that is, whether each household is emigrant or nonemigrant. The technique lets us estimate directly the probability of an event occurring. Table 9.3 displays coefficients that measure the effects of each independent variable on the logit of probability of emigration for each social class.

References

Baker, Hugh D. R. 1979. *Chinese Family and Kinship*. New York: Columbia University Press.

Bodnar, John, Robert Simon, Michael P. Weber. 1982. *Lives of Their Own: Blacks, Italians, and Poles in Pittsburgh, 1900–1960.* Champaign-Urbana: University of Illinois Press.

Borjas, George J. 1990. *Friends or Strangers: The Impact of Immigrants on the US Economy.* New York: Basic Books.

Bott, Elizabeth. 1957. *Family and Social Network; Roles, Norms, and External Relationships in Ordinary Urban Families.* London: Tavistock Publications.

Boyd, Monica. 1989. "Family and Personal Networks in International Migration: Recent Developments and New Agendas." *International Migration Review* 23(3):638–671.

Burt, Ronald. 1992. *Structural Holes: The Social Structure of Competition.* Cambridge, Mass.: Harvard University Press.

Calzavara, Liviana Mostacci. 1983. "Social Networks and Access to Jobs: A Study of Five Ethnic Groups in Toronto." Research Paper 145. University of Toronto, Centre for Urban and Community Studies, November.

De Jong, Gordon F., Ricardo Abad, Fred Arnold, Benjamin Carino, James Fawcett, and Robert Gardner. 1983. "International and Internal Migration Decision Making: A Value-Expectancy Based Analytical Framework of Intentions to Move from a Rural Philippines Province," *International Migration Review,* 17(3):470–484.

Findley, Sally E. 1987. "An Interactive Contextual Model of Migration in Ilocos Norte, The Philippines." *Demography* 24(2):163–190.

Granovetter, Mark. 1974. *Getting a Job. A Study of Contacts and Careers.* Cambridge, MA. Harvard University Press.

Granovetter, Mark. 1982. "The Strength of Weak Ties: A Network Theory Revisited." Pp. 105–130 in *Social Structure and Network Analysis,* edited by Peter V. Marsden and Nan Lin. Beverly Hills, CA: Sage.

Grunig, James. 1971. "Communication and Economic Decision Making Processes of Columbia Peasants," *Economic Development and Cultural Change* 19:580–597.

Hugo, Graeme. 1981. "Village-Community Ties, Village Norms, and Ethnic and Social Networks: A Review of Evidence from the Third World." Pp. 186–224 in *Migration Decision Making,* edited by Gorden F. De Jong and Robert W. Gardner. New York: Pergamon Press.

Ikels, Charlotte. 1983. *Aging and Adaptation: Chinese in Hong Kong and the United States.* Hamden, CT.: Archon Books.

Jasso, Guillermina, and Mark Rosenzweig. 1990. *The New Chosen People: Immigrants in the United States.* New York: Russell Sage.

Kwong, Paul C. K. 1991. "Emigration and Manpower Shortage." Pp. 297–338 in *The Other Hong Kong Report, 1990,* edited by Richard Y. C. Wong, Joseph Y. S. Cheng. Hong Kong: The Chinese University Press.

Kwong, Paul C. K. 1993. "Internationalization of Population and Globalization of Families." Pp. 147–174 in *The Other Hong Kong Report, 1993,* edited by Choi Po-king and Ho Lok-sang. Hong Kong: The Chinese University Press.

Lau Siu-kai. 1985. *Society and Politics in Hong Kong.* Hong Kong: The Chinese University Press.

Lau, Siu-kai, and H. C. Kuan. 1988. *The Ethos of the Hong Kong Chinese.* Hong Kong: The Chinese University Press.

Light, Ivan H. 1972. *Ethnic Enterprise in America.* Berkeley: University of California Press.

Lopez, M. E., and Mary Hollnsteiner. 1976. "People on the Move: Migrant Adaptation to Manila Residence." Pp. 227–250 in *Philippine Migration Decision: Papers and Proceedings of Experts' Meeting,* edited by Rodolfo A. Bulatao. Makati: Population Center Foundation.

Man, Guida. 1994. Paper presented at the 89 annual meeting of the American Sociological Association, Los Angeles, CA. August, 8, 1994.

Massey, Douglas S., Rafael Alarcon, Jorge Durand, and Humberto Gonzalez. 1987. *Return to Aztlan: The Social Process of International Migration from Western Mexico.* Berkeley: University of California Press.

Massey, Douglas S., and Felipe Garcia Espana. 1987. "The Social Process of International Migration." *Science* 237:733–738.

Portes, Alejandro. 1976. "Determinants of the Brain Drain." *International Migration Review* 10:489–508.

Portes, Alejandro, and Julia Sensenbrenner. 1993. "Embeddedness and Immigration: notes on the Social Determinants of Economic Action,." *American Journal of Sociology* 98(6):1320–1351.

Richmond, Anthony H., and Ravi P. Verma. 1978. "The Economic Adaptation of Immigrants: A New Theoretical Perspective. *International Migration Review* 12(1):3–38.

Salaff, Janet. 1998. "The Gendered Social Organization of Migration as Work." *Asian and Pacific Migration Journal* 6(3–4):317–342.

Salaff, Janet, and Wong Siu-Lun. 1994. "Exiting Hong Kong: Social Class Experiences and the Adjustment to 1997. Pp. 205–250 in *Inequalities and Development,* edited by Lau Siu-kai, Lee Ming-kwan, Wan Po-san, and Wong Siu-lun. Hong Kong: Hong Kong Institute of Asia-Pacific Studies, The Chinese University of Hong Kong

Skeldon, Ronald. 1991. "Emigration, Immigration and Fertility Decline: Demographic Integration or Disintegration?" Pp. 259–274 in *The Other Hong Kong Report, 1991,* edited by Sung Yun-wing and Lee Ming-kwan. Hong Kong: The Chinese University Press.

Spear, Allan H. 1967. *Black Chicago: The Making of A Negro Ghetto, 1880–1920.* Chicago: The University of Chicago Press.

Stark, Oded. 1984. "Migration Decision Making: A Review Article." *Journal of Development Economies.* 14:251–259.

Sung, Yun Wing. 1991. *The China-Hong Kong Connection: The Key to China's Open-Door Policy.* Cambridge: Cambridge University Press.

Temple, G. P. 1974. *Migration to Jakarta: Empirical Search for a Theory.* Ph.D. Dissertation. Madison: University of Wisconsin.

Watson, J. L. 1975. *Emigration and the Chinese Lineage: The Mans in Hong Kong and London.* Berkeley: University of California Press.

Wellman, Barry. 1990. "The Place of Kinfolk in Personal Community Networks", *Marriage and Family Review* 15(1/2):195–228.

Wellman, Barry, and Scott Wortley. 1990. "Different Strokes from Different Folks: Community Ties and Social Support." *American Journal of Sociology* 96(3): 558–588.

Wickberg, Edgar, and Harry Con. 1982. *From China to Canada: A History of the Chinese Communities in Canada.* Toronto: McClelland and Stewart, in association with the Multiculturalism Directorate.

Wong, Thomas W. P., and Tai-lok Lui. 1992. "From One Brand of Politics to One Brand of Political Culture." Hong Kong: Institute of Asia Pacific Studies, The Chinese University of Hong Kong, Occasional Paper No. 10.

Zhou, Min. 1992. *Chinatown: The Socioeconomic Potential of an Urban Enclave.* Philadelphia, Temple University Press.

10

Net-Surfers Don't Ride Alone: Virtual Communities as Communities

Barry Wellman and Milena Gulia

Hope, Hype, and Reality

Can people use the Internet to find community? Can online relationships between people who never see, smell, or hear each other be supportive and intimate?

The debate fills the Internet, the airwaves, and especially the print media. Enthusiasts outnumber critics, for as the prophet Jeremiah discovered millennia ago, there is more immediate reward in praising the future than in denouncing it. Unfortunately, both sides of the current debate are often Manichean, presentist, unscholarly, and parochial.

The *Manicheans* on either side of this debate assert that the Internet either will create wonderful new forms of community or will destroy community altogether. Dueling dualists feed off each other, using the unequivocal assertions of the other side as foils for their own arguments. Their statements of enthusiasm or criticism leave little room for the moderate, mixed situations that may be the reality. The up-to-the-minute participants in this breathless debate appear to be unaware that they are continuing a century-old controversy about the nature of community, albeit with new debating partners. There is little sense of history.

Brave New Net World?

Enthusiasts hail the Net's potential for making connections without regard to race, creed, gender, or geography (Van den Boomen 1998). As Amanda Walker asserts online:

Every advance in communication changes the nature of reality as we experience it. . . . The Internet is yet another revolutionary method of communication. For the first time in the history of the world, I can have an ongoing, fast-moving conversation with people regardless of their physical location, schedule, or other such constraints. . . . The world is changing, and we're the ones that are doing it, whether we realize it or not.[1]

Phil Patton similarly asserts that "computer-mediated communication . . . will do by way of electronic pathways what cement roads were unable to do, namely connect us rather than atomize us, put us at the controls of a 'vehicle' and yet not detach us from the rest of the world" (1986, p. 20). John Perry Barlow, cofounder of the Electronic Frontier Foundation, goes further in prophesying the radical and positive social transformation that the Net will bring about:

With the development of the Internet, and with the increasing pervasiveness of communication between networked computers, we are in the middle of the most transforming technological event since the capture of fire. I used to think that it was just the biggest thing since Gutenberg, but now I think you have to go back farther. (p. 36) . . . In order to feel the greatest sense of communication, to realize the most experience . . . , I want to be able to completely interact with the consciousness that's trying to communicate with mine. Rapidly. . . . We are now creating a space in which the people of the planet can have that kind of communication relationship. (in Barlow et al. 1995, p. 40).

Lost in Cyberspace?

By contrast, critics worry (mostly in print, of course) that life on the Net can never be meaningful or complete because it will lead people away from the full range of in-person contact. Or, conceding half the debate, they worry that people will get so engulfed in a simulacrum virtual reality, that they will lose contact with "real life."[2] Meaningful contact will wither without the full bandwidth provided by in-person, in-the-flesh contact. As Texas commentator Jim Hightower warned over the ABC radio network:

While all this razzle-dazzle connects us electronically, it disconnects us from each other, having us "interfacing" more with computers and TV screens than looking in the face of our fellow human beings. (Fox 1995, p. 12).

Or as Mark Slouka, author of *War of the Worlds: Cyberspace and the Hitech Assault on Reality* (1995), worries: "Where does the need come from to inhabit these alternate spaces? And the answer I keep coming back to is: to escape the problems and issues of the real world" (Barlow et al. 1995, p. 43.)

Social Networks as Communities
(Virtual or Otherwise)

Although broad references to Gutenberg and McLuhan are often made (e.g. Press 1995), both sides of the debate are *presentist* and *unscholarly*. Consistent with the present-oriented ethos of computer-users, pundits write as if people had never worried about community before the Internet arose. Yet sociologists have been wondering for over a century about how technological changes (along with bureaucratization, industrialization, urbanization, and capitalism) have affected community (Wellman and Leighton 1979; Wellman 1988a). Have such changes led community to (a) fall apart, (b) persevere as villagelike shelters from mass society, or (c) be liberated from the clasp of traditional solidary groups? Like Jim Hightower today, until the 1950s, sociologists feared that rapid modernization would mean the *loss of community*, leaving a handful of transitory, disconnected, weakly supportive relationships (e.g., Tönnies 1887; Stein 1960). Since then, more systematic ethnographic and survey techniques have demonstrated the *persistence of community* in neighborhood and kinship groups (e.g., Young and Willmott 1957; Gans 1962).

More recently, sociologists have discovered that such neighborhood and kinship ties are only a portion of people's overall community networks because cars, planes, and phones can maintain relationships over long distances (Wellman 1988a, 1993). They realized that communities do not have to be solidary groups of densely knit neighbors, but could also exist as *social networks* of kin, friends, and workmates who do not necessarily live in the same neighborhoods. It is not that the world is a global village, but, as McLuhan (1965) originally said, one's "village" could span the globe. This conceptual revolution moved from defining community in terms of space—neighborhoods—to defining it in terms of social networks (Wellman 1988a, 1994).

Social network analysts have had to educate traditional, place-oriented, community sociologists that community can stretch well beyond the neighborhood. By contrast, members of virtual communities take for granted that computer networks are also social networks spanning large distances (e.g., Rheingold 1993; Jones 1995; Hiltz and Turoff 1993; Stoll 1995). Such *computer supported social networks* (CSSNs) come in a variety of types, such as electronic mail (e-mail), bulletin board systems (BBSs), multiuser dungeons (MUDs), newsgroups, and Internet Relay Chat (IRC). All CSSNs provide companionship, social support, information, and a sense of belonging. But do they? The *Manichean* pronouncements of pundits—pro and con—most likely overstate the actual nature of virtual community life. (Perhaps it is difficult for a pundit to get media attention without unequivocally asserting that virtual community will greatly change life as we know it—for good or ill.) Although naysayers have recently received some press (e.g., Stoll 1995; Slouka 1995), most scholarly accounts of online interactions have been quite positive. Although we share this basically positive evaluation, we also suspect that this enthusiasm is partially attributable to the fact that most research has been done by academics and those working for private organizations who have had vested interests in showing that CSSNs work. With the best will in the world, people developing or evaluating online systems want them to work and have invested a large part of themselves in the apparent success of the systems in which they have been involved (Garton 1995).

Much of the analysis that does exist is *parochial*. It almost always treats the Internet as an isolated social phenomenon without taking into account how interactions on the Net fit with other aspects of people's lives. The Net is only one of many ways in which the same people may interact. It is not a separate reality. People bring to their online interactions such baggage as their gender, stage in the life cycle, cultural milieu, socioeconomic status, and offline connections with others (O'Brien 1998).

Just as previous generations worried about whether community had been destroyed or transformed by earlier "new technologies," —such as the telephone (Fischer 1992) or the automobile, —the pundits of the 1990s have identified the Internet as the ultimate transformer (see the reviews in Wellman and Leighton 1979; Wellman 1988a). We think it useful to examine the nature of virtual community in the light of what we have learned about social networks of "real-life" community. Unfortunately, anecdotal assertions about virtual community outweigh careful accounts. These resemble the old genre of "travelers' tales," accounts of adventurous trips from the civilized world to newly discovered, exotic realms. General interest magazines appear weekly with stories about dating (Cybergal 1995) or doing witchcraft on the Net (Davis 1995). *Wired* magazine appears to run such an account almost every month.

Unfortunately, there have been few detailed ethnographic studies of virtual communities, no surveys of who is connected to whom and about what, and no time-budget accounts of how many people spend what number of hours virtually communing.[3] We review here what research there is about virtual community, supplemented with findings from another more widely studied domain of computer-supported social networks: "computer-supported cooperative work" (reviewed also in Garton and Wellman 1995; Sproull and Kiesler 1991; Wellman 1997; Wellman et al. 1996). To fill in gaps with first-order approximations, we add germane anecdotes and travelers' tales, including our own experiences.[4] Our key questions are:

1. Are relationships on the Net narrow and specialized or are they broadly based? What kinds of support can one expect to find in virtual community?
2. How does the Net affect people's ability to sustain weaker, less intimate, relationships and to develop new relationships? Why do Net participants help those they hardly know?
3. Is the support given on the Net reciprocated? Do participants develop attachment to virtual communities so that commitment, solidarity, and norms of reciprocity develop?
4. To what extent are strong, intimate relationships possible on the Net?
5. What is high involvement in virtual community doing to other forms of "real-life" community involvement?
6. To what extent does participation on the Net increase the diversity of community ties? To what extent do such diverse ties help to integrate heterogeneous groups?
7. How does the architecture of the Net affect the nature of virtual community? To what extent are virtual communities solidary groups (like traditional villages) or thinly connected webs? Are virtual communities like "real-life" communities? To what extent are virtual communities entities in themselves or integrated into people's overall communities?

Question 1: Are Online Relationships Narrowly Specialized or Broadly Supportive?

The standard pastoralist ideal of in-person, villagelike community has depicted each community member as providing a broad range of support to all others. In this ideal situation, all can count upon all to provide companionship, emotional aid, information, services (such as child-care or health care), money, or goods (be it food for the starving or saws for the renovating).

It is not clear whether such a broadly supportive situation has ever been the case—it might be pure nostalgia—but contemporary communities in the Western world are quite different. Most community ties are specialized and do not form densely knit clusters of relationships. For example, our Toronto research has found that, except for kin and small clusters of friends, most members of a person's community network do not really know one another. Even close relationships usually provide only a few kinds of social support. Those who provide emotional aid or small services are rarely the same ones who provide large services, companionship, or financial aid. People do get all kinds of support from community members, but they have to turn to different ones for different kinds of help. This means that people must maintain differentiated portfolios of ties to obtain a variety of resources. In market terms, they must shop at specialized boutiques for needed resources instead of casually dropping in at a general store (Wellman and Wortley 1989, 1990; Wellman, Carrington, and Hall 1988; Wellman 1990, 1992b).

Although much of the current literature shows that one can find various kinds of social resources on the Net, there is no systematic evidence about whether individual relationships are narrowly or broadly based. Our reading of travelers' tales and anecdotes suggests that while people can find almost any kind of support on the Net, most of the support available through one relationship is specialized.

In one respect, the Internet has continued the trend of technology fostering specialized relationships. Its structure supports a market approach to finding social resources in virtual communities. With more ease than in almost all "real-life" situations, people can shop around for resources within the safety and comfort of their homes or offices. Travel and search time are reduced. It is as if most North Americans lived in the heart of densely populated, heterogeneous, physically safe, big cities rather than in peripheral, low-density, homogeneous suburbs.

Net members have participated in more than 80,000 topic-oriented collective discussion groups by April 4, 1998 (Smith 1998), more than three times the number identified on January 27, 1996 (Southwick 1996; see also Kling 1996; Kollock and Smith 1996). Their topics range from the political (such as feminist groups, etc.) and technical (computer hardware and software groups), to the social (abuse-recovery groups, singles groups) and recreational (book reviews, hobby groups, sexual fantasy groups). On synchronous chat modes such as the IRC, people can browse through various specialized "channels" before deciding to join a particular discussion (Reid 1991; Danet, Ruedenberg, and Rosenbaum-Tamari 1998). Such groups are a technologically supported continuation of a long-term shift to communities organized by shared interests rather than by shared place (neighborhood or village) or shared ancestry (kinship group). See the discussions in Craven and Wellman 1973; Fischer 1975; Wellman and Leighton 1979.

As Net groups can focus on very specific topics, relationships in these virtual communities can be narrow, existing mostly for information-processing. The nature of the medium supports such relationships since people can easily post a question or comment and quickly receive information in return (Sproull and Faraj 1995). This can be important when efficiency and speed are needed. Everyday examples are the arrangement of group get-togethers, but the Net has also been used to marshal resources, such as after the Oklahoma City bombing in April, 1995. Within hours after the explosion, university students in Oklahoma had created special information sites and electronic bulletin boards on the Internet (Sallot 1995). Among other things, these information resources provided a list of names of the wounded, hospitals servicing these wounded, and locations of emergency blood-donor clinics. Not only was this source of information speedy, but it was often more accurate than television news. Social movements also have been organized online, For example, striking Israeli university professors recently used both private and group messages on the Net to coordinate their fight against the government (Pliskin and Romm 1994; see also Johnson-Lenz and Johnson-Lenz 1993; Marx and Virnoche 1995; Ogden 1994).

If the Net were solely a means of information exchange, then virtual communities played out over the Net would mostly contain only narrow, specialized relationships. However, information is only one of many social resources exchanged on the Net. Many Net members get help in electronic support groups for social, physical, and mental problems, along with information about treatments, practitioners, and other resources. For example, women experiencing the same physical and emotional strains associated with menopause have found online support in knowing that others are going through the same symptoms, feelings, and concerns (Foderaro 1995). Similarly, the Net provides emotional and peer-group support for recovering alcohol and drug addicts; the virtual encounters provided by electronic support groups are important supplements to regular attendance at "real-life" meetings or recovery groups (King 1994).

In at least a few cases, emotional therapy itself is explicitly provided through the Net. One psychiatric social worker in New York "sees" dial-in clients on a BBS:

> The dynamics of the in-person interactive process itself is missing. But what online work can accomplish is to enable people to begin to explore their own thoughts and feelings without being judged. . . . Because I encounter words on screen only, my sensitivity to style as a communication itself and subtle changes in patterns of "speaking" has been heightened. Knowing what a word means to the "speaker" is particularly crucial where the communication is words on screen only. As a result, I tend to ask about the meaning of more words than I might in person. . . . Email or bulletin boards . . . can open a door for people who would not ordinarily reach out for help (Cullen 1995, p. 7).

Electronic support groups are not the only electronic groups where Net-surfers can find emotional support and companionship. Peter and

Trudy Johnson-Lenz have facilitated online groups for more than twenty years, working to build self-awareness, mutually supportive activities, social change, and a sense of collective well-being. In 1978 they coined the term "groupware" to describe "computer-mediated culture": "Some parts are embodied in software, other parts in the hearts and minds of those using it" (1990, p. 1). At the heart of their workshops is a "virtual circle," based on non-Western traditions of passing around sacred "talking sticks." Software tools rearrange communication structures, vary exchange settings, mark group rhythms, and encourage noncontributing lurkers to express themselves (Johnson-Lenz and Johnson-Lenz 1990, 1994).

Even when online groups are not designed to be supportive, they often are. As social beings, those who use the Net seek not only information but also companionship, social support, and a sense of belonging. For example, while most elderly users of "SeniorNet" reported joining the Net to gain access to information, nearly half (47%) had also joined to find companionship. The most popular activity was chatting with others. Over a four-month period, the most heavily used features of SeniorNet were e-mail, "forum," and "conferencing" (social uses), whereas such information access features as "news," "bulletin board," "library," and "database" were the least used. SeniorNet also provides access to grief counselors who would otherwise be inaccessible. One member noted that "if I am unable to sleep at night, all I have to do is go to my computer and there's always someone to talk to, laugh with, exchange ideas...." (Furlong, 1989, p. 149).

There are many other examples of the online availability of emotional support, companionship and advice in addition to information (e.g., Hiltz, Johnson, and Turoff 1986; Rice and Love 1987; McCormick and McCormick 1992; Walther 1994; Rheingold 1993; Meyer 1989; Sproull and Faraj 1995; Kraut et al. 1995; Parks and Roberts 1998). An informal support group sprang up inadvertently in a "Young Scientists' Network," which had been established to provide postdoctoral physicists with job-hunting tips, funding information, and news stories (Sproull and Faraj 1995). Similarly, the private mailing list "Systers" was originally designed for the exchange of information among female computer scientists, but turned into a forum for companionship and social support (Sproull and Faraj 1995). In another case, the members of a university computer science laboratory use e-mail extensively for emotional support. As much of their time is spent online, it is natural for them to use e-mail to communicate their problems to confidants. When confidants receive an online message of distress on their own screens, responding by e-mail is easy for them (Haythornthwaite, Wellman, and Mantei 1995; Haythornthwaite and Wellman 1998).

Emotional support, companionship, information, making arrangements, and providing a sense of belonging are all nonmaterial social resources that are often possible to provide from the comfort of one's computer. They usually do not require major investments of time, money, or energy. But skeptics (e.g. Stoll 1995) ask about the quality as well as the narrowness of such support. Consider the following colloquy:

> On the Internet . . . , people would put words like "grin" or "smile" or "hug" in parentheses in a note. It's a code meaning cyberhugs, cybersmiles, cyberkisses. But at bottom, that cyberkiss is not the same thing as a real kiss. At bottom, that cyberhug is not going to do the same thing. There is a big difference. (Mark Slouka in Barlow, et al. 1995, p. 42.)

> Yes, there is a difference. But I wasn't without the warmth of my friends. I got a lot of hugs during that period, and I still get them. My community was around me. I mean, it wasn't a case of either/or. I didn't have to give up the human embrace in order to have this other, slightly larger form of human embrace, a kind of meta-embrace. One supplemented the other. (John Perry Barlow in Barlow et al. 1995, p. 42.)

To address this issue, we can only be like Slouka and Barlow and provide anecdotes, rather than more persuasive evidence from controlled experiments, detailed ethnographies, or systematic surveys. Many people have received significant emotional support online. For instance, when David Alsberg, a forty-two-year-old computer programmer, was murdered in New York City, his Net friends organized online to solicit recipes and compile an electronic cookbook whose proceeds support a trust fund for the Alsberg family (Lewis 1994; Seymour 1994). In another case, when Mike Godwin's belongings were destroyed in a blaze while moving to Washington, his "cyberspace neighbors" on "the WELL" (an institutionalized virtual community) responded by sending boxes and boxes of books to him for six months (Lewis 1994).

An estimated 20% of U.S. households were online by the end of 1997 (up from 13% a year before), with nearly 60% of these households accessing the Net (Seidman 1998; see also Georgia Institute of Technology 1997). The high rate of Net growth has led some pundits to worry that the Net may be becoming a repository of misleading information. For example, a *Wall Street Journal* article proclaimed that the "pioneers" or veteran users of the Internet were rejecting the electronic medium, overwhelmed by the "sludge" of information that is overpowering Usenet (Chao 1995). Thus one partial scan of the Net found 11,472,741 messages between February 2 and April 4, 1998. These had been posted by 1,597,110 account holders discussing 7,973,251 "threads" in 81,725 newsgroups. Approximately 30,000 new threads were started every day (Smith 1998; see also Kling 1996, Table 1). Critics worry about the overwhelming number of people "who don't have a clue, who are posting

questions because they can, not because they have something to offer"
(James Bidzo, president of RSA Data Security and a twenty-year veteran
of online communication, quoted in Chao 1995). This concern is shared
by health-care professionals who criticize online services for functioning
as repositories of incorrect information and bad advice (Foderaro 1995).

Such worries discount the fact that people have always given each other
advice. Before life on the Net, people did not always go to experts, be they
mechanics for their cars, doctors for their bodies, or therapists for their
psyches. For example, the health-care literature has many accounts of "lay
referral networks" giving people advice on what their ailments were,
which remedies to use, and appropriate doctors or alternative healers to
see (Pescosolido 1986; Wellman 1995). To some extent, the Net has just
made the process more accessible and more visible to others, including experts whose claims to monopolies on advice are threatened (Abbott 1988).

Yet information supplied over the Net is not like information flows
through other relationships, for the Net's speed and greater connectivity
can accelerate the spread of (mis)information when people often send
messages to scores of friends and to large distribution lists (DLs) (Dantowitz and Wellman 1996). For example, the night we were completing a
draft of this article, we received an e-mail warning from a friend about a
"brand-new Good Times computer virus" that was transmitted by e-mail
and could destroy our hard disk. Yet we had received the identical warning about the alleged Good Times virus eleven times in the past four
years. Although the initial warning message was a hoax, the persons who
sent it on did so in good faith and were thoroughly alarmed about the
possibility of their friends' computers becoming infected. While the
speed of the Net allows such information to be disseminated speedily
and quickly, fortunately the ability of Net mail systems to maintain logs
of who sent and received messages aids the correction of misinformation.

It seems as if messages transmitted through the Net can merge the
"two-step flow of communication" (Katz and Lazarsfeld 1955) into one
step, combining the rapid dissemination of mass media with the persua-
siveness of personal communications. The warnings about this nonexistent virus usually come in clusters, so that when one comes it is likely to
be followed by several others. This redundant clustering occurs because
messages are broadcast to friends, and such friends are often friends of
each other (Rapoport 1957).

Question 2: In What Ways Are the Many
Weak Ties on the Net Useful?

Virtual communities may resemble "real-life" communities in the sense
that support is available, often in specialized relationships. But, Net

members are distinctive in providing information, support, companion-ship, and a sense of belonging to persons they hardly know offline or who are total strangers. Anecdotes from virtual communities and more systematic accounts of computer-supported cooperative work provide ample evidence of the usefulness of acquiring new information from weak ties on the Net (Constant, Sproull, and Kiesler 1996; Pickering and King 1996; Garton and Wellman 1995; Harasim and Winkelmans 1990; Carley and Wendt 1991). For example, 58% of the online messages in an organization's DL came from strangers to the recipients (Finholt and Sproull 1990; Kiesler and Sproull 1988).

A few commentators have warned about the consequences of making affiliations in an electronic medium teeming with strangers whose biogra-phies, social positions, and social networks are unknown (Stoll 1995; Chao 1995; Sproull and Faraj 1995). Yet Net-users usually trust strangers, much like people gave rides to hitchhikers in the flower-child days of the 1960s. For example, some Net-users hide their identities and addresses by using a remailing service that claims to accept all messages and forward them to designated recipients while hiding the original sender's name and e-mail address. Although such a service could be of use to those wanting to dis-turb the established order or to harass others, users must trust that the ser-vice will keep their identities secret and forward their messages to the in-tended recipients. The best-known service (now defunct) claimed to be in Finland, but for all the users knew it might have been operated or moni-tored by the CIA, the KGB, the Mafia, or Microsoft.

This willingness to communicate with strangers online contrasts with in-person situations where bystanders are often reluctant to intervene and help strangers (Latané and Darley 1976). Yet bystanders are more apt to intervene when they are the only ones around (and most reluctant when there are many others) and requests are read by solitary individu-als, alone at their screens. Even if the online request is to a newsgroup and not to a specific person, as far as the recipient of the request knows, there may be no one else available who could provide help. Yet online as-sistance will be observed by the entire newsgroup and positively re-warded by its members (Kollock and Smith 1996). Moreover, it is easier for people to withdraw from problematic situations when they are on-line—all they have to do is "exit" the Net session—than it is to withdraw from face-to-face interactions.

The lack of status or situational cues can also encourage contact be-tween weak ties. Often the only thing known about others is their e-mail address, which may provide minimal or misleading information (Slouka 1995). The relatively egalitarian nature of Net contact can encourage re-sponses to requests. By contrast, the cues associated with in-person con-tact transmit information about gender, age, race, ethnicity, lifestyle and socioeconomic status, and clique membership (Culnan and Markus 1987; Garton and Wellman 1995; Hiltz and Turoff 1993; Weisband, Schneider, and Connolly 1995). Online interaction can also generate a culture of its own, as when humorous stories (or virus warnings) sweep the Net, coming repeatedly to participants. Indeed, the Net is fostering a revival of folk humor. At times, the velocity and proliferation of this communication can have consequences as when the broad circulation of "Intel Inside" jokes helped create successful pressure for replacing faulty Pentium computer chips.

Online and offline, weak ties are more apt than strong ties to link people with different social characteristics. Such weak ties are also better means than strong ties of maintaining contact with other social circles (Feld 1982; Granovetter 1982; Lin, Dean, and Ensel 1986). This suggests that the kind of people you know is more important for obtaining information than the number of people you know. For example, in one large organization, people were better able to solve problems when they received online suggestions from a small number of people who had a wide range of social characteristics than when they received suggestions from a large number of socially similar people (Constant, Sproull, and Kiesler 1996).

Question 3: Is There Reciprocity Online and Attachment to Virtual Communities?

It is a general norm of community that whatever is given ought to be repaid, if only to ensure that more is available when needed. Repayment of support and social resources might be as exchanges of the same kind of aid, reciprocating in another way, or helping out a mutual friend in the network. For example, the "real-life" communities of the Torontonians we are studying are reciprocal and supportive overall. Almost all can get a wide range of help from somewhere in their network. Their diversified portfolios of ties provide access to a variety of network members and resources (Wellman, Carrington, and Hall 1988; Wellman and Nazer 1995).

The problem of motivation for giving support in a virtual community arises when we consider that many of the exchanges that take place online are between persons who have never met face-to-face, have only weak ties, and are not bound into densely knit community structures that could enforce norms of reciprocity. Some analysts have suggested that the greater the social and physical distance between the support seeker and provider (i.e., the weaker the tie), the less likely that reciprocity will take place. This suggests that there may be little motivation for individuals to provide assistance, information, and support to physically and socially distant others on the Net since they are less likely to be rewarded or receive support in return (Thorn and Connolly 1987; Constant, Sproull, and Kiesler 1996).

Nevertheless, there is substantial evidence of reciprocal supportiveness on the Net, even between weak ties (Hiltz, Johnson, and Turoff 1986; Walther 1994). Constant, Sproull and Kiesler's (1996) study of information-sharing in an organization suggests two explanations for this reciprocity (see also Constant, Kiesler, and Sproull 1994). One is that the process of providing support and information on the Net is a means of expressing one's identity, particularly if technical expertise or supportive behavior is perceived as an integral part of one's self-identity. Helping others can increase self-esteem, respect from others, and status attainment.

Meyer's (1989) study of the computer underground supports this social-psychological explanation. When they are involved in illegal activities, computer hackers must protect their personal identities with pseudonyms. If hackers use the same nicknames repeatedly, this can help the authorities to trace them. Nevertheless, hackers are reluctant to change their pseudonyms regularly because the status associated with a particular nickname would be lost. With a new nickname, they would have to gain the group's respect again. If they are not seen to contribute, the hackers would not be recognized as community members.

Norms of generalized reciprocity and organizational citizenship are another reason that people help others online (Constant, Sproull, and Kiesler 1996). People who have a strong attachment to the organization will be more likely to help others with organizational problems. Such norms typically arise in a densely knit community, but they appear to be common among frequent contributors to distribution lists and newsgroups. People having a strong attachment to an electronic group will be more likely to participate and provide assistance to others. As Kollock and Smith argued:

> Whatever the goal of the newsgroup, its success depends on the active and ongoing contributions of those who choose to participate in it. If the goal of the newsgroup is to exchange information and answer questions about a particular topic, participants must be willing to answer questions raised by others, summarize and post replies to queries they have made themselves and pass along information that is relevant to the group. (1996, p. 116).

Group attachment is intrinsically tied to norms of generalized reciprocity and aiding mutual friends. People having positive regard for the social system in which requests for assistance are embedded are likely to show respect for the system by offering their help either directly to others who have helped them in the past or to total strangers (Constant, Sproull, and Kiesler 1996). Rheingold, a regular participant in the WELL community writes that, "the person I help may never be in a position to help me, but someone else might be" (Rheingold 1993, p. 60). Moreover, one of us has observed that those who have contributed actively to the BMW car network get their requests for advice answered more quickly and more widely. That is probably why people reply to the entire group when answering an individual's question.

In addition to aiding self-expression, organizational attachment and generalized reciprocity, the Net's technological and social structures assist the provision of social support in other ways. The logistic and social costs of participating in electronic gatherings is relatively low (Sproull and Faraj 1995). People can easily participate within the comfort and safety of their own homes or offices, for any length of time they choose, and at their own convenience. Moreover, it can be easy to provide assistance to others when the group is large. The accumulation of small, individual acts of assistance can sustain a large community because each act is seen by the entire group and helps to perpetuate an image of generalized reciprocity and mutual aid. People know that they may not receive help from the person they helped last week, but from another network member (Rheingold 1993; Barlow 1995; Lewis 1994).

Question 4: Are Strong, Intimate
Ties Possible Online?

Even if weak ties flourish in virtual communities, does the narrower bandwidth of computer-mediated communication work against the maintenance of socially close, strong ties? When people chat, get information, and find support on the Net, do they experience real community or just the inadequate simulacra about which Jim Hightower and Mark Slouka have warned?[5] The test is to see whether the Net creates and sustains the socially close, strong, intimate ties that are the core of community. Personal-relationship theorists tell us that the stronger a tie, the more intensely it exhibits these characteristics:

- (1) a sense of the relationship being intimate and special, (2) with a voluntary investment in the tie, and (3) a desire for companionship with the tie partner;
- (4) an interest in being together as frequently as possible, (5) in multiple social contexts, (6) over a long period;
- (7) a sense of mutuality in the relationship, (8) with the partner's needs known and supported;

- (9) intimacy often bolstered by shared social characteristics such
  as gender, socioeconomic status, stage in the life cycle, and
  lifestyle (Duck 1983; Perlman and Fehr 1987; Blumstein and
  Kollock 1988; Feld 1982; Homans 1961).

In practice, many strong ties do not contain most of these characteristics. For example, intimates living abroad may rarely be seen or offer social support, while many frequently seen relationships are with neighbors and coworkers whose relationships are rarely intimate, voluntary, or supportive (Wellman, Carrington, and Hall 1988). So this list of nine characteristics is more a typology with which to evaluate the strength of online relationships than it is an accurate depiction of the actual nature of strong ties.

Strong ties that are online have many characteristics that are similar to strong offline ties. They encourage *frequent, companionable* contact and are *voluntary,* except in work situations. One or two keystrokes are all that is necessary to begin replying, facilitating *reciprocal, mutual support* of tie partners' needs. Moreover, the placelessness of e-mail contact aids *long-term* contact, without the loss of the tie that so often accompanies geographical mobility.

But if the relationships are companionable and supportive, are they truly intimate and special enough to be strong ties, and do they operate in multiple social contexts? Part of the fears of pundits about the inability of the Net to sustain strong ties is wrongly specified. Pundits, both enthusiasts and critics of virtual community, often speak of relationships as being solely online. Their fixation on the technology leads them to ignore the abundant accounts of community ties operating both online and offline, with the Net being just one of several ways to communicate. Despite all the talk about virtual community transcending time and space sui generis, much contact is between people who see each other in person and live locally. Our research into a less trendy communication medium, the telephone, found that Torontonians spoke more with people who live nearby than they did with those far away. Their calls filled the gaps between in-person meetings, and made arrangements for future get-togethers (Wellman, Carrington, and Hall 1988; Wellman and Tindall 1993).

Yet some relationships are principally sustained online. Can they be strong? Some analysts have argued that the comparatively low bandwidth of computer-mediated communication cannot by itself sustain strong ties (Beniger 1987; Jones 1995; Stoll 1995). They argue that without physical and social cues or immediate responses, e-mail can foster extreme language, difficulties in coordination, and group polarization (Daft and Lengel 1986; Short, Williams, and Christie 1976; Kiesler and Sproull

1992; Hiltz and Turoff 1993; Latané and Bourgeois 1996). Perhaps the medium itself does not support strong, intimate relationships; or as neo-McLuhanites might say, the medium may not support the message (McLuhan 1965). Thus Clifford Stoll (1995, p. 24) worries that intimacy is illusory in virtual community: "Electronic communication is an instantaneous and illusory contact that creates a sense of intimacy without the emotional investment that leads to close friendships."

The debate is not yet resolved because scholarly research thus far has focused on the presence of supportive, intimate relationships in online work situations rather than in virtual communities. (However, as noted above, the supportiveness of online coworkers has been an unexpected outcome of what had originally been seen as an instrumental, limited-bandwidth medium focused on the exchange of information.) In one study, some participants came to feel that their closest friends were members of their electronic group, whom they seldom or never see (Hiltz and Turoff 1993). Walther (1995) similarly argues that online relationships are socially close, suggesting that groups of people interacting on the Net become more personal and intimate over time (see also McGrath and Hollingshead 1994). He points out that most research experiments analyze social interactions within a limited time, missing the nuances of later interactions and the potential for relationships to grow closer over time. He argues that the medium does not prevent close relationships from growing but simply slows the process. Relational development takes longer online than in face-to-face interactions because communication is almost always asynchronous (and slower) and the available bandwidth offers less verbal and nonverbal information per exchange. Walther's experiments comparing groups of undergraduates' online and in-person meetings suggest that, over time, online interactions are as sociable or intimate as in-person interactions. In other words, the Net does not preclude intimacy.

There has been little systematic analysis of the nature and longevity of online intimacy, other than experiments with university students or serendipitous observations of intimacy observed in computer-supported cooperative work (reviewed in Garton and Wellman 1995; Haythornthwaite, Wellman, and Garton 1998). Despite lurid media reports, there may not be much antisocial behavior online other than uttering hostile "flaming" remarks and "spamming" individuals and DLs with profuse junk mail. However, social-psychological studies report that CSSNs seem to foster uninhibited discussion, nonconforming behavior, and group polarization (Hiltz, Johnson, and Agle 1978; Kiesler, Sproull, and Eccles 1985; Siegal et al. 1986; Sproull and Kiesler 1991; Lea et al. 1992; Walther, Anderson, and Park 1994). Studies of Usenet groups (e.g. Kollock and Smith 1996) report extensive free-rider "lurking" (reading others' comments without contributing). Although lurking does not support the group (because it is not easily observed online), it is less detrimental to group morale than is similar behavior in face-to-face situations.

With respect to longevity, there are few statistics about how *long-lasting* Internet relationships are, although one study shows that people are more apt to participate actively in those online groups that they perceive to be long-lasting (Walther 1994; Parks and Roberts 1998). We do note that the durability of "real-life" strong ties may be more pastoralist myth than current reality. For example, only 27% of Torontonians' six socially closest "real-life" community ties remained close a decade later (Wellman et al. 1997).

To be sure, there are many anecdotes about antisocial behavior online, such as confidence men betraying the innocent, entrepreneurs "spamming" the Net with unwanted advertisements, online stalkers harassing Net members, and scoundrels taking on misleading roles (e.g., Cybergal 1995). The most widely reported stories are about men posing online as women and seducing other women (e.g. Slouka 1995), but the accounts suggest that these are probably rare incidents. Moreover, masquerading can have a playful, creative aspect, allowing people to try on different roles: Such systems as the real-time IRC (Reid 1991; Bechar-Israeli 1995; Danet, Ruedenberg and Rosenbaum-Tamari 1998) and the asynchronous Electronic Information Exchange Service (EIES) (Hiltz and Turoff 1993) encourage role-playing by permitting participants to communicate by nicknames.

A much greater threat to community relationships is the ease by which relationships are disrupted. The literature on flaming shows that the narrower bandwidth of communication facilitates the misinterpretation of remarks and the asynchronous nature of most conversations hinders the immediate repair of damages.

What of *multiplexity*, the strengthening of relationships through interactions in multiple roles and social arenas? In multiplex relationships, a neighbor may become a friend, or a friendship may broaden from a single shared interest. The Net supports both narrowly specialized and broadly multiplex relationships, although online relationships often broaden over time (Parks and Floyd 1996). Usenet groups and distribution lists focus on special interests. For example, one of us has observed that frequent participants on the BMW DL know little about each other besides the types of cars they drive and their level of expertise about repairs. Indeed, the rules of that DL forbid comments unrelated to BMWs.

Our observations of such groups suggest that many online interactions are what Wireman (1984) calls "intimate secondary relationships": informal, frequent, and supportive community ties that nevertheless operate only in one specialized domain. Although Wireman originally studied in-person voluntary organizations, her concept is useful for analyzing relationships online (see also Calhoun 1987).

Question 5: How Does Virtual Community
Affect "Real-Life" Community?

Several writers have expressed fears that high involvement in virtual community will move people away from involvement in "real-life" communities, which are sustained by face-to-face, telephone, and postal contact. Certainly there are stories of "cyberaddicts" whose involvement in online relationships turns them away from "real-life" relationships with family and friends (Hiltz and Turoff 1993; Barlow 1995; Rheingold 1993; Kling 1996; *Newsweek* 1995). Addiction may even create "cyberwidows," as when O'Neill (1995) reports: "I was coming home later and later. My wife thought I'd started drinking again. I lose all sense of time once I get on-line. I'm an addict."

Such fears are misstated in several ways. For one thing, they treat community as a zero-sum game, assuming that if people spend more time interacting online, they will spend less time interacting in "real life." Second, such accounts demonstrate the strength and importance of online ties, and not their weakness. As we have seen in the previous section, strong, intimate ties can be maintained online as well as face-to-face. It is the siren call of the virtual community that is luring some people away from "real life." We believe that critics who disparage the authenticity of such strong, online ties are being unwarrantedly snobbish in disregarding the seriousness with which Net participants take their relationships.[6]

Third, we suspect that the excitement about the implications of e-mail for community implicitly sets up a false comparison between e-mail-based virtual communities and face-to-face-based "real-life" communities. In fact, most contemporary communities in the developed world do not resemble rural or urban villages where all know all and have frequent face-to-face contact. Rather, most kith and kin live farther away than a walk (or short drive), so that telephone contact sustains ties as much as face-to-face get-togethers (Fischer 1982; Wellman, Carrington, and Hall 1988). Indeed, even community members living in the same neighborhood rely on telephone contact to maintain relationships between face-to-face encounters (Wellman 1996). Although people now take telephone contact for granted, it was seen as an exotic, depersonalized form of communication only fifty years ago (Fischer 1992). We suspect that as online communication is rapidly becoming widely used and routinely accepted, the current fascination with it will soon decline sharply. It will be seen much as telephone contact is now and letter-writing was in Jane Austen's time: a reasonable way to maintain strong and weak ties between people who are unable to have a face-to-face encounter just then. Indeed, there are times when people prefer e-mail contact to face-to-face contact because they can better control their communication and presentation of self, and they do not have to spend time at that moment dealing with the other person's response.

Fourth, people do not neatly divide their worlds into two discrete sets: people seen in-person and people contacted online. Rather, many community ties connect offline as well as online. It is the relationship that is the important thing, and not the communication medium. E-mail is only one of multiple ways by which ties are sustained. For example, university researchers intermingle in-person and e-mail communication, often using e-mail to arrange for in-person get-togethers (Haythornthwaite, Wellman, and Mantei 1995; Haythornthwaite and Wellman 1998; see also Eveland and Bikson 1990; Finholt and Sproull 1990). In another example, employees in a small office communicate by e-mail while they physically work side by side. This allows them to chat while giving the appearance of working diligently at their computers (Garton 1995). In such situations, conversations started on one medium may continue on others. As with the telephone and the fax, the lower bandwidth of e-mail may be sufficient to maintain strong ties between persons who know each other well. Thus "invisible colleges" of scholars communicate over wide distances through e-mail and other media (Carley 1990; Kaufer and Carley 1993), while kinship networks use the Net to arrange weddings and out-of-town visits.

Fifth, although many online relationships remain specialized, the inclusion of e-mail addresses in messages and DL headers provides the basis for more multiplex relationships to develop between participants (Rheingold 1993; King 1994; Hiltz and Turoff 1993). For example, 58% of recovering addicts on electronic support groups also contacted their online acquaintances by phone, postal mail, or face-to-face (King 1994). His findings corroborate Walther's aforementioned hypothesis (1995): The longer addicts frequented the electronic support group, the more likely they were to contact others offline. Such multiplexity has also been found elsewhere:

> During and following Conference '72, many participants altered their business and vacation travel plans to include a face-to-face meeting with each other. (Hiltz and Turoff 1993, p. 114).

As in this situation, the development of multiplexity can involve the conversion of relationships that only operate online to ones that include in-person and telephonic encounters. Just as community ties that began in-person can be sustained through e-mail, online ties can be reinforced and broadened through in-person meetings. Without social and physical cues, people can meet and get to know each other on the Net and then decide whether to take the relationship into a broader realm. For example, in a newsgroup devoted to the topic of planning weddings, one of us observed a woman explaining that some of her guests would include people she has never seen but has known for some time from the Net.

In sum, the Net supports a variety of community ties including some that are quite close and intimate. But while there is legitimate concern about whether true intimacy is possible in relationships that operate only online, the Net promotes the functioning of intimate secondary relationships and weaker ties. Nor are such weaker ties insignificant. Not only do such ties sustain important, albeit more specialized, relationships, but the vast majority of informal interpersonal ties are weak ties, whether they operate online or face-to-face. Current research suggests that North Americans usually have more than one thousand interpersonal ties: Only a half-dozen of them are intimate and no more than fifty are significantly strong (Kochen 1989; Wellman 1990, 1992b). Yet, taken together, a person's other 950+ ties are important sources of information, support, companionship, and a sense of belonging.

Question 6: Does the Net Increase Community Diversity?

To this point, we have considered the ability of the Net to support community *ties*. Yet a community is more than the sum of a set of ties: its *composition* and *network structure* affects how it supplies companionship, supportiveness, information and a sense of identity.

Consider two types of communities. The traditional communities of pastoralist nostalgia have been densely knit, villagelike structures composed of socially similar community members. Their composition and structure give them the communication capacity to coordinate and control the supply of supportive resources to needy community members. Yet they tend to be all-encompassing, with less scope for innovation. In contemporary Western societies, such traditional communities are typically found in isolated rural areas or enclaves of poor immigrants (e.g., Gans 1962; Walker 1993), but even such communities have significant ties with the outside world (Allan 1989; Allen and Dillman 1994).

Most contemporary Western communities do not resemble preindustrial villages for they are socially diverse, sparsely knit, and well connected to the outside world (Wellman, Carrington, and Hall 1988; Wellman 1988a). These are only partial communities that do not command a person's full allegiance. Rather, each person is a limited member of multiple communities such as kinship groups, neighborhoods, and friendship circles. These heterogeneous, low-density communities do not control people and resources as well as community villages do, for disgruntled participants can always shift their attentions to other arenas. Although such communities do not control resources as well as villagelike structures, they are better at acquiring resources from elsewhere. Yet, these multiple, ramifying communities expose each person to a more diverse set of social worlds, with heterogeneous, nonredundant sources of information and social support (Greer 1962; Wellman and Craven 1973; Fischer 1975).

Although MUDs and similar role-playing environments at times resemble villagelike structures in the ways they capture some participants' attention (Reid 1998; DuVal Smith 1998), people rarely spend their full time in these environments. Rather, the tendency of the Net is to foster participation in multiple, partial communities. People often subscribe to multiple distribution lists and newsgroups. They can easily send out messages to personal lists of their own making, perhaps keeping different lists for different kinds of conversations. Moreover, they can vary in their involvements in different communities, participating actively in some, occasionally in others, and being silent "lurkers" in still others.

Such communities develop new connections easily. The Net makes it easy to ask distant acquaintances and strangers for advice and information via e-mail (distribution lists, newsgroups, etc.). When one's strong ties are unable to provide information, one is likely to find it from weak ties. Strong ties are more likely to be socially similar and to know the same persons; hence they are more apt to possess the same information. By contrast, new information is more apt to come through weaker ties better connected to other, more diverse social circles (Granovetter 1973, 1982).

The Net encourages the expansion of community networks. Information may come unsolicited through distribution lists, newsgroups, and forwarded messages from friends who "thought you might like to know about this." Friends forward communications to third parties, and in so doing they provide indirect contact between previously disconnected people who can then make direct contact. Newsgroups and distribution lists provide permeable, shifting sets of participants, with more intense relationships continued by private e-mail. The resulting relaxation of constraints on the size and proximity of one's "communication audience" on the Net can increase the diversity of people encountered (Lea and Spears 1995).

The Net's relative lack of social richness can foster contact with more diverse others. The lack of social and physical cues online makes it difficult to find out if another Net member has similar social characteristics or attractive physical characteristics (Sproull and Kiesler 1986), and Net norms discourage asking outright if someone is high or low status, handsome or ugly. (As one pooch in a *New Yorker* cartoon says to another, "On the Internet, nobody knows if you're a dog.") Thus the Net's lack of in-person involvement can give participants more control over the timing and content of their self-disclosures (Walther 1995). This allows relationships to develop on the basis of communicated shared interests rather than be stunted at the onset by differences in social status (Hiltz and Turoff 1993; Coate 1994; Weisband, Schneider, and Connolly 1995).

This focus on shared interests rather than on similar characteristics can be empowering for otherwise lower-status and disenfranchised groups. Consider, for example, "Amy's" situation in Douglas Coupland's novel, *Microserfs*:

> [Amy] told me that all her life people had only ever treated her like a body or a girl—or both. And interfacing with [her virtual lover] Michael over the Net [where she used the gender-obscure alias, "Bar Code"] was the only way she could ever really know that he was talking to *her*, not with his concept of her. "Reveal your gender on the Net, and you're toast." She considered her situation. "It's an update of the rich man who poses as a pauper and finds the princess. But fuck that princess shit—we're both *kings*. (1995, p. 334)

As Amy/Bar Code observes, social characteristics do not disappear entirely from the Net. Women, in particular, may receive special attention from male Net members and may feel uncomfortable (or be made to feel uncomfortable) in participating actively (Shade 1994; Herring 1996). This may well be a function of the high ratio of men to women on the Net (Pitkow and Kehoe 1995).

Possibilities for diverse communities also depend on the population of the Net having diverse social characteristics. Yet a survey of Web-users in Spring, 1995, found that women comprised less than one-fifth of their sample, although the proportion of women users had doubled in the previous six months (Pitkow and Kehoe 1995; the authors note that their convenience sample may not be representative). The survey reported that about two-thirds of the sampled Web-users had at least a university education, had an average household income of US$59,600, and three-quarters lived in North America (Gupta, Pitkow, and Recker 1995).

Because most friends and relatives live a long drive or airplane ride away, sustaining relationships online is often easier than meeting face-to-face (Wellman 1988a, 1992a; Wellman, Carrington and Hall 1988). Indeed, people's allegiance to the Net's communities of interest may be more powerful than their allegiance to their neighborhood communities because those involved in the same virtual community may share more interests than those who live on the same block. Howard Rheingold expresses his attachment to the parenting conference on the WELL in the following terms: "People you know as fierce, even nasty intellectual opponents in other contexts give you emotional support on a deeper level, parent to parent, within the boundaries of 'Parenting,' a small but warmly human corner of cyberspace" (Rheingold 1993, p. 18).

Community based on shared interests can foster another form of homogeneity. Despite the medium's potential to connect diverse cultures and ideas, we suspect that people are generally drawn to electronic groups that link them with others sharing common interests or concerns. Sole involvement in one Net group may have a deindividuating effect, where the lack of information about personal characteristics may promote an attraction between people solely on the basis of their membership in that group (Lea and Spears 1992).

Question 7: Are Virtual Communities "Real" Communities?

Despite the limited social presence of online links, the Net successfully maintains strong, supportive community ties, and it may be increasing the number and diversity of weak ties. The Net is especially suited to maintaining intermediate-strength ties between people who cannot see each other frequently. Online relationships are based more on shared interests and less on shared social characteristics. Although many relationships function offline as well as online, CSSNs are developing norms and structures of their own. They are not just pale imitations of "real life." The Net is the Net.

The limited evidence available suggests that the ties people develop and maintain in cyberspace are much like most of their "real-life" community ties: intermittent, specialized, and varying in strength. Even in "real life," people must maintain differentiated portfolios of ties to obtain a variety of resources. But in virtual communities, the market metaphor of shopping around for support in specialized ties is even more exaggerated than in "real life" because the architecture of computer networks promotes marketlike situations. For example, decisions about which newsgroups to get involved in can be made from topical menus that list available choices, while requests for help can be broadcast to a wide audience from the comfort of one's home rather than having to ask people one by one. Thus while *online ties* may be specialized, the aggregate sets of ties in *virtual communities* are apt to provide a wide range of support.

The provision of information is a larger component of online ties than of "real-life" ties. Yet despite the limited social presence of online ties, companionship, emotional support, services, and a sense of belonging are abundant in cyberspace. Although sending material goods over the ether is not possible, the Net supports arrangements to supply goods as well as services. The mechanism or functions involved with maintaining supportive network ties exist in both virtual and "real-life" community networks. Like other forms of community, virtual communities are useful means of both giving and getting social support.

Virtual communities differ from "real-life" communities in the basis upon which participants perceive their relationships to be intimate. People on the Net have a greater tendency to develop feelings of closeness on the basis of shared interests rather than on the basis of shared social characteristics such as gender and socioeconomic status. So they are relatively homogeneous in their interests and attitudes, just as they are relatively heterogeneous in the participants' age, social class, ethnicity, life-cycle stage, and other aspects of their social backgrounds. The homogeneous interests of virtual community participants may be fostering relatively high levels of empathetic understanding and mutual support (Lazarsfeld and Merton 1954; Verbrugge 1977; Feld 1982; Marsden 1983).

The architecture of the Net may encourage significant alterations in the size, composition, and structure of communities. Although no study has yet provided a count of the number of ties in the virtual community, its architecture supports the maintenance of a large number of community ties, especially nonintimate ties. Distribution lists and newsgroups routinely involve hundreds of members while people easily send hasty notes or long letters to many friends and acquaintances. The distance-free cost structure of the Net transcends spatial limits even more than the telephone, the car, or the airplane because the asynchronous nature of the Net allows people to communicate over different time zones. This allows latent ties to stay in more active contact until the participants have an opportunity to meet in person. By supporting such online contact, the Net may even foster more frequent in-person meetings between people who might otherwise forget each other.

With regard to the structure of communities, the Net is nourishing two somewhat contradictory phenomena. Specialized newsgroups, distribution lists, and the like foster multiple memberships in partial communities. At the same time, the ease of group response and forwarding can foster the folding-in of formerly separate Net participants into more all-encompassing communities.

Operating via the Net, virtual communities are simultaneously becoming more "glocalized," as worldwide connectivity and domestic matters intersect. Global connectivity de-emphasizes the importance of locality for community; online relationships may be more stimulating than suburban neighborhoods. At the same time, people are usually based at their home, the most local environment imaginable, when they connect with their virtual communities. Their lives may become even more home-centered, if telework proliferates (Salaff and Dimitrova 1995; Wellman et al. 1996). Just as was prevalent before the industrial revolution, home and workplace are being integrated for teleworkers, although gender roles have not been renegotiated. The domestic environment of teleworkers is becoming a vital home base for neo–Silas Marners sitting in front of their computer screens. Nests are becoming well-feathered, and teleworkers will be well situated to provide the eyes on the street that are the foundation of neighboring (Jacobs 1961).

Pundits worry that virtual community may not truly be community. These worriers are confusing the pastoralist myth of community for the reality. Community ties are already geographically dispersed, sparsely knit, connected heavily by telecommunications (phone and fax), and specialized in content. There is so little community life in most neighborhoods in Western cities that it is more useful to think of each person as having a *personal community:* an individual's social network of informal interpersonal ties, ranging from a half-dozen intimates to hundreds of weaker ties. Just as the Net supports neighborhoodlike *group communities* of densely knit ties, it also supports personal communities, wherever in social or geographical space these ties are located and however sparsely knit they might be.

Both group communities and personal communities operate online as well as offline. Thus Wellman gets widely distributed e-mail daily from his group communities of BMW aficionados and social network analysts. He reads all their online discussions, and all of the groups' members read his. Messages to group communities narrowly focus on the concerns of that group (Hiltz and Turoff 1993). For example, no other member of the social network analysis group is interested in BMWs, and vice versa.

At the same time, Wellman also maintains an e-mail address file of more than 1,800 members of his personal community. As the creator, maintainer, and center of this network, he is the only one who initiates communications with this personal community. Usually, correspondents respond privately to his messages, although his e-mail software allows replies to all who have received a message. By its very nature, this personal community cuts across specialized, partial communities. Hence it provides the basis for crosscutting ties that link otherwise disconnected social groups.

It is even possible that the proliferation of computer-mediated communication may produce a countertrend to the contemporary privatization of community. In this century, community in the Western world has moved indoors to private homes from its former semipublic, accessible milieus such as cafés, parks, and pubs. There is abundant evidence that people in the Western world are spending less time in public places waiting for friends to wander by and to introduce friends to other friends (Wellman 1992a). Even the French are going out to cafés less often (*Economist* 1995). Instead, by-invitation private get-togethers and closed telephone chats have become the norm. This dispersion and privatization mean that instead of dropping in at a café and pub and waiting for people they know to drop by, people must actively get in touch with community members to keep in contact. The result probably is a lower volume of contact between community members.

Computer-mediated communication accelerates the ways in which people operate at the centers of partial, personal communities, switching rapidly and frequently between groups of ties. People have an enhanced ability to move between relationships. At the same time, their more individualistic behavior means the weakening of the solidarity that comes from being in densely knit, loosely bounded groups (Wellman 1997).

Yet virtual communities provide possibilities for reversing the trend to less contact with community members because it is so easy to connect online with large numbers of people. For example, one of us has a personal "friends" list of eighty persons and frequently sends them jokes, deep thoughts, and reports about life experiences. Such communication typically stimulates ten to twenty direct replies, plus similar messages sent out by others to their online friends. Communities such as online chat groups usefully stimulate communication in another way. Because all participants can read all messages—just as in a barroom conversation— groups of people can talk to each other casually and get to know the friends of their friends. "The keyboard is my café," William Mitchell enthuses (1995, p. 7).[7]

Thus even as the Net might accelerate the trend to moving community interaction out of public spaces, it may also integrate society. The Net's architecture supports both weak and strong ties that cut across social milieus, be they interest groups, localities, organizations, or nations. As a result, cyberlinks between people become social links between groups that otherwise would be socially and physically dispersed (Durkheim 1893; Breiger 1974; Wellman 1988b).[8]

We have concluded this chapter more like pundits and tellers of tales than researchers. As others before us, we have argued often by assertion and anecdote. This is because the paucity of systematic research into virtual communities has raised more questions than even preliminary answers. As one of Bellcore's chief technologists noted, when

> scientists talk about the evolution of the information infrastructure, . . . [we don't] talk about . . . the technology. We talk about ethics, law, policy and sociology. . . . It is a social invention. (Lucky 1995, p. 205).

It is time to replace anecdote with evidence. The subject is important: practically, intellectually, and politically. The answers have not yet been found. The questions are just starting to be formulated.

Notes

We have benefited from the advice of our colleagues in the Virtual Social Research Network: Janet Salaff, Dimitrina Dimitrova, Emmanuel Koku, Laura Garton, Keith Hampton, Nancy Nazer, and Caroline Haythornthwaite. We appreciate the advice provided by Peter Kollock and Mark Smith, and by our computer science colleagues in the now-completed Cavecat and Telepresence projects: Ronald Baecker, William Buxton, Marilyn Mantei, and Gale Moore. Financial support for this chapter has been provided by the Social Science and Humanities Research Council of Canada, Bell Canada, the Ontario Ministry of Science and Technology, the Information Technology Research Centre, and Communications and Information Technology, Ontario. A preliminary version appears in Smith and Kollock (1998). We dedicate this chapter to science-fiction personage Judith Merril, who surfed cyberspace for fifty years until her death in September, 1997.

1. Message on the Net to the Apple Internet Users group, August 3, 1995. Fittingly, the message was forwarded to Wellman in Toronto by Steven Friedman, a discussion-list (DL) member and friend of Wellman's who lives in Israel. Yet the interaction is not solely a product of virtual community. The relationship between Wellman and Friedman developed out of a close childhood friendship of Wellman's wife and was reinforced when the Wellmans spent April, 1995, visiting Israel.

2. We put "real life" in quotation marks because we believe that interaction over the Internet is as much real life as anything else. However, we continue to use "real life" in this chapter because it is useful to make the contrast between online relationships and other types of community ties.

3. The first scholarly study was announced as we went to press (Kraut et al. 1998). Preliminary analysis from an atypical sample suggested that Net activity may increase depression and loneliness, and substitute weak online ties for strong in-person ties.

4. We focus in this chapter on computer-mediated communication (CMC) systems that are primarily text-based and are used for personal and recreational reasons. These include both synchronous and asynchronous modes of CMC such as the Internet, dialogue or chatlines (i.e., Internet Relay Chat), E-mail, newsgroups, bulletin board systems, commercial networks such as America Online or MUDs. Although some of these systems are, strictly speaking, not part of the Internet, they are rapidly becoming connected to it. Hence, unless we are making special distinctions, we refer here to the sum of all these systems as the "Internet" or simply "the Net." Indeed, the Net has never been a single entity. Rather, it is a "network of networks," a form first identified by Craven and Wellman (1973). We exclude here analyses of picturephones, videoconferencing, and other forms of video-based computer-mediated communication that now are mainly used in large organizations or experimentally by academics. For information on desktop videoconferencing, see Mantei et al. 1991; Buxton 1992; Garton 1995.

5. Devotees of computer science and science fiction are already aware that virtual community members in the near future will interact via simulacra. Instead of sending text messages, animated figures will interact with each other (*Com-*

munications of the ACM 1994). Several preliminary chat systems using graphical "avatars" already exist, such as AlphaWorld on the Internet and WorldsAway on the CompuServe network (Damer 1996). Nongraphical "agents" have proliferated rapidly on the Net since 1995. Although these agents have largely been used to search the World Wide Web for relevant information, they should soon have the capability of interacting with the Net denizens (from files to humans) they encounter. See Stephenson (1992) for a fictional account of agents and avatars in future virtual communities, and Maes (1995) for a report on implementations.

6. Our own study of "real-life" community in Toronto provides support for accepting people's own accounts of strong ties. We asked study participants to distinguish between their intimate and less strong relationships, and we independently coded for intimacy ourselves. The correlations were extremely high (> 0.90) between the participants' own reports and our "expert" coding.

7. The ultimate in this is Isaac Asimov's science-fiction world (1957) where all contact is by virtual reality because in-person meetings are taboo. By contrast, in recently developed "cybercafés," people physically get together in cafes equipped with Internet access. This creates a situation where strangers are sitting side by side, each separately interacting online with members of their respective virtual communities. Presumably the physical proximity and similar interests will encourage some café denizens to get to know those sitting near them.

8. Of course all intergroup contact may not be benign. The Guardian Angels, a volunteer group formed in 1979 to patrol public spaces in New York City, have created "CyberAngels" to patrol the Net for "suspicious activity" that might indicate crimes against children or intergroup hatred. As the privatization of in-person community has emptied the streets, the Guardian Angels are going where the action is (*Atlanta Journal-Constitution* 1995).

References

Abbott, Andrew. 1988. *The System of Professions: An Essay on the Division of Expert Labor*. Chicago: University of Chicago Press.

Allan, Graham. 1989. *Friendship*. London: Harvester Wheatsheaf.

Allen, John, and Don Dillman. 1994. *Against all Odds: Rural Community in the Information Age*. Boulder: Westview Press.

Asimov, Isaac. 1957. *The Naked Sun*. Garden City, NY: Doubleday.

Atlanta Journal-Constitution. 1995. "Angels to Patrol the Net." August 6.

Barlow, John Perry. 1995. "Is There a There in Cyberspace?" *Utne Reader,* March-April:50–56.

Barlow, John Perry, Sven Birkets, Kevin Kelly, and Mark Slouka. 1995. "What Are We Doing On-Line?" *Harper's,* August:35–46.

Bechar-Israeli, Haya. 1995. "From <Bonehead> to <cLoNehEad>: Nicknames, Play and Identity on Internet Relay Chat." *Journal of Computer-Mediated Communication* 1 (November): online URL: http//www.usc.edu/dept/annenberg/journal.html

Beniger, James. 1987. "Personalization of Mass Media and the Growth of Pseudo-Community." *Communication Research* 14:352–371.

Blumstein, Philip, and Peter Kollock. 1988. "Personal Relationships." *Annual Review of Sociology* 14:467–90.

Breiger, Ronald. 1974. "The Duality of Persons and Groups." *Social Forces* 53:181–90.

Buxton, Bill. 1992. "Telepresence: Integrating Shared Task and Person Spaces." Presented to the Graphics Interface '92 Conference, May, Vancouver.

Calhoun, Craig. 1987. "Computer Technology, Large-Scale Social Integration and the Local Community." *Urban Affairs Quarterly* 22:329–349.

Carley, Kathleen. 1990. "Structural Constraints on Communication: The Diffusion of the Homomorphic Signal Analysis Technique through Scientific Fields." *Journal of Mathematical Sociology* 15(3–4):207–246.

Carley, Kathleen, and Kira Wendt. 1991. "Electronic Mail and Scientific Communication: A Study of the Soar Extended Research Group." *Knowledge: Creation, Diffusion, Utilization* 12(June):406–440.

Chao, Julie. 1995. "Net Loss: The Pioneers Move On." *Toronto Globe and Mail*, June 20.

Coate, John. 1994. "Cyberspace Innkeeping: Building Online Community." Online paper: tex@sfgate.com.

Communications of the ACM. 1994. Special issue on Intelligent Agents 37 (July).

Constant, David, Sara Kiesler, and Lee Sproull. 1994. "What's Mine Is Ours, or Is It? A Study of Attitudes About Information Sharing." *Information Systems Research* 5:400–421.

Constant, David, Lee Sproull, and Sara Kiesler. 1996. "The Kindness of Strangers: The Usefulness of Electronic Weak Ties for Technical Advice." *Organization Science* 7(2):119–135.

Coupland, Doug. 1995. *Microserfs.* New York: HarperCollins.

Craven, Paul, and Barry Wellman. 1973. "The Network City." *Sociological Inquiry* 43:57–88.

Cullen, Diana List. 1995. "Psychotherapy in Cyberspace." *The Clinician* 26(Summer):1, 6–7.

Culnan, Mary, and M. Lynn Markus. 1987. "Information Technologies" Pp. 420–443 in *Handbook of Organizational Communication*, edited by Fredric Jablin, Linda Putnam, Karlene Roberts, and Lyman Porter. Newbury Park, CA: Sage.

Cybergal. 1995. "The Year of Living Dangerously." *Toronto Life Fashion Magazine*. September:104–109.

Daft, Richard, and Robert Lengel. 1986. "Organizational Information Requirements, Media Richness and Structural Design." *Management Science* 32:554–71.

Damer, Bruce. 1996. "Inhabited Virtual Worlds: A New Frontier for Interaction Design". *Interactions*, September:27–34.

Danet, Brenda, Lucia Ruedenberg, and Yehudit Rosenbaum-Tamari. 1998. "Hmmm . . . Where's All That Smoke Coming From? Writing, Play and Performance on Internet Relay Chat." Pp. 41–76 in *Network and Netplay: Virtual Groups on the Internet*, edited by Sheizaf Rafaeli, Fay Sudweeks, and Margaret McLaughlin. Cambridge, MA: MIT Press.

Dantowitz, Aaron, and Barry Wellman. 1996. "The Small World of the Internet." Presented to the Canadian Sociology and Anthropology Association, June, St. Catharines, Ont.

Davis, Erik. 1995. "Technopagans." *Wired* (July):126–133, 173–181.

Duck, Steve. 1983. *Friends for Life*. Brighton, UK: Harvester.

Durkheim, Émile. 1893 [1993]. *The Division of Labor in Society*. New York: Macmillan.

DuVal Smith, Anna. 1998. "Problems of Conflict Management in Virtual Communities." Pp. 134–160 in *Communities in Cyberspace,* edited by Marc Smith and Peter Kollock. Berkeley: University of California Press.

Economist, The. 1995. "Mais Où Sont les Cafés d'Antan." June 10:50.

Eveland, J. D. and Tora Bikson. 1990. "Work Group Structures and Computer Support: A Field Experiment." *ACM Transactions on Office Information Systems* 6:354–379.

Feld, Scott. 1982. "Social Structural Determinants of Similarity among Associates." *American Sociological Review* 47:797–801.

Finholt, Tom and Lee Sproull. 1990. "Electronic Groups at Work." *Organization Science* 1:41–64.

Fischer, Claude. 1975. "Toward a Subcultural Theory of Urbanism." *American Journal of Sociology* 80:1319–1341.

Fischer, Claude. 1982. *To Dwell Among Friends*. Berkeley: University of California Press.

Fischer, Claude. 1992. *America Calling: A Social History of the Telephone to 1940*. Berkeley: The University of California Press.

Foderaro, Lisa. 1995. "Seekers of Self-Help Finding It On Line." *The New York Times,* March 23.

Fox, Robert. 1995. "Newstrack." *Communications of the ACM* 38(8):11–12.

Furlong, Mary S. 1989. "An Electronic Community for Older Adults: The Senior-Net Network." *Journal of Communication* 39 (Summer):145–153.

Gans, Herbert. 1962. *The Urban Villagers*. New York: Free Press.

Garton, Laura. 1995. "Linking Social Networks: A Case Study of Communication Media Use in One Organization." Report to Centre for Information Technology Innovation. Laval, Que., June.

Garton, Laura, and Barry Wellman. 1995. "Social Impacts of Electronic Mail in Organizations: A Review of the Research Literature." *Communication Yearbook* 18:434–53.

Georgia Institute of Technology. 1997. "Graphic, Visualization, and Usability Center's 8th WWW User Survey." December. Website: http://www.gvu.gatech.edu/user_surveys/.

Granovetter, Mark. 1973. "The Strength of Weak Ties." *American Journal of Sociology* 78:1360–1380.

Granovetter, Mark. 1982. "The Strength of Weak Ties: A Network Theory Revisited." Pp. 105–30 in *Social Structure and Network Analysis,* edited by Peter Marsden and Nan Lin. Beverly Hills, CA: Sage.

Greer, Scott. 1962. *The Emerging City*. New York: Free Press.

Gupta, Sumit, Jim Pitkow, and Mimi Recker. 1995. "Consumer Survey of WWW Users." Website: http://www.umich.edu.sgupta/hermes.html. August 10.

Harasim, Linda, and Tim Winkelmans. 1990. "Computer-Mediated Scholarly Collaboration." *Knowledge* 11:382–409.

Haythornthwaite, Caroline, Barry Wellman, and Laura Garton. 1998. "Work and Community via Computer-Mediated Communication." Pp. 199–226 in *Psychology and the Internet,* edited by Jayne Gackenbach. San Diego: Academic Press.

Haythornthwaite, Caroline, and Barry Wellman. 1998. "Work, Friendship and Media Use for Information Exchange in a Networked Organization." *Journal of the American Society for Information Science* 49(12):1101–1114.

Haythornthwaite, Caroline, Barry Wellman, and Marilyn Mantei. 1995. "Work Relationships and Media Use: A Social Network Analysis." *Group Decision and Negotiation* 4(3):193–211.

Herring, Susan C. 1996. "Gender and Democracy in Computer-Mediated Communication." Pp. 476–89 in *Computerization and Controversy: Value Conflicts and Social Choices,* edited by Rob Kling. 2d ed. San Diego: Academic Press.

Hiltz, Starr Roxanne, Kenneth Johnson, and Gail Agle. 1978. "Replicating Bales Problem Solving Experiments on a Computerized Conference: A Pilot Study." Report to Computerized Conferencing and Communications Center, New Jersey Institute of Technology.

Hiltz, Starr Roxanne, Kenneth Johnson, and Murray Turoff. 1986. "Experiments in Group Decision Making: Communication Process and Outcome in Face-to-face Versus Computerized Conferences." *Human Communication Research* 13(2):225–252.

Hiltz, S. Roxanne, and Murray Turoff. 1993. *The Network Nation.* 2d ed. Cambridge, MA: MIT Press.

Homans, George. 1961. *Social Behavior: Its Elementary Forms.* New York: Harcourt Brace Jovanovich.

Jacobs, Jane. 1961. *The Death and Life of Great American Cities.* New York: Random House.

Johnson-Lenz, Peter, and Trudy Johnson-Lenz. 1977. "On Facilitating Networks for Social Change." *Connections* 1(2):5–11.

Johnson-Lenz, Peter, and Trudy Johnson-Lenz. 1990. "Rhythms, Boundaries, and Containers: Creative Dynamics of Asynchronous Group Life." Working Paper, Lake Oswego, OR: Awakening Technology.

Johnson-Lenz, Peter, and Trudy Johnson-Lenz. 1993. "Community Brain-Mind: Groupware Tools for Healthy Civic Life." Presented to the Healthy Communities Networking Summit Conference. San Francisco, CA.

Johnson-Lenz, Peter, and Trudy Johnson-Lenz. 1994. "Groupware for a Small Planet." Pp. 269–84 in *Groupware in the 21st Century,* edited by Peter Lloyd. London: Adamantine Press.

Jones, Steven. 1995. "Understanding Community in the Information Age." Pp. 10–35 in *Cybersociety: Computer-Mediated Communication and Community,* edited by Steven Jones. Thousand Oaks, CA: Sage.

Katz, Elihu, and Paul Lazarsfeld. 1955. *Personal Influence.* Glencoe, IL: Free Press.

Kaufer, David, and Kathleen Carley. 1993. *Communication at a Distance: The Influence of Print on Sociocultural Organization and Change.* Hillsdale, NJ: Lawrence Erlbaum.

Kiesler, Sara, and Lee Sproull. 1988. "Technological and Social Change in Organizational Communication Environments." Working Paper. Carnegie Mellon University.

Kiesler, Sara, and Lee Sproull. 1992. "Group Decision Making and Communication Technology." *Organizational Behavior and Human Decision Processes* 52:96–123.

Kiesler, Sara, Lee Sproull, and Jacquelynne S. Eccles. 1985. "Pool Halls, Chips, and War Games: Women in the Culture of Computing." *Psychology of Women Quarterly* 9:451–462.

King, Storm. 1994. "Analysis of Electronic Support Groups for Recovering Addicts." *Interpersonal Computing and Technology* 2 (July):47–56.

Kling, Rob. 1996. "Social Relationships in Electronic Forums: Hangouts, Salons, Workplaces and Communities." Pp. 426–54 in *Computerization and Controversy: Value Conflicts and Social Choices*, edited by Rob Kling. 2d ed. San Diego: Academic Press.

Kochen, Manfred, ed. 1989. *The Small World*. Norwood, NJ: Ablex.

Kollock, Peter, and Marc Smith. 1996. "Managing the Virtual Commons: Cooperation and Conflict in Computer Communities." Pp. 109–128 in *Computer-Mediated Communication*, edited by Susan Herring. Amsterdam: John Benjamins.

Kraut, Robert, Vicki Lundmark, Michael Patterson, Sara Kiesler, Tridas Mukopadhyay, and William Scherlis. 1998. "The Internet Paradox." *American Psychologist* 53(9):1017–1031.

Kraut, Robert, William Scherlis, Tridas Mukhopadhyay, Jane Manning, and Sara Kiesler. 1995. "HomeNet: A Field Trial of Residential Internet Services." *HomeNet* 1(2):1–8.

Latané, Bibb, and Martin Bourgeois. 1996. "Experimental Evidence for Dynamic Social Impact: The Emergence of Subcultures in Electronic Groups." *Journal of Communication* 46(Sept.):35–47.

Latané, Bibb, and John Darley. 1976. *Help in a Crisis: Bystander Response to an Emergency*. Morristown, NJ: General Learning Press.

Lazarsfeld, Paul, and Robert Merton. 1954. "Friendship as Social Process." Pp. 18–66 in *Freedom and Control in Modern Society*, edited by Morroe Berger, Theodore Abel, and Charles Page. New York: Octagon.

Lea, Martin, T. O'Shea, P. Fung, and Russell Spears. 1992. "Flaming in Computer-Mediated Communication: Observations, Explanations, Implications." Pp. 89–112 in *Contexts of Computer-Mediated Communication*, edited by Martin Lea. New York: Harvester Wheatsheaf.

Lea, Martin, and Russell Spears. 1992. "Paralanguage and Social Perception in Computer-Mediated Communication." *Journal of Organizational Computing* 2:321–342.

Lea, Martin, and Russell Spears. 1995. "Love at First Byte? Building Personal Relationships Over Computer Networks." Pp. 197–233 in *Understudied Relationships: Off the Beaten Track*, edited by Julia T. Wood and Steve Duck. Thousand Oaks, CA: Sage.

Lewis, Peter H. 1994. "Strangers, Not Their Computers Build a Network in Time of Grief." *New York Times*, March 8.

Lin, Nan, Alfred Dean, and Walter Ensel. 1986. *Social Support, Life Events and Depression*. Orlando, FL: Academic Press.

Lin, Nan, and Mary Dumin. 1986. "Access to Occupations through Social Ties." *Social Networks* 8:365–86.

Lucky, Robert. 1995. "What Technology Alone Cannot Do." *Scientific American* 273(Sept.):205.

Maes, Patti. 1995. "Artificial Life Meets Entertainment: Lifelike Autonomous Agents." *Communications of the ACM* 38(11):108–114.

Mantei, Marilyn, Ronald Baecker, Abigail Sellen, William Buxton, Thomas Milligan, and Barry Wellman. 1991. "Experiences in the Use of a Media Space." Pp. 203–208 in *Reaching Through Technology: CHI '91 Conference Proceedings*. Reading, MA: Addison-Wesley.

Marsden, Peter. 1983. "Restricted Access in Networks and Models of Power." *American Journal of Sociology* 88:686–717.

Marx, Gary, and Mary Virnoche. 1995. "'Only Connect': E. M. Forster in an Age of Computerization." Presented to the American Sociological Association, Washington, August.

McCormick, Naomi, and John McCormick. 1992. "Computer Friends and Foes: Content of Undergraduates' Electronic Mail." *Computers in Human Behavior* 8:379–405.

McGrath, Joseph and A. B. Hollingshead. 1994. *Groups Interacting with Technology.* Thousand Oaks, CA: Sage.

McLuhan, Marshall. 1965. *Understanding Media.* New York: McGraw-Hill.

Meyer, Gordon. 1989. "The Social Organization of the Computer Underground." Masters' thesis. DeKalb: Department of Sociology, Northern Illinois University.

Mitchell, William. 1995. *City of Bits: Space, Time and the Infobahn.* Cambridge, MA: MIT Press.

Newsweek. 1995. "Cyberaddicts." December 18:60.

O'Brien, Jodi. 1998. "Gender on (the) Line: An Erasable Institution?" Pp. 134–160 in *Communities in Cyberspace,* edited by Marc Smith and Peter Kollock. Berkeley: University of California Press.

O'Neill, Molly. 1995. "The Lure and Addiction of Life On Line." *New York Times,* March 8.

Ogden, Michael. 1994. "Politics in a Parallel Universe: Is There a Future for Cyberdemocracy?" *Futures* 26(7):713–729.

Parks, Malcolm, and Kory Floyd. 1996. "Making Friends in Cyberspace." *Journal of Computer Mediated Communication* 1 (4):Online URL, http://jcmc.huji.ac.il/vol1/issue4/parks.html.

Parks, Malcolm, and Lynne Roberts. 1998. "'Making MOOsic': The Development of Personal Relationships On Line and a Comparison to Their Off-Line Counterparts." *Journal of Social and Personal Relationships* 15(4):517–537.

Patton, Phil. 1986. *Open Road.* New York: Simon and Schuster.

Perlman, Daniel, and Beverley Fehr. 1987. "The Development of Intimate Relationships." Pp. 13–42 in *Intimate Relationships,* edited by Daniel Perlman and Steve Duck. Newbury Park, CA: Sage.

Pescosolido, Bernice. 1986. "Migration, Medical Care Preferences and the Lay Referral System: A Network Theory of Role Assimilation." *American Sociological Review* 51:523–540.

Pickering, Jeanne M., and John Leslie King. 1996. "Hardwiring Weak Ties: Interorganizational Computer-Mediated Communication, Occupational Communities and Organizational Change." *Organizational Science* 6(4):479–86.

Pitkow, Jim, and Colleen Kehoe. 1995. "Third WWW User Survey: Executive Summary." Report to Graphic, Visualization and Usability Center, Georgia Institute of Technology.

Pliskin, Nava, and Celia T. Romm. 1994. "Empowerment Effects of Electronic Group Communication: A Case Study." Working Paper, Department of Management, Faculty of Commerce, University of Wollongong.

Press, Larry. 1995. "McLuhan Meets the Net." *Communications of the ACM* 38(6):15–20.

Rapoport, Anatol. 1957. "Contribution to the Theory of Random and Biased Graphs." *Bulletin of Mathematical Biology* 19:257–77.

Reid, Elizabeth M. 1991. "Electropolis: Communication and Community on Internet Relay Chat." Honors Thesis, University of Melbourne.

Reid, Elizabeth. 1998. "Hierarchy and Power: Social Control in Cyberspace." Pp. 105–133 in *Communities in Cyberspace,* edited by Marc Smith and Peter Kollock. Berkeley: University of California Press.

Rheingold, Howard. 1993. *The Virtual Community: Homesteading on the Electronic Frontier.* Reading, MA: Addison-Wesley.

Rice, Ronald, and Gail Love. 1987. "Electronic Emotion: Socioemotional Content in a Computer-Mediated Communication Network." *Communication Research* 14(February):85–108

Salaff, Janet, and Dimitrina Dimitrova. 1995. "Teleworking: A Review of Studies of this International Business Application of Telecommunications." Toronto, Centre for Urban and Community Studies, University of Toronto.

Sallot, Jeff. 1995. "Internet Overloaded after Bombing." *Toronto Globe and Mail.* April 27.

Seidman, Robert. 1998. "More Fun with Numbers: Results from IDC's Semiannual 1997 World Wide Web Survey of Home and Business Users." *Seidman's Online Insider* 5 (April 5). Website: http://www.onlineinsider.com.

Seymour, Jim. 1994. "On-Line Ties that Bind" *PC Magazine,* March 29:99–100.

Shade, Leslie Regan. 1994. "Is Sisterhood Virtual? Women on the Electronic Frontier." *Transactions of the Royal Society of Canada VI* 5:131–42.

Short, John, Ederyn Williams, and Bruce Christie. 1976. *The Social Psychology of Telecommunications.* London: Wiley.

Siegel, Jane, Vitaly Dubrovsky, Sara Kiesler, and Timothy W. McGuire. 1986. "Group Processes in Computer-Mediated Communication." *Organizational Behavior and Human Decision Processes* 37:157–87.

Slouka, Mark. 1995. *War of the Worlds: Cyberspace and the High-Tech Assault on Reality.* New York: Basic Books.

Smith, Marc. 1998. "Netscan: A Tool for Measuring and Mapping Social Cyberspaces." April 4. Website: http://netscan.sscnet.ucla.edu/index.html.

Smith, Marc, and Peter Kollock, eds. 1998. *Communities in Cyberspace.* London: Routledge.

Southwick, Scott. 1996. "Liszt: Searchable Directory of E-Mail Discussion Groups." Report to BlueMarble Information Services, January 27. Website: http://www.liszt.com.

Sproull, Lee, and Samer Faraj. 1995. "Atheism, Sex and Databases: The Net as a Social Technology." Pp. 62–81 in *Public Access to the Internet*, edited by Brian Kahin and James Keller. Cambridge, MA: MIT Press.

Sproull, Lee, and Sara Kiesler. 1986. "Reducing Social Context Cues: Electronic Mail in Organizational Communication." *Management Science* 32:1492–1512.

Sproull, Lee, and Sara Kiesler. 1991. *Connections*. Cambridge, MA: MIT Press.

Stein, Maurice. 1960. *The Eclipse of Community*. Princeton, NJ: Princeton University Press.

Stephenson, Neal. 1992. *Snow Crash*. New York: Bantam.

Stoll, Clifford. 1995. *Silicon Snake Oil: Second Thoughts on the Information Highway*. New York: Doubleday.

Thorn, B. K. and T. Connolly. 1987. "Discretionary Data Bases: A Theory and Some Experimental Findings." *Communication Research* 14:512–528.

Tönnies, Ferdinand. 1887 [1955]. *Community and Organization*. London: Routledge and Kegan Paul.

Van den Boomen, Marianne. 1998. "Utopia in Cyberspace: Virtual Communities and Reality." Annual meeting of the International Communal Studies Association, Amsterdam, July.

Verbrugge, Lois. 1977. "The Structure of Adult Friendship Choices." *Social Forces* 56:576–97.

Walker, Karen. 1993. "Between Friends: Class, Gender and Friendship." Ph.D. thesis, Department of Sociology, University of Pennsylvania.

Walther, Joseph B. 1994. "Anticipated Ongoing Interaction Versus Channel Effects on Relational Communication in Computer-Mediated Interaction." *Human Communication Research* 20(4):473–501.

Walther, Joseph B. 1995. "Relational Aspects of Computer-Mediated Communication: Experimental Observations Over Time." *Organization Science* 6(2):186–203.

Walther, Joseph B., Jeffrey F. Anderson, and David W. Park. 1994. "Interpersonal Effects in Computer-Mediated Interaction: A Meta-Analysis of Social and Antisocial Communication." *Communication Research* 21(4):460–487.

Weisband, Suzanne, Sherry Schneider, and Terry Connolly. 1995. "Computer-Mediated Communication and Social Information: Status Salience and Status Differences." *Academy of Management Journal* 38(4):1124–1151.

Wellman, Barry. 1979. "The Community Question." *American Journal of Sociology* 84:1201–31.

Wellman, Barry. 1988a. "The Community Question Re-evaluated." Pp. 81–107 in *Power, Community and the City*, edited by Michael Peter Smith. New Brunswick, NJ: Transaction Books.

Wellman, Barry. 1988b. "Structural Analysis: From Method and Metaphor to Theory and Substance." Pp. 19–61 in *Social Structures: A Network Approach*, edited by Barry Wellman and S. D. Berkowitz. Cambridge: Cambridge University Press.

Wellman, Barry. 1990. "The Place of Kinfolk in Community Networks." *Marriage and Family Review* 15(1/2):195–228.

Wellman, Barry. 1992a. "Men in Networks: Private Communities, Domestic Friendships." Pp. 74–114 in *Men's Friendships*, edited by Peter Nardi. Newbury Park, CA: Sage.

Wellman, Barry. 1992b. "Which Types of Ties and Networks Give What Kinds of Social Support?" *Advances in Group Processes* 7:207–235.

Wellman, Barry. 1993. "An Egocentric Network Tale." *Social Networks* 17(2):423–436.

Wellman, Barry. 1994. "I was a Teenage Network Analyst: The Route from The Bronx to the Information Highway." *Connections* 17(2):28–45.

Wellman, Barry. 1996. "Are Personal Communities Local? A Dumptarian Reconsideration." *Social Networks* 18:347–354.

Wellman, Barry. 1997. "An Electronic Group is Virtually a Social Network." Pp. 179–205 in *The Culture of the Internet*, edited by Sara Kiesler. Hillsdale, NJ: Erlbaum.

Wellman, Barry, Peter Carrington, and Alan Hall. 1988. "Networks as Personal Communities." Pp. 130–84 in *Social Structures: A Network Approach*, edited by Barry Wellman and S. D. Berkowitz. Cambridge: Cambridge University Press.

Wellman, Barry, and Barry Leighton. 1979. "Networks, Neighborhoods and Communities." *Urban Affairs Quarterly* 14:363–90.

Wellman, Barry, and Nancy Nazer. 1995. "Does What Goes Around Come Around? Specific Exchange in Personal Community Networks." Presented to the International Social Network Conference, London, July.

Wellman, Barry, Janet Salaff, Dimitrina Dimitrova, Laura Garton, Milena Gulia, and Caroline Haythornthwaite. 1996. "Computer Networks as Social Networks." *Annual Review of Sociology* 22:211–238.

Wellman, Barry, and David Tindall. 1993. "Reach Out and Touch Some Bodies: How Social Networks Connect Telephone Networks." *Progress in Communication Sciences* 12:63–93.

Wellman, Barry, Renita Wong, David Tindall, and Nancy Nazer. 1997. "A Decade of Network Change: Turnover, Mobility and Stability." *Social Networks* 19:27–50.

Wellman, Barry, and Scot Wortley. 1989. "Brothers' Keepers: Situating Kinship Relations in Broader Networks of Social Support." *Sociological Perspectives* 32:273–306.

Wellman, Barry, and Scot Wortley. 1990. "Different Strokes from Different Folks: Community Ties and Social Support." *American Journal of Sociology* 96:558–588.

Wellman, Beverly. 1995. "Lay Referral Networks: Using Conventional Medicine and Alternative Therapies for Low Back Pain." *Sociology of Health Care* 12:213–238.

Wireman, Peggy. 1984. *Urban Neighborhoods, Networks, and Families*. Lexington, MA: Lexington Books.

Young, Michael, and Peter Willmott. 1957. *Family and Kinship in East London*. Harmondsworth, UK: Penguin.

About the Editor and Contributors

Yanjie Bian is associate professor of sociology at the University of Minnesota and the Hong Kong University of Science and Technology (1997–99). He is the author of *Work and Inequality in Urban China*. (sobian@ust.hk)

Karen E. Campbell is associate professor of sociology at Vanderbilt University, Nashville. She has studied women's and men's job searches, gender differences in social support, neighborhood networks, and women's suffrage movements in American states. (karen.e.campbell@vanderbilt.edu)

Alain Degenne is the former director of CNRS-LASMAS (Caen and Paris). His research has focused on methods of studying the formal properties of social networks. (degenne@mrsh.unicaen.fr)

Vicente Espinoza is a researcher at the Institute of Advanced Studies (IDEA), University of Santiago, Chile. He has taught at the Pontifical Catholic University of Chile, and has been a consultant for the United Nations and a number of governmental and non-governmental organizations. His interests include social movements, social networks inequality, and social policy. (vespinoz@rdc.cl)

Alexis Ferrand is professor of sociology at the University of Sciences and Technologies in Lille and has been a visiting researcher at CNRS-LASMAS (Paris). He has studied friendship, sexual behavior, and the emergence of norms in networks. (alexis.ferrand@univ-lille1.fr)

Eric Fong is associate professor of sociology and research associate at the Centre of Urban and Community Studies, University of Toronto. His research interests include ethnic economies, and racial and ethnic residential patterns. (fong@chass.utoronto.ca)

Milena Gulia is completing her doctorate in sociology at the University of Toronto where she is studying immigration, housing, and the sociology of community. (gulia@chass.utoronto.ca)

Barrett A. Lee is professor of sociology and a faculty associate of the Population Research Institute at Penn State University. In addition to local social networks, he is studying urban homelessness, residential segregation, neighborhood change, and racial and ethnic diversity. (bal6@psu.edu)

Lise Mounier is a researcher at CNRS-LASMAS (Caen and Paris) where her research has included studies of friendship and sexual behavior in networks. (mounier@mrsh.unicaen.fr)

Shinsuke Otani is professor of sociology at Kwansei Gakuin University near Osaka. He has a longstanding interest in comparing Japanese and North American communities. (qyf11536@niftyserve.or.jp)

Stephanie Potter's principal interests are in research and policy with respect to immigrant integration. She is completing her doctorate in sociology at the University of Toronto, studying indicators of immigrant settlement in Canada. (potter@chass.utoronto.ca)

Janet W. Salaff is professor of sociology at the University of Toronto and studies family economies in Chinese societies. She is the author of *Working Daughters of Hong Kong*. (salaff@chass.utoronto.ca)

Endre Sik is professor of sociology at the Department of Human Resources, Budapest University of Economic Sciences. His research examines migration and the informal economy under communism and post-communism. (sik@tarki.hu)

Barry Wellman is professor of sociology at the University of Toronto and a research associate of the Centre for Urban and Community Studies. He founded the International Network for Social Network Analysis, co-edited *Social Structures: A Network Approach*, and is now studying networks of work and community on and off the Internet. (wellman@chass.utoronto.ca)

Wong Siu-lun is professor of sociology at the University of Hong Kong and director of its Centre for Asian Studies. He is studying Chinese entrepreneurial behavior. (slwong@hku.hk)

Index